THE
IBM
WAY

THE IBM WAY

*Insights into the World's Most
Successful Marketing Organization*

F. G. "Buck" Rodgers

with Robert L. Shook

PERENNIAL LIBRARY

HARPER & ROW, PUBLISHERS, New York
Cambridge, Philadelphia, San Francisco, Washington
London, Mexico City, São Paulo, Singapore, Sydney

THE IBM WAY. Copyright © 1986 by Francis G. Rodgers and Robert L. Shook. Foreword copyright © 1986 by Harper & Row, Publishers, Inc. All rights reserved. Printed in the United States of America. No part of this book may be used or reproduced in any manner whatsoever without written permission except in the case of brief quotations embodied in critical articles and reviews. For information address Harper & Row, Publishers, Inc., 10 East 53rd Street, New York, N.Y. 10022. Published simultaneously in Canada by Fitzhenry & Whiteside Limited, Toronto.

First PERENNIAL LIBRARY edition published 1987.

Designer: C. Linda Dingler

Library of Congress Cataloging-in-Publication Data

Rodgers, Buck.
  The IBM way.

  Includes index.
  1. International Business Machines Corporation.
2. Computers—Marketing—Case studies. 3. Electronic office machines—Marketing—Case studies. 4. Marketing—Case studies. I. Shook, Robert L., 1938-
II. Title.
HD9696.C64I4875   1987   338.7'61004'0973   85-45223
ISBN 0-06-091417-3 (pbk.)
ISBN 0-06-337048-4 (international ed.)
ISBN 0-06-337043-3 (U.K. ed.)
ISBN 0-06-337047-6 (Indian ed.)

87 88 89 90 91 MPC 10 9 8 7 6 5 4 3 2 1

This book is dedicated to
Helen, Christy Ann, Scott and Kathy.
They have been my love, joy and inspiration.

CONTENTS

FOREWORD

By Thomas J. Peters

"IBM has been built on some simple ideas and principles ... like thoughtfulness, courtesy and integrity." Buck Rodgers, IBM's top marketing executive for ten years, provides the first comprehensive behind-the-scenes look at marketing in the world's most successful company. The secrets he reveals are obvious, as the above passage suggests. Yet in my view they are the clear-cut reasons, oddly hidden from competitors, which explain IBM's tremendous success.

I hope that one chapter title rings in the ears of every American manager: "Creating a Totally Sales-Oriented Environment." Rodgers speaks with dismay of the many companies that take their people and their customers for granted. He talks about a different world at IBM: "The Company Heroes" are the marketing people—IBM's VIPs. The logic: "Let's face it, the salesperson is the source from which everything in business starts." Moreover, *everyone* is involved in sales at IBM. Every job description in the various marketing divisions—even accounting and personnel—spells out a "customer connection" with the customer orientation being part of every performance evaluation. Engineers, financial people, and executives alike are regularly in the field. And heaven help the IBM branch managers who fail to keep in touch with their top customers.

The sales orientation, though, is just the beginning. The relationship with the customer is what ultimately counts: "Most companies are a lot better at prospecting for new customers and selling those prospects than they are at maintaining the existing customer base." With that,

Rodgers lays out the Alpha to Omega of IBM's awesome approach to service.

These are the simple but impressive themes. The supporting details are there by the bucketful: job descriptions, account review processes, quota setting, recognition programs, the ins and outs of IBM's compensation plans, training, recruiting, customer listening. He goes so far as to describe such little touches as having the marketing reps introduce the local IBM accounts-receivable team to their customers. Everybody becomes a part of the IBM-customer bandwagon.

I have been accused regularly of having discovered the obvious; one very successful business person even went so far as to call my work a "blinding flash of the obvious." Buck Rodgers could be tarred with the same brush. And I presume he will be as delighted as I. From grocery chains to steel companies to car dealerships, when I have observed excellence it has always resulted from applying common sense and common courtesy—to one's people and one's customers. And this is Rodgers' message.

It's hard to complicate the message. One wonders, then, why so few follow—and, more important, persist at— these common sense strictures. I don't know, frankly. We seem to have become so ensnared in complexity that we have lost sight of these basics.

There is, it is clear, a revolution afoot. Companies and their managers are fundamentally rethinking their approaches to doing business. What they most need is a role model. There can be none better than IBM; there can be no better role model or voice than thirty-four-year veteran executive (1950–1984) Buck Rodgers. He saw and led through IBM's growth from $250 million to $50 billion. We can all consider ourselves lucky for his having laid bare the IBM marketing story. It's simple. I just hope we listen—and act on what Buck says.

ACKNOWLEDGMENTS

During the past few years, I began to think about the possibility of writing a book—not an autobiography, but a book about the IBM corporation and the subject of marketing. Every now and then, my family would urge me on, as would some close friends inside and outside IBM.

The more contact I had with customers, universities and industry associations, the more convinced I became that IBM's story was a special one and that others could benefit from what this corporation and its people do on a day-to-day basis. Also, the art of marketing was coming into its own, with businesses large and small realizing that the customer really does come first and excellence can be a way of life. Frankly, the thought of doing the book was intriguing, but I wondered whether I could do it, let alone find the time. The idea became feasible when I decided to retire from IBM two years earlier than planned. (As you may know, IBM has a policy wherein key officers are required to relinquish their positions at age sixty.) I was spending a considerable amount of time and energy in outside speaking engagements as part of my job as vice-president of marketing. So why not do two things? Write a book and start a new career on the lecture circuit.

However, the catalyst of my decision to write this book was Bob Shook, whom I met in 1979 when he was writing *The Ten Greatest Salespersons,* in which I was included. Through Bob's initiative and my family's encouragement, I decided to go ahead. As an accomplished writer, he was invaluable in coordinating *The IBM Way.*

One other person who worked closely with me during

the final manuscript preparation was my daughter Christy. She was a constructive critic and a significant editorial contributor.

Again, my main thrust was to convey the beliefs and values of IBM, since these principles had such a profound effect on my life, as well as to describe for the first time the specific details of how IBM markets. Sure, there has been some sensitivity about describing IBM's marketing, in light of the tough competitive marketplace that exists today. However, I have discussed our tactics and strategies hundreds of times in public over the years and know that the real difference is in the execution.

I wish there were some way to thank individually the literally thousands of IBMers who played an important role in my career. I can only hope that this book will in some way be a tribute to their great skills and valued friendships.

Also, I thank my parents, Harry and Hazel, for instilling in me a sense of integrity and a desire to do what's right.

The following people were interviewed for this book and contributed meaningful insights into the world of IBM: Dale Antonik, Stan Barchan, Dean Beckwith, Harry Bernhard, Ed Bullard, Connie DeLoca, Bob Erwin, Bob Evans, Chuck Francis, Steve Haeckel, Jack Hammond, David Hendrickson, Dick Kirkley, Don Laidlaw, Stan McElroy, Doug McMillan, David Miller, Jim O'Connell, Pete Schavoir, Bob Siegel.

SPECIAL ACKNOWLEDGMENT

Irv Levey, as editor of this book, was a practitioner of excellence. He was the creative force in the rewriting of the manuscript. Any success the book may have will be a reflection of his dedicated efforts.

THE
IBM
WAY

INTRODUCTION

There really *is* an IBM way of marketing and managing. Like the title of this book, IBM's approach to business, technology and people has nothing clever or slick about it. *How* it functions, and *why*, have more to do with IBM's success than *what* it does. Because that's true, all of the traits and characteristics that make IBM great can be emulated by any company of any size. I don't think a company or a business person anywhere can fail to learn something worthwhile from IBM.

Since we in the United States became self-conscious about the downward trend of productivity in our country, and the need to improve quality, scores of business books have been written. Some have been scholarly examinations of what's wrong with American companies and what's right with their Japanese competitors. They analyze and dissect, turn us inside out and leave us bloody on the operating table. Some show us how easy it is to climb the corporate ladder. Others reveal how to become rich and powerful, with the emphasis on looking out for number one. Still others concentrate on management theory and a fast-paced approach to becoming a more effective manager.

Every now and then—about as often as Halley's Comet streaks across the sky—a book like *In Search of Excellence* comes along and gets right to the heart of things. Without award-winning prose or mind-dulling jargon, it deals with failure by elucidating success, simply but not simplistically.

So why a book about IBM? For one thing, this $50 billion American company, which now employs 400,000 people and is the most profitable business in the world, is poised to double its revenues by the end of the decade. What makes this phenomenal growth possible, and what forces drive the company, are important, because what IBM does and how it does it have a tremendous impact on the business community and on society at large. Millions of people are directly affected by this company's activities.

To understand IBM's success and its unshakable optimism, one needs some insights into its marketing systems and philosophy, and its unique relationship with employees and customers. That's where I can be helpful. I know IBM from the inside out. For the past dozen or so years, I've been invited to speak with representatives of every type of business imaginable; and since my early retirement, I've not only increased my speaking engagements but also acted as consultant for some of the world's finest companies. They want to know how IBM does it. They're as fascinated by this company's amazing ability to roll with the punches, to change and adjust, as they are by its spectacular growth. I'm in demand because I know why IBM has the most highly motivated and productive marketing organization anywhere. Even the most successful companies want to know how an organization of such high achievers was put together and managed. They want to know how it's possible to sustain its level of excellence, year after year.

Among other things, *The IBM Way* will explain what it means to be a customer-driven organization; how IBM's marketing and sales orientation permeates every aspect of its operation; how its profound concern for the customer goes far beyond guaranteeing satisfaction; how the IBM "personality" is shaped by the company's insatiable quest for excellence.

This is the first book ever written about IBM by an IBM officer. A quick sketch of my IBM career will give you an idea of the depth of my involvement with the company, especially my connection with their sales and marketing operations:

Like almost everyone who ever held a managerial or an executive position at IBM, I started as a trainee and moved up through the ranks. I was a marketing rep who sold everything from electric typewriters to stored program systems; a special rep responsible for installing one of the very first large-scale computer systems; an administrative assistant to the executive vice-president, who was responsible for all IBM engineering, manufacturing, marketing and financial functions; a branch manager; the head of IBM's banking, finance, and brokerage business; Eastern Regional Sales Manager, responsible for more than a hundred branch offices; general manager for the Western Region; and president of the Data Processing Division, the U.S. marketing operation for all IBM computer products. Then, finally, I became the company's chief marketing strategist, vice-president of marketing, with worldwide responsibility. That was my job for the past ten years. I now serve on five corporate boards of directors and four university advisory councils, and I lecture on eight university campuses each year. Activities such as these provide insight into the world outside IBM, as they broaden personal perspectives.

I'm a marketing person. A salesman. I've been referred to as a "salesman's salesman," and I consider that the greatest compliment. Marketing and sales are so tightly woven into IBM's past, present, and future successes that they are inseparable.

Although I was part of the IBM marketing operation for thirty-four years, and responsible for that function for ten years, this is not going to be a book on management theory. Nor will it be a company history, and it sure won't be a kiss-and-tell book. Even if I hadn't been a satisfied employee and an admirer of this awesome giant, I wouldn't write a book to satisfy the gossip collector's appetite. It's not my style.

I have made two absolutely right decisions in my life: the first was to marry Helen; the second, to join IBM in 1950. While at IBM, I was offered the opportunity of becoming CEO of a variety of companies, including many in the computer industry. Though the offers were attractive, I was always challenged by my IBM assignments and remained a born-and-bred, dyed-in-the-wool IBMer.

The IBM Way will expose the heart and soul of IBM: how it thinks and behaves behind closed doors; what goes into its decisionmaking; what it deems important and how it stacks its priorities; why the great majority of its employees, recruited right out of college, never leave the company; why IBM's hundreds of thousands of employees never had a union; what kind of people become members of our army of blue-suiters; what's the truth about the much-talked-about dress code and relocation policy. Mostly, you'll get a good look into IBM's sales and marketing operation. I'll talk about everything that makes IBM IBM.

If because of this book other companies increase their level of productivity and profit, we all will benefit. And if competitors improve their operation and make an effort to close the gap, IBM will feel the heat and enjoy the challenge.

1

A BUSINESS AND ITS BELIEFS

The only sacred cow in an organization is its principles.

With more than 400,000 employees, annual sales that exceed $50 billion, and offices in almost every country in the world, IBM can be mind-boggling in its vastness, fascinating in its accomplishments. But to appreciate this business phenomenon, you must understand its corporate attitudes, feelings and behavior. Some people may have difficulty imagining that a corporation the size of IBM has humanistic characteristics, but it does. And I'm convinced that it's these very human qualities that are responsible for IBM's incredible success.

I don't know how many companies have actually had a code of behavior articulated for them, but that's what Thomas J. Watson, Sr., did for IBM when he founded it in 1914. Like any ambitious entrepreneur, he wanted his company to be financially successful, but he also wanted it to reflect some of his personal values. These values, which he put down on paper, became the foundation for his new company; and anyone who worked for him thereafter knew exactly what Tom, Sr.'s, company was all about.

Watson's tenets, which were reaffirmed by his son, Thomas Watson, Jr., in 1956, when he became IBM's second CEO, are uncomplicated and can be easily understood by everyone from the CEO's office to the mailroom. They are:

1. The individual must be respected.
2. The customer must be given the best possible service.
3. Excellence and superior performance must be pursued.

These commitments, which remain at the heart of the company's operation, are so revered and encompassing that every action and policy is directly influenced by them. I think that anyone who studies the development of IBM will agree that Watson's philosophy has more to do with the company's success than do its technological innovations, marketing skills or financial resources. IBM doesn't have a patent on corporate values, principles and philosophies. However, I don't think any company can become great without them. Principles, though, can quickly become empty slogans. They're like muscles that turn soft and weak if they're not exercised regularly. To be important in a business environment, principles must first be clearly understood by everyone in management. They must be articulated to every employee, repeated so often that everyone understands just how seriously they are to be taken. IBM conscientiously drives home its philosophical messages at meetings, in internal publications and memos, at company gatherings and in private conversations. None of this would mean anything, of course, if IBM's management did not demonstrate, by personal deeds and actions, what these beliefs mean. It requires diligence, but it works. Employees understand that not only the company's success is dependent upon their faithful adherence to Tom Watson's principles; but so is their personal success. And that means all of IBM's employees. It takes time, but once your people believe you, every facet of your business is positively affected.

THE FIRST COMMITMENT

The individual must be respected. No one can be against this. At least, no one would admit to it.

After all, respecting the rights and dignity of the individual has been advocated by many cultures and religions throughout history. But while almost everybody agrees with the idea, seldom is it found in the doctrine of a business, let alone practiced. Of course, IBM isn't the only company that advocates this, but not enough companies do.

Far too many employers abuse their employees. They may demean them by overtly outrageous actions or they may chip away at their self-esteem subtly and covertly; often, they look the other way while their supervisors and managers do the dirty work. Such behavior bothered Tom Watson, Sr., as it bothers some of us today. He couldn't solve the problem universally, but he could do something about it in his own company. He truly wanted the people who worked for him to feel good about themselves and their work. No one could be paid enough money to be compensated for being made uncomfortable and unhappy by his supervisors.

Tom, Sr., was particularly intent on building the self-respect and self-confidence of his marketing reps. For years, when he was a salesman in the field, he may have suffered from low esteem. Those were the days of the "drummer," and selling was not a respected career—especially traveling salesman.

He said, "I want the IBM salesmen to be looked up to. Admired. I want their wives and children to be proud of them. I don't want their mothers to feel that they have to apologize for them when asked what their sons are doing."

His early emphasis on human relations was not motivated by altruism alone, but as Tom Watson, Jr., put it, "by the simple belief that if we respected our people and helped them respect themselves, the company would certainly profit."

The Watsons understood that people, not money or things, are a company's greatest asset. Ever since IBM's earliest days, an ongoing campaign has stressed that *each individual makes a difference.* So that nobody feels like a number, the company tries to create a small-business atmosphere. Branch offices are kept small, and the company is pretty successful at maintaining a one-to-twelve manager-to-employee ratio. All managers understand the value of job satisfaction, and the need to motivate their people continually. Superior performances are rewarded by recognition, promotions and money. Compensation will be discussed fully in a later chapter, but I'll say here that there are no automatic raises for IBMers, no cost-of-living increases—and it's possible for a fairly new marketing rep to earn more than one who has been with the company for many years. Each person gets paid on the basis of what he produces, not on his longevity. Those who do exceptionally well are paid accordingly.

Since IBM opened its doors, the company has had a full-employment tradition. This is as true today, with nearly 400,000 employees, as it was when there were only hundreds of people in the company. An employee who produces always has an assignment, preferably a meaningful one. In nearly fifty years, no person employed on a regular basis has lost as much as one hour of working time because of a layoff. Like all businesses, IBM has had its share of difficult times. It has taken careful planning and commitment to maintain full employment. Perhaps the most dramatic way to help achieve this is through retraining, which often requires career changes and/or relocation. For example, during the economically troubled years 1969–72, more than twelve thousand IBM employees moved from plants, labs and headquarters with light workloads to locations where they were needed. More than five thousand employees were retrained for new careers in sales, customer engineering, field administration and programming. Most ended up with comparable or better jobs.

Again, in 1975, during the severe recession, nearly 3,800 employees were placed in new positions to balance a workload. It cost a lot of money, but it was important. This doesn't mean the company is benevolent and paternalistic to the degree that nobody has ever been terminated. People are dismissed for poor performance, usually early in their career.

IBM couldn't afford to spend so much to reward the good performers if it had to subsidize those who do not produce.

Productive people need challenging assignments. It's vital for them to go home at night feeling that they did something worthwhile. And when they enjoy their work and know the company cares about them, they want to contribute to its growth.

IBM's practice is to promote people from within. In all my years with the company, I recall only three executives—all in highly specialized fields—who were brought in from the outside. Everyone knows that if he works hard and aspires to a higher position, he will have an opportunity to advance. It's frustrating and demoralizing for an ambitious person to work his tail off, striving for a certain job, only to have someone from the outside come in and get it. I know the argument that promoting only from within can lead to inbreeding, but I don't accept it. The negative effect that bringing in outsiders has on morale far outweighs the hazards of inbreeding.

IBM has many programs to let a person know he or she can make a difference, and I'll discuss a few of them later. But there is a host of little things that you might notice at IBM headquarters in Armonk, New York. For instance, there are no titles on any doors or desks, no bathrooms designed for "executive use only," no reserved parking spaces, no executive dining room. All in all, it's a very democratic environment, where everyone is treated with the same respect. Even IBM's equal opportunity policy and affirmative action programs go far beyond government guidelines. In fact, the company's minority population equals or exceeds the minority percentage mix of the U.S. population.

IBM strives to be a responsible corporate citizen. From a dollar perspective, the company's 1984 contributions to social, cultural and educational programs exceeded $145 million. IBM's attitude toward the individual extends far beyond company headquarters. Management treats everyone who works at IBM with respect and, in turn, expects everyone to treat customers, suppliers and even the competition the same way. The company's code of conduct states that no IBMer shall disparage any competitor; that selling must be done on the merits of products and services: sell strengths and never try to exploit someone else's weaknesses. The code also advises not to boast about the company's size, success or position in the industry; or about how much is spent on research and product development; or about how many systems engineers there are to work with customers. It's all right to talk about the *quality* of IBM's products or services, the resources and people that represent a commitment to the customer and the concept of excellence. It's O.K. for a rep to tell the customer about an IBM educational facility that is staffed and equipped to give him the best possible service. That's not boasting of bigness; it's a fact and it's relevant to the customer's needs.

The Watsons believed that when one respects the individual one shows consideration for *all* people—in and out of the company. And that belief must be reinforced constantly by one's actions.

The first time I met Tom Watson, Jr., I quickly learned that he practiced what he preached. I was new to the company and completing the final sales training program at the sales school in Poughkeepsie, New York. Although I was happy and excited about getting an opportunity to work for IBM, I was at the same time under considerable personal strain. My wife was pregnant and expecting to deliver at any moment. Though we had agreed that I must complete this initial phase of my training, no matter what, I was having second thoughts. I wanted to be with Helen, but I was afraid to ask for the time off—especially since I didn't know exactly when the baby would be born. It could be happening right now, it could be tomorrow or next week—or longer.

Watson spoke to the class, and when he was finished he

moved around the room, chatting with the trainees. I was wondering if I had time to call home, when he approached me.

"How are things going? What's happening?"

Well, he asked so I told him. I hadn't got the words out of my mouth when he interrupted.

"What are you doing here? You should be home with your wife. Get on a plane and get back to Ohio immediately."

Within the next few minutes, IBM's CEO made arrangements for this trainee to get to Cleveland, and I was airborne that same afternoon.

In the lectures, I heard a lot about respect for the individual, but the message was made crystal clear when Watson demonstrated how he placed my family and personal worth above the business.

Among the flowers that were delivered to the hospital room after the arrival of my daughter was a beautiful arrangement from Tom Watson.

"Do we know him?" Helen asked.

In 1969, I wrote to the twenty-eight thousand people in my division:

Respect for the individual is not a platitude. It is a constant in IBM, the initial belief on which our business was founded. Its effectiveness depends entirely on the extent to which it is encouraged by every manager in this company, and practiced by every employee.

But respect for the individual can become a platitude, if it is not continually reemphasized and consciously made a part of our day-to-day business relationships.

The dramatic changes of our business increase rather than diminish our need to respect one another.

THE SECOND COMMITMENT

Customer Service. When Tom Watson, Sr., said that he wanted IBM to provide *the best service in the world*, he referred to service by any company, not just in his own industry. To accomplish this, he mandated that IBM would be a *customer-oriented company*. That is, every part of its operation would focus on the customers' requirements. Every employee's job description is somehow related to IBM's goal of providing customers, prospects and vendors with the best possible service.

It's a shame, but in America today when we get good service we are surprised by it. People don't expect it, they don't demand it, and they settle for a lot less than they should. When customers are first exposed to IBM's brand of service, they are usually taken aback. But it's easy to get used to the kind of treatment that makes you feel important. And every customer with every company should be made to feel that way.

To let the customer know how important he is, IBM tries to respond to, if not resolve, any complaint within twenty-four hours of its receipt. When a customer requests a service call, the response is even quicker—frequently within the hour. Similarly, IBM has introduced more efficient ways of providing service to its customers. IBM specialists are available via toll-free numbers to solve service and software problems over the phone. Lower-priced carry-in and mail-in service agreements have been added to give customers a wider range of choices. In addition, IBM has established guidelines requiring that each new IBM product be superior in quality to the one it replaces, and to comparable products in the marketplace. IBM strives to provide its customers with superior products and service.

The quality of its service depends upon an organization's training and educational capabilities. In this area, IBM believes that it has made the largest financial commitment of any company in the world. Its training and educational programs are unparalleled in business. The hours logged in the classroom are believed to exceed those spent in any major university. Each year, every IBM manager is given forty hours of training, and that extends down through the organization. Even customers are routinely invited to participate in a variety of classroom programs. In an industry where repeat business is essential for long-term growth, it is essential to make sure that the initial order is only the beginning. Outstanding service is what keeps bringing the customer back to do more business.

THE THIRD COMMITMENT

Watson's third mandate is *excellence*—the pursuit of all tasks with the idea that they can be accomplished in a superior fashion. The constant goal is zero defects, in product and service. Though Watson of course knew that perfection is never possible, to aim for less would lower expectations and weaken his program. In its striving for the impossible, the company established certain satisfaction indexes so it could regularly sample the marketplace to establish the quality of its service. More about that later.

Excellence begins with the recruiting program. IBM believes that the best students selected from the nation's best colleges may be the most responsive to the company's intensive training program and the most highly motivated to do superior work. So a lot more is involved than simply attracting the outstanding young people. To achieve excellence, they need superior training and must feel compelled to succeed. At IBM, a highly competitive environment creates an atmosphere that nurtures excellence. Needless to say, a great deal of peer pressure exists. Nobody owns a job at IBM. With the intensity of competition and the continual emphasis on education, there's no room for individual complacency. The insistence on peak performance sets a rigid pace. People begin to think that anything can be achieved—that anything is possible. That attitude generates excitement. You feel it in the air.

When an organization demands and gets excellence from its people, the excitement eventually becomes contagious. Its customers, too, become optimistic and enthusiastic, and think: "This is the kind of organization I want to do business with."

THE ONLY SACRED COW

Tom Watson, Jr., said: "For any organization to survive and achieve success, there must be a sound set of principles on which it bases all of its policies and actions. But more important is its faithful adherence to those principles." Does Watson's credo hold up in times of change?

In business, everything about an organization's operation is subject to change. Locations change. People change. Products change. (IBM originally manufactured butcher scales and time clocks.) Names change. (Until 1924, IBM was known as the Computing-Tabulating-Recording Company.) We live in a world of constant change, and in business, one's survival is dependent upon a capacity to change. (In the 1950s, I was involved with the installation of the largest and most expensive system of its time, the 705 computer. It had a price tag of approximately $1,500,000 and took up an entire room. Today, the three-thousand-dollar Personal Computer that sits on my desktop at home has more capacity than the 705!) In an era of high technology, change is both frequent and swift. Marketing programs that don't respond to the changes can destroy a company. You either go forward or go backward; you can't stand still.

The only sacred cow in an organization is its principles. A company must never change them. No matter what its nature or size, there must be certain bedrock beliefs to serve as its guiding force. While a company must be flexible, always regrouping and changing with the times, its beliefs must remain irrevocable, deeply embedded throughout time. IBM's three basic beliefs are so fundamental to success that any deviation is unthinkable.

I wish that every business would establish a set of principles to serve as a guide for its people. Although the best time to do it is upon starting a business, few fledgling entrepreneurs think in such terms. They are too busy making a living to formulate principles that will guide them in what seems the distant future. However, at some point their philosophies should be recorded; and once formulated, they should not be kept a secret, but be loud and clear to everyone.

When a business is small, its owner generally has personal contact with his key people and conveys his convictions on a one-to-one basis. If he doesn't discuss his philosophy with his employees, he certainly demonstrates it by example. As an organization grows and prospers, it must make sure every level of management understands and practices the same established principles. For the most part, if you study outstanding American organizations that have weathered the test of time, you will find well-articulated philosophies behind their behavior. The success of a business is measured in more than dollars and cents. As Al Williams, a former IBM president, said: "It is not bigness we seek, it is greatness. Bigness is imposing. Greatness is enduring."

An organization must constantly communicate its beliefs to its people. At the onset of the IBM training program, new people are introduced to the philosophy of the company, along with its history and tradition. However, it's one thing to talk about beliefs and values, and quite another to incorporate them into the very fabric of your organization. An Emerson quote comes to mind: "What you are . . . thunders, for I cannot hear what you say." Actions, tactics, strategies, implementation, inspection, measurement, recognition and commitment—those are what's important. Not just words. I believe *In Search of*

Excellence, by Tom Peters and Bob Waterman, was so successful because it struck a nerve in America: not because it told us anything new, but because it confirmed that which we already understood. It reaffirmed that paying attention to detail, doing things right the first time, practicing good human relations and being market-driven separate the leading organizations from the rest.

IBM marketing trainees see the company's code of behavior at work, in the office and in the field, during their very first week on the payroll. They learn what IBM means by respect for the individual. They see how they're personally treated. Nobody is ever too busy to help them with a problem. They see how customers are treated, and hear the praise given to the helpful marketing reps, systems engineers and service reps. They're surrounded by people striving for excellence. Soon, what appeared to be rhetoric becomes reality. Examples of the IBM beliefs are printed regularly in many company publications, and reports of outstanding service are repeated in classrooms, at branch office meetings and customer conferences. A major effort is constantly at work to keep the company's ideals alive, healthy and valued.

The three tenets—respect, service and excellence—are as important to IBM today as when first uttered by Thomas Watson, Sr., in 1914. The Watsons didn't simply communicate a set of principles to hear themselves say something nice. They lived by their beliefs in their day-to-day work.

To me, Tom, Jr., was a great man—but he wasn't perfect. He had a pretty good temper and could be very impatient with what he thought to be inconsiderate behavior. When I was president of the Data Processing Division, he sent a message to my office asking that I come to a meeting at three o'clock that same afternoon. It was a special session, with little advance notice, and I was already on my way to New Jersey to see a customer. Arriving at the customer's office, I received a call from my secretary: Watson had called a meeting and wanted me there. The customer situation was a difficult one, and I didn't get back to Armonk until six-thirty that evening. As an object lesson, Watson hadn't started the meeting, so everyone was waiting for me. Now, as much as I admired the man, I didn't want to be on the receiving end of his wrath, and I assumed that he was building up a pretty good head of steam.

As I walked into the room, he said, "When I call for a three o'clock meeting, I expect *everybody* to be there at three o'clock."

I took a deep breath. "Tom, how many times have you said, 'The customer comes first'? I was with one in New Jersey who had a very serious problem."

Watson's face softened. "Buck," he said, smiling, "you have the right priorities."

There was a brief pause; he turned to the others and said, "We shall now commence the meeting."

As IBM prospered over the years, both Watsons showed an enormous amount of flexibility in responding to the changing times. But neither would ever bend or compromise the basic values that are at the heart of the company's very existence. Nor would I.

2
LEADERSHIP

---

*A real leader has the ability to motivate others to
their highest level of achievement; then gives them
the opportunity and the freedom to grow.*

The Watsons were role models for just about everyone who ever climbed IBM's organizational ladder. I was no exception. It was easy for me to incorporate their business values into my own style of leadership, which often differed from but never seriously conflicted with theirs. It was easy because I truly believed in their approach to people and problems.

Fortunately for me, the Watsons provided a nurturing environment that allowed me to develop. They considered my success their success.

Too many people work under insecure leaders, whose paranoia stifles the growth of everyone around them. A leader who runs scared fills the environment with tension, hostility and tentativeness. He batters the self-esteem of his people, frightening them just as he is frightened. He kills incentive in the very people he must motivate in order to achieve his prescribed goals. This kind of manager can cripple an organization, and is a leader in rank only.

I promise not to fill this chapter with sports analogies, but you can certainly see a variety of leadership styles, on any weekend, by switching your TV dial from one sports event to another—from Indiana's explosive Bobby Knight to Dallas's cool Tom Landry.

Regardless of his style, *a real leader, through his or her actions and words, has the ability to motivate others to their highest level of achievement; then gives them the opportunity and the freedom to grow.*

In this chapter, I'll tell you what I think it takes to be a good leader; how I led a marketing group that numbered tens of thousands of bright, ambitious people; and which of my characteristics helped me get the job done.

I've received a lot of recognition for my work at IBM, in and out of the house. Today, major corporations everywhere pay me handsome fees to address their top management conferences. I've been asked so many questions about my own style of leadership that I've been forced to analyze it.

Here are some personal traits that affected the way I manage, and have helped me become successful:

1. *I like people.* I like them better than computers, sports or books. I love to talk and I like to listen, and couldn't imagine working in a position that isolated me from others.

2. *I feel good about myself.* I'm comfortable with my values and my personal philosophy. Whenever I consider doing anything that conflicts with those values, warning lights flash in my brain and I reevaluate and rethink my motives.

3. *For me, to be given responsibility is an honor.* I know that the greater the responsibility, the greater the challenge. The greater the risk, the greater the reward. Although I've made my living for more than thirty years as a motivator, and know how important "incentives" are, I've always been more motivated by the challenge of responsibility than by the promise of financial gain. Of course, I've never turned down any money that IBM offered, but I don't think it was the money that made me perk. On the other hand, I might have developed a different attitude if IBM had been less generous.

4. *I like to solve problems, and believe that any problem that can be uncovered and articulated can be solved.* A trouble-free position would bore me.

5. *My temperament is such that I don't have to win every point to have been in a successful debate.*

You can see that I believe a successful leader must have a good sense of self-worth and purpose.

THE SIAMESE TWINS

You can't talk about leadership without talking about responsibility and accountability; as far as I'm concerned, you can't separate the two. A leader must delegate responsibility and provide the freedom to make decisions, and then be held accountable for the results. It seems simple enough, but leadership often runs into roadblocks right from the outset. Frequently it's the fault of the person who delegates. That's because he does it with his fingers crossed. He goes through the ritual of delegating but he just can't let go. Perhaps he has second thoughts about the decision, or maybe he's afraid that he's weakened his own power base. Whatever the reason, he intends to keep an eye on things. Soon he is breathing down the neck of his newly appointed manager, scrutinizing every action, criticizing every decision, allowing little or no room for expression or experiment. He renders his manager helpless and then holds him accountable for the results. The poor guy doesn't have a chance. He stops trying to be innovative, and by not exercising his authority, returns the decisionmaking to his boss. He becomes an implementer, which is probably what he was before his promotion. The people who work under this manager know that he's powerless—and they resent it. They want to work for a winner. His promotion may have added something to his paycheck, but it can never be enough for what it cost him in self-esteem and peace of mind. He was a victim of the "captain of the ship" syndrome, in which the person at the top assumes all the responsibility.

There are times when the opposite occurs. A person is given the responsibility, authority and freedom to get a job done, but is never held accountable. A business can be driven into the ground because a leader recklessly delegates responsibility as if he were getting rid of a hot potato, then detaches himself from the delegate and his decisions. It catches up with him eventually, when a crisis surfaces that he can't avoid. This kind of leader doesn't want to be held accountable, but somehow doesn't hold the other person accountable either. It seems impossible, doesn't it? But it happens somewhere every day. Personally, I want to be held accountable and responsible for whatever decisions I have the freedom and authority to make and to implement.

IMPLEMENTING SOMEONE ELSE'S DECISIONS

There are times when a person in a leadership position has to implement a decision that he didn't make and may not completely agree with. At one time or another, everyone in management is involved in a frustrating or unpopular decision: maybe a budget cut, or the scrapping of a project or product. More than once in my career I found myself in that position, and I have firm beliefs about what a strong leader must do in such a situation.

If I was part of the decisionmaking process, I would certainly argue my point of view. Until the decision was reached, I'd do everything possible to swing the others involved to my way of thinking. But once the decision was made, even though my point of view did not prevail, I would treat that decision as if it were my own. Furthermore, I would implement it with the same interest and enthusiasm as if it were. Sometimes that's difficult, especially if it turns out to be an unpopular decision. But for a strong leader it's imperative. Besides, what about the times when the shoe is on the other foot, and my decision has to be implemented by people who may have opposed it?

In situations like this, weak leaders go to their people and say, "Look, this decision comes from top management. I don't like it any more than you do. Believe me, I tried to shoot it down but failed. Now we're stuck with it, and it's up to us to make it work."

He apologizes for the decision! He separates himself from management. He says, "Hey, I'm not one of them, I'm one of you."

By encouraging a "we-they" attitude, he hurts the company, causes dissatisfaction and unrest, and most of all, demeans himself as a manager and a leader. He thinks that he's strengthening his position with the troops. He's wrong! He's presenting the decisionmaking process as a confrontation in which there are winners and losers; he's telling his people, loud and clear, that he's a loser. He's also demonstrating that when some people don't get their way, they bad-mouth those who do.

Well, such a leader certainly undermines his staff's perception of his effectiveness. When a person in a leadership position separates himself from the decisionmakers, his people take notice and begin to question his ability to manage. The change in their attitude toward him may be so subtle that he does not see it happening, but once he puts himself on the sidelines he is no longer taken seriously.

These so-called leaders would not be part of my team for long—not the dictator who can't delegate responsibility, or the procrastinator who avoids making a decision. None of my people could flip-flop in and out of management and survive. These types weaken the managerial structure of a company. They are usually a major source of rumors and gossip. They confuse the people in their department and, as they try to be on the popular side of any company issue, more often than not add fuel to any smoldering fire.

Although I believe that a good manager carries out the

decisions of his superiors as though they were his own, I'm not advocating blind allegiance. Every person should know, and set, his limits. If what you're expected to implement is contrary to your basic values, you must resolve it to your satisfaction, one way or another—but never by underhandedly trying to sabotage the decision.

I have said that I consider it my responsibility to argue my point of view in the decisionmaking process. That is true, but I'm a pragmatist who carefully picks and chooses the fights I get involved in. I'm not interested in winning a battle if I end up losing the war. We all know people who fight for every point as if their life depended on it. They get a reputation for being argumentative, hardheaded and unreasonable. After a while you can't tell which points are important to them and which aren't. Before long, this kind of person is left out of the decisionmaking process whenever possible—and isn't taken too seriously when he can't be avoided.

SETTING PRIORITIES

A good manager and leader has to be able to set priorities, not only in the battles he opts to get into, but in just about everything he does. So let's talk about priorities.

In a large corporation, priorities have to be set at every level. The corporate goals have a tremendous impact on the priorities of everyone in management. At IBM, how those goals are to be achieved affect the priorities of everyone in all functions—engineering, manufacturing, marketing, etc. I can visualize a company's priorities as a set of boxes that nestle, one into another—starting with a large box, symbolizing the corporate priorities, and ending with a small box, which might symbolize the papers piled up in each individual's in box. A good leader has to be the master of his own in box. He has to know how to prioritize its contents or he'll be buried in details, wondering where the time went and why so little was accomplished. I've known people who immerse themselves in minutiae, sometimes giving to a routine memo, which requires only a minimal response, the same time and attention they devote to a more serious matter. Some people hide in their in box. It's a way for them to put off dealing with things that may be difficult but should have a high priority.

The best managers know how to stack their priorities, quickly and with certainty, and do not get caught up in details that erode their time and managerial effectiveness.

There are so many options today, so much to choose from, that one must constantly sort out things one needs from those one wants or yearns for. Too many managers have an insatiable desire for more people, more money, more resources. Necessity versus desirability is a frequent conflict. Too often desire wins out—usually at the company's expense. An executive who gives in to desire may put too much fat into his head count or spend too much of his budget on nonessential programs. You must be able to make a clear distinction between what is desirable and what is necessary.

Priorities—they are a continuous consideration. Do you build on your strengths or do you struggle to improve your weaknesses? Do you invest in a training program so that you can promote from within, or do you spend the money for higher-priced outside talent? How much quality are you willing to give up for price? Good leaders constantly think in terms of priorities. They pick and choose, and are aware of the impact of each decision. They also keep assessing their ordering of things and carefully restack them if necessary. One thing is sure: if most of your time is spent on items that are not very high on your list of priorities, you're headed for trouble.

I must say this for IBM: regardless of its size and complex structure, its leaders have never been bureaucratic paper shufflers. They try to keep things simple and paperwork at a minimum.

I decided a long time ago that if I was to be a really topnotch manager, I'd have to limit the number of things that I could get deeply involved in. Somewhere along the way, I set the limit at five. Five objectives, five items on my list of priorities; and I insisted that the people who worked for me also limit their objectives to five. The problem rarely was getting them to stretch to five—rather it was inducing them to cut back on objectives. That doesn't mean I didn't permit myself or them to be involved in more than five things. Simply, we were expected to devote most of our time and energy to the five most important things on the agenda. The upside of this is obvious. There was less shifting of gears, fewer distractions. The most important things got done more efficiently and more quickly. You need your priorities, all right, but you can't have such a long list of them that you spread yourself too thin.

There was a downside to limiting myself to five major areas of interest, but it was minimal. When I narrowed the focus of my attention, I became less of an authority about things on the periphery, or outside my primary interests. At first it bothered me. I thought that people expected me to have an answer to almost any question right on the tip of my tongue, and I didn't like disappointing them. But it didn't take long for me to come up with an acceptable response:

"I don't know, but I'll find out and get back to you." What made it acceptable was my never failing to follow up. No one had to ask me twice. This approach is a lot better than "hip shooting" an answer and then wishing you hadn't responded so fast.

HAVING INTEGRITY

If you're to be a successful leader you must have integrity. People must know what to expect from you. Once you make a commitment to a person or a task, you must honor it. I try to live by that, down to the smallest detail. I return phone calls promptly; I answer letters; I meet deadlines. I work at doing things right the first time, and everybody knows it. To me, there's no greater compliment than for people to say, "I can always count on Buck Rodgers." It's a matter of living up to my word, time after time. And since the people I work with can count on me, I feel that I have every right to expect as much from them.

From the time I was a marketing rep, I established myself as dependable, especially where my customers were concerned. I did that by never making a promise I couldn't keep. It wasn't always easy. I remember rough times in the mid-sixties when we were having some difficult production problems. To guarantee a specific delivery date wasn't always possible, and often the sale hinged on that issue. It was tempting to come up with a date that would satisfy the customer, figuring that you'd dance around the problem when the disappointed customer confronted you. But I never "danced." It was more difficult to sell, but I made a special effort to be totally realistic with each customer, never misleading him about our ability to deliver. It may sound corny, but I was determined to establish the fact that my word was my bond. I could never do business any other way—and I'm lucky that I worked for a company that never attempted to put a strain on that value. As a rep, I felt that I was IBM's front man. What the customer would think about me, he would think about IBM. As the president of a large division, and then an officer of the company, I felt the same way—not only about the customer but also about the thousands of IBMers for whom I represented top management.

I said earlier that a good leader is a motivator, one who inspires superior performance by his actions and words. I had my role models at IBM. Among them were Vincent Learson, Frank Cary and L. H. (Red) La Motte. Learson followed Tom Watson, Jr., as CEO. He was tough and demanding, but fair. Cary, his successor, was a master strategist, who at the same time encouraged creative thinking. La Motte, executive vice-president during the Watson era, was a great people motivator, who proved that nice guys can finish first. Just as these men were my role models, I consciously tried to be one for others.

A good role model is almost always a good performer. He does his job so well that it's obvious to the people he works with. He treats his position with respect and his mission or goals with commitment. I don't mean that he exudes solemn staidness and gets carried away with himself—I do mean that he doesn't belittle the importance of his position, his work or the goals he's expected to achieve.

Every time I took a new assignment at IBM, I received what we called a mission statement; some companies call them job descriptions. I'd study these statements and then I'd throw them away. I wasn't being rebellious, but I knew that I couldn't possibly do everything covered in the statement. I felt I had to decide just what was necessary to accomplish the goals set forth, and which of my experiences and skills would help me get the job done. I never believed in trying to press a person into a mold I designed for him. For myself, I wanted to help create the positions to which I was assigned, and I wanted the same for the people who were my responsibility. I wanted them to treat their mission statements as I did: as guidelines.

ENERGIZING THE ENVIRONMENT

I love to work. I'm an enthusiastic person by nature, and so it's with great enthusiasm that I approach every assignment. I considered it my responsibility to charge the atmosphere with excitement and optimism. I was fully aware that the attitude of any leader, positive or negative, which characterizes his style, rubs off on the people he works with. Unfortunately, too many people in leadership positions are terrible role models. They enervate rather than energize their people. An old adage says: "Age may wrinkle the face, but lack of enthusiasm wrinkles the soul." I believe that; but I think that lack of enthusiasm wrinkles the face too.

Still, I must caution you that a good leader's optimism must be realistic. Unfounded optimism can be as destructive as unfounded pessimism. For instance, they take great pains, at IBM, in setting attainable sales quotas for reps. Often it is necessary to stretch to bring in the forecasted sales, but the stretch is considered a realistic part of the projection. Plenty of companies announce sales quotas that are 30, 40, even 50 percent higher than they honestly expect to achieve. I consider that to be poor management at best, and possibly even deceptiveness.

I never wanted reps to go into the field feeling that the company had stacked the cards against them. Once they entered customers' offices, they had to project IBM's enthusiasm and mine. And a person can't do that if he thinks he's getting a raw deal. The blending of realism and optimism is the key to an upbeat selling season.

A WINNING ATTITUDE

A successful leader in marketing projects a winning attitude to his people, and through them to the customers they serve. You'll see what a high premium we put on winning when I discuss compensation and motivation later on. I've always admired the former professional football coach George Allen, who used to tell his players, "Winning is living. Every time you win, you are reborn. Every time you lose, you die a little." That may be excessive, but I agree that winning is an incredibly exhilarating experience, and losing is a bummer.

Because I'm a high-energy person and have a reputation for always striving for "a little more," people who don't know me very well could get the idea that I'm a workaholic. They're wrong. I've known people who are proud to say that they reached the pinnacle of their profession by working sixteen or eighteen hours a day, six or seven days a week. They brag that they haven't had a vacation for years, and when they do take a day off, they call the office three or four times.

I'm not interested in judging other people, but I could never consider myself successful if I had to devote my life to my work. I said that I love to work, and I do. But somewhere along the line I developed the philosophy of working to live rather than living to work. When I'm on the job—in or out of the office—I give the task at hand my complete attention and concentration, and whatever energy is needed to get the job done. I pace myself. I don't want to run out of steam, physically or mentally. It bewilders me when managers demand 120 percent from their people, when I've never been able to give 100 percent of myself, except in short spurts. You really need to know when an extra effort is required, and that's when you must inspire people to reach back and draw upon their reserves. I've missed my share of dinners with my family and given up a few weekends to my work, but these were the exceptions. I never saw a correlation between hours worked and work accomplished that gave me any reason to believe the workaholic was the most productive kind of performer. It doesn't make sense to me that he would be. Most things done in excess are exhausting, and tired people cannot be the most efficient workers. But what really bothers me is what happens to the workaholic's field of vision, his interests and his personal relationships.

It's unfortunate when a family is sacrificed because a person can't work out a balance between work, family and play. A notably productive salesperson recently confided that he never had a meal with his family except on Sundays, never attended his children's graduations or watched them perform in a school event; he worked six days a week from 7 A.M. until 10 P.M. throughout his career—and considers himself to be one of the most successful salespeople in the world. Not in my book! I'm not condemning this workaholic. I feel sorry for him. It's too bad that a person has to give so much of himself, and his family and his freedom, to do a job that someone else could do just as well expending reasonable time and energy.

In my thirty-four years at IBM, I never shirked a responsibility or put out less than the job required. In fact, I always gave a little extra. I can say the same about my performance as a family man. I even manage to get in some time for myself. In addition to running five miles a day, I am a three-handicap golfer and an "A" tennis player. That's not too shabby for a guy my age.

BALANCING ACT I

I advocate balance in one's life. Of course, you have to give a fair day's work for a fair day's pay. If your family and your sense of social responsibility and your value system aren't high, or if your compulsion to work drives everything else out of your life, then you've got a serious problem. Regarding social responsibility, I think we all have a "civic rent" to pay during our lifetime. Happily, our society has moved from the "me" generation to what I refer to as the "be" generation. This means you can be anything you want to be, depending on your skills and capabilities. People want to *be* something; they want to contribute; they can't just be takers. What we choose to do is personal, whether it's working in a drug abuse program or for a charitable organization or toward getting band uniforms for the local school. Every good leader I know encourages his people to find ways to express themselves outside their work life. Not only do they and their community benefit; so does their company.

Recently, I was invited to speak to the top management of a multibillion-dollar manufacturer. The thrust of one of my messages was that every business person should get involved in civic activities, away from the business. The group seemed a little uneasy, and I sensed that I had hit a nerve. Later, in a private conversation, the chairman of the board told me that it wasn't unusual for the key people in the audience to work six or seven days a week. That was the pace he personally set—and demanded. It had been his style of management for many years, and his company was successful; but he agreed that perhaps there was a changing value system to be dealt with, and said that my ideas were worth considering. Shortly afterward, he invited me to serve as a consultant to his company. I was flattered, and pleased to accept.

SEEKING ADVICE

Not only do I give advice when asked, I also never hesitate to seek it. Yet for some people I know, asking for advice is more difficult than asking for money. They somehow feel that it's a display of weakness, or that it makes them vulnerable to criticism. Well, I learned a long time ago that there are people much brighter than I, who at times have the ability to cut through a complex problem that has had me buffaloed. I also found that often the best advice comes from someone who brings to the table a totally different point of view. The most successful leaders feel comfortable asking for the advice of others whenever they need it. They make no attempt to project an image of an all-knowing, omnipotent executive. There are lots of good reasons to ask for advice, but high among them is that it's the greatest compliment you can give, demonstrating that you think enough of someone to involve him in a problem you have. Asking for advice should become part of every leader's repertoire of management techniques.

When you're in a highly structured organization, you may be inhibited from going for advice to someone below or above you on the organizational chart. Most people feel O.K. about asking their immediate supervisor or a peer for advice; but what about your boss's boss? Will you be stepping on someone's ego? Or what about going to someone two or three rungs down the ladder from you? Would that be considered a tactical error in your company? Frankly, I go to whoever I think can help me—whether it's for advice or for information. And that seems to work pretty well throughout IBM. I don't see any reason to stand on ceremony when you need help. You should know who has the expertise in your organization, and make use of it. I welcome anyone into my office, whatever his or her position in the company. I'm delighted when someone comes to me to find out what it takes to "make it" at IBM. When an executive purports to have an "open door policy" but people rarely take advantage of it, it's usually because he is sending out double messages—one being "Don't take my invitation seriously." Either that, or people are being discouraged from going over the heads of their managers.

Just as I've never been shy about asking for advice, I've never been afraid to surround myself with the best staff possible. It's one of the easiest ways to get a reputation for being a first-rate manager. The leader who selects his staff with the insight of a topnotch casting director is certain to have an easier time of it than the manager who defers to his personnel department. Everybody who's ever worked in a corporation has heard of the manager who is so insecure that he actually avoids hiring the best people. He is afraid that the "new kid on the block" will show him up or somehow make him look bad, and eventually push him out of his job. It's another form of job paranoia, of running scared. I never thought in those terms. I always tried to find the best of the best, and when they met my expectations I saw to it that they advanced. If they chased after my job, so much the better. They performed at a higher level than they might have done otherwise.

PRAISING IN PUBLIC, CRITICIZING IN PRIVATE

Not everyone I hired performed as well as I had hoped. Even the best of them had occasional lapses of good judgment, just as I did and sometimes still do. When someone you give responsibility to doesn't live up to expectations as a leader, you are faced with one of your most difficult tasks—confronting the person and criticizing the performance. Some managers find it almost impossible to handle a confrontation with someone they are closely associated with. At times, they fail to do their own job properly by letting the mediocre or incorrect work slide by, with barely a mention. On the other hand, I've seen managers who seem to delight in chewing out an employee—often in front of his co-workers. I can understand, but not tolerate, the manager who wants to avoid a scene, and I have no respect at all for the tyrant. I don't think anyone should be humiliated or demeaned because of his errors or bad judgments. Nor should a leader allow the quality of work to become low because he's too weak to demand that it remain high.

I think that at one time I was perceived as an easygoing type of manager with a superior staff of people. That's because I always praised in public and criticized in private. I never thought it necessary to let others know that someone in my department didn't do his job properly. When a problem arose, I dealt one-on-one with the person involved, in private. I never raised my voice to frighten anyone into doing what was right. I discovered that people are smart enough to know who holds their pay card, so scare tactics are as unnecessary as they are unfair. I entered each of these private conversations with the assumption that both of us wanted to accomplish the same thing: perform our job with the highest degree of excellence possible. And, with a minimum of bruised feelings, correct our mistakes and get on with the job.

On the other hand, if somebody did something exceptionally well, something beyond our expectations, I made sure that as many people as possible knew about it. I always acknowledged new ideas in front of others. This encouraged others to bring ideas to me, because they knew I wouldn't plagiarize them. Whenever possible, I praised our top performers on special occasions such as branch office meetings, sales banquets and customer conferences, as well as in our company newsletter and other publications. I never met anyone who didn't enjoy the attention. The praise must be sincere, though; otherwise you come across as a back-slapper, and lose your credibility.

BEING ABLE TO ANTICIPATE

One of the toughest and most important traits a good leader must acquire is the ability to anticipate and develop a strategy. The generals of the world know that strategy is the craft of the warrior; they understand their own strengths and weaknesses as well as their enemies'. They then analyze these facts before they plan their attack.

No crystal ball or Ouija board will help you. First, you must put together a long-term strategic plan and a short-term operating plan that everyone agrees is realistic and attainable. Then you say, "Look, we made our commitment. Now let's see if we can stretch beyond that." This is known as a goal level, but the resources and commitment are set on the base plan. Second, you must prepare a definitive risk plan in case things go wrong, so you have something to fall back on. Thus you can avoid making dangerous, hip-shooting decisions, because you already thought through the problems during calm times, before they occurred.

Wayne Gretzky understands the need to anticipate. Considered perhaps the greatest hockey star in the history of the sport, he is the only professional player to score more than fifty goals in fifty or less games in a single year. He's done this for three consecutive seasons, while leading the league in scoring for the past five years. When asked his secret, he says matter-of-factly: "I skate to where the puck is going to be, not where it has been."

I don't think anyone is a born leader. A person who aspires to a high managerial position can develop the necessary skills if he or she is ambitious and dedicated enough. I believe that. But I know you have a head start if you like people and yourself, and adhere to a strong sense of integrity.

3

CREATING A TOTALLY SALES-ORIENTED ENVIRONMENT

. . . at IBM everybody sells! . . . Every employee has been trained to think that the customer comes first—everybody from the CEO, to the people in finance, to the receptionists, to those who work in manufacturing.

Successful salespeople understand the importance of long-term customer connections. The size of their paycheck is determined to a large extent by their ability to develop sound, lasting relationships with enough customers. For the best of them, it's easy enough. They are respectful and thoughtful and go out of their way to be helpful. Most companies appreciate the need for good salespeople. Even so, what puzzles me is that so many companies have a shortsighted view of what selling is all about. They have the mistaken idea that the only salespeople in their organization are pounding the pavement, or toting a sample bag, or working the showroom. The rest of the organization is not considered as part of their marketing operation, and that's a serious mistake. Such companies may be selling a product or a service, but they aren't running a sales-oriented business. There's no way to quantify the loss in sales their tunnel vision incurs.

Doing business with a company that is not sales-oriented is usually an unpleasant experience—one we're all too familiar with. Your phone call is answered with, "One moment please," and before you have a chance to say hello, you're on hold. The receptionist scowls at you for interrupting a personal conversation and sends you through a maze of halls with vague directions. As you look for your destination, obviously lost, you pass a dozen employees and no one offers assistance. If this company thinks you missed a payment on its Friendly Budget Plan, you are treated as if you held them up with a gun; and when you prove that its accounting department screwed up, it is shrugged off without an apology. I could go on and on, but we all are familiar with people and companies who should take a course in creating a totally sales-oriented environment, emphasizing good old-fashioned courtesy.

It doesn't make any sense to invest in a sales organization or to build an advertising program designed to project a caring attitude, and then have all your good work sabotaged by someone in the credit department, or by a receptionist or secretary, or even by an unthoughtful CEO.

IBM is a sales-oriented company. That's because at IBM, *everybody sells!* That's not a slogan or a gimmick. It's a fact. Walk into the IBM building in New York or into any of its offices throughout the world and you'll get the idea. Every employee has been trained to think that the customer comes first—everybody from the CEO, to the people in finance, to the receptionists, to those who work in manufacturing.

To me, it seems utterly obvious that every employee should feel a part of the selling effort. Let's face it—everybody's salary comes out of the revenue generated by sales. When there are no sales, there is no income, and no business. It's as simple as that. Everyone in a company must understand and respect that fact, and also understand the part he or she plays in the sale.

At the same time, all employees must realize how their jobs relate to the sales force, the company's first line of attack. After all, the sales reps are the liaison people—the spokespersons who interface with the customer.

The sales-oriented shipping department understands that it can either enhance a sale or play havoc with it. As much as any service department, shipping personnel give the salespeople credibility. If because of negligence or displaced priorities an order doesn't get out of the warehouse when it was promised by the salesperson, everybody suffers. Not just the customer and the rep. Employees in the sales-oriented shipping department realize that and handle every order as if they wrote it themselves.

The sales-oriented credit department is, in a sense, an extension of the sales department. Its personnel know that if they drag their feet and delay the opening of a new account, they will cause the loss of selling time, and could even have a negative effect on their company's inventory turnover and cash flow. They think sales.

In a sales-oriented company, like IBM, all personnel who have any contact with a customer, directly or indirectly, are made to feel that they are involved with their own customer. They must also feel a responsibility toward him, never forgetting that they are being paid, in part, by that customer.

Any IBM employee you might meet, then, is trained to assume that you are a customer or a prospective customer, and should treat you as if his or her job depended on your satisfaction.

Unfortunately for the business world in general, there are too few sales-oriented, customer-driven companies. I suppose that the silver lining to that cloud is the fact that so long as this situation exists, firms that operate the way IBM does will have an edge on their competition.

EVERYBODY SELLS

IBM takes great care to project an honest-to-goodness sales-oriented environment, for customers, or anyone who visits the facilities, are expected to leave with positive feelings.

It starts with the job description of every marketing position—line or staff. Each clearly spells out the job's "customer connection," explaining how it fits into the sales effort—how each position is part of an overall customer support system.

IBM begins imbuing its employees with its sales-oriented philosophy even before they're hired, at the very first interview. To some, the word "imbuing" connotes brainwashing, but I don't think there's anything negative or heavy-handed in what is done. Basically, anyone who wants to work for IBM is told: "Look, here's how we do business. At IBM, the customer comes first. We have some very specific ideas about what that means—and if you work for us we'll teach you how to treat our customers. If our attitude about customers and service is incompatible with yours, we'll part ways—and the quicker the better."

Once a person joins IBM, he or she quickly learns just how serious the company is about being a customer-oriented organization. The concept permeates the training program of every employee, regardless of position or department. Everyone learns that the bottom line is customer satisfaction, and regardless of his or her job, an employee is expected to contribute in some way to the overall marketing effort.

A firm doesn't have to be big or rich to create a sales-oriented environment. It has to be determined and sometimes hard-nosed about its attitude. Businesses that, for whatever reason, have their employees locked into rigid job descriptions must make a special point of building the sales orientation into everyone's day-to-day activities. An IBM marketing job description not only implies each employee's responsibility to the customer but also explains that it is an important factor in the employee's performance appraisal. I think it's crucial to let people know in advance that they are going to be appraised—and exactly what for. In the case of a marketing staff person, one must establish the evaluation criteria. For example, one might say: "You are expected to spend 15 percent of your time in the field with our marketing reps"; or "We expect you to participate in eight industry conferences"; or "You are to keep in contact with ten customers."

You get the idea: It's essential that everyone realize how important the sale and the customer are, what part the employee has in the sale, and how he or she will be evaluated. It's vital that everyone be geared to respond to the customer. This certainly applies to all IBMers. In *In Search of Excellence*, Peters and Waterman verified how the best-operated companies are customer-driven. They reported: "The good news from excellent companies is the extent to which, and the intensity with which, the customers intrude into every nook and cranny of the business—sales, manufacturing, research, accounting."

MONEY ISN'T EVERYTHING

Today, most companies provide incentives for their sales force, and that's fine, especially if a substantial part of a salesperson's income is directly tied into his or her sales production. Unfortunately, most companies do not have any kind of incentive program for those who support or service the salespeople. I'm not advocating the same commission arrangement for the support staff, but I do think it's very important for everyone to think marketing, and to be rewarded for specific achievements or performances.

Of course, the most serious motivator is the job itself. Anyone who hopes to enjoy a long career with IBM must perform at a prescribed acceptable level. But if you want your people to stretch toward an excellent performance, to go beyond what's "acceptable," or even "very good," you should reward them with proper recognition and appreciation.

The least that can be done for an employee who does something especially nice for a customer or for a salesperson is to thank him, privately and publicly. (I almost deleted the preceding sentence because it seems so obvious, but the sad truth is that a great many employers and managers take the genuine contributions of their staff for granted and rarely think to express their appreciation.)

Simple awards for responsive sales- or customer-connected ideas can promote goodwill, and point up management's interest in sales and customers. Their name on a plaque or their idea with proper credit in the house organ can give people a real lift.

Tangible recognition is always welcomed and doesn't have to be a big deal to be effective. Dinner and a show for two is certainly a suitable way to show appreciation. IBM calls it "A Night on the Town."

A weekend at a nearby resort or at a local luxury hotel makes a nice bonus for a deserving employee. You can be as generous as you feel is appropriate to a particular contribution.

At IBM, some big bonuses have been given to behind-the-scenes people to let them know how much their customer responsiveness was appreciated. Sometimes the trappings are rather elaborate, but the "dramas" do make a lasting impression. At a company affair, a suitcase or a small wheelbarrow filled with a large number of dollar bills may be dumped on a table as the emcee invites the recipient to "Please come here and pick up your money!" Then the emcee explains what outstanding support to the marketing function occasioned this award. Any size business can give a plaque, a television set or a check to express gratitude for extraordinary behind-the-scenes sales support. At IBM, it's not unusual for a secretary or a technician to be given a small cash award or another form of recognition when the company receives a letter from a customer that commends some outstanding service rendered. Nothing beats praise when it's deserved. No matter what size a company is or what position an individual holds, he or she gets a real boost when a manager walks into the office and says, "I think you did a terrific job with . . ."

While the orientation should always be to praise, you must also let people know when they're not performing satisfactorily. If you accept mediocre work, you are certain to end up with a mediocre bottom line. Criticize on a one-to-one basis, but don't be bashful about conveying your disappointment when someone lets down a customer or the field salespeople.

Every sales-oriented employee—no matter what his or her position—strengthens a company's sales and marketing efforts. It's like adding extra manpower to a work force. They become goodwill ambassadors, on and off the job, and that's important. IBM doesn't hype people to behave as though they were zealous members of some religious cult out to convert the world. But they are motivated to project a company image that radiates care for the customer, and for society in general.

Every employee is encouraged to act as if he or she were the only personal contact the customer has with the company—and to behave as if the entire company's image is dependent upon the impression that employee projects. In some cases, a behind-the-scenes person may be the only contact a customer has with the home office. In a competitive sales situation, the way a telephone inquiry is handled can be very important to the sale.

The ill will created by a lackadaisical attitude in an employee not directly involved in the selling effort can have a devastating impact on its outcome. Most businesses must realize this. It's bewildering that so few of them do anything about it.

I can't understand why any company that produces a high-quality product would allow rude, surly or apathetic employees to represent them in any phase of their operation. The installer who leaves a mess in a customer's house, the mumbler who loses patience when he's misunderstood, the clerk who acts as if he's doing a favor when he answers a question—these people make it tough on the company they work for. They should be goodwill ambassadors. They are handicaps. I'll tell you this: they wouldn't work for IBM very long.

LINE VERSUS STAFF

I must admit that when I headed IBM's U.S. computer marketing operations—a line position—I didn't encourage corporate staff involvement. It wasn't as if corporate people weren't interested in sales; some watched the daily sales reports as avidly as a stockbroker watches the ticker tape. However, my attitude was that I had enough resources in the division to get the job done, so why complicate things. It's a fact of life that every line executive wants to run his own show without a lot of bureaucratic involvement. A bit of proprietorship seeps into your psyche, meaning: "Keep off my turf." The secret is not to build these barriers to where they become detrimental to getting the job done. It's important to know when to open the doors and ask for help.

After I joined the corporate staff, I felt the line divisions couldn't get along without my direction and involvement. This viewpoint may seem contradictory or even humorous, but it really isn't. It simply came about as a result of IBM's practice of moving its key people back and forth, between line and staff, so they clearly understand the responsibility of each assignment. At the same time, it emphasizes the sensitivity of a person, regardless of the job he holds, in wanting to get the day-to-day sales job done. Today, I continue to be an unabashed advocate of executive involvement in the world of sales and marketing. It's as important to have a sales-oriented corporate headquarters as it is to have a sales-oriented warehouse or credit department. It's more than just a case of vantage point.

IBM's corporate headquarters is populated with people who worked themselves up through the sales and marketing departments, but it's easy to lose your sales orientation if you are separated from your sales force and your customers for any length of time. What about companies that are headed by management who never sold the products they produce, who have no sales orientation at all? How understanding and responsive can they be to their people in the field, or to their customers?

Without real understanding, a salesperson not uncommonly complains: "If I didn't know better, I'd think the home office people were purposely trying to undermine my sales effort. It's as if they're sabotaging everything I accomplish in the field. If they won't assist me, the least they could do is stay out of my way!" When I hear sales reps talking like this, it's generally a good indication that the organization they work for has turned inward, and really doesn't understand why it's in business.

IBM's people are rotated fairly routinely between staff and line positions. It's not always convenient, but having a strong sales-minded organization is a very reasonable trade-off. Generally, once in a staff position, employees of most companies remain in some staff slot as long as they survive the corporate wars. I think that going from line to staff is usually considered a demotion, but this is not so at IBM.

ON THE FIRING LINE

Now, it's not possible to rotate every single employee, but it is very important for your key people to have firsthand exposure to customer situations. I can't think of a better way to let the engineering, manufacturing and financial people know what goes on in the field than to *put them out in the field with a salesperson calling on customers*. It's an incredible education. You'll hear comments such as: "It's totally different from what I had imagined." "I knew the sales reps were having a problem, but my interpretation was completely off base." "I didn't understand; no wonder my solutions were wrong." "I thought I had a fix on the customer's problems, but now that I've been taken through his plant, I know what we have to do at our end."

Recently, General Motors has had factory people spend time in dealership showrooms, mingling with the customers. Not only do they see, firsthand, the customers' reactions to their product, but they also have the opportunity to hear the salespeople's "pitch" and to listen to their complaints. The factory people go back to their plant jobs with a different perspective.

Many times I've seen IBM people develop new attitudes about customer problems after only a short time in the field. An employee handling accounts receivable gets a feel for the kind of confusion that's created when a customer is invoiced incorrectly. "He wrote and we spoke on the phone, so I knew that he was unhappy," a staff person said, "but it really hit home when he looked me in the eye and said, 'If the company can't bill me properly, and can't quickly expedite the correction, then how do you expect me to believe it can successfully install a computer system for us?' " In the field, you realize that the customer perceives the company as a whole, and that the foul-up of one department affects the total perception.

It's a common practice at IBM for all levels of management to meet regularly with customers. Everyone does it— department heads of accounting, education, research and development, manufacturing, and the company's top executives, as well. As corporate vice-president of marketing, I met with customers all over the world, both formally and informally.

At one lunch with a key customer, I asked about our service and if there were any problems. He answered, "Well, Buck, overall I think your people are terrific. However . . ." He hadn't planned to complain, but we had become friendly and he felt comfortable telling me about his company's dissatisfaction with our service in one part of the country. As I probed, I discovered that one of our senior people on the account apparently had not kept up to date with certain technical aspects of the business, and the customer wasn't satisfied with this IBMer's knowledge. That afternoon I asked our regional manager to investigate discreetly. The customer's complaint was legitimate, and a serious problem was averted by getting our senior rep into a new educational program.

Sure, in my capacity as IBM's marketing vice-president I was expected to be out there mingling with customers. Well, it should be expected of *all* officers of a truly sales-oriented company. Everyone in a key managerial position should be out there constantly probing and asking the customer, "How are we doing?" Take a leaf from New York Mayor Koch's book. He asks that question so often you might think he's patented it—but it's a good question, and if you ask it you may learn a lot from the responses you get. Then you've got to follow up quickly, or the customer will get the idea that your interest was merely rhetorical. Report back to him. Let him know what's being done. Your customer will be flattered to know how seriously you took his complaint.

THE CUSTOMER ON YOUR TURF

There are times when, instead of going to your customers, you invite them to visit you. Whether you invite one or a group, it's a great idea. At IBM, it frequently is done in a big way, with customer conferences ranging in size from fifty to a thousand participants. At these meetings, product planners, development engineers and other key technical people get an opportunity to mix and exchange ideas with these very important people. Several times a year, specific customers and a variety of industry groups—representing, say, a cross-section of the banking or the insurance field—are invited, for discussion of their industry's problems and assessment of how IBM products are meeting customers' expectations. These are important dialogues, and line and staff people are encouraged to participate. Incidentally, it's very reinforcing to hear customers say positive things about the company and not just air the problems.

Perhaps the most exciting customer sessions conducted by IBM are its Chief Executive Officers Classes. Here are brought together in a classroom leaders from industry, education and government. They're really impressive groups. The representatives of industry are either presidents or chairmen of the boards of companies that do at least a billion dollars' business a year. The educators are presidents of leading universities, and the politicians are usually state governors. These five-day classes are held at the company's Poughkeepsie and San Jose facilities and are in session from eight in the morning till eight at night. The meetings are not a hard sell on IBM products. They focus on how customers' operations can be improved through the use of advanced management techniques and new computer technologies. For ten consecutive years, I had the privilege of being the wrap-up speaker at these sessions. And during their chairmanships, Frank Cary and John Opel also participated.

Now you may be thinking: "Sure, IBM brings in CEOs of billion-dollar companies, but how does that apply to my business?" Naturally, I realize that smaller firms can't duplicate these CEO classes or, for that matter, the industry councils. However, they can do something similar on a smaller scale. Any company can give a luncheon or dinner, for example, to pay tribute to its customers. Depending on your budget, a prominent national or local guest speaker could address the group. It's not the size that matters; it's the environment you create when you bring your employees and your customers together, to share ideas and problems. It's surprising to me that so many companies don't get around to inviting any of their customers to see their operation and meet with their people, something every company should do regularly. While you might not get every customer to accept your invitation, I can promise you, at the very least, that they'll all be flattered to have been invited.

THE GLUE THAT BINDS

What IBM calls account-planning sessions are conducted annually. Here, both line and customer-support people spend from three days to a week reviewing the entire status of an account. With a major customer like Citibank or General Motors, as many as fifty IBM people could be involved. In the case of a small account, the session might include a handful of IBMers.

At these meetings, the customer's business conditions are discussed, and both long-term and short-term strategies are examined. There is review of all applications and installations of the customer's systems, its backlog, maintenance records, and so on. An action plan is set up and participants address the question: Where are we going to take this customer? What is the competitive situation? What is the right set of products? How do we give him value? These questions are discussed with the customer and his participation is a vital part of the development of the plan. A wonderful partnership arrangement evolves. The customer has a well-documented action plan that covers the upcoming year as well as years to come.

One of the best things about the account-planning sessions is the productive working relationship that develops between the customer and IBMers. It's not simply a matter of marketing reps and system engineers working closely with the customer. Many others can be involved—planning people, engineers, service people, administrative employees, and others—all working closely with the customer. While many good things result from these sessions, one obvious benefit is a very enlightened support system to back up the marketing rep.

The IBM account-planning session should give a business of any size some constructive ideas. In the majority of cases, these meetings are conducted on a much smaller scale than what I have just described, but the same basic principle is applied. Time is allocated to reflect upon IBM's relationship with each customer, and to put together a brief history that facilitates an action plan. A small company can do the same thing. It might take only a single afternoon session at your office, or at the customer's place of business. The important thing is to get all your people, particularly the behind-the-scenes ones, involved in working with the customer and developing a partnership relationship.

THE TOP 100

I could visit an IBM branch anywhere in the United States, Canada, South America, the Far East, Europe and Asia and ask: "What can you tell me about your top accounts?" I would then be shown an extensive up-to-date file on every one of them. There'd be a booklet containing data ranging from current systems installed to the education programs in effect. These documents are kept current to make sure the needs of each of these customers are understood, and if there's a change in the sales force, new people can be informed quickly on the status of the account.

The short-term and long-term plans for major customers were always available not only to me but to all senior management, including the president and the chairman of the board.

Every business should keep similar data on its top accounts, but by no means is 100 a magic number. Just how many and how you arrange them depends on a number of variables. Sales volume and sales potential are basic orientations, or maybe you will focus on what I call "leadership" accounts, those that are the most prestigious and make the greatest impact on their industry. And while you are committed to giving outstanding service to all your customers, certain ones are what I refer to as your company's family jewels. You've worked very hard to obtain them, and you want to stay on top of things so you *never lose them.*

These account profiles and action plans are an important tool and should be available for review at the drop of a hat. You should not have to go digging for information when a problem develops with a top account. Although I know of many companies whose executives didn't even know who their top customers were, such a situation at IBM is inconceivable to me.

EXECUTIVE INVOLVEMENT

A company cannot afford to excuse its high-ranking executives from participating in its sales effort. IBM believes that. The executive who gets his "feel" for the marketplace from reports, trade publications and an occasional meeting with a customer is going to have a shallow understanding of the problems in the field. Consequently, top IBM executives not only spend some of their time traveling with reps, but also have key customers assigned to them. These executives—who are responsible for working with perhaps three or four customers—are from all parts of the company: marketing, manufacturing, development labs, etc. They stay in touch with their accounts in person and by phone. They ask for suggestions, make recommendations, present updated information about technology and express thanks for the business. Sometimes they invite a customer to spend a day at a plant, laboratory or headquarters; at other times, they take a few key IBMers out to visit the customer. The objective of this program is to develop a sales-oriented executive group—the most sensitive possible. It avoids management's living in an isolated cocoon, out of touch with reality.

This work with customers is always done with the co-operation and help of the local IBM marketing rep. Thus, besides a firsthand view of some of the day-to-day problems of the customer, the executive gets a real education about selling in the field. Other benefits gained include a possible short-circuiting, by customer and rep, of company bureaucracy. Over the years, some companies I worked with included United Airlines, Bank of America, Dow Chemical, Carter Hawley Hale, Standard Oil of California, and Boeing Corporation. The people in these companies felt comfortable contacting me directly as well as working through the IBM branch office, and I particularly enjoyed being on an informal, first-name basis with all levels of their management. For some executives in other areas of the business, these assignments are especially exciting and enlightening because they afford a rare firsthand knowledge of the marketplace.

THE COMPANY HEROES

The real heroes in every truly market-driven company are the sales reps. It is they who find out what the customers want and need, and that's where it all begins. Thanks to the marketing reps, IBM's engineering and manufacturing departments build what the customer needs. Our reps are never told, "Here's a product that we've created—now you go out and create a need for it." All employees know that salespeople are the catalysts who generate the company's business.

It bewilders me that some companies consider their sales force to be a necessary evil, something they wish they could eliminate—an expense they are forever whittling away at.

These companies have little or no respect for their salespeople and more often than not treat them as though they were adversaries. They cut territories unnecessarily, raise quotas unrealistically, reduce commission rates whenever they can, and try to bully their salespeople into performing. The company usually gets what it deserves—a sales force that's angry, unhappy, unresponsive and nonproductive.

Companies like this give the sales force only minimal headquarters support, and cry out in pain when everything they try falls short of their expectations.

These are not sales-oriented companies. Staff doesn't communicate with line—the left hand doesn't know what the right hand is doing. Salespeople are generally left stranded in their territories without selling tools and information. And the customer is a victim of such companies' foolishness and inefficiency. In time, these companies self-destruct. Sadly, they are poisoning themselves, and they won't know it until it's too late. They have only to realize that it doesn't take a great deal of money or brains to build a successful sales-oriented company. A little money, a few brains and a lot of caring will do it.

I wear my admiration for creative salespeople like a badge for all to see. Every company, starting with its highest management, should make it known to every one of its employees that the salesperson is a VIP. That is how he or she is treated at IBM. It's not unusual for a small group of the top salespeople to be invited to the home office for informal meetings, a private lunch or dinner meeting with top management, and a friendly chat with the chairman of the board. In addition to being great morale-builders for the salesperson, these meetings have a tremendous impact on the total organization. If the chairman and other top executives think enough of sales reps to have these small get-togethers, it makes a strong statement about how selling is valued by the company! It's such a natural thing for IBM to do, but other companies simply don't think in these terms. I know of a salesperson who was the leading producer not only in his company but in his entire industry, and yet he had never met the company's president or chairman. Even when he let it be known that he'd like to meet them, his request was denied. I can't understand the mentality of that company's management! They had a golden opportunity to give well-deserved recognition that would have had a ripple effect on the entire organization. No wonder salespeople too often accuse management of not coming down from their ivory tower!

Praise and recognition are fundamental at IBM, but I must admit that an extra effort is devoted to recognizing exceptional performance in the marketing arena. Some salespeople reach star or celebrity status not only in the company but in the industry—and they deserve it. Let's face it—the salesperson is the *source* in business.

Finally—and it should go without saying—a company must be generous in compensating its sales reps. Underpaying them clearly tells everyone you think they're not important. If they *are* valuable to your business, they deserve to be compensated accordingly. You have to put your money where your mouth is. It's important for IBM to maintain a leadership role through its compensation plan. To ensure this, the total compensation package is routinely evaluated against other information-processing companies, as well as businesses outside the industry. IBM simply wants to make sure that its sales force receives a premium for outstanding performance. This practice helps attract, and retain, top performers.

CREATING MORE SELLING TIME

In a truly sales-oriented environment, everyone is working in harmony to make the sales rep's time more productive. Everyone is asking questions like: "How can I get the order processed sooner?" "How can I guarantee quick delivery?" "How can I improve my job to support the customer?" "How can I enhance the quality of the product?" When everyone in the company is thinking along these lines, the sales rep is going to get the kind of support that is needed to serve the customer.

I don't like it when a salesperson who works all day in the field is burdened with hours of paperwork in the evening. Good reps save their paperwork for nonselling time, and those extra long hours are bound to take their toll in energy, if not in enthusiasm. IBM gives constant attention to reducing unnecessary detail work by the sales rep, and wherever possible tries to mechanize his paperwork. For example, every IBM salesperson has available a terminal that can be used to look up a customer's account in a matter of seconds and access everything needed to provide fine service.

Shortly after I was named president of IBM's Data Processing Division in 1967, I initiated a program for the thousands of employees who worked with me. I wanted everyone to be more responsive to the customer, and a campaign was set up requesting suggestions for improvements on our ways of doing things. New in my position, I asked everyone to give me advice on running the division. Each employee was invited to finish the statement: "If I were president of the Data Processing Division . . ." I announced that I would respond to every suggestion, and recognition, from dinners to money awards, would be given for the best ideas. The program was a huge success, generating several thousand suggestions from marketing reps, service personnel, systems engineers, programmers, secretaries, branch officers and headquarters people. The most striking thing about the responses was that people were concerned not only with current operations but also with the future. Proposals covered every conceivable subject related to the success of the division, including customer relations, asset management, recruitment, personnel development, education, policy and marketing programs. These ideas were considered by the division, and were also forwarded to IBM's

Suggestion Plan, where they became eligible for corporate awards. I think it worked so well because people took it seriously—and knew that they would be taken seriously.

One thing I learned from listening to the people in the field is that the bureaucracy of a corporation can really handicap a sales organization that's designed to react swiftly to the needs of its customers. Rules, regulations and procedures are never intended to stifle, but unless there's a conscious effort to keep them in check, they can be suffocating. What developed at IBM is a pretty good example of what can happen.

Over the years, an extensive library of procedures and directives, called branch office manuals, was built. In every branch office, bookcases were packed with thousands of pages of "how to" and "what for" material. Volumes instructed, in minute detail, how to process an order, how to submit reports, how to acquisition supplies, when to raise the flag, etc., etc. This stuff was taken very seriously by management people. Each new page that was added to this ever-growing body of knowledge was one more headache for the rep in the field. I must admit that as president of the division, I could avoid most of the irritating procedures that filled the manuals. (The fact that people in high positions are usually immune to this type of paperwork, some of which they author, contributes to the problem.)

Well, the complaints from the field got to me and I decided to do something. Accompanied by several headquarters executives, I flew to Salt Lake City unannounced and physically removed the complete set of IBM branch office manuals.

The first reaction was: "How can we operate without them? How will we know what to do? It will be chaos!"

"Use common sense," I replied. "Do what's right for the customer, and above all, make it easier for the IBM people to do business. Rewrite the book so we can be more responsive, lighter on our feet." Then I flew to Saint Louis and went through the same thing at our branch there.

Within ninety days we had a new set of guidelines,

which became the standard operating procedure for the entire division. The revised manual was a quarter of the original. More important, hours of unnecessary paperwork had been eliminated.

The ease of modern communication is usually considered a blessing, but sometimes it can be abused. When a few of our branch managers complained about the amount of paper that was crossing their desks, I wanted to get a feel for what they were up against, and asked the mailroom to send me every piece of paper the branches were receiving. In a week, my desk was covered with so much material that there was no room for anything else. Obviously, the complaints from the field were justified.

Our branch offices were being deluged with paper from all over the division: from product managers complaining that their product was not selling in some area, and wanting the branch manager to initiate a new program for them; from education centers asking for help in filling a class; from financial managers wanting to borrow a few people for a week to participate in a task force. Along with requests that had branch managers juggling their staff at the same time they were trying to meet their own objectives, there was an inundation of promotional material, product information, directives, price changes, procedural modifications. You name it, they got it. To relieve the situation and free our people for selling, installing and servicing, I ordered a control point where information was prioritized. Not only was the flow of unnecessary paper curtailed; the number of people who could communicate directly with the branch offices was reduced.

Bureaucracy, with the paper it generates, can take on a life of its own. It can exist for its own sake, insensitive to the mission and goals of a company. For me, there must be a continuous effort to improve the ability to serve the customer, by creating more selling time for the sales reps and the branch managers.

4

BUILDING A SUPERIOR MARKETING ORGANIZATION

. . . top management should spend 40 to 50 percent of its time educating and motivating its people . . .

Thomas Watson, Sr., believed that IBM's annual investment in education, training and internal communication should increase at a rate that is greater than the company's rate of growth. He wanted the people who worked for him to understand the goals of the company, and to know that each person's contribution was important toward achieving those goals.

Watson, who had been employed by National Cash Register, first as a marketing rep and then as a sales manager, recognized the striking parallel between a salesperson's success and the amount of home office support he received. He knew that a salesperson needed not only proper sales training and product knowledge but also inspiration, and a dynamic organization ready with backup support. Watson's successor, Tom, Jr., began his IBM career in sales and, like his father, understood the importance of the marketing rep. Since its earliest days, then, "Everybody thinks selling" has been a dominant theme at IBM.

Like the Watsons and thousands of other IBMers who have had management positions, I began my career with the company as a marketing rep. In this chapter, I will discuss IBM's marketing operation. Much of what has made that company great can be emulated by any sales organization.

THE TALENT SEARCH

IBM recruits top people.

Although I don't believe in a "naturally born" salesperson, I do think some candidates have greater potential than others. IBM doesn't hire people at random. Its recruitment program is truly a selective talent search.

IBM recruits from approximately 350 colleges across the country, focusing on 100 top schools. Selected executives act as liaisons to thirty-two key schools, including Harvard, Illinois, Penn State, Purdue, the University of Texas and UCLA. Grades, student activities, athletics, leadership roles and communications skills are important considerations. About half of the recruits have technical degrees in hard sciences, such as math, engineering and physics; about 40 percent have business degrees, and the rest are art and science majors. Approximately 40 percent are women.

In 1984, the average student recruit had a 3.65 grade point average. But this did not rule out the C student who made an outstanding impression during his personal interview—the most important factor of the selection process.

To the surprise of many placement officers, only first-line managers do the actual hiring for IBM. After all, if you hold these managers accountable and responsible for the company's objectives, then you give them the freedom to pick and choose the people they want.

IBM has a corporate recruiting organization that sets guidelines, teaches techniques, maintains liaison with the various college placement offices and coordinates recruiting activities among the various divisions. Because of its size, IBM needs this superstructure. In 1984 alone, the company had more than 1,300,000 job applications!

While most marketing people are recruited on college campuses, others apply on their own, or respond to IBM advertisements for individuals with specific skills. One important source of talent is referrals. Unlike many companies, IBM encourages its employees to recommend friends and relatives, considering it a wonderful endorsement. I could never agree with company policies that prohibit hiring immediate family of employees. However, all hiring and all promotion are based on individual merit and nobody receives special preference. There are regular complaints by IBMers whose children are not hired. It's a source of great personal pride that my three children all joined IBM in marketing and are enjoying successful careers with the company.

Since IBM operates with a well-defined value system, it's essential that the young people recruited into the company are comfortable and compatible with those values. Important as it is for the interviewer to do an honest job of describing the company and its opportunities, it's even more important for the interviewee to speak his mind and present his wares. He must be given the time to sell himself.

An applicant is expected to know something about IBM and have an idea of why and how he might fit in. After all, he is applying for a position in marketing!

I like an applicant who is assertive and asks questions about the company's philosophy, its pay range, how people are promoted, the training program. The questions show thoughtfulness and intelligence. An applicant shouldn't attempt to overwhelm the interviewer with his or her personality. I advise young people to ask questions that show their interest in establishing a long-term partnership with the company.

I don't believe in just taking from the campus. A person successful in business has what I've called a "civic rent" to pay. There are many creative programs at schools across the country where business people can become involved. I myself have participated in the Executive in the Classroom programs at Purdue and Tennessee, Penn State's Distinguished Speaker program, and the Colgate Darden School program at the University of Virginia. Though my purpose in being on campus wasn't to recruit, I met many outstanding students, some of whom subsequently joined IBM.

Every executive should visit at least one or two college campuses every year. The campus is a good place not only to find out what young people in this country think but also to become energized. You should let students know that ethics, rewards and excitement exist in the world of American business. It's vital for students to get a mixture of the theory being taught in the classroom and the practicality of the business world. This type of participation builds a better bridge of understanding between classroom and boardroom. Although business people are welcomed on college campuses today, there were periods when we were not so well received. At such times, a special effort must be made to hear the students' message and make sure they hear yours.

THEORY AND PRACTICE

IBM would never send an untrained or a partially trained person into the field. What representatives say and do, and how they say and do it, is too important to the company's image and credibility. And it could shorten the career of a potentially good salesperson to go into the field unprepared.

IBM's training program is well funded, planned and structured, so by the time the trainee is finished, he has the skills to meet the customer with confidence. A weak training program almost guarantees high turnover—and that always costs more than an effective training program. Turnover can shatter a sales organization's morale and frustrate the customer who is dependent on the rep for service and advice. In recent years, IBM lost less than 3 percent of its first-year marketing reps, so from the company's point of view, the recruiting and training programs work.

IBM sales and systems engineer trainees receive twelve months of initial training—field experience combined with formal classroom work. About 75 percent of the training is at the branch office location and 25 percent at one of IBM's national education centers. A branch office training manager will oversee the IBM trainee's education program, which includes self-paced modules on everything from the company's culture, values and beliefs to basic knowledge of the full product line. Trainees spend time with marketing people on customer calls to get a feel for the business. In addition, it is not uncommon for the new kid on the block to make his first formal product demonstration to the most critical audience—the veteran reps—at a branch office meeting. Sometimes the constructive criticism can be devastating, but the trainee gains confidence and earns the respect of his peers. The branch office takes great care in ensuring that its trainees are ready for each phase of marketing training. Just as IBM would never send an unqualified rep to meet with a customer, it would never send an unqualified trainee to one of the schools. It simply doesn't make good business sense.

The first marketing school covers some of the more formal aspects of the way IBM does business, including sales policies and marketing practices, in addition to computer concepts and IBM products. Learning to sell begins on the second day of class. (Many organizations barely discuss the art of selling in their training sessions, dealing with it almost as an afterthought.) In the classroom, IBM trainees learn about the company's support structure and how to use it. They study the competition and begin to develop general business skills.

This process of theory and practice continues as the IBM trainee moves closer to becoming a qualified sales rep or systems engineer. The trainee sees the practical side of the classroom work when he or she returns to the branch. The fieldwork is followed by another four weeks of classroom sessions, referred to as "heartbreak hill": intense schooling from 8 A.M.

to 6 P.M., and homework that keeps the trainee working past midnight. The courses were designed so that no one could finish them, and for a reason. In the world of business, people must learn how to manage their time. They must determine "What is enough effort?" "Is it better to stay up all night rather than study until ten?" In the beginning of the program, the trainees are graded as if they were in college—that is, tests are objective, and the results are based on how much information is retained. As they progress in the program, the testing becomes more subjective. Trainees perform sales demonstrations, and although they might have their facts down pat, they might get a poor grade because of a weak presentation. The facts must be presented in simple terms that spell value and benefits. A customer won't judge a salesperson on what he knows, but on how well he communicates what he knows. The business world is subjective, so that's what sales trainees must be prepared to deal with.

Occasionally trainees think and act as if they are still in college, and object to a specific phase of the training program. "We don't think it's fair that the instructors have all the power and decide the curriculum. We think we should have more say about it." Student power!

When this happens, they're told: "You probably paid fifteen thousand dollars a year to go to school. Now we're paying you. So we decide what's best. This is the economic imperative and one of the first things for you to learn about business." It's a welcome-to-the-real-world lesson, and the demands for student power have always been short-lived.

Generally, the trainees thrive on IBM's rigorous training program, the long hours and the stiff competition. It really is tough on them—fourteen to fifteen hours of intense study each day—but seldom does anyone complain, and rarely does anyone drop out.

The top people IBM recruits are highly motivated, and in the formal training program these individuals want to perform to the best of their abilities. One reason the trainees take the education program so seriously is that students are evaluated each step of the way. At the conclusion of marketing training, an Excellence in Marketing award is presented and a class president designated.

WHO MAKE THE BEST TEACHERS?

Many companies assign the job of training new people to their least productive sales reps. Unwilling to give up the revenue of top producers, they think they are saving money. I believe that the sales force is far too important to be trained by mediocre people. The best teachers are a company's top sales staff, for not only do they understand selling techniques; they have the keenest perceptions, and marketing acumen that is second to none. It's important, too, that your instructors be heroes and role models. Proud of their accomplishments in the field, they should be able to project that pride in the classroom. It probably *will* cost some sales to pull the top producers out of the field, but a well-trained sales force will pay back the short-term losses in spades.

Not every top salesperson is able to teach, so IBM has been very careful in selecting its instructors. Marketing instructors go through rigorous training before they are permitted to lead a class. An IBM instructor teaches for no more than eighteen to twenty-four months, so there is an influx of fresh experiences, brought in by up-to-date salespeople. The assignment has proved to be a stepping-stone for the marketing people, as 75 percent of instructors are promoted to first-line manager positions.

IBM's instructor-trainee ratio is one to ten. In addition, top marketing and systems engineering reps are invited to be guest instructors for each class. Trainees hear straight from the source how a significant order was won—or lost—just a few days before, and benefit from an even closer instructor-trainee ratio. At the same time, the guest instructor is, in a sense, auditioning for a new assignment.

TEAM SELLING

Unlike students in most classrooms, IBM trainees are taught to work as a team. For sixteen years of schooling, students are told, "Don't look at anyone's paper. Do your own work." Now, for the first time, IBM trainees are told, "Here's the problem. The four of you must solve it together." Initially, most trainees don't know how to react to this different approach to problem solving. They have to learn to share and cooperate intellectually, as they work on a single assignment that requires each of them to fulfill specific tasks. The problem cannot be solved unless they work together. This closely approximates the type of team effort and cooperation that the rep will be expected to display in the field. In our industry, sales reps are constantly working with and relying upon the skills of others—specialists in accounting and manufacturing, inventory control and engineering. Since reps assigned to large national accounts always work in teams, it is essential for trainees to become productive team members as soon as possible. At the same time, the entrepreneurial spirit must be maintained.

THE STRUCTURED SALES CALL

Teaching the structured sales call is a fundamental part of IBM marketing training. Not a single day goes by during the entire first year without it being part of the trainee's education program. I am not implying that a "canned" sales presentation is used; it's not possible in our business. However, IBMers learn certain basic messages and techniques, which are incorporated into every presentation.

The objectives of the demonstration or presentation are always stated. This includes why you are there and what you hope to accomplish. The features, functions and benefits of the product are clearly articulated and demonstrated. Trainees learn questioning techniques and listening skills, how to manage objections and ask for the order. If the customer says the product costs too much, you must first find out if this is a valid objection. A cost-justification proposal won't get the order if other factors underlie the objection.

IBM is constantly refining and honing the sales methodology that is taught in every sales school. There's continual role-playing in the classes, with the instructor as customer, whose problems the trainees demonstrate their ability to solve. These sessions are closely monitored and the trainees are critiqued on both strengths and weaknesses. A student is assessed and measured in several key areas, including communication skills, presentation/demonstration techniques, customer interaction and general business knowledge. For every sales call and product demonstration a student gives, he receives personal feedback from his instructor.

IBM conducts one of the most ambitious and sophisticated techniques ever developed for sales training—the Armstrong Case Study, focusing on a fictitious international conglomerate with hotel chains, marinas, retail outlets, and manufacturing and sporting goods divisions. There are detailed profiles of engineers, financial executives, marketing people, the chief operating officer and the chief executive officer. The profiles incorporate personality characteristics, attitudes and even past decisions.

IBM created an incredibly lifelike environment, with instructors enacting Armstrong personnel. The trainees are required to make a series of complicated calls on various people within the organization. Facing dozens of problems and challenges, they must deal with almost everyone in the Armstrong organization, from receptionists to the board of directors. The study is so realistic and the "actors" so convincing that every participant treats the case study as seriously as IBM intended. The exercise culminates in a simulated customer meeting which includes presentation of the study findings, the IBM solution and getting the order.

CUSTOMERS IN THE CLASSROOM

Not only does IBM bring its top sales and technical people into the training centers; it invites customers as well. Their participation creates a real-world atmosphere because they discuss specific problems affecting their businesses. The trainee learns that salespeople can cost the customer money in terms of valuable time, and that a business person is selective about whom he will see. The customer will quickly terminate a sales presentation that doesn't immediately interest or benefit him. Hearing this from someone he or she may someday call on makes a strong impression on the trainee. Customers are usually flattered to participate in education, so don't be shy about seeking their cooperation and counsel.

THE PROFOUND DIFFERENCE

During the three years that I was president of the Data Processing Division, I made it my business to meet with every individual who completed our rigorous sales training program. When I became vice-president of marketing, I continued this practice as often as I could.

This meant addressing twenty to twenty-five final sales training classes and delivering what might be called the graduation speech. Each year, I was able to meet, face to face, with five hundred to a thousand IBMers who were about to go into their first sales territory assignment.

I got a pretty good fix on the quality of our recruiting efforts and the effectiveness of our training program. In addition, I was able to provide tactical and strategic direction, and at the same time challenge the group to meet their objectives.

From the students' perspective, they met firsthand with the president of the division. A trainee in a corporation of thousands of people can feel a million miles away from the company's management. Obviously I didn't want that. Besides, I wanted them to know that their top management understood the marketplace and was willing to listen to any problems or new ideas they might have.

Recently, I addressed a class of IBM marketing trainees in New York City at the wrap-up session of their training program. In the new IBM Madison Avenue building, surrounded by these highly trained reps, I could feel their camaraderie and high spirits. This was the gist of my message to them:

You know that you have participated in a superior training program, and that you will represent a product line that's the envy of the industry. You feel secure with the knowledge that you have both technical and application support systems to help you provide value to the customer. All of this gives you a sense of great strength. And it should, because you know that you have the means to get the job done. Of course, the real test comes when you walk out the door and are on your own. At times you will call on prospects and even some customers who won't be impressed by the name and reputation of IBM, or care how much we invest in research and development. They have a multitude of problems that need solutions. They want answers, information, new ideas. In order to help them, you must draw upon your personal strength and all that you have learned during your training. This is the challenge you face. And part of the beauty and excitement of selling comes with the knowledge that you—one person—can make a profound difference.

THE DISCIPLINED SALES REP

When a customer is receptive, a sales career seems like a piece of cake. It doesn't require discipline to make calls when everything is going well. That's easy.

However, if he makes enough calls, a rep will have doors slammed in his face sooner or later. It's something that comes with every territory. Rejection hurts the best of us, but when a sales rep gets shot down several times in a row, it takes discipline to keep going, especially when there's nobody following him to make sure he keeps plugging away. The best and most effective discipline is self-imposed.

In the 1950s, like all IBM marketing reps I was required to submit, weekly, an hour-by-hour, day-by-day plan of how I would spend my time in the field. This was not only burdensome; it was a nightmare to administer. The company eliminated these reports in the 1960s, thinking that with the right people, it wasn't necessary to dictate how hard they must work to achieve success. IBM no longer uses formalized call activity forms. In effect, IBM said to the people in the field: "We have enough respect for you to believe that you're going to give us a fair day's work for a fair day's pay." However, the marketing rep's day-to-day work habits eventually surface when a documented account plan for each customer is reviewed.

Although the individual doesn't report his daily activities, IBM develops accurate records by a quarterly survey of the entire sales force. Every marketing organization needs to have a formalized method for getting information from its sales force—it must know how its people are spending their time in the field. IBM's Field Reporting System provides the company with information on how much time is being spent selling and servicing a specific product. From this reporting system it also gets the expense-to-revenue ratios by product, which help in setting the right price and determining the real profit being generated per product. IBM also finds out if the support structure is functioning as it should for all product categories. Perhaps more manpower is required to support a particular product. With effective reporting, the company may discover that more education and training than had been originally planned is needed to sell some of its products. As you can see, the field report is more than simply a device to measure an individual's sales activity.

FIRST IMPRESSIONS

When people hear the name IBM, I'm sure many different images come to mind, especially for those who don't really know the company. A while back, I heard it said that IBM stood for "I've Been Moved." People thought of IBM as an impersonal monolithic organization that disregarded the rights and feelings of its employees; a company with no wild ducks, its representatives all cloned to fly in formation. Over the years, many myths developed, and that can't be controlled. But when the opportunity arises (like now), I am delighted to project an IBM image that is rooted in reality.

One of the first questions asked by the curious is not about IBM's size or its products or its history, but rather: "Is it true that IBM requires you to wear a dark conservative suit, winter or summer, a white shirt and a quiet tie?" That's the number one question! Now, IBM has no written policy that tells a person how to dress: that's a fact. But to be completely truthful, there is an unwritten dress code that's as effective as if it were engraved in steel—or as if it had a loaded gun behind it. So the honest answer to the question is "Yes," or at least, "Sort of." The first reaction to this is often feigned surprise: "In the mid-eighties? You gotta be kidding!"

Well, let's talk about uniforms for a minute. In all kinds of businesses, people work in uniforms and no one thinks anything about it. The uniform is usually designed to help the wearer perform his job as efficiently as possible. A surgeon does his work in a gown, a dentist in a white coat, a policeman in blue; an athlete wears an outfit that will give him the most freedom and the best protection, and make him easily identifiable to any spectators who may be present. Musicians in a symphony orchestra wear formal dress, and I imagine that if you attended a concert and found each of them dressed in informal attire of their choice, you'd be disconcerted. And have you ever played tennis or golf with a person who was "out of uniform?" Weren't you distracted?

That's one of the points of IBM's unwritten dress code. Clothes should not be such as to distract people. Men and women who are on the job representing IBM wear business suits. That's because IBM is serious about its business and wants that attitude projected to its customers by its front people. Besides, what's wrong with dressing for the occasion? Or being expected to? I don't wear a business suit when I'm at a sports event or a casual dinner or a neighborhood movie. And if I wore a suit at a backyard barbecue, would the proponents of "wear whatever turns you on" applaud me for my individuality? I doubt it.

Some of the critics of the business suit complain that it's an uncomfortable way to dress. That makes no sense to me at all. What makes a loud plaid sport jacket more comfortable than a blue suit jacket? The colors? Certainly not the material or the cut. If your suit fits you, it will be comfortable. And the only time that I felt uncomfortable in a white shirt was when I tried to squeeze my 16 neck into a 15½ collar.

One of the most frequent complaints IBM hears is this:

"When you impose a dress code you're inhibiting self-expression, individuality and creativity." My response is usually: "Baloney!" No company has put more time and money into developing the creative talents of its staff than IBM; and none of its research or observations leads IBM to believe that the way its employees dress is in any way a negative. In fact, the conviction is that IBM people's mode of dress is a real plus for them and the company. I'll explain.

Everyone who calls on a customer or prospect for IBM wears a suit—that includes service people, those who call on an account to repair a typewriter or a computer. I know that most people expect a repairman to show up in a pair of coveralls, or some other form of work clothes. Tom Watson, Sr., had observed service people with other companies who were not treated with the same respect as salespeople who dressed in business suits. That didn't seem right to Watson. He wanted those talented technicians to be respected and he wanted them to have self-esteem. For this reason, all IBM repair people and installers have always dressed the same way as the marketing reps. It's greatly influenced their reception in the field, and I'm sure it makes them feel better about themselves.

About a half century after Tom Watson decided that the way you dressed affected the way you were perceived, and the way you were perceived affected the way you were treated, John T. Molloy wrote *Dress for Success*. Watson's beliefs were supported, time after time, by the studies done for this best-selling book. Receptionists who ignored the fellow in the sport jacket were warm and friendly to the one dressed in a pin-striped suit. Executive secretaries who wouldn't set up an appointment for a person with a stylish but flamboyant hairdo set one up without a hitch for the person with a fresh conservative haircut. It goes on and on.

Incidentally, almost all the criticism of IBM's "dress code" comes from outside the company. Neither employees nor customers complain. Enough said about clothes.

Now, for the record, it's true that in the past IBM did move a lot of people around. It was partly the times. After World War II, it seemed that half the households in the nation were on wheels, traveling between cities on cavernous moving vans. IBM contributed its share to the traffic jams. The relocations almost always involved a promotion and an improved opportunity for the employee; not good was management's dim view of anyone who turned down an opportunity when it was offered. The future of the employee was not nearly as bright as it would have been had he complied.

Sometimes it takes a while, but attitudes change. Society began looking with a critical eye at the whole idea of families being uprooted. And so did IBM. It became a moral issue. Was it right to relocate an employee, and of course his or her family, strictly for the company's convenience? IBM wisely and happily responded to the changing times by revising its relocation policies. In addition to the personal problems relocation caused, it was very expensive to the company and often disruptive to the customer. Today, no IBMer can be transferred at the whim of his manager. At least three other candidates must be considered for a position. Nor can anyone be moved within two years of the date of a previous relocation without having both his immediate manager and the division president approve it. When a manager carries the decision up the line, people are less likely to be moved indiscriminately. Of course, IBMers may still be relocated, but not as often and never out of fear of losing their jobs or crippling their careers.

It's been years since IBM changed its policy, and I don't hear the "I've Been Moved" jokes very often anymore; but it took a long time to shake it. There's something to be learned from that—you're stuck with the image you project, and you're perceived that way for a long time, so you have to give a good deal of thought to what you do and how you do it.

STAY-IN-TOUCH MANAGEMENT

When I moved into management, I was determined not to be viewed as one of those executives who, following a promotion, divorced himself from the selling end of the business. I knew I would be most effective in marketing if I had firsthand knowledge about what was happening in the field. I made up my mind that I would never be too busy to visit our customers, in the company of the marketing rep responsible for each account. I would thank them for their business, talk about IBM's strategies and listen to their views of our products and services. And it was exhilarating for me. Besides, it gave me the opportunity to show off a little, to demonstrate that the person at the top was as knowledgeable as were the people on the firing line. Marketing reps want action-oriented management. A sales force loses confidence in managers who isolate themselves in ivory towers. And so do the customers.

As president of IBM's computer division in the U.S. and later as vice-president of marketing, I spent at least 25 percent of my time meeting with customers, either in the field or at industry meetings. Each year I committed myself to a specific number of customer calls.

COMMUNICATING WITH THE SALES FORCE

IBM has one of the largest sales forces in the world. And because it's spread out all over the globe, the problems of communicating with this army of marketing reps, systems engineers and administrative people are especially complicated. But the sales force has a compelling need for information, and it's the responsibility of management to get that information to them.

Just how management goes about it is determined by the nature of the information and its degree of urgency. Information of general interest may appear in *Think,* an IBM in-house bimonthly publication that's distributed to more than 200,000 U.S. employees and thousands more overseas. Each division and facility has its own in-house publication. Bulletin boards at every IBM location contain news of a more immediate nature.

Some important messages are first given to a group of high-ranking executives, who relay them to the rest of the organization. Early each January, for example, IBM's CEO delivers to the company's assembled top officers the plans and goals for the next twelve months and for years ahead. I vividly recall John Opel's calling out at one such meeting the four goals set by IBM for the 1980s to ensure its continued leadership: One, to grow with the industry, not only in traditional areas such as mainline computers but also in newer areas. Two, to exhibit leadership both in the development and production of high-quality, reliable products and in sales and service. Three, to be *the* most efficient and effective in everything it does—*the* low-cost producer, *the* low-cost seller, *the* low-cost servicer and *the* low-cost administrator. And four, to sustain profitability, which funds the growth of the business.

The January meeting lasts only one day, but as many as 250 people attend from all over the world. Following that, each executive who attended passes down the company's goals through his chain of command. Every branch manager around the world holds a special kick-off meeting that highlights the corporate goals and specifically addresses the divisional and local targets. These are, in essence, sales rallies to motivate the field force.

One year, when we were excited about a significant change, I thought its importance would be dramatized if the sales force got the information directly from me. Our communications people videotaped my message and copies were forwarded immediately to all branches. A day or two later, my speech was delivered to thousands of reps throughout the entire marketing organization. On other occasions, IBM rented movie theaters in large metropolitan areas to make important announcements via closed-circuit television.

In 1981, when IBM's marketing was completely reorganized, there was concern about the magnitude of the change and its effect on the individual IBMer. A vast sophisticated educational program was launched, which utilized slides, videotapes, written question-and-answer handouts, as well as a personal presentation by an IBM executive. The message was delivered simultaneously throughout the country.

Nothing is more frustrating for a rep than to have a customer give him a bit of information about his company that he didn't already know. Sometimes the "news" slips out prematurely and quickly feeds the rumor mill. More often than not, it's misinformation, which needs to be quickly dispelled. This kind of problem is handled by getting on the phones right away or by sending the correct information to the branches via our telecommunication system.

When I assumed the management of IBM's Western Region, I wanted to let everyone in each of my sixty branch offices know what kind of guy they were going to have to deal with. I decided that the best way wasn't necessarily the quickest—or the easiest. I would visit all sixty branches and meet everyone in person. It took two weeks and lots of hours in the air—covering every major city in the western United States, from L.A. to Dallas to Seattle to San Diego. I traveled with the heads of Personnel and Service, and almost every day we had breakfast, lunch and dinner in a different city, meeting with IBMers, making speeches and conducting private conferences. It was a very tiring trip, and we joked about the number of times my companions had to listen to me speak. I'd coax them, "Please keep from falling asleep while I'm delivering my speech."

At the end of the tour, the three of us were exhausted, excited and fulfilled.

Then, in 1965, we experienced some difficult times as a result of a slump in the aerospace industry, a major source of the Western Region's business. Numerous changes had to be made, which many times meant physically moving people to other areas of opportunity. In order to get our people to extend themselves so that we could meet our goals for the year, I ran a motivational program which had the theme "The Winning of the West." Wall-sized posters were sent to all the branch offices, and weekly meetings with twenty-five IBMers at a time were conducted at my office in Los Angeles. It took six months, but I met with every marketing rep in the region—hundreds of them. I would explain our strategy in great detail and ask each rep for a personal commitment. A lot of hoopla and fun were incorporated into these gatherings. As we began to turn things around, special awards of appreciation were given for productivity and valuable feedback from the field.

It's vitally important for all levels of management to have some form of one-to-one communication with its sales force. It's a matter of finding out, firsthand, what's going on, and it does wonders for the salespeople's morale. You must let them know you care; if you can't do that, you can't manage them effectively. Every field manager stays in close phone contact with people in remote locations who are not seen daily or even weekly. I believe that a manager should feel as close to his salespeople as if they were sharing the same office.

Besides spending time in the field with the reps, and seeing them at meetings or conferences, at least every three months I'd bring a group to our headquarters to spend a day with me. I knew what they did day to day, and I wanted them to get a sense of what I did and what goes on at corporate headquarters.

The branch office meeting is emphasized. While it has been mandatory to have a minimum of one per month, some branch managers hold meetings biweekly and even weekly.

IBM communicates with its sales force by providing terminals for them at the branch offices. In fact, IBM is one of the largest users of computers in the world. At the terminal, a rep can review new announcements; check on the status of orders; validate prices or terms; get information for an account, etc. The terminal also helps a rep sell by providing information about new product usage in a given industry. One salesperson might put into the system a message that describes a new solution to a problem. That information is now available to the entire organization. In effect, a central information data bank is available, where anyone can deposit or withdraw ideas, problems and solutions. A marketing rep also can keep up to date on his own annual quota status. He can see what he has to produce to meet his financial goals and how much a given transaction is worth to him.

The bigger an organization becomes, the harder its management must work at communication. Regardless of a company's size, I think, no more than eight to ten people should report directly to a single manager. This ratio assures each person of individual attention, without overburdening the manager. When a manager has too many individuals to supervise, it's almost impossible to maintain discipline and recognition. And of course nothing is more frustrating and demoralizing than to work for a manager who doesn't have adequate time for his staff.

IBM has a fundamental program that's designed to enhance communications as it boosts morale. The Executive Interview offers an employee a scheduled but rather informal conference with management one level above the person he or she works for. The idea is for the employee to know that someone other than his manager is aware of his accomplishments. The discussion is free-flowing, giving the employee every opportunity to express himself and to ask questions about the company and the business. This is very exciting to me because the program got started when Bob Woodworth, a very creative manager, came to me in the mid-sixties and outlined the need for enhanced employee communications. I immediately implemented the Executive Interview in my area of responsibility, the western United States. It was so successful that it became a valued addition to our companywide personnel programs. This program works because it's exercised: these things have to be more than good intentions to be meaningful.

I suppose every company has some form of "Open Door" policy. At IBM, it's a basic communication channel, a policy that's deeply ingrained in the company's history. It's based on the conviction that every employee has the right to appeal the actions of those who are immediately over him or her in authority.

The employee is encouraged to discuss a problem with a manager or manager's manager, a personnel manager or the site manager. If a problem is not solved at that level, he can go to the president or the general manager of the division or subsidiary. Finally, if the employee isn't satisfied, he may cover the subject with the chief executive officer, either by mail or, if the CEO feels it is appropriate to the resolution, personally.

Some people outside IBM who know of this policy say, "How can you make your CEO accessible to over 400,000 employees in this busy and complicated world of business?" How can you *not* be interested in what one person thinks or feels? These practices work because management believes in them, and most important, so does everybody else.

A VERY IMPORTANT SURVEY

Even though IBM does its best to see, hear, feel and understand the mind and mood of the sales force, it worries that something important might be missed. Every year, the total field force is required to answer a questionnaire (no signature is necessary) that asks such things as: Are you being challenged by your job? What work pressures do you have? Do you think IBM is still practicing respect for the individual? How do you evaluate your pay in light of your duties? What do you think about our pay compared with that in other companies? Are you satisfied with your career planning? How do you feel about headquarters management? Are they responsive to you? Are they providing you with enough tools to get the job done? How do you evaluate your manager? How do you evaluate your manager's manager?

This information is reviewed at each level of management, from the branch office to the summit. If a problem seems to have a pattern, action is taken.

At one time, the marketing reps' opinion of a particular division's management had dropped significantly. The complaints were justified. We gave the division president ninety days to get things turned around, or he would be replaced. We had to replace him.

The company always responds to the opinion surveys. A composite of what the reps say—pro and con—is distributed to everyone at branch office meetings, with management's reaction—pro and con. Most problems that surface are caused by managers who are unable to listen with understanding and communicate clearly. The key to an open and honest survey is voluntary participation coupled with a quick response from management.

In addition to the annual survey, every ninety days each sales rep and system engineer answers a series of questions related to customer satisfaction: do the reps think the company is doing a good job? As a follow-up, IBM customers are surveyed by both the company and independent sources. An independent survey that does not inform the customer that IBM is the sponsor facilitates a candor that might not otherwise surface. Basically, the same questions are asked of the sales force and the customer, to see how well IBM people are tuned in to their accounts. These surveys help uncover both negative and positive trends.

THERE IS NO SATURATION POINT IN EDUCATION

The above words are etched in stone at the entrance to IBM's education center in Endicott, New York. Thomas Watson, Sr., believed that top management should spend 40 to 50 percent of its time educating and motivating its people, and this practice, handed down through Tom, Jr., has been carried on to the present.

It doesn't make sense to have a rep go through a one-year training program—no matter how thorough—and have it end there. Anyone who stops learning goes backward. Like any professional—from tax accountant to physician—an IBM representative must keep up to date with what's happening. This is particularly essential in so complex an industry as IBM's. It's not enough for marketing rep or systems engineer to know the new technological advances made by the company and by the information-processing industry. He must stay on top of what's happening in his area of specialization, whether it be banking, insurance, transportation or whatever. It's estimated that an experienced IBM marketing rep will spend fifteen days each year in the classroom, attending special industry schools and conferences.

Although there is no required reading list, considerable material is distributed to the field to be studied. Each week, the company announces an average of ten different products plus new programs, so the marketing people must deal with a continuous flow of information. All in all, it's estimated that 15 percent of their time is devoted to education.

In 1984, IBM had 42,000 managers and 1,500 people in executive positions throughout the world. In keeping with the idea that if it is important to train a person to sell, it is equally important to train a person to manage, the company promotes from within. Whatever a person's credentials, he or she must go through IBM's basic training program. An exceptional person could emerge as a management candidate in five years, but it takes an average person seven to ten years to make it.

A first-line manager receives eighty hours of classroom training during his first year on the new job. It's mandatory that within thirty days of his promotion, the new manager attend a one-week class at IBM's Management Development Center, a campus that occupies twenty-six acres of the corporate headquarters site in Armonk, New York. The program covers the company's history, beliefs, policies and practices, as well as basic managerial skills, including the motivation, appraisal and counseling of people. An emphasis is placed on strengthening employee-manager communications and keeping managers updated in a constantly changing environment. Flexibility is vitally important. A good manager must be able to adapt to change while preserving IBM's basic beliefs and philosophies. The material used in each class is this: "Will it be useful next week, when the manager returns to his office?" Every year thereafter, the managers, all 42,000 of them, spend at least forty hours in the classroom.

There is also a Middle Managers School, founded upon the recognition that special skills are needed to manage other managers. The classes concentrate on effective communications and people management, but also cover business concerns and strategies. Then, too, there are schools for the experienced middle manager and the senior manager. These deal with more sophisticated matters, such issues as external factors, both social and economic.

A company can't rely on executives to rise from its ranks by chance. It must be actively engaged in a continuous talent hunt. It's essential to find the very best people and prime them for future managerial positions. IBM's Executive Resources program seeks out and plans the careers of those who are considered to have especially high potential. All managers participate by identifying their superstars.

In another training program, promising young people are brought in as assistants to high-ranking company executives—one might be an assistant to the chairman's office, another to the president's office. After I had been with IBM for seven years, I served as administrative assistant to an executive vice-president, which gave me tremendous exposure and insight.

To broaden their perspective, future managers attend educational programs outside the IBM environment: the Menninger Clinic, Harvard's Advanced Management Program, the London School of Economics, MIT's and Stanford's Sloan Program. They may last from a week to a year. Those who excel attend the Advanced Managers School, a program given in about forty colleges, including Harvard, Columbia, Virginia, Georgia and Indiana. IBM's highest-ranking executives may attend an executive seminar on federal government activities, given at the Brookings Institute, and a two-week international executive program is attended by the company's top two hundred executives. The program covers a broad range of subjects, from what's happening in South America and the Middle East, to the trade deficit and the federal budget. Topical events are studied with a special regard for their implications for the company today and in the future, and people like Henry Kissinger, Martin Feldstein and David Broder participate.

A few executives may enroll in the Aspen Institute of Humanistic Studies, which covers such diverse subjects as religion, astronomy and South American literature. Its purpose is to help the individual take a fresh look at his value system. It can activate a midlife awakening—stimulating ideas that haven't been considered for years.

IBM invests a lot of money in its people. Total estimated expenses for educating and training ran in excess of $600 million in 1984. But since the future of a company depends on the quality of its people, the investment is an imperative.

5
FUTURE-ORIENTED MARKETING

Sometimes the manager must perform with the courage and agility of a circus performer, carefully crossing the highwire between short-term problems and long-term objectives.

Marketing is the process used by an organization to relate creatively and productively to the environment in which it sells its products and services. *Effective* marketing requires the talent to speak in a language the marketplace understands; the insight and skill to find solutions to customers' problems; and the commitment to give value. To accomplish this, a company must be willing and able to use all its resources.

Remember that while selling tries to get the customer to want what you have, marketing tries to have what the customer wants. There is a fundamental difference between these two perspectives.

To IBM, marketing is a source of pride and joy. It is the vehicle upon which the company moves its goods, and it provides a voice that articulates what IBM is, what it believes in, and what it hopes to accomplish and contribute.

There's a lot to marketing—product planning, marketplace segmentation, pricing, distribution, advertising and promotion. Each of these requires the making of decisions based on assumptions about the future.

Shortsighted people deal almost exclusively with today's problems, programs, motivations and sales results. Of course, all these are tactically important, but well-managed companies keep looking ahead. They know that while today's actions are essential, the impact of these actions on the future must be predetermined.

The higher you are in management, the more important it is to think strategically. The responsibility of spelling out long-term strategies belongs to top management, who must make a clear statement on the importance of strategic planning and ensure that a long-range plan is in place—a plan that establishes definite goals. Everybody must be made aware of the impact of his daily activities on those long-term objectives.

My management style is based on the belief that while you are doing your best to get today's job done, a part of you must be aware of your influence on the future.

I have always told everyone who worked with me that I preferred them to spend more time on long-term matters than on day-to-day issues. What's needed are people who can conceptualize, who can visualize what's going to happen four and five years ahead.

You may decide today that by cutting your head count or reducing your advertising expenditures you can meet this quarter's goals and enhance the bottom line at the year's end, but you might regret it down the road. You'd better have a good fix on the future before implementing any immediate decision.

BALANCING ACT II

Sometimes the future-oriented manager must perform with the courage and agility of a circus performer, carefully crossing the highwire between short-term problems and long-term objectives.

A decision to invest in a project that cannot produce a quick profit can cause the decisionmaker to suffer migraine headaches, sleepless nights and more. The expenditures needed to get the new project off the ground will surely lower the current year's profit picture and possibly even have an adverse effect on the value of the company's stock. You must anticipate the reactions to all the negatives before putting the plan into motion. It takes a great deal of careful preparation, thoughtfully presented, to ward off potentially hostile stockholders who might try to climb the pole and cut the highwire before you make it across.

Many marketing managers give in too easily to the guardians of the bottom line. They'll squeeze every last sale out of a tired marketing program or product. They'll enjoy cheap sales for a short period because the start-up costs have long been amortized. For a while, fewer sales may produce a higher than usual profit margin, but the day of reckoning is certain to come. Before he knows it, the shortsighted marketing manager is faced with an eroding share of the market; his product, its packaging and the sales program are old and worn out, and he has nothing in the pipeline.

Of course, you want to get the most mileage out of your investments, but as with an automobile, you have to know when to tune them up, when to overhaul them and when to scrap them.

IBM is a master of balancing its long-term and short-term goals without sacrificing acceptable profit levels. If the information-processing industry grows to a trillion-dollar level in the 1990s, IBM, growing at the same rate, could be a $185 billion company.

Since 1979, IBM has invested about $13 billion in its factories to improve quality and reduce breakeven points. IBM spent $350 million to convert its twenty-five-year-old factory in Lexington, Kentucky, into one of the U.S.'s most automated plants. Before the plant was automated, labor accounted for about one third of manufacturing costs. By 1986, when the plant is running full bore, that figure will shrink to 5 percent. Consistent with IBM's practice of job security, the company spent $5 million to retrain its Kentucky workers.

These massive investments—bets on the future—came during the 1970s, when IBM's growth rate (based on revenue) had slowed to about 13 percent. IBM pumped money back into the business in prodigious amounts. And it took some heat. One heard comments that IBM had lost its zip and was getting complacent. None of these criticisms, it turned out, was accurate. As an IBM financial expert said, "The company took a short-term hit." When you make such investments, there isn't a payback until the future. Well, the future has arrived.

THE EXTERNAL FACTORS

No matter how well you plan ahead, there will always be unexpected external factors that you must deal with—changes in government regulations, politics, inflation, trade imbalances, unemployment, the prime rate. . . . There may right now be on the drawing board government regulations that can make a product obsolete. When the EPA set clean-air standards, the automobile manufacturers had to invest billions of dollars switching to low-lead-gasoline-fueled cars; and oil companies had to make changes in their service station equipment as well as their gasoline production. When the prime rate rose to record heights, the housing industry, for one, was hit hard. Banking responded with variable interest rates and real estate developers switched from building single dwellings to building multifamily projects. President Reagan's grain embargo on Russia was an external factor that had a devastating impact on the small American farmer, who is especially vulnerable to external factors—government actions, natural disasters, banking practices, etc.

Women have created a series of problems and opportunities that most marketing departments are wrestling with today. In entering the work force en masse, women have changed their buying habits and what they consider their necessities. In the past, the automobile industry virtually ignored women as factors in marketing strategy. The industry can no longer turn its back on them, since women participate in 81 percent of all new car and truck purchase decisions. It's tougher now to market to women in the home, because fewer of them are home. On the other hand, mail order businesses are thriving because working women have less time to visit retailers during regular store hours. Of course, there are many more examples. Women must be reckoned with by marketing departments.

Sometimes an unexpected external factor can result from a company's own technology and marketing successes. Rapid technical enhancements made the computer available to almost every school, millions of homes and small businesses. Because so many people spend hours at the computer keyboard—and a lot of these people are children—the industry had to react to concern about the computer's effect on mind and body. In some European countries, governments are attempting to regulate such things as the height of keyboards and the clarity of video display terminals. IBM is dealing with these concerns and others now, although federal guidelines on visual display terminal (VDT) ergonomics standards are not presently anticipated.

An unexpected external problem in the computer field is the invasion of privacy by so-called hackers, who attempt to access confidential information. Unlawful access has become commonplace: people attempt to change their credit ratings, students alter grades, competitors steal secret data. For this reason, IBM offers its customers an option of new hardware and software features to protect their data. In the immediate future, I believe, the demand for this kind of security will be so high that it will be a major consideration in buying computer systems.

There are times when external factors may cause an organization to reevaluate itself top to bottom. At the end of the review, the company concludes that its best course of action is to go right on conducting business as usual—changes aren't necessary. This was what happened after the U.S. Justice Department antitrust suit against IBM, filed in 1968, ended thirteen years later, in 1981, in what had become the longest such case in this country's history. Some 2,500 depositions were taken, and more than 66 million pages of documents were involved. IBM's former chairman Frank Cary alone spent forty-five days making depositions and many more days preparing for them. As vice-president of marketing, I, too, spent days having depositions taken. Later, as the first IBMer called to testify at the trial, I again expended considerable time that could have been utilized more productively.

The government had charged IBM with attempting to monopolize the general-purpose computer market and sought to break up the company into smaller pieces, or at least change some of its practices. During this period, approximately twenty-five other suits were filed by competitors such as Greyhound, Memorex and Teletex, accusing IBM of utilizing its marketing practices to achieve what's referred to as "a dominance of the marketplace." Needless to say, we were distracted from the day-to-day job, and the time and money that went into such things as legal fees, paralegal people and preparation to protect ourselves was very costly. When it was all over, the Department of Justice completely vindicated IBM of any wrongdoing. The court had ruled: "The suit was without merit."

When the verdict was out, CEO John Opel said: "IBM prevailed, first and foremost, because we were blameless. For all its efforts over those thirteen long years, the Government failed completely to show any violation of that principle to which we adhere: IBM will not tolerate unfair or unlawful conduct anywhere in the business. That principle still stands. We'll continue to compete aggressively, as we always have, but always uncompromisingly within the letter and spirit of the law." IBMers rejoiced because it had been proved that a corporation, regardless of its size, can achieve any level of penetration of a market as long as that penetration has been realized through excellence and fairness.

The case caused IBM to be very sensitive to the way it did business, and carefully analyze everything about itself. But in the end, IBM concluded that there was nothing to apologize for. The company had been conducting business at the highest ethical level, and reaffirmed its commitments to provide outstanding service and excellence in everything it did.

The antitrust suits filed against IBM illustrate that certain external factors can demand a great amount of a company's resources, but may not cause change. Nonetheless, you can't ignore the external factors around you, because they can have devastating consequences. Had IBM been found guilty of the antitrust charges, the law would have required the company to change substantially the way it did business. Yet IBM was so certain that it had done nothing wrong, a contingency plan was never prepared. Nor, during the thirteen-year period, did the case cause overreactions and changes in marketing practices that would have weakened IBM's position in the marketplace.

It is to be hoped that you never get involved in a long-drawn-out lawsuit that drains your resources of time and money. Even when a company wins the case, it ends up paying a high price. Yet, like every external factor you can't ignore, hoping it'll go away, you must give anything that turns up your absolute attention.

Each time an operating or a strategic plan is developed, a set of environmental assumptions should be made. You have to look down the road as far as you can and build as many safeguards as possible into your plans. Of course, you can't have contingencies in place for external factors that cannot be predicted. But you must have people who are sensitive to environmental changes, who can see beyond the confines of your business and can react quickly when confronted with the unexpected.

THE INTERNAL DANGER SIGNS

If you are going to be able to manage people sensibly, you have to know what's happening *within* your own organization. Trouble may be brewing that won't be reflected in numbers alone. Probe around, talk, listen, observe your people: you find out by reading the signs. You have to be sensitive to mood changes and varying energy levels. *In Search of Excellence* calls it "management by wandering around." Maybe there are three resignations from one branch, or grumblings about inadequate recognition, or complaints about the size of raises.

A while ago, IBM suffered a higher-than-normal attrition in its sales force in Australia. Upon investigating the problem, IBM found that to speed up the ability to meet the demands in that country, the branch offices had been hiring a higher proportionate number of professional people as compared to university students. These experienced people left at a higher rate than usual, to work for other organizations within the information-processing industry. This abnormal voluntary attrition resulted from inadequate new employee orientation. They simply hadn't been exposed to IBM's culture.

A manager can observe many danger signs about an individual who works with him: There may be change in a person's physical appearance, level of concentration and attitude. These may accompany a drop in the person's productivity and the quality of his work. The number of customer calls made by a marketing rep takes a nosedive, or he may stay late at the office every night. You must find out what is causing this behavior. Is it something personal? Perhaps he's not getting along well with his spouse and doesn't want to go home. Or he may tell you, "I haven't enough administrative people around here to support me, so here I am, filling out forms when I ought to be in front of the customer."

For instance, a regional manager might notice that one of his branch managers is no longer spending the proper amount of time out in the field with his reps, meeting customers. Investigation might reveal that the reps are no longer inviting the branch manager to make calls because they feel he's lost touch with the marketplace.

There are countless internal danger signs, but you've got to put in the time to look for them. You have to be as sensitive to the people you pay as you are to the people you sell.

CHANGING VALUES

Civil rights. The Kennedy and King assassinations. Vietnam. Watergate. Women's liberation. Consumerism. The energy crisis. The events and movements of the past quarter century have caused America to reexamine its values and to initiate changes. A well-run marketing organization must be sensitive to what I call *forces of change.*

Because of these events and developments, people today are very concerned with the quality of their life. Personal values are changing and IBM works at staying on top of those changes when making marketing and managing decisions. Changing attitudes about sex, marriage, family roots, religion, education and drugs have to be considered. People are more sophisticated, less trusting—thank goodness. They want to know what they're eating and what their kids are being taught and what things really cost. They're not as quick to buy Madison Avenue's pitch or blindly follow the fashion designers' bidding. For many, small really is beautiful.

Any company that doesn't think that these changing values are factors to be understood and dealt with is headed for trouble. Changing values is one of the reasons this country's growth rate in production began to slip in 1965, just when West Germany's showed a dramatic increase and Japan's began to soar. As you will well remember, it was the beginning of a decade of unrest throughout our country, and the workplace was certainly affected. Companies responded in different ways to the social changes. Some became as loosely structured and undisciplined as many sixties college campuses. IBM responded too—its change in relocation policies is an example—but it would not relent in its philosophical commitments to respect for the individual, service for the customer and excellence of performance. The result? IBM's productivity rate did not slip.

THE BEST SOURCE OF INFORMATION

The customer is perhaps your best source of information for long-term planning. After all, to survive, you must understand the customer's problems so you can provide solutions that withstand hard scrutiny over a period of time. Surveys and studies may be useful, but every small business can go directly to its customers for information. It's simple. Talk to them during your initial stages of planning. Ask for their opinions of designs, price and packaging. Involve them. Make them part of the decisionmaking process. It will make sense to them too. And keep going back to them as your plan progresses.

There are times when a customer enters into a Joint Study Agreement with IBM. After a nondisclosure compact is executed, IBM may install a preproduction prototype of a machine yet to be introduced to the marketplace. Customers help the company assess the new product's performance in a real-world environment. The customer benefits by having the product developed to fit his specific requirements.

On other occasions, IBM invites a dozen or so customers to a specific industry council—for example, top banking executives attend a Bankers Council. Here customers critique IBM's practices and policies, as well as describe their needs and problems.

On a larger scale, IBM conducts what it calls industry conferences. Several hundred customers attend a convention at which the latest technology and most advanced applications are presented. The users share their experiences with one another. A company that has its customers working with other customers represents marketing at its finest.

A small company can't always afford to conduct a seminar or expect the top executives of a particular industry to attend. But a small industrial company could fly its top engineer, head of manufacturing and pricing manager to visit one or more of its leading customers. Most companies are satisfied to stay home, sit back and surprise their customers with new products or programs. What they miss by not taking the time to preview their plans could prove to be catastrophic. To their dismay, their new product may have missed the mark. Go to your customers and ask what they think their future needs are. You don't have to be shy or coy with them. Be direct. A small company that does this will get the information it needs. This is *not* an expensive venture, and the customer is complimented by the visit.

A NEW OPPORTUNITY—A NEW PRODUCT

Although IBM is supersensitive to movement in the marketplace and responds with new products with what I consider remarkable agility, you might be surprised at the company's studied approach to change. IBM has a large staff of people who study the marketplace in order to determine future needs of specific industries. This industry marketing unit, made up of former reps, systems engineers and professional hires, has in-depth knowledge of all aspects of a particular industry. It monitors the changes taking place in that industry, and speculates about the future.

IBM's marketing people are responsible for discerning the existing opportunities for new products. The various marketing division managers take a broad view of opportunities and submit what is called a Statement of Opportunity. In the document, a manager might predict that the retail industry is going to grow faster than the projected GNP rate. He'll supply as much data as possible to support his assumptions. His conclusion might be: "More people will be buying. The graying of America will continue and the baby boom will expand." Therefore, he might recommend that IBM put more dollars into products catering to retailers.

A typical report may include an explanation of perceived opportunity, analysis of the competitive environment, and a description of the product the manager thinks will sell.

IBMers refer to these situations as "windows of opportunity." That means: "Urgent! We'd better get this out fast or somebody else will beat us to it." Just how fast a company responds to a particular opportunity depends on how quickly its parts can react. And IBM is geared up to act, not just to react. Every department has to move—you can't afford to have anyone dragging his feet once the commitment is made and the time frame is set.

Once marketing identifies what they believe the new opportunity should be, the development and manufacturing staffs take over. Responsible for establishing specific product requirements, the technical staff is given the freedom to select the best technology to produce the product.

After a commitment is made to introduce a new product at some future date, additional marketing research determines just how receptive the marketplace will be. And before any dollars are actually allocated to production, a research study is done to support the initial assumptions and validate the product's practicability. Several checkpoints are established, the first perhaps three to six months after the product's conception. The plan is then reassessed by engineering, manufacturing, marketing and finance before funds are allocated for tools and parts. About ninety days later, the opportunities are reevaluated, this time by taking a hard look at the revenue and profit picture. With all costs known, before the product is actually manufactured another review establishes what is considered a realistic price. A formal review is then made by both line and staff to determine whether the original commitment is still valid. It's a continuous procedure from checkpoint to checkpoint, reevaluating and going on.

This may seem unnecessary, but I assure you that it's time and money well spent. It's a safeguard against manufacturing a product that makes little or no profit and has no reality in the marketplace. I can't emphasize enough how important it is to keep a formal dialogue and frequent checkpoints going throughout the stages of a product's development. This is nothing more than "interlocking" all of a company's internal functions before the final release of the product to the marketplace.

IBM's recent entry into the personal computer field represents a different approach to its past marketing efforts.

I must tell you that the Personal Computer has been a marketing challenge for IBM. The product couldn't absorb the high costs of IBM's traditional marketing system, and forced the company to look at less expensive selling methods.

Off to a late start, with many competitors already in the field, IBM established a task force to pursue the development and distribution of this new product. As it turned out, the personal computer opened up several new marketplaces for us—as well as new challenges. New markets included students, and people who use it in the home.

In order to effectively reach this vast number of potential buyers, a bold marketing decision was made. For the first time in the company's history, dealers would sell a significant volume of an IBM product. The real test was to find quality dealers who would let IBM educate and train them to perform at a level equal to its own sales force. After analyzing various industries, we concluded that IBM could make it work. By insisting that its beliefs about sales and service be respected and adhered to, IBM felt certain that the dealers selected would live up to the commitment IBM made to its customers. The goal was that customers would not see a difference between doing business with IBM and buying from its dealers.

To accomplish this, every support function had to be examined. It was vital for the company to provide the consumer with immediate service. The consumer needed convenient locations where his Personal Computer could be dropped off for servicing, in addition to the option of IBM service at his own site. From some remote areas, a customer would have to ship his Personal Computer to a central maintenance depot. The proper service strategy was as necessary as an effective selling strategy.

IBM established a series of education programs that not only trained the dealers on the product itself but taught them better ways to manage their people and their dollars. And finally IBM developed its first consumer advertising campaign.

This new opportunity has presented IBM with a continuous flow of challenges that have kept our people excited and busy.

THE LITTLE TRAMP

IBM never advertised widely to attract new prospects until the introduction of the Personal Computer, so its experience in this area was limited. I think the Charlie Chaplin character as spokesman for the IBM PC was a stroke of brilliance by the advertising agency. The "Little Tramp" personifies the qualities the company wants to project for the new product—uncomplicated, unintimidating and fun.

Traditionally, IBM's corporate advertising program has been institutional in nature. An overall corporate point of view was projected to a general audience: "The computer is something to want, not fear." "Our products make life easier for you; we have educational applications, and solutions for your business problems." "Here is IBM, and we're involved in a variety of products and services, all providing some benefit for you."

Appearing in newspapers, national magazines and on television (IBM was a major sponsor of the 1984 Olympics, and such specials as *The Nutcracker* and *A Christmas Carol*), the ads have been designed to create goodwill and promote the company as a worthy corporate citizen. The audience is told that IBM products are of the finest quality; that IBM people have been trained to give the best service; that the company is innovative and caring, solution-oriented and responsive—not some gray, monolithic giant. IBM wants everyone to know that it cares about its customers and people who work for it; that it has a sense of humor and, above all, is approachable.

Product advertising, on the other hand, mainly zeroes in on a specific market, perhaps focusing on a particular piece of equipment. It's more "hard sell" and aims at generating the interest to buy. These solution-oriented advertisements often appear in "vertical" media such as trade and business publications, including *American Banker, Petroleum Week, Chemical Week* and *Aviation Week.* However, like the corporate advertising, they also appear in "horizontal" media, including the *Wall Street Journal,* the *New York Times, Fortune, Business Week, Time* and *Newsweek.*

In the past, when IBM's business was strictly marketed by its blue-suit organization and a medium-sized computer had a price tag in the hundreds of thousands of dollars, advertising was used almost exclusively to support the sales force. No attempt was made to move products the same way automobiles or appliances are sold. Corporate advertising in horizontal media almost always promoted the company flag rather than specific products. It wasn't until the 1980s, when technological advances lowered computer prices and broadened the marketplace, that IBM beefed up its product advertising budget, and focused on promoting sales of the Personal Computer.

The majority of the company's revenues, however, have always come from larger systems, sold by marketing reps, which are only minimally helped by advertising. Until the scope of the market was expanded by alternatives to the traditional distribution system, it didn't make much sense to do a great deal of advertising, even for smaller items like typewriters, copiers and work stations. IBM wasn't geared then to take advantage of the prospects a national advertising campaign would attract. Now the advertising has changed. The company is no longer limited to the one-on-one selling of reps; and can also count on IBM Product Centers, independent dealers, catalogs and the telemarketing program.

I do not doubt that advertising is an effective stimulator. It piques a prospect's curiosity and provokes him to make a phone call or go looking for a product. It's a terrific support for a selling force—who can close orders with fewer calls—and since an industrial call can cost almost three hundred dollars, effective advertising is a welcome aid.

IBM doesn't view advertising as an expense but as an investment in increased sales productivity. Helping the sales departments to keep pace with the manufacturing department's ability to turn out products, advertising speeds up inventory time and shortens the selling cycle.

Surveys have proved that IBM's advertising has successfully created new customers at the retail outlets. To a seven-city survey that asked customers what had brought them into the stores, 46 percent of respondents replied that it was advertising and direct mail. In Baltimore, as a four-month test market, expenditures on local advertising were increased to two and one half times the going rate. Store traffic and sales more than doubled. So advertising at IBM is no longer considered simply a tool to assist the sales force; it is a marketing tool to generate orders.

IBM attempts to decentralize its advertising as much as possible. Typically, international companies have a global advertising campaign, created at their corporate headquarters and disseminated around the world, translated into the language of each country where they conduct business. IBM's ads have a different look in each country. For example, IBM Germany and IBM United Kingdom have the freedom to run their own product advertising, subject to an overview from

European headquarters in Paris, where IBM standards of professionalism, honesty and quality are monitored.

In compliance with IBM's emphasis on fairness, the advertising focuses on selling the merits of products and services. While it may be in vogue today to knock the competition, IBM disagrees with the tactic. Just as marketing reps are not permitted to disparage a competitor, neither is the advertising department. Personally, I avoid doing business with companies whose advertising message is what's wrong with the competition.

Of course, advertising isn't worth a nickel if you don't have the distribution system to make the products readily available. And it's not worth much, in the long run, if the products you're selling and the service you're providing are inferior.

THE CONTENTION SYSTEM

In a mom-and-pop operation, mom argues that they should do this and pop argues that they should do that. And if they don't settle on what to do between themselves, they go to a third party (a son-in-law, their accountant, etc.) to aid their decisionmaking.

On a more formal basis, IBM does the same thing. The corporation encourages debate and a multiplicity of views. If staff and line don't agree, for example, they'll try to thrash it out until they come to some sort of meeting of minds. To keep people from getting their way by winning a shouting match, the divergent points of view are carefully documented. On occasion, I had heated debates with division presidents about the allocation of marketing resources, and whether we had too many or too few people. Through our management system, the differences were eventually resolved by a formal committee of top-ranking IBM officers. Happily, a lot of arguing is done at IBM—about new products, changes in pricing, revisions of terms and conditions, restructuring of the organization and overall long-term objectives.

Depending on the subject and its importance, IBM's contention system can go all the way up the organization and require different parties to meet in the boardroom with the president and/or chairman, who presides over the debate. As marketing head, I might want a new product to be developed and ready for market by a given date in order to meet competition. The engineering head might disagree, believing that a new product wasn't even needed, that the enhancement of an existing product would do. Each of us would present his views, and top management would serve as arbitrator. In a case of this nature, a clear-cut decision in favor of one view could be made, or a compromise suggested. Or the response could be: "You're both wrong. Go back and do your staff work."

One of the real values of this sort of contention system is that while people may disagree, they don't have to compromise themselves in order to settle an issue. At IBM, it is called the "right of nonconcurrence." Once a decision is made, there's no animosity. It's not a game of win or lose; everybody is playing on the same team. Both line and staff are held accountable for the final results.

SHIFTING GEARS

Businesses as well as entire industries have fallen by the wayside because they failed to perceive themselves correctly. The example most frequently cited is the buggy whip industry, which failed to realize it was in the transportation business; and as we all know, the movie industry almost suffered a knockout blow when television hit the scene in the 1950s. It took at least a decade for the moguls to realize that they were in the entertainment business and stop perceiving themselves as filmmakers whose products had to be viewed in theaters. This is Ted Levitt's thesis, highlighted in his classic article "Marketing Myopia," which appeared in the *Harvard Business Review* in 1960.

A business can suffer other forms of myopia. It can bask in the luxury of its own success. Of course, a company that slows down and rests on its laurels is headed for trouble.

Back in the fifties, when IBM was considered the leader in the information processing industry, Tom Watson, Jr., boldly led the company from the world of punch cards to the world of stored programming. I was fortunate to be among its marketing pioneers. A small group of us attended one of the first commercial electronic data processing schools, to be trained away from the old concepts. From a technical as well as a marketing point of view, this was a drastic change in direction. It was perhaps the most significant change in the company's history.

In 1964, after investing $5 billion, IBM announced a new family of computers, called the System/360. The retooling investment was huge. The new product would not be compatible with IBM's existing systems. Talk about risk! At the time IBM was ready to make the move, its "old" product accounted for well over half of IBM's revenue and profit. New programming required new skills. IBM customers could have rejected the company's new baby and converted to the competition. To many, it was a foolish gamble. Some doubting IBMers dubbed the program "You Bet Your Company." Cynics cried out, "If it ain't broke, don't fix it." It certainly would have been easier to stick with a successful product. But enough visionaries believed that standing still was equivalent to going backward.

The most insidious disease in business is complacency.

People reflect too long on their accomplishments. Success is fleeting and should never be expected to last forever. As you work to retain it, you continue to seek new opportunities. Pioneering is risky, but business myopia is riskier. A successful company doesn't wait for outside influences to shape its destiny. It looks ahead. It asks itself "What if?" questions: "What if there's inflation?" "What if there's a recession?" "What if the competition does this?" It might not always come up with the right answers, but it's rarely taken by complete surprise.

While the computer industry is highly volatile and constantly changing, IBM is sometimes characterized as a great big monolith, never experiencing disruption. The company has been compared to a snowball rolling downhill, getting bigger and bigger. I assure you this is not an accurate assessment.

It's easy to look at the present company and think that everything simply fell into place. However, had the company failed to read the tea leaves, the IBM the world knows today would be a far different organization. IBM, like any company, has not been impervious to external factors and internal upheavals; both Watsons adhered to the principle: "We will change everything about our corporation. We will alter our terms and conditions, we will change our organization and its products. We will change our policies. We will do whatever is necessary to keep our people challenged and motivated; to assure that we have the money to invest in people, research and development; and to give our customers the best possible value. We will change everything except our beliefs."

Obviously, IBM hasn't shied away from making major changes when necessary. I mentioned the switch from keypunch card to stored programming products. Another bold marketing change was made in 1969, when IBM switched from selling its products in a "bundle" (one price purchased all components in a package) to pricing components separately and allowing the customer to pick and choose. IBM began to unbundle at a hectic time, when several new domestic competitors as well as the Japanese were entering the market, and it took two years to implement. It would have been easier to make this change in calmer waters. But that simply wasn't IBM's style in making hard decisions. Most important, from a customer point of view, the time was right for change.

In 1981, IBM made a major overhaul in its marketing structure. Three divisions had been selling IBM products: one handled typewriters, copiers and word processing equipment; another sold only small and medium-sized computers; and the third sold large computer systems. Reps often called on the same customers, causing an overlap of proposals and activities. When customers became confused, IBM began to consider alternatives.

Consequently, the three divisions were merged into two. The National Accounts Division sold the full product line to the top two thousand IBM customers, and the National Marketing Division sold the full product line to a wider customer base, ranging from small offices to major accounts not assigned to NAD.

At the time of these changes, IBM was enjoying prosperous times and some thought it was a mistake to rock the boat. And it would have been far easier to let the complaints slide. But we knew that the reorganization would enable IBM to give better service to its customers and to optimize our resources, so the company went ahead with it. It was a massive undertaking to reeducate our salespeople and match skills with customer needs. And it took incredible resolve for those in the field to adjust to the new demands. It was not a painless changeover and there were risks. But it was a thoughtful gamble that worked. IBM's sales volume and net profits have since reached record highs.

As a further example of meeting the needs of an ever-changing marketplace, in January 1986, IBM merged and then geographically split these two U.S. divisions to form the North-Central Marketing Division and the South-West Marketing Division. Each field office now sells the full product line to all companies, regardless of size, within its geographic area. IBM has never been afraid to revamp its marketing organization, with each change being right for the time.

NEW CHANNELS OF DISTRIBUTION

One of IBM's most intellectually challenging, exciting and difficult changes has been the development of alternate channels of distribution. Throughout the company's history, products were always sold via the direct interface of marketing reps and systems engineers. Even so, the challenge for any company is to make its sales force even more productive, and to deploy them as intelligently as possible.

The introduction of the Personal Computer and other low-cost products dictated new and complementary approaches to the basic IBM selling and installation approach. A broad distribution system had to reach more customers than ever before—at competitive prices. IBM set out to be not only the low-cost producer but the low-cost seller as well.

Corporate marketing was asked to review what was happening throughout the industry and recommend a course of action. This study analyzed our direct mail, telephone selling and other marketing programs. We visited and conferred with companies that utilized dealers and distributors outside the computer industry.

One key factor was the forecast that by 1988 approximately 35 percent of the total industry's information-processing revenues would be generated from nontraditional sales approaches. Clearly we needed to move quickly, since only a very small percentage of IBM's future revenue was expected to come from these new techniques.

I presented this scenario at a top management conference in Woodstock, Vermont. From there, Frank Cary and John Opel didn't hesitate to tell the line executives to initiate creative actions and establish a dual marketing strategy. We would continue to enhance our existing branch office structure, but at the same time expedite the use of a complementary network of distribution channels.

In 1983, the National Distribution Division was formed to sell high-volume, low-cost products through alternate distribution channels. Besides the approximately one hundred IBM Product Centers in the U.S., an increasing number of retail stores and independent dealers are selling IBM products. In addition, there are hundreds of companies that buy IBM products, add substantial value to them, usually in the form of software or additional hardware, and resell them to customers. In 1984, there were approximately 10,000 dealer outlets worldwide selling selected IBM products.

IBM is also reaching thousands of potential customers through catalogs and direct mail campaigns. With its toll-free telephone number for selected customer orders, IBM Direct receives ten thousand calls daily, generating a revenue flow that amounts to several million dollars a day.

The results have been impressive. In 1984, sales through nontraditional channels accounted for a growing percentage of IBM's total revenue. But it hasn't been easy. First of all, marketing representatives were worried about their future role. At our recognition events and other meetings, we constantly had to reassure them. No way did we want to turn our representatives against the channels of distribution or the channels against our marketing force.

Some problems still exist where IBM's field force initiates the interest, then the customer goes to a Computerland, Businessland, Sears Roebuck or other dealer to buy the system. Progress is being made and most of the problems have been overcome. In addition to changing IBM's thinking, the experience has affected pricing practices and made the company more competitive.

We live in a changing world and the future cannot be predicted with certainty. That's an obvious statement, but how we deal with change and the future is not so obvious. Change can be an ally when your company is alert and sensitive and has its antennae reaching in all directions, picking up all the signals around you. Of course, change will be your enemy if it catches you by surprise. You must control change—or change will control you. To the fearful, change is threatening. They know that things will somehow get worse. The hopeful have faith that change will make things better. But to those special people who love a challenge and are "light on their feet," change is stimulating and exciting. They are the people who can make a difference. They can make a company. The people who make things happen are in demand and should be guarded jealously. Those who watch things happen and those who aren't sure what's happening are left behind.

OCCURRENCE MANAGEMENT

Managers who fail to understand the potential that modern technology offers will fall by the wayside in this highly competitive world. The requirement is not to convert people into technologists, but rather to have a sense of awareness of what these devices can and cannot do.

We are finally reaching a stage in our society when computer technology in the hands of truly creative people is being used as it's meant to be: *to amplify man's intelligence and provide a business life-style that is more rewarding and productive.*

For the foreseeable future, there will be a continual flood of paperwork and administrative trivia, and a need to communicate better. This dictates the need to simplify the information flow and separate out that which is important. Having visited organizations all over America during the past several years, I have observed that progressive managers no longer want to deal with information of a historical nature—other than to look at the past for its heritage value. Today the emphasis is on what I call *occurrence management,* which concentrates on identifying a potential problem and taking action before it happens. It also requires concentrating on your organization's strength. If a product is selling well in Dallas but poorly in Seattle, you go to Dallas to find out what they're doing right, not to Seattle to find out what's wrong. A computer system can be the tool to help accomplish this.

Modern technology also enables a business to effectively identify who, within its own organization, is the best source of information. For this reason, many companies are switching from a vertical style of management to a horizontal one— which I have always preferred. I never cared where a person was in the management hierarchy, but went to whoever I felt could provide me with the most timely and accurate response. I respected the individual's intellect and capability.

6
SOLUTION-MINDED SELLING

People buy products for what they can do, not for what they are.

When I'm asked, "What products does IBM sell?" I answer, "IBM doesn't sell products. It sells solutions." The answer may sound kind of flip, but its meaning is quite serious. People buy products for what they can do, not for what they are. They buy products to solve problems. If a person's problem is straight straggly hair, when the fashion is a halo of ringlets, the solution may come in the form of a curling iron, plastic rollers, a chemical compound or a visit to a hair stylist. It's not the product that is important to the buyer; the solution to the problem is what matters. All the buyer wants is curly hair.

The information processing business is all problem solving and solution selling. If I call on you, I try to convince you that I can make your job easier, improve your cost structure and help you provide better service for your customers, and I'll probably get your attention. But one thing you can count on: I'll never try to sell you a typewriter, a copier or a computer. An IBM marketing rep's success depends totally on his ability to understand a prospect's business so well that he can identify and analyze its problems and then come up with a solution that makes sense to the customer. Don't be surprised if that solution involves an IBM system, but it doesn't always. It might involve reprogramming the existing equipment or buying a new set of application packages. You can be sure, though, that there will be no attempt to "sell" a piece of equipment that isn't an integral part of a solution.

I said the rep has to know the customer's business in order to understand his problems; he also has to know his own product line if he is going to be of any help to the customer. And he has to know what the competition has to offer—its quality, pricing, delivery, etc. The people in the field have to be a combination of analyst, consultant, applications specialist, technologist and salesperson—and they have to be good in every area. Too many companies think of their reps only as salespeople, their primary and perhaps only function being to persuade a prospect to buy their product. If the prospect doesn't need the product, the salesperson is expected to create an illusion of need—then get the money and run before reality settles in. That's not IBM's approach.

Today's salesperson has to be a lot more to the customer than a genial, back-slapping, joke-telling Willy Loman type, who drops in each season to entertain and show his wares. He's performing best when he really understands the concept of solution selling.

YOU CAN'T GET AN *A* IF YOU DON'T DO YOUR HOMEWORK

I've never known a successful salesperson who doesn't do his homework before he calls on a customer.

It goes without saying that the rep should know his product line like the back of his hand. How, otherwise, can he relate his products to customers' needs? A company that sends an improperly trained salesperson into the field is insulting its customers and wasting their time.

I go further than that—I think it's just as bad to call on a customer without first giving that customer some serious thought and study.

Your particular business may determine what kind of information you'll find helpful. But almost any rep will benefit from scanning the customer's annual report and 10K—especially if it's a new customer or a prospect.

As IBM's marketing vice-president, I reviewed the action file that is kept on every key IBM customer before I made a call. I couldn't imagine walking in cold, thinking I'd just wing it. I do the same kind of homework when speaking to a group of customers at an industry conference. My staff helps me get information from the field so I can speak to the problems of my audience. Just as I don't believe in canned sales pitches, I don't believe in canned speeches. I don't think they ring true.

It's important to update yourself regularly on even those customers you've known for years. Recently I made a call on a very large insurance company that I hadn't been to for quite some time. Although I knew the company well, I spent a half hour reviewing its latest 10K and annual reports. The thirty minutes were well spent. I learned of three recent major investments, and of some significant reorganization that I hadn't heard about. During the course of my conversation with some of the insurer's top executives, my homework paid off. They were flattered that I knew what was going on and that I cared enough to remember the "numbers" involved in their recent acquisitions.

I had learned enough in the half hour of homework to know that their expansion would involve challenges that IBM could help with right from the outset.

It doesn't matter who the customer is; you're paying him a wonderful compliment when you demonstrate that you know something about his business—information that required research and thought. This approach is head and shoulders above the salesperson who walks in off the street and says, "I was in the neighborhood and thought I'd drop in."

Once you get your foot in the door, it takes more than a look at the prospect's annual report to win his business, especially when you're up against stiff competition. Years ago, I was asked by a marketing rep to join him in making a visit to a multibillion-dollar bank. We had our work cut out for us. The bank claimed that it was satisfied with its existing equipment, installed by one of our competitors—and to make matters even more difficult, the competitor's president sat on the bank's board of directors.

We did our homework well. Our strategy was to demonstrate unconditionally that our people were solution-oriented. That they were knowledgeable in the banking field. That we had the expertise to serve the bank's present and future needs. That IBM's marketing and engineering organizations were equipped to anticipate the banking industry's problems and needs during the next five to ten years. We worked hard to prove that we could be an important asset to them. I made more than a dozen calls on the bank over a period of several months, and during that time, arranged for its people to visit with other leading banks around the country to see firsthand how we perform. Then we took them to our education centers and said, "These are the people who will come to you and train your staff in preparation for the installation of the IBM equipment. This is just the beginning of our partnership with you and the commitment we will make."

We made it obvious that our interest went far beyond the sale of equipment. It was important that the bank executives meet with our product planners and highly skilled engineers, to convey their views and to get to know the people who would modify our equipment to meet their needs, if necessary. They were impressed that we would come to their premises and set up an entire education program for their people—top to bottom. They were impressed, too, with the banking knowledge of our systems engineers, who were thoroughly trained in the particular products the bank would need. We convinced them that our specialists would be on hand with solutions to whatever problems could occur. No area was left unexplored. We demonstrated that we not only knew where their industry was headed but could fully see its future needs. We got the business, because we sold them our people and their ability to solve problems—and convinced them that we were much more than just a producer of business machines. Like the person with straight straggly hair, they wanted their problems solved and didn't care if the solution came in a bottle or a crate.

ROLE-PLAYING THE CUSTOMER

IBM has a two-week course for its sales force that requires the marketing rep to role-play an IBM customer. Conducted with Harvard, it's called the President's Class. Here the salesperson is confronted with a series of problems and conditions a customer might face. The purpose is to help the marketing people understand how an executive thinks and what he does on a day-to-day basis.

Every organization can put its salespeople through a similar exercise. Role-playing requires only two people—they can alternate as customer and salesperson. One successful real estate agency I know has its trainees alternately play agent and customer, actually showing each other through homes. Experienced salespeople hired by the firm from competitive realtors and put through the role-playing exercise have realized how different the perspective became when they walked in the shoes of a potential buyer.

Of course, every customer is different, so a rep must learn to put himself in many pairs of shoes.

Many times the most direct way to get to a customer's problem—and often the only way—is to listen to him. Asking penetrating questions and listening to the answers: what could be simpler? Unfortunately, few people know how to listen, and salespeople are no exception. It's a major deficiency in our whole communication system, and our private, professional and public lives suffer because of it. I don't mean to get on a soapbox, but I think that it's a weakness in our educational system not to have courses in listening, and make the passing of them a requirement for graduation. The idea that the supersalesperson is a glib, fast-talking peddler is a complete misconception. The best professional salespeople are the best listeners. They know the importance of giving the customer time to think through and then verbalize his problems and concerns. It's important not only because the rep will learn a lot, but because it's flattering to the customer, who becomes an ally. Instead of the rep being the aggressor and the customer the defender of his pocketbook (and his eardrums), the two work together at defining and solving a problem. If they are both successful, a sale will be made. If the salesperson wasn't able to contribute to the solution, he didn't deserve to make the sale. And if his listening skills are weak, he's starting off with a handicap.

SPECIALIZATION—THE ONLY WAY

IBM's customer list covers many different industries, and because a number of its products and programs can be tailor-made to handle specific tasks, it's imperative to build a sales force of industry specialists. It's imperative, that is, if the intention is to run a solution-minded business. A salesperson can't be expected to be an authority on the automobile industry *and* the textile industry *and* the shipping industry. No matter how competent, he or she simply cannot call on a bank and talk about demand deposits and trust accounting, and then meet with an industrial company across the street to discuss an inventory or engineering problem.

As anyone in business knows, it's a full-time job to be

expert in one field—to understand its problems, decode its jargon, bring direction and fresh ideas to its future. So IBM specializes. There are fifteen major industry classifications, and each has subdivisions. In transportation, there are specialists in airlines, motor freight and railroads. In retailing, there are department store and supermarket specialists. In banking, there are savings and loan specialists and finance specialists. These people zero in on their specialty as if they were going to become a leader in that industry—as if they were going to become a banker or run a railroad. When calling on their customers, they bring expertise and insight that a salesperson who is strictly a product-seller could never bring.

Some companies think this procedure is too expensive. It's true that several of your people might be driving down the same highway, headed for the same city—one to call on an insurance company, one to see a grocery chain, another to visit an airplane plant. The quality of work accomplished by the specialists more than pays for the added expenses.

In the large metropolitan areas, IBM branch offices are organized by industry to service their market. Where there are several branches, each has its own specialization. Training centers specialize in a particular industry and are involved in education programs at various universities. Years ago, I established a program at Rutgers University for our banking specialists. I chose Rutgers because it was one of the best banking schools, where the bankers send their people for special training. The program focused on what's new in the banking industry. It gave our people a better view of the important issues facing top banking executives.

Several hundred experts in division headquarters work with the field people, assisting them with industry applications. These specialists design applications and implement systems for a cross-section of American business. One might go to a particular city with a marketing rep to consult with a customer who has a serious inventory control problem. With a true understanding of his business, he can evaluate the problem and design a solution.

One Houston branch specializes in the petroleum industry and has a team of specialists who work only in the area of mining. When they designed a large system for a major seismic petroleum concern, it also became *the* system for the mining industry. Specialization by industry isn't only for large corporations. Many smaller companies, out of necessity or choice, serve a single industry. These organizations may not have the manpower and financial resources to do otherwise, but by becoming experts in servicing a particular industry they may, in time, become recognized as the leaders in their field and build a terrific business around this reputation.

SHOWCASING A CUSTOMER

IBM relies heavily on its customers to help its marketing efforts—especially those customers that are considered to have leadership roles in their industry. IBM *showcases* these customers whenever it can. In a business like IBM's, most of the creative effort takes place in the field. The customers are the real innovators and their premises often are IBM's laboratory. It's up to IBM's marketing people to share their successes with other customers.

Sometimes, no matter how much time and effort a marketing rep puts into describing his products and services, making a truly outstanding presentation, the prospect still can't comprehend the end result. The best solution is to visit a successful customer installation. A satisfied customer speaking in your behalf is an ideal endorsement. It means a great deal when he tells your prospect: "Here's what we are accomplishing from this program. Here is the improved application. Here is the improved productivity. This is the savings we realized. This is the end result."

For the most part, customers are delighted to cooperate. Of course, don't expect an oil company to show a leading competitor a new mathematical model that finds oil in the ground! Nor will an automobile manufacturer in Detroit agree to showcase one of its IBM engineering display terminals containing model designs for the next three years.

The future-oriented marketing industry conferences I have mentioned are in part an extension of this idea of showcasing. Industry leaders attend these IBM-sponsored conferences at their own expense, and enthusiastically share their experiences with other companies in their industry. The conferences include sessions of special interest to financial, personnel, legal and marketing executives, but most exciting and effective is when these prestigious leaders describe their problems and share their solutions with everyone else. It's incredibly important to IBM, since it was, in most cases, a partner in finding the solution.

THE BITS AND BYTES

Since IBM is very serious about selling solutions, not products, its marketing reps don't try to dazzle their clients or prospects by dumping a lot of technical jargon on them. That doesn't mean that they're ignorant of the technology behind the products that implement the solutions. They're not like the car salesman who told me, "Look, I don't know what's under the hood. I'm not a mechanic. If I talked about gear ratios and horsepower, I'd scare people away."

I don't buy that line about not needing the technical knowledge. IBM's marketing reps spend months learning about their products and they're regularly updated throughout their careers, learning more and more about bits and bytes. If a salesperson doesn't know the latest specifics about his product, how can he understand its application for solving the customer's problem?

However, a salesperson is only as good as his ability to describe his product so that a customer can understand it. While understanding its bits and bytes is vital, he must also know how much information is useful to the customer. An engineer might have a keen interest in a computer system's basic technology. He's likely to ask about its capacity to switch information at a millisecond or microsecond rate. On the other hand, if you're talking to the company's chief financial officer, he's more interested in the end result: the application of the machine. You must be able to walk both lines—knowing when selling the bits and bytes is appropriate. Too much technical detail can dilute the selling effort.

A salesperson entering the field could become smitten with the jargon, but it doesn't take long for him to realize the importance of using "computer talk" sparingly. To me, people who fill their conversation with foreign phrases come off as affected snobs—and that includes technical jargon.

A CONSTANT SEARCH

At IBM, it's often said: "Nothing is successfully sold until it's successfully installed. Nothing is ever installed until it's properly sold." *Sell—Install:* the two words go together, never one without the other. When an initial sale is consummated, it is generally for a specific application. Two or three applications at most. But the sale doesn't end there. The delivery and installation phase of a sale might take as long as a year; meanwhile the customer must be educated in applying the product properly. IBM is constantly working with its customers, always trying to find new applications to further justify the equipment.

For instance, a marketing rep sells a piece of IBM equipment to the chief financial officer of a manufacturing firm, to handle its payroll. Later, he meets with the company's engineering and manufacturing people, and finds that with the same equipment they can speed up the orders on the shop floor and improve the inventory turnover. And when he talks to the people in purchasing, he learns that it takes five days to process those purchase orders. The processing time might be cut dramatically with minor additions to the existing machine: another disk drive, or additional tapes, or maybe another printer. The point is, a good marketing rep makes an ongoing effort to find new applications for the customer's equipment. The more problems uncovered and the more solutions, the greater the company's value to the customer.

I don't believe in trying to do too much at first with a new account. It's better to start off with a single application, as in payroll or accounts receivable, and demonstrate how the equipment will perform. My advice to a new account has been to do things gradually, justify the equipment on one or two applications. Once it is demonstrated that this is right for the customer, with no disruption in his business, *then* IBM will move forward with additional applications. Over the years, I have found that when you try to have a solution for everything right away, you tend not only to overpromise but to overwhelm the customer.

A computer system often has the guts of a customer's business tied up in it. Anything that could go wrong with it must be anticipated, so it can keep performing around the clock, 365 days a year. As with the space shuttle, redundancies are built in to minimize any problems. But it gets back to a sale not being successful until the equipment is satisfactorily installed and working. IBM is in a repeat business, and *must demonstrate value every day.*

I have often said that each proposal must be cost-justified from the customer's point of view. But there are factors involved that can't always be controlled. For example, a product like the Personal Computer or System/36 will free up some time on your calendar or perhaps allow your administrative people and secretaries to get more done in less time, but unless that "extra" time is used productively, the proposal doesn't save the customer money.

The values of some applications are more difficult to quantify than those of others. It's easy to justify an inventory control application. That's something tangible that you can put a dollar figure on. In the airlines industry, nothing is more perishable than an airplane seat. If it can be proved that a computerized reservations system will help fill those empty seats, that's tangible and cost-justifiable. On the other hand, handling more reservations in less time and responding to inquiries more quickly are intangible benefits. While the airlines know that they're providing a convenience for their customers, they can't measure an exact value received. I think it's always more difficult to cost-quantify an intangible reason for making a buying decision, but that is not to say a real value doesn't exist.

Finding new applications isn't limited to the computer industry, nor is growing with your customer base. Every salesperson should sell conservatively in securing the initial order. What's important is *getting the business,* and then performing so outstandingly that your customer will never go elsewhere to solve his problems.

VALUE-ADDED SELLING

In today's competitive business world, product superiority alone isn't enough for making it in the marketplace. Firms with inferior merchandise are destined to fail, of course, but I've also seen companies collapse even though they had fine products. They knew they had a superior product and didn't take their competition seriously. You should assume your competition also has a good product and that you must offer something extra. At IBM, this is referred to as *value-added selling*.

Value-added selling comes in many forms. It's often the difference that separates great organizations from the rest of the pack. The quality of a product should be the tip of the iceberg. I preach that "The actual sale doesn't begin until after the equipment has been installed." This means what you do for the customer after he's signed on the dotted line is every bit as important as what you did to earn the sale.

Value-added selling is why IBM was able to convince the major bank I mentioned earlier to use our computer systems. We demonstrated in no uncertain terms that we would do much more than just sell them machines: We had the qualified people to meet their long-term needs; we would educate their people, and together we'd come up with innovative applications on an ongoing basis. They *knew* that once our equipment was installed, it was only the beginning of a long-term partnership.

Not every company can go to such great lengths to win accounts with value-added selling, but I sincerely believe that every organization must somehow convey some added value in what it does—perhaps an important convenience or service or guarantee.

It's not always the company that offers the "best deal" pricewise that does the most business. I once bought a car because the dealer convinced me that he'd give me outstanding service. As I was looking at some models in the showroom, he said, "While you're here, I want you to walk through our service department with me. See how clean it is. See the working habits of our people. I want you to see the large parts inventory we have, so you'll know that if something goes wrong, we're not going to say, 'This job will take about three weeks.' I also want you to meet our service manager. He's been with us for fifteen years." Not that the price of the car wasn't a factor. It was. But I was impressed with how the dealer showed me the total resources available to me. I liked the pride he and his people had in their organization. They made me feel good about putting my confidence in their ability to give dependable service.

In this case, the value added made the difference. I don't care what the product is—it's what you offer over and above the basic product and how you perform that builds a solid business.

Many companies do have excellent support functions, but too often their people fail to let the customer know what's available. If my auto dealer hadn't coordinated his service department's and his sales force's efforts, I wouldn't have known what added value I was getting when I bought my car. Support functions such as IBM's education and office systems centers won't do anyone much good unless they are utilized by all systems engineers and all marketing reps with their customers.

Everything IBM does is influenced by its effort to excel in value-added service. If a customer is lost, you can bet it's not because of IBM's apathy or smugness. And you can also bet that IBM takes its competition seriously. If they intend to take away a customer, they'll have to care about that customer as much as IBM does.

7

BEING RESPONSIVE TO THE CUSTOMER

. . . the world is filled with the kind of customers who deserve the care and attention I advocate, and I'd be willing to jump through hoops to win and keep them.

If you had the idea, before getting into this book, that IBM became great because it had vast resources or a product that couldn't be duplicated by others, you must realize by now that IBM's greatness has been built on some very simple ideas and principles. Nothing very complicated or profound—little things that, I hope, are still being taught to children by their parents, teachers and religious leaders. Things like thoughtfulness, courtesy and integrity.

No magic formula or guarded secret keeps customers "married" to IBM long after their equipment is installed and their check deposited. It's just that IBM approaches the customer, *after* the sale, with the same interest and attention as when he was the prospect to be courted.

IBMers are not Pollyannas or altruists; they're pragmatists—realists who know which side their bread is buttered on. They know they'll be out of work if there are no customers. They also know that although their ambitions may be boundless, there's a limit to the number of customers they can acquire. So while they work very hard to get a new customer, they work even harder to hold on to the ones they have. Someone once said I behaved as if every IBM customer were on the verge of leaving, and that I'd do anything to keep them from bolting. There's a bit of truth in that. IBM is part of a huge industry, and I've always respected the competition. If they want to garner a larger share of the market, they have to compete head-on with IBM. They have to be innovative and smart—and they're both. That's why I might be caught looking over my shoulder, acting a little paranoid. But there is no truth to the suggestion that I'd have done *anything* to get or hold on to a customer. I would never do anything that either I or IBM considered improper or unethical.

There are certain places in the world where the mode of doing business includes bribes and kickbacks. Lots of companies go along with this: "When in Rome, do as the Romans do." Well, I don't buy this kind of thinking and neither does IBM. I don't understand how you can have one set of principles for the United States and another set for other parts of the world. No, I wouldn't do *anything* to make a sale, and there were times when I'd refuse to sell someone, on a matter of principle. Fortunately, the world is filled with the kind of customers who deserve the care and attention I advocate, and I'd be willing to jump through hoops to win and keep them.

It seems to me that most companies are a lot better at prospecting for new customers and selling those prospects than maintaining their customer list. They are *sales*-driven, putting money into campaigns designed to bring in leads. They can easily measure how successful they are: how many leads the promotion pulled in and how much each lead cost them. Leads are then turned over to their sales force, and again they can easily measure their success and compute the cost. That's O.K. as far as it goes, but it's not far enough for a *market*-driven organization. Of course, sales is a very important part of marketing—for some businesses it is the most important part—but it's not the whole thing, and I think that too many companies fail to realize this. By separating selling from the marketing function, they often separate the customer from their long-range plans. At IBM, our field people are called marketing reps, not sales reps, for a good reason: They know that their involvement with a customer just begins with closing the sale. It's much more difficult to measure the cost of keeping a customer than to calculate the cost of getting him in the first place. As far as I'm concerned, customer maintenance is imperative to doing business—and can be the difference between a company that struggles to stand still and one that enjoys healthy growth.

Anyone who stops worrying about a customer once he's delivered his goods should mull over the idea of the *inverted organizational structure*. Take your pyramidal organizational chart and upend it: the longer you look at it, the more sense it makes. The traditional structure shows the chief executive officer in the top box; below him are the top-ranking officers, followed by middle management, and at the bottom of the chart are the marketing or sales reps. Below them, implied if not shown, are the customers. Too often, that's where they're relegated by the people who depend on them most—to the bottom of the heap. But once you set that chart on end, with the CEO on the bottom and the customers on top, it illustrates what should be your company's priorities and goals.

In a truly market-driven organization, the customer is considered first and foremost. Of course, everyone loves this concept *as a customer*—at a restaurant, in a department store, buying a car, or whatever. IBM's customers are in that enviable position at the top of the organizational chart. That's why IBM's so tough to beat.

BEING BIG, ACTING SMALL

There's a tendency today to look back with bittersweet nostalgia at the time when we were a nation of small shopkeepers. Many people are saddened that the mom-and-pop businesses have given way to big chains and large corporations. Expensive research, ever-growing competition and the tremendous cost of doing business made it impossible for many businesses to stay small; to stay small often means to self-destruct. We can't turn back the clock and become again a nation of craftsmen and tradespeople. Even most of those kids of the sixties who abhorred the way our society was headed have given up their communes and their idea that *only* small is beautiful or worthwhile. And those who lament the loudest for the good old days would probably fight to keep their cars and TVs and long-distance telephone calls—none of which could be produced and operated by a simple proprietorship.

What we long for, I think, is the personal touch of the small business person—the grocer who knew our name, the fruit and vegetable peddler who brought his produce to our door. The doctor who made house calls. Well, I don't think a company has to be small to act small. Even a giant can be gentle and helpful and kind. It's not the size of a corporation or the number of people it employs that alienates customers, making them yearn for the good old days. It takes only one or two insensitive corporate employees to convince a person that he's dealing with an impersonal monolithic giant. After all, few people get entangled in a big company's bureaucracy when they make a purchase. How many employees does it take to negotiate a car deal with you? No more than your great-grandfather dealt with when he purchased a handmade carriage from a local craftsman. And there's no doubt in my mind that there were plenty of short-tempered, impatient business people in the good old days. The point is, it's foolish to blame bad manners on big business. If you walk into an IBM Product Center tomorrow to inquire about a personal computer, and a salesperson treats you with respect and willingly spends whatever time is necessary to satisfy your interest, you're going to feel good about the experience. You're not going to give a hoot if that rep is part of an organization that employs 400,000 people or if he's the proprietor.

It may be more difficult for the folks at IBM to project a

personal one-on-one attitude because of the company's size, but they do it. They do it because the customer is considered their number one priority. If IBM can do it, with hundreds of thousands of employees, and tens of thousands of managers, in hundreds of locations spread all over the world, then any company can do it.

There's no way of quantifying how many customers are lost because of little human errors—not returning a phone call, being late for an appointment, failing to say thank you, taking an account for granted. As far as I'm concerned, these "little" things can be the difference between a very successful company and a failure.

LITTLE THINGS

If you don't return phone calls promptly or answer your mail quickly, if you break appointments at the last minute, without a darned good reason, or have people sitting on their hands because you're late to appointments you do keep—what kind of message are you sending out? You're saying, "Hey, customer, you're not really very important to me or my company." I'll tell you this—I wouldn't want to do business with you. If I'm not sure that you'll return my phone calls, how can I feel sure that you'll expedite my order?

I wonder about the ability of people who don't have the time to answer letters and return phone calls. My job kept me as busy as anyone in our business, but I always found time to respond to customers' letters or phone calls within a day. If I was traveling, an assistant let them know when I'd respond— and I don't think I ever made a liar out of anyone. If I told a customer I would phone him by a certain time, and found that for some reason I couldn't, that customer received a call from my office. If I discovered that I'd be late for an appointment—even a few minutes late—whoever expected me was notified. I respected my customers' time just as I respected my own.

I wrote a lot of notes. Whenever I visited a customer or one visited me, I wrote to thank him for the time he spent with me, and to review whatever we discussed. If I was his guest for lunch or he was mine, I dropped him a thank-you note. None of these people were taken for granted. You have to let customers know how important they are. Every time a customer is lost, you weaken the sales base; the longer you keep a customer, the greater the equity in the marketing investment.

Too many companies start off on the wrong foot with a new customer by mishandling the initial order. Errors in setting up the account, which lead to wrong billings; a foul-up by the credit department, which delays the order and perhaps embarrasses the customer; improper handling of the paperwork by the shipping department—all errors that could have been avoided with a little care—can negate the good work the salesperson did to bring in the new account. Errors can be corrected, of course, but they're held against you and keep you scrambling. Life is easier when you do things right the first time. Casey Stengel said: "When you hit a home run you can take your time running the bases."

From the customer's point of view, nothing could be more frustrating than a continual battle with a supplier's billing department. Hours can be wasted in trying to untangle the mess one or two sloppy entries can cause. IBM makes mistakes too, and some of them could have been avoided. But it makes a continual conscious effort to eliminate them. By that, I mean that IBM doesn't simply wait for an error to occur and then quickly react—although I can assure you that it does quickly react. But it also tries to study the areas where little frustrating mistakes are likely to happen and nip them in the bud.

I've advised marketing reps to introduce new customers to the accounts receivable person—in person. In my opinion, nothing beats having internal people interface with the customers they serve. And it's good to get out of the office and meet the customers on their turf. It's important for people who have to deal with one another on money matters to develop a personal relationship. People should have a better understanding of an account than they can get from credit applications and cold numbers. At times, it can be more difficult when it comes to asking for money; because the relationship is more personal, it must be done with more care and sensitivity—but from my point of view, that's good. Some companies think that when it comes to asking for money, the less personal the relationship, the better. And their dun letters reflect their attitude. They're cold and curt and single-minded, and too often they offend the customer. And frequently they're off base. I completely disagree with this approach, and believe that it wastes a golden opportunity to strengthen a relationship with a customer. I don't ever want to lose a customer because of a billing mixup, or because we can't go after owed money with sensitivity.

A customer's ego, like anyone's, needs massaging at times. I don't believe in complimenting someone insincerely, but there are plenty of opportunities for honest flattery or attention. Years ago, I was called in on a highly competitive situation by a West Coast rep. We were trying to convince the management of a large aerospace company to let us handle certain applications that were being processed on a competitor's system. About twenty of our people were working with them, but the decisionmaker was obviously pleased that someone at my level in the company had come to participate. In fact, he said so. Frankly, I was flattered that he was flattered, and I said, "Look, if we put this deal together, I'll visit you once a month. You and I will sit down together and review how we're doing in meeting the specific installation target dates. This includes the application programming, people training, systems delivery dates, and all aspects of our joint effort." We got the business. I don't know what my commitment to those monthly meetings contributed to getting the order, but it may have been very important, even critical. The point is, you must use all your resources if you want to win a customer. You have to be sensitive to customers' needs, and sometimes those needs include a factor that is not product-connected. Incidentally, I kept my promise and, in time, established a wonderful relationship for IBM and for me personally. Of course, I couldn't make the same promise to every customer—it's a matter of putting one's time to the best possible use.

I called on many customers while I was in IBM management. I always followed up the visit with a letter, thanking them for their time and their business, and summarizing our discussion and whatever plans we made. Then, at the appropriate time, depending on the situation, I phoned to be sure that the customer was satisfied with the results.

It takes time and energy and a good tickler system to build a solid relationship with a customer, but it's important. And if anyone says that what I'm describing is busy work, I say that person doesn't understand marketing.

In all my years with IBM, I never considered the amount of business involved when it came to solving a customer's problem. When I was corporate vice-president of marketing, a complaint addressed only to "The Marketing Manager" was forwarded to me. An elderly man who had one of our first typewriter models was upset because his order for three black typewriter ribbons was shipped in the wrong color. He said that he had been trying to straighten out this problem but received no satisfaction. I wrote immediately, expressing my regret that we had inconvenienced him and assuring him that his order would be expedited promptly and properly. A few days later, I phoned to make sure that he had received the ribbons. And you can be sure that I investigated to find out why the error occurred. This was no grandstand play. Little problems can be symptomatic of big problems—and the time to solve them is when you hear about them.

It's essential to convey to every customer that you value his business, regardless of size. The bigger your organization is, the more important it is for you to relay this message. You never want your small customers to perceive that they're being treated indifferently, or differently from your big customers. I've been told, "If I don't give you my business you're not going to worry about it, because IBM has thousands of customers that are more important than my company." Nothing is further from the truth. The combined impact of IBM's small customers on annual sales volume is tremendous. It's the composite of these individual customers that formed the foundation of the company, and it has grown and prospered as a result of their support. When it comes to any policy or marketing decisions, IBM considers the small customer, just as it considers the big one. I've heard people say, "In our business, 80 percent of our income comes from 20 percent of our customer list, so our policies are designed to keep the 20 percent happy. The rest have to look out for themselves." In the long run, that kind of attitude will be destructive, and it's one I cannot accept. As a matter of fact, I've always been so sensitive about a small customer's perceiving a slight that I've doubled my efforts to prove him wrong.

Brilliant ideas or an expensive PR campaign isn't necessary to improve the way a company is perceived by its customers. It can usually be done by attending to the little details. It's an important part of taking care of business. After I addressed an industry conference recently, someone said: "There's a lot of talk about excellence in business today, Buck. What does it mean to you?" I answered with the first thought that popped into my mind: "Excellence means doing the little things well—doing a thousand things one percent better rather than doing one thing a thousand percent better. It's demonstrating to your customer and peers that you're willing to give extra effort, and take an extra step to assure a good job." It all gets back to value-added selling. You simply can't neglect the little things and be successful.

THE OCCASIONAL SACRIFICE

When I told you that I wasn't a workaholic, I meant it. My private time is very important to me, but every so often a business situation comes up that dips into the hours I usually set aside for myself and my family. I never resent putting in that extra time, especially when it benefits a customer. It's an investment that always pays off.

From the beginning of my IBM career, I realized that an excellent performance required that my customers be happy with what I did. When I was a neophyte marketing rep, I sold a computer system to a wire spring company in Cleveland. It was my biggest sale at the time, and I wanted them to be as pleased and excited as I was. They had a difficult payroll problem, and were worried about the time it would take to transfer everything from a manual system onto punch cards and then into the computer. I spoke with our systems engineers and we agreed to do something special for this new customer. We worked through the weekend—forty-eight hours straight—and when the company opened for business Monday morning, the system was in place and the payroll ready to be processed. The customer was elated and grateful, and I had the satisfaction of knowing that the systems engineers and I had done an excellent job. It was a rewarding experience, especially so early in my career. I liked the good feeling and was happy to repeat it whenever it was necessary.

No one should be expected to operate in overdrive continuously, but there are times when an extra effort and a small sacrifice can be very important to you and your customer. If repeat business is as important to you as it is to IBM, you must be committed to the extra effort. A seductive advertising campaign and a price with most of the profit squeezed out of it are not enough. It's one thing to get the initial order, but quite another to have the customer stay with you year after year.

During my tenure as head of marketing, IBM grew from a $10 billion company to a $50 billion company, and we didn't do it by selling price. Most customers are not looking for the cheapest solutions to their problems. They expect to pay a fair price for what they buy. And what they are buying from companies like IBM is usually a real solution to a problem—not a quick fix. The quality of the equipment they invest in is certainly important to them, but even more important is the quality of the people whom they must depend on to service it. *They're buying peace of mind and a good night's sleep.* Customers perceive IBM as a company they can count on in a crisis. There's no doubt in my mind that IBM has earned that perception not because it tries to project a caring image in its advertisements—but because it is willing to make an extra effort and an occasional sacrifice to help a customer. Any customer.

Here's an interesting "case." After Irv Levey acquired this book for Harper & Row, he noticed that almost every business machine in the publisher's New York headquarters was an IBM. He asked Bill Baker, the company's comptroller, "How come? Are they cheaper? Are they superior? Why IBM?" They're not cheaper; Bill Baker was sure of that. And he couldn't swear that they were absolutely the best machines available. But one thing Baker was sure of: IBM's service organization was the best in the world. They were totally dependable and, at times, did incredible things for their customers. Then he told Irv about a time when the company's main computer, in Scranton, Pennsylvania, went down because a very inexpensive small part malfunctioned. It was very unusual for this part to cause a problem, and there was no replacement for it anywhere in the area. However, IBM quickly located one in Colorado, sent a jet to pick it up, and had the computer in full operation within twenty-four hours of the mishap. It took an extra effort by IBM to keep this customer happy. It paid off many times over. And although the incident took place years ago, before Bill Baker became a top executive at Harper's, it was one of the first things that popped into his mind when he was asked, "Why IBM?"

AVOIDING END ZONE SAVES

No football coach wants to see his team put in a position where the quarterback is forced to pass on the last play of the game. It's especially frustrating if he has the win in his pocket and fumbles it away. Desperation plays cause ulcers. At IBM, everything possible is done to avoid having to make desperate moves to keep an account on the books. It's tough enough when you lose an initial order in a competitive situation, but it's really rough when you're losing a customer you had previously won. The situation becomes intolerable when it's happening because of customer neglect. To me, neglecting an established account is as great a marketing sin as not following up on a bona fide lead.

A company that keeps in touch with its customers is rarely surprised by the kind of problem that loses accounts. To avoid having to make "end zone saves," you must build into your marketing program a way of keeping in touch with your customer *even when you have nothing to sell.* You never want to be in the position of hearing a distraught customer say: "Where were you when this problem was developing? You're the experts—you would have spotted it had you been here. Why are you showing up now that we put one of your competitors on the case?"

As far as I'm concerned, the most effective contact you have with a *satisfied* customer is that contact between sales—

even if you don't know when the next sale might be made. Many sales organizations disagree completely with me on this. They say that an account with no immediate need for their product is off limits to the rep. Once you sold them, stay away—why look for trouble? Besides, it's too expensive to call on an account unnecessarily. Such organizations are short-sighted. They can't see beyond today's call report.

I wanted our people to find a good reason to call on the satisfied account, even if it took some creative thinking. They can check out the system, making sure there are no minor problems; they might drop off an interesting article that appeared in a trade journal not readily available to the customer, or pass on information regarding an industry meeting. Whatever. Becoming used to seeing the rep—and not only when he's trying to sell—the customer should think: "This guy really does have my interest at heart. He's accessible. If I have a problem, I'll go to him first."

When companies, or reps, develop this kind of relationship with a customer, the odds are that they'll never find themselves trapped into making desperation moves to keep the relationship going.

THE PROGRAM OF RECONCILIATION

Although IBM does everything a company can do to prevent the loss of a customer, occasionally one is lost. Let's face it, IBM's marketing organization is tens of thousands of individuals who have minds and wills of their own and are at various levels of development so far as their business skills are concerned. The company does a marvelous job of recruiting and training, but it's not perfect. Well, whatever the reason for losing an account, IBM doesn't take the loss lightly. It wants that customer back. Once it knows for certain that a customer has a firm commitment with a competitor, IBM steps aside until the competitor has had an opportunity to install his equipment on that specific application. There's no legal reason for this—but IBM thinks it's a tasteful way of doing business, and has made it a matter of policy. It's the same kind of thinking that's behind the company's policy never to knock a competitor. However, it doesn't make IBM any less intense or committed to getting the customer back.

The first step in the reconciliation, as with any other failed relationship, is to find out what went wrong. It might be a misunderstanding between the customer and an IBM service organization. It might be a personality conflict between the customer's contact and the rep. It could be a political problem in the customer's house—a new authority wanting to make his presence felt. Or maybe the competitor's rep did a terrific job of convincing the customer that he could deliver a superior product.

Once the cause of the failure is understood, a solution is sought. It could be a new approach, a redesigned program, a change in equipment or a shift in personnel.

IBM people are patient but persistent. Just as they never take their customers for granted, neither should the competitors. Sometimes it requires a year or more to win back a lost account, but IBM's average in recouping lost business is quite high.

Why is losing a customer so challenging? For one thing, a lost customer has an immediate impact on sales volume. The company invests a lot to get the customer in the first place. It counts on repeat business, equity in the existing customer list. Turning over inventory is exciting—turning over a customer list is frightening. When you lose an account, you risk a snowball effect. A dissatisfied customer may complain to ten others and influence them negatively. The competitor who won the customer from you might broadcast his victory to all who will listen. That can't help your image and can have a demoralizing effect on the rep in the field. And you don't increase your sales base by replacing a lost customer. Every time you lose a customer, you have to sell another one just to stand still.

TRUE PARTNERSHIPS

It's easier to keep an account than it is to regain one. Easier, that is, if your orientation is long-term relationships. And the basis for an enduring association is, of course, understanding and concern. A company that views a business relationship strictly from a selfish vantage point has no right to expect loyalty from the other principal. I don't see how you can be successful, in the long run, if the customer isn't strengthened by his involvement with you. I honestly believe that any good that is done for the customer is good for you. And the flip side of that is just as true. If you hurt the customer, you hurt yourself. That's why IBM wants its field people to represent the customer with as much zeal as he devotes to IBM. I assure you that there is no conflict of interest when it's done properly.

A team of IBMers asked me to help them with a customer that was one of the nation's largest banks. It was a tough competitive situation. Another computer company had made a strong pitch for the business, and as the meeting, at the bank's headquarters, progressed, it became evident that the executives were leaning toward the other company. The bank's president was very impressed with the technological aspects of the competitor's presentation. He was obviously caught up in the bits and bytes, and I would have antagonized him had I debated their relative value.

I listened very attentively as he had his say, and when he was finished I responded. "I have only one thing to ask, and nothing more," I said. "Do you want to do business with a hardware vendor or do you want a partner?"

There was nothing tricky or clever about the question. It was honest. I truly believed that we had something very special to offer this account, something that went far beyond the technology of our machines—our sincere interest in their well-being.

"I want a partner," he said, after considering the question for a few moments. Then he walked over to me, extended his hand and said, "Buck, shake hands with your new partner."

I always wanted every customer to feel a partnership relationship with IBM. Like friendship, marriage or a legal partnership, the kind of relationship I advocate requires a greater commitment, and acceptance of more responsibility, than any ordinary buyer-seller relationship. The seller should never do anything that is self-serving, anything for short-term gain, anything that might jeopardize a long-term relationship. It's a very nice way of doing business. It casts both parties in roles that are far removed from those of adversaries, each trying to squeeze the "best deal" out of the other.

The highest-profile IBM "partnerships" are those with the national accounts. General Motors is an example. A team of IBMers, headed by an account executive, works full-time with GM. IBM has offices at their headquarters and manpower located at each of their many divisions. It's not unusual for a marketing rep to report daily to one such account, where he spends 90 percent of his time.

Customers sometimes confuse the IBM staff with theirs. It was always music to my ears when they said, "I forget who's on my payroll and who's on yours."

When you work that closely with a customer, you know that you have reached the highest level of customer-partner satisfaction.

A lot of salespeople make a go of it by taking the path of least resistance. "Give 'em what they want, and let them worry about it if they make a mistake" is a common attitude. That doesn't work if you believe in partnership selling. I've been in competitive selling situations where the customer wanted a smaller, less expensive installation than I *knew* he needed. I could not sell him what he wanted, without feeling that I wasn't benefiting him. Not if I had done my homework. Not if I had spent days on his shop floor studying his operation, interviewing his foremen, engineers and production people. It's exactly the same if I concluded that what the customer wanted was more equipment than he needed. When I tried to increase or decrease a client's order, it was because I *knew* I was right. It's a matter of integrity. There's a time when you have to take a stand, even if it means losing the order. Of course, taking such a stand wouldn't make sense in all selling situations. If a customer wanted ten typewriters and I thought he needed twelve, I wasn't going to walk away from the order. No harm done, and when he found out I was right, he'd order more. But I'd have to take a stand in a case where I was selling a complex installation that might require equipment modifications and a custom-designed program. An error by the customer could cost him a great deal in terms of future work disruption and investment.

Sticking to your guns may not be the easiest way to get the initial order, but it pays off in the long run.

In our business, sometimes a customer outgrows his system more quickly than he or we expected. Forecasting future needs is hardly an exact science, so at IBM an attempt is made to document every assumption that went into the decision to install a particular product. It's good to have that documentation in those instances when, a year or two after a sale is made, the customer comes in anguish and says, "How did this happen? I can't handle these increases in volume. How could such a mistake have been made?" Of course, the company's assumptions are rooted in the forecasts made by the customer. So long as there are records of those expectations, IBM can demonstrate that the decision at the time was right. The purpose is not to hide behind those numbers but to help the customer understand IBM's response to them.

The quality of a company's relationship to its customers is affected by its morality and expertise. Although it's said that you can't legislate morality, when it comes to the way IBM's people relate to its customers, IBM tries. And its people are expected to become experts in whatever marketplace they are asked to service. It's IBM's way of making sure that the company's response to any customer's inquiry or problem will be authoritative, intelligent and fair.

Although the teams it sends into the field are highly trained in their area of expertise, IBM still goes to outside sources for reinforcement—consulting firms and universities, for example. It goes to the outside on a regularly scheduled basis, as well as ad hoc. Each year, for example, a group of Harvard MBAs is invited to study a particular problem. The point of this is to maintain a certain balance in IBM's interpretation of customers' needs. Many professors with outstanding expertise in business and industry are available for consultation. It surprises me that more companies—especially small firms—don't take advantage of this rich source of knowledge.

The major manufacturers and packagers of consumer products do a tremendous job of collecting data to better understand their customers. Their market researchers, through in-depth surveys and diligent probing, have learned that the average American puts 3.2 ice cubes in his soft-drink glass; blows his nose 256 times a year; writes 24 checks a month; consumes 95 hot dogs, 283 eggs, 5 pounds of yogurt, nine pounds of cereal and 2 pounds of peanut butter per year. Incredible! They even know that 47 percent of us put water on our brush before we apply the toothpaste and 15 percent water the brush after the toothpaste is applied. I've never been a trivia game player, but this is fascinating stuff. But what's really impressive is the depth of the inquiry. The companies that sponsor this type of consumer survey are in the most competitive of businesses. They have to know their customers so well that they can anticipate and respond to their questions, concerns and worries. Most businesses don't have to think in terms of their average customer, nor do they need to deal with consensus opinions. They can communicate directly with their customers, and uncover their needs and concerns. And respond in a thoughtful, courteous, honest way—if they appreciate the importance of holding on to a customer, and are smart enough to do it. You don't have to be a genius.

8

SERVICE, SERVICE, SERVICE . . . AND MORE SERVICE

While everybody wants it, most don't want to give it.

S ervice is a tremendous source of revenue for IBM. In fact, if the revenue generated by IBM's domestic service alone went into a separate corporation, that company would rank within the top 100 companies of 1985 in the Fortune 500 listing.

IBM pioneered the idea that *selling* and *servicing* were inseparable parts of the marketing function. And although *Roget's Thesaurus* doesn't consider the two words to be synonyms, IBM does. Seventy-plus years ago, when Tom Watson, Sr., proclaimed service to be the backbone of sales, selling was almost entirely a battle of wits: a contest between the sellee, who had some money in his pocket, and the seller, who wanted it.

Selling in general has changed since those days. The contest between buyer and seller is more subtle; more civilized. Today's salespeople study the art of persuasion, and take courses in negotiating. Too often they concentrate on buzzwords, angles and hooks, rather than quality and service.

Psychologists are paid to come up with clues to a prospect's vulnerability, then wordsmiths and media specialists zap him with messages that make products irresistible.

Today, some products are hyped in a way that purposely ignores quality. Yes, selling has changed since 1914, when

Watson, Sr., began implementing his notion about the art. It seems to me, however, that the changes aren't really fundamental. They are mostly changes in style, format and technology.

I sold service during my entire professional life. I bought IBM's line not because it was glib or slick but because service worked for me. It made me a topnotch salesperson.

Why haven't more companies recognized the fact that the most reliable contributor to building a solid sales base is giving the customer the best possible service?

Modern business has certainly focused its attention on convenience. You don't have to go far to spend your money today. It seems that you can buy just about anything without leaving your home. Merely dial 1-800 and have your credit card number ready.

Of course, I'm not putting down convenience. IBM has its 800 numbers too. But convenience is not enough, and sometimes it's a misnomer. Buying a product without leaving one's easy chair may seem convenient until the product arrives in a thousand pieces, with instructions that are loosely translated from the Japanese. What happens when one of the parts is missing and the 800 number is connected to an answering machine hundreds of miles away?

When business turned its attention to new channels of distribution, it certainly made an important impact on our buying habits, and our expectations. In many ways it's been a bonanza for lots of businesses. However, companies like IBM, which have enthusiastically committed themselves to giving the best possible service to their customers, have also experienced prosperity, *plus* the security of an ever-growing customer base.

The general attitude about service is an interesting paradox. While everybody wants it, most don't want to give it. Some individuals may consider giving service to be a downer— a throwback to the days of the obsequious servant. But I'll tell you this—I doubt if any of IBM's thousands of service people feel demeaned by what they do for a living. More about that in a moment, but what about businesses that struggle against a difficult economy, foreign competition and an unending stream of new products that vie for the customer's allegiance? Why don't these companies understand the importance of service? I think it's partly because they can't quantify its value, especially after they've made the sale. They consider the costs involved to be nonrecuperated expenses. To me, it doesn't matter how you account for the cost of servicing a customer; the important thing, in the long run, is to consider it an investment in the future.

I'm concerned here about the service that takes place *after* the sale is made. Some businesses, of course, have no contact at all with a customer once the goods and money change hands. Having one product to sell per customer, with little or no chance of repeat business, they are totally sales-driven. But too many firms that *do* depend on repeat business to keep afloat seem to forget the customer once they land him. At least, they behave that way.

IBM can't forget the importance of its old customers or its commitment to give them the best service possible. It is part of IBM's creed, and it's reaffirmed every working day by everyone in the company.

When it comes to service, IBM may have written the book. It took more than a simple commitment to reach the company's present level of excellence—it took a major investment in time, research, manpower and money. And the work and investment are ongoing. It's worth it. When IBM tells a customer that the product it buys from the company is only the tip of the iceberg, IBM means it. A marketing rep may sell a machine or an application, but what he delivers is the concern and expertise of a tremendously talented and committed staff. Included are administrative people, technical specialists, systems engineers, service representatives and managers who work in every capacity throughout the company. The service provided goes far beyond making certain that the product sold delivers what was promised. IBM people share their market research, and what they know about advertising and even accounting. They invite customers to IBM-sponsored industry seminars and conferences, providing an environment where customers learn not only from IBM but from each other.

The size of a customer's purchase is not a factor in determining what IBM provides in service. The in-depth service described above is available to every customer.

IBM decided years ago that to be the most successful company in the world, it must have an exciting, flexible, sensitive service program to maintain old customers, create new ones and make people want to do business with IBM. A good service program would not be satisfactory. It had to be better than that. When IBM's commitment to being the best service organization in the world, bar none, regardless of industry, was announced to employees, the spirit within the company soared. An IBM culture was created, which started with recruits in their basic training program. That spirit would prevail throughout their entire careers. Everyone was sharing the same commitment—to provide an overwhelming level of service, unequaled by anyone, and to achieve the highest level of customer satisfaction.

Think of the pride of the salesperson who can tell a customer: "If you incorporate my ideas and products into your operation, we will never let you down. Servicing your company will be our top priority." He can say it without fear because his organization will not let him down.

IBM doesn't want to lose a customer, ever. It tries to give superior day-to-day service so that customers wouldn't even consider doing business with anyone else. But one is lost occasionally, and when it happens it stings IBMers' pride. They never blame it on the customer. They want to know what went wrong, and when they find out, they take steps to prevent a recurrence.

Any company can strengthen its position with current customers by improving its service program. It probably wouldn't take additional real estate or a big investment in equipment or personnel. What it takes is a major commitment of the company's top management, and the resolution that, in time, every employee must make the same commitment.

BUILDING SERVICE INTO THE PRODUCT

Service can't be an afterthought. It must be an important part of the marketing plan, and a serious consideration throughout the development of the product, from its very inception. A new product should never be introduced before service has been thought out and tested.

At IBM, service people live at the development site of a new product. They design the maintenance techniques and deal with such questions as: What training will be required to service the product? What diagnostics can be built into it? What is the appropriate support delivery system? Where should spare parts be stocked? In what quantities?

An interlock process during the initial planning integrates engineering, manufacturing, marketing *and servicing*. For a product to get a development go-ahead, each of the four functions is required to verify that it has the skills and resources to do its part.

Of course, it's a lot easier for an engineer to design a product if he doesn't have to worry about its maintenance; and if he doesn't look down the road, it may seem cheaper. But it isn't. I've heard of companies that quickly designed a product, then rushed it into the marketplace without any consideration for its maintenance. Soon they discovered that the cost of servicing it was prohibitive, and the entire project was scrapped. It's almost impossible for anyone with an IBM orientation to fathom this, but I know it happens.

IBM's engineers know that a product's design must be practical and economical. A product mustn't be overdesigned or underdesigned if it's to be serviced with minimal difficulties. And as the product is being developed, the company must be kept apprised of the servicing problems that are foreseen. Important servicing questions must be resolved by the time the product is ready for the market. Are the skills needed for servicing already in the house and available when needed? Must some of the service reps be retrained or do additional people have to be hired? Is there a shortage of the kind of skilled service people needed for this new product? If there is a shortage, is it so acute that it's necessary to build redundancy into the product to reduce the need for specific service?

Just as cost-effective redundancy is built into the design of a product to reduce the possibility of a customer's equipment going down, a program of preventive maintenance is put into motion right from the point of sale. Service schedules are established for every product IBM produces, including typewriters, copiers, terminals, and small and large computers. Service reps make regular calls and inspect the equipment. Sometimes the call is for a specific maintenance procedure, or because a certain component may have developed a troublesome history and the service person wants to shortstop a potential headache. Sometimes the call is for a general checkup. The rep isn't looking for trouble; he's just testing to make sure there isn't any.

IBM people don't want to interrupt the customer's operation, so when trouble does develop, they do everything possible to eliminate the down time entirely or at least limit it to the barest minimum. If a service rep identifies the problem as being in hardware, he replaces the faulty element with a new one. Not only is this the quickest way to get the equipment running; it's also the most economical.

The important thing is to have the service people work hand in hand with the technical people. When IBM built a new typewriter in Lexington, Kentucky, hundreds of service reps worked on the manufacturing line. It was essential that they have firsthand knowledge of how the product was made. After all, they were the ones who would be sent into the field to service it. They had a complete understanding of the machines, and were able to foresee the type of servicing problems that might occur, so they argued that additional redundancy be built into units. Because they did, the service time needed for these typewriters was greatly reduced.

Often, to enhance its *ease of use*, a product is brought into an IBM test center. Here, nonprofessionals read the product's promotional materials, study the application code and operate the new machines. They do this while being observed by engineers and "human factor" people. What is learned has a marked effect on the finished product.

At times, the service people request that a particular product be introduced on a stage basis, with testing in perhaps eight major cities to study the product's service needs before it is distributed nationally.

In a sense, IBM reinvents service every time it creates a new product.

THE DIFFERENCE-MAKERS

Service rep—the IBMer who actually services a customer's equipment—is a job classification that carries great responsibility and respect. (As noted, "service person" in IBM parlance is far from the proverbial guy in rumpled coveralls with grease under his fingernails. IBM service reps come to work dressed in the same fashion as a marketing rep or an executive. And why not? They're very important business people and IBM wants its customers to sense immediately that they are dealing with a very special breed of service person.)

To IBM's more than 25,000 field service people, *the customer comes first, absolutely.* They know that the equipment IBM installs is vital to the operation of a company. If it goes down, a whole plant can go down. This is especially true in a catalytic operation such as a petrochemical company, where the entry of its gasoline and crude oil is based upon a process control system, and if one computer system fails, the plant grinds to a halt. And it's true of manufacturers that rely to a great extent on robots, or any business whose inventory is computer-controlled. Customers depend on the service reps to keep their operation running smoothly twenty-four hours a day.

A service rep can be either a generalist who services a variety of machines (typewriters, copiers, word processors, small computers) or a specialist in, say, large computers. In either case, he is thoroughly trained before he's put in a customer environment. The service division has a strict rule never to allow anyone to service a product he isn't completely familiar with, even if it's closely related to a piece he has mastered. While there might be little doubt that he could service it, the company won't relax the rule and risk an error.

As is true with every IBMer who works in this field, the service rep's performance is enhanced when he understands the meaning of being on a team, and takes advantage of the company's available resources to do the job at hand. He must learn which resources to tap and where to go to get the information to satisfy the customer. He depends on *teamwork.*

Besides the mechanical and technical training they receive, service reps go through IBM's basic orientation and educational program along with the marketing reps and the systems engineers.

For the past few years, a *Fortune* magazine survey has proclaimed IBM to be the most admired company in America.

It's an honor that everyone at IBM is proud of and rightfully shares in, but if there's any single facet of IBM's operation that has "the best" written all over it, it's service. Creeds, policies and programs document the company's desire to serve, which may even border on compulsion; but it really comes down to the people, to this army of good citizens, dressed in their business suits, proudly representing IBM and willingly helping every customer. It's a matter of pride and integrity to them and to the company.

The way people view IBM is fascinating to me. What they're really impressed with, I think, is the adherence to common courtesy and old-fashioned values. It seems a little strange, considering the fact that so many business people ignore those values in their own business relationships. Their indifference bothers me. I call it "psychosclerosis": a hardening of the attitudes. Their heads are filled with thoughts like: "It's someone else's problem, not mine." "Why should I get involved?" "If I'm off the hook contractually, the heck with them." If your attitude is one of apathy and avoidance, you can't expect those who represent you to be any different.

CALENDAR INTEGRITY

I can't tolerate bad manners or sloppy work. I always expected the people I worked with to be considerate to me, to their co-workers and, of course, to our customers. I'm a nut on what I call calendar integrity. I want meetings to start on time, and I want everyone who's supposed to participate to be there. I want my phone calls returned and my memos answered and deliveries made when promised. People who can't do those things have no business in a sales-oriented, customer-driven company. Personally, I don't know what business they do belong in.

A company can't give good service—not what I consider

good service—unless its people are committed to calendar integrity. Everyone who ever worked for me knows exactly what that term means to me. They know that when they have an appointment with me and are late—even a few minutes late—I don't let it slide by. It's not the few minutes that matters; it's the lack of respect for someone else's time. I come down hard on those who do not perform the simple courtesies and tasks, and I'm consistent.

Once, I had an appointment with the president of a multibillion-dollar manufacturing company near Chicago. I flew in from New York and, with a group of IBMers, went to his office for a 10 A.M. meeting. We were right on time, but were ushered into a reception area by a secretary, and waited half an hour. Finally, I said to the people with me, "We've waited long enough. Let's go."

They felt somewhat uneasy about leaving. "But, Buck, we have to work with these people on a day-to-day basis."

"That's baloney," I told them. "There's no reason for anyone from our company to be treated this way." And we left.

The manufacturer's president called me that afternoon at the local IBM office and said, "Hey, Buck, I thought we had an appointment set up for this morning."

"A ten o'clock appointment," I said, "and I was there."

He immediately rescheduled the meeting, and I guarantee you it started exactly on time. And it was a good one. Calendar integrity must be practiced across the board. I live by it, and I expect others to do the same.

Good values and good business are not contradictory. IBM isn't the only company in the world that's proved that. But I'd like to see the day when the nice things a company does are not viewed as modern business anomalies.

Giving good service is doing a lot of little things right the first time. It starts with each individual taking care of business, hour by hour, day by day. It's the water-drop principle: Each little act, no matter how insignificant it appears, is tremendously important.

THE CLOSER THE BETTER

One of IBM's real strengths is the local support available to the customer. Typically, sales and service people are located in the same building, where strong emphasis is placed on day-to-day dialogue between the two groups. It's vital that they work as a team and understand and respect each other's problems and expertise. The close relationship makes it possible for the reps to sell IBM's service without hesitation. They know that what they promise will be delivered and they're grateful for that. On the other hand, the service people know that their success is directly tied into the new business generated by the salespeople. This kind of interdependency could cause stress and friction between the two groups, but it doesn't—the relationship is warm, friendly and harmonious. Throughout the organization there's a continual meshing of sales, service and education, which is brought as close to the customer as possible. For example, located at most of IBM's regional offices are small groups of specialists called Application Transfer Teams. They focus on leading edge applications; learn every justification, and then help the reps sell it to specific customers. Equally important, they participate in the installation of these applications from one customer to another. Their function is primarily one of passing on outstanding new applications. But, as with many things IBM does, the effort reaps its eventual rewards. The most satisfied customers are those who get the maximum benefit from their investments. If Application Transfer Teams can come up with more uses for the equipment than the customer bargained for, it's a bonus the customer won't forget.

Along the same line, there are Application Marketing Centers across the country where seminars, product demonstrations and business systems planning programs are conducted. There, IBM specialists train customers to maximize the use of their equipment by accessing decisionmaking data within their own organization.

Some of these centers concentrate on the needs of the retailer; a customer can come to learn about optical scanning systems, for example. Other centers focus on office systems, and there a customer might spend several days learning how the flow of office information can be mechanized.

WHEN YOU CAN'T GET AS CLOSE AS YOU'D LIKE

Sometimes a customer needs information, or has an equipment problem, and it's not feasible for him to get to one of the IBM centers, nor for the company immediately to dispatch a service person to his facility. Happily, IBM has developed incredibly successful remote service systems. A customer with an equipment problem can make a toll-free call to an IBM Support Center and describe his problem to one of the technicians there. This expertly trained technician quickly taps into a central data base to search for any similar or identical problems that occurred elsewhere with the same type of equipment. He then finds out how they were diagnosed and corrected. Actually, all IBMers have access to a worldwide network of data banks that contain up-to-the-minute solutions to every kind of equipment or systems problem imaginable.

Via telecommunications, engineers and service people in Poughkeepsie can see exactly what's happening with a machine on the customer's premises in San Francisco, and solve its problem without leaving the IBM facilities. If repairs are required, the necessary service people are sent to do the work.

It's also possible to forecast and prevent an equipment problem by on-line diagnostics. A terminal can be linked to a mainline computer, and then, by using a mathematical model, technicians can locate an impending problem, and correct it before it happens!

Also adding to service productivity are more effective measuring tools. There is, for example, a portable device that plugs into an ailing machine and does everything but take its temperature. This helps to analyze difficult technical problems, saving a tremendous number of man-hours.

Another remote service is performed by connecting a customer's computer with one at the company, which is programmed to analyze the problem.

Here's a statistic that might surprise you: *About 85 percent of the called-in problems are solved immediately on the telephone!* By now it won't surprise you that the company tries to respond to all problems within twenty-four hours.

IBM products need immediate service when there's trouble. It can be catastrophic if a system containing the guts of a business goes down. The closer the customer, the easier the problems are to deal with. But whether next door or halfway around the world from the problem, IBM has the same sense of responsibility.

THE IMAGE-BUILDERS

When IBM says it wants its customers to sleep well at night, that it can be counted on to keep their equipment operating, it's completely serious. IBM's reputation for being perhaps the most service-oriented company in the world isn't the result of a successful advertising campaign or PR hype. It's a reputation that came about through years of consistent hard work, and occasionally some downright heroics by service people.

Here are a few legendary episodes:

A service rep based in Phoenix was driving to Tempe to deliver a small part a customer needed to restore a malfunctioning data center. But what was usually a short, pleasant drive turned into a nightmare. Torrential rains transformed the Salt River into a rampaging rapids, which closed all but two of the sixteen bridges that crossed over to Tempe, causing a bumper-to-bumper traffic jam that changed the normal twenty-five-minute drive to a four-hour crawl. Determined not to lose the entire afternoon to the traffic, the service rep remembered that she had a pair of roller skates in the trunk of her car. She pulled out of the line of traffic, donned the skates, and skated across the bridge and to the customer's rescue!

I could fill a book with this kind of a story. About a service rep who traveled four hundred miles to make a typewriter repair. About a team of our people who traveled by helicopter to get to a lumber mill in a remote section of Oregon.

And we all remember the New York City blackouts. Wall Street came to a standstill; both the New York and the American stock exchanges were shut down, and banking firms were in turmoil. Everyone in IBM's New York City branch offices worked relentlessly to keep every customer's lost time to an absolute minimum. Finding, transporting and installing needed parts and machines was almost a magic act.

During a twenty-five-hour power failure brought on by a heat wave, with outside temperatures in the mid-nineties and no air conditioning, with no elevators and of course no light, IBM people climbed stairs in some of the tallest buildings in New York (including the World Trade Center) in order to service customers' machines.

A few years ago, on the day before Thanksgiving, a fire broke out on the fifteenth floor of the Reliance Insurance Company in Philadelphia—the site of its computer room. The IBM field manager was notified at 5 A.M., but wasn't allowed to survey the damage until 8:30 that morning. He discovered that all conduit wires were melted and a lot of machines were damaged—twenty keypunches, ten disk drives, a laser printer, twenty tape drives, five communication systems and eighteen key entry units. Using emergency lighting the first twenty-four hours, teams of IBM service people worked in round-the-clock shifts. By Monday morning, Reliance was fully operational. Because IBM service people worked throughout the three-day holiday, Reliance hardly missed a beat.

Hundreds of incredible customer service stories were reported during the "great blizzards" of 1977 and 1978 in the American Midwest and Northeast. However, such servicing is an everyday occurrence for the IBM service reps working with the Alyeska Pipeline Service Company. The Trans-Alaska Pipeline moves 1.6 billion barrels of crude oil about eight-hundred miles every day, past a series of ten pump stations, each built specifically for arctic conditions. Each station contains IBM terminals linked to a mainframe computer in Anchorage. Alyeska's state-of-the-art computer tracks the oil as it passes through the line, schedules oil into tankers, handles the payroll and word processing, and enables workers at any pump station to order parts instantly.

The two biggest problems for servicing the pipeline are the harsh weather and the remote locations of the pump stations. It's not uncommon for service reps to be exposed to temperatures of forty degrees below zero. They carry winter survival items in their cars—snow boots, blankets, arctic parkas, heavy mittens, and camp stoves to melt snow for water. Travel by small plane to remote places—taking off and landing on Alaska's barren North Slope—makes these frequent trips anything but joyrides. Sometimes it's a major feat simply to open the frozen door of the aircraft. Because of the infrequent scheduled commercial flights into the areas, an otherwise fifteen-minute service call often takes ten hours or more.

Many customers present truly challenging service problems. But coming up with solutions to those problems is part of what IBMers do for a living. Customers expect it of them, and that's the way they want it.

It's no simple task to service the Norfolk Navy Base, with more than 3,100 ships entering and leaving the port every year, but it has to be done. There are all kinds of servicing problems: getting through the tight security; frequent exposure to the open seas; having to cut a hole into the side of a ship to deliver a machine five decks down, by means of slings and dollies; dealing with the rust caused by a nuclear wash-down drill (the spraying of salt water on board to wash off radiation in the event of a nuclear leak); working in incredibly cramped quarters (one service rep described the repairing of a computer on board a submarine as "like trying to fix a typewriter in a telephone booth"). IBM sells service. It has to deliver.

PLANNING FOR MONTHS, MOVING IN HOURS

Moving for any business is stressful, and it's particularly so when an organization's computer operation must be relocated. When a major customer makes the decision to move, IBM service people have their work cut out for them. When you're dealing with a computer system that is vital to the ongoing operation of a company, it's more than packing, shipping and unpacking. The task is approached with the sensitivity and urgency of a surgical team in an operating room. That may sound overdramatic, until you think of the information and important applications stored in the memory of these machines.

The amount of work and time involved in a move can be tremendous. Twenty-four service reps working around the clock, in teams of eight, put in a total of more than seventeen thousand man-hours to relocate the computer system of the McDonnell Douglas Automation Company when their Saint Louis headquarters moved to a seven-building campus.

It took eighteen months of advance planning to move the Arco (Atlantic Richfield Co.) Oil and Gas Division's data processing operation from Dallas to Plano, Texas, about twenty miles away. An estimated four thousand detailed tasks were identified and tracked, using a computerized management control and scheduling system. The move was planned with minute detail and precision, including the schedule for individual trucks, what each would carry, and what would happen when they arrived at the new location. In order for Arco, as well as its fifteen hundred time-sharing users, to have the maximum use of its system during the operation, the move was spread out over several months' weekends and holidays. As always, everything possible was done to keep disruptions to a minimum. Throughout the move, more than fifty-five agencies continued to use the center, with three thousand terminals supporting their on-line users.

For IBM, with its thousands of customers, relocating is an everyday occurrence, yet no two moves are exactly alike. There's nothing automatic about them. Each requires the service reps' individual attention.

During my thirty-four-year career, I witnessed innumerable situations that, in their uniqueness, required not only conscientious but creative servicing. Organizations like the FBI, the CIA, the World Bank, the U.S. Supreme Court, the Nuclear Regulatory Commission, the White House presented special problems. But whether government agencies, or special enterprises like the 1984 World's Fair and the 1984 Olympics, or small entrepreneurs are in need, the resourcefulness, flexibility and commitment of IBM's service people stand ready to meet every challenge head-on. I tell you this, knowing that the world's greatest field service organization is making every function in the company run more smoothly makes life easier—especially marketing.

9
MEASUREMENT AND COMPENSATION

IBM doesn't want its people to get frustrated and restless because it has them reaching for carrots they can't quite grasp.

I've taken great care to let you know how IBM feels about its marketing people, but let's face it, we didn't build one of the world's greatest sales organizations by *just caring* for our people. Being concerned helps, all right, but it doesn't build homes, educate children, or pay for cars, boats or vacations. It doesn't assure anyone of a financially trouble-free retirement. Those things take money. And the kind of marketing people who succeed in IBM are as interested in their personal bottom line as the "numbers people" are in the corporation's bottom line. IBM wants its people to be concerned not only with their own financial health but with the company's too. They will be if they are treated fairly. Every leader of IBM, since the days of Tom Watson, Sr., has known that fair compensation is an important part of fair treatment.

As you already know, this company puts tremendous effort and resources into selecting, recruiting and training its marketing and systems engineering people. It would be foolish to make such an investment in these young people, then waste their potential by using a compensation package that promises a lot more than it delivers.

IBM doesn't want its people to get frustrated and restless because it has them reaching for carrots they can't quite grasp. It doesn't want them to envy competitors' employees, or to look for greener pastures in other industries.

Some companies actually make an effort to turn over their salespeople frequently. By keeping investment in the marketing staff low and getting rid of people before they build up any equity, these organizations think they profit on the turnover. But that's not IBM's style. A professional marketing organization that's capable of building long-lasting relationships with customers is the goal. And IBM is successful at keeping its marketing force pretty much intact. Less than 5 percent leave voluntarily each year, and that includes quite a number who choose to take early retirement. A few are enticed by lucrative offers from companies just starting out in some phase of the industry and are willing to pay dearly for the IBM expertise. Often it's an offer of some sort of partnership. Very few leave to go to the competition. One important reason people don't leave voluntarily is that the IBM money and benefit package is good.

Coming up with a system of compensation that makes sense for everyone is no simple matter. Of course, the total money package must be fair to the employee and to the company, but *how it's paid* can make a difference in how satisfied the employee is, and how well he or she performs.

At IBM, the compensation strategy has to accomplish several things:

1. *It has to provide employees with a sense of security.* IBM wants them to concentrate on making their objectives when they're in the field representing the company. They should not be distracted with basic money worries—that is, money needed to feed, clothe and house their family. Their salary should take care of those things, if they manage their affairs sensibly. I'm not suggesting that all employees are told, "Submit your personal budget to us, and we'll come up with a guaranteed salary to cover it." But they do know what they're assured of getting, and can budget accordingly. There is an

attitude in some companies that sets up the salesperson to sweat out the very minimum. I don't go along with that.

The security aspect of IBM's compensation is enhanced by the reimbursement of travel and other territory expenses, and a generous package of benefits that is one of the best offered by any company, anywhere. When a person receives a substantial part of his or her income in the form of guaranteed salary, insurance, paid vacations, retirement plans and other benefits, the company has the right to "manage" that employee in a way that's not possible with one who works on straight commission or free lance. So when it comes to guarantees, there are pluses and minuses for both the employer and the employee.

2. Besides providing security for the employee, *the pay package must include strong incentives and motivation.* Some people are satisfied enough with the base pay, fringes and expenses. IBM tries not to hire such individuals, but is after sales and marketing people who want more than a fixed salary and expenses, and will respond when given the right opportunity. It's necessary to come up with incentives that not only will encourage excellent performances and high levels of productivity but will deliver a higher income when the reps succeed. The point is, IBM is willing to pay a premium for excellence and achievement. Therefore, an incentive system that works is crucial to the overall success of the company's entire compensation program.

3. In addition to salary and commission, IBM likes to sweeten the lives of especially deserving employees with *awards and rewards.* They're not always announced in advance, and usually come as a surprise to the recipient. They come in the form of cash, gifts or trips, and are tokens of the company's appreciation of superior performance or a specific accomplishment. Even when spontaneous, they are both objective and subjective gestures.

MONEY IN THE BANK

First, about the salary: Pay packages are designed so that, on average, about one half of the total income of marketing reps, marketing managers and branch managers is derived from their guarantees, or base pay. There are a number of factors that go into a marketing person's base pay: the position, the employee's length of service, and the quality of the employee's overall performance. These reflect the increasing value of experience, expertise and maturity. Along with the growing value of fringe benefits and the retirement package, it's the employee's equity in the company, the return on his or her investment in time and loyalty.

While an employee's salary and job are secure so long as he or she performs effectively, no one has tenure at IBM. (For thirty-four years I kept listening for those footsteps; some days they were louder than others.) There's pride in the fact that no one has ever been laid off because of cutbacks in programs, departments, products or budgets; but a person will be discharged, regardless of position or longevity, who violates the company's ethics, or falls down on the job and fails to respond to assistance in correcting his or her performance.

Every person has the right to an annual performance appraisal and a face-to-face discussion about it with his manager. If the manager is doing his job properly throughout the year, there should be no surprises at the annual appraisal meeting. That is, he should be on top of things, and his people should be apprised, on an ongoing basis, of any developing problems or dissatisfaction. This evaluation of an employee's performance helps determine the size of his merit increase. It is possible for an employee to go through a year without receiving an increase in salary, because IBM does not give cost-of-living increases. However, it rarely happens two years in a row. The other purpose of the annual appraisal meeting is to discuss the goals and objectives for the upcoming year, and any performance modifications needed to achieve them. It's really important for a person to understand exactly what is expected of him, and what impact his performance may have on his base pay. As far as I'm concerned, the underpinning of respect for the individual is the performance appraisal process. An honest, straightforward discussion of a person's strengths and weaknesses forms the cornerstone of the IBM merit pay philosophy.

BREAKING THE BANK

Each year, IBM wants to present an incentive package that will treat everyone evenhandedly and will do its job—that is, motivate. In a nutshell, it works like this: Every regional manager begins the fiscal year with a new quota and a set of goals to achieve. His quota is split up among his branch managers. Each branch manager then divides his quota among the marketing managers who report to him. The marketing managers make the final quota allocations, determining the bogey for each marketing rep. If this sounds a little like the Abbott and Costello "Who's on first" routine, believe me, it's worse. We have tens of thousands of territories, and no two are alike.

There is a lot to factor into each quota: the size of the territory, the types of customers, their potential to expand, the kind of systems they can use, their service requirements, the rep's involvement in team projects, the conditions affecting the marketplace, product availability. There's more, but you get the idea. To complicate matters, no one is simply handed his quota. At each level, the factors and sometimes the numbers are debated. Think of this as a tops-down plan with bottoms-up input. The key philosophical point is that each individual, regardless of job level, is being measured against the same set of factors.

There are two basic quotas each person must deal with:

one for products and one for installations, which is really revenue growth. They are the critical factors in determining how much money, over salary, these tens of thousands of people will receive by the time the curtain falls at the end of the year. The salesperson has mighty good reasons to sell as much as he can, and to install everything he sells.

The system may seem cumbersome, but it's complex only because IBM wants to be absolutely fair to the people in the field, and to the company too. It could be simplified but in this case simpler isn't better, because streamlining would eliminate the aspects that make one territory different from another.

Mistakes are made, by setting the goals either too high or too low. When that happens, there are adjustments, sometimes to the delight of the reps. But other times things happen unexpectedly, things that could blow the reps away. Management has to deal with reality; it can't simply say, "Oops, sorry. We set the quotas, and you're stuck with them." Whether a war breaks out, or the economy takes a nosedive, or there's an Arab oil embargo, the quotas have to be realistic. At the local level, the rep's earnings shouldn't be wiped out because his major account went bankrupt. Nor should he become rich simply because a major customer moved into his territory just as the fiscal year was coming to a close.

To cover unusual circumstances, each person's annual sales plan has built into it a safety net that can be implemented by each manager. Changes in the quotas, though necessary at times, are not made easily or frequently. IBM wants its people to believe in and respect the sales package they receive. It doesn't want them to think that the numbers delivered at the beginning of the year are just a starting point and that they'll fluctuate throughout the next twelve months. IBM plays hardball, but plays it equitably.

What about the service the company is so proud of? Where is the dollar incentive for all that hard work? This will take some explaining. First, it's part of the salary, and the true payback comes from having a satisfied customer. But there is also a takeback provision. Specifically, when a customer cancels or discontinues any IBM equipment, all previously paid commissions are charged back to the marketing rep presently handling the account. While this sounds harsh, it serves as a key factor in making sure field people are paying attention to their customers, even during periods when little selling or installation is taking place. This approach centers on a corporate purpose of maintaining old customers, creating new ones, and making people want to do business with IBM through value-added selling.

IBM simply doesn't want to lose any business, and when it does, it investigates why. Monthly win-loss reports were prepared by the domestic and international marketing divisions from information supplied by their branch managers. These reports highlighted the significant wins as well as the circumstances that precipitated a major revenue or key customer loss. They were signed by division presidents and sent to IBM's top line management, with copies distributed to other high-ranking executives. It is distasteful, besides being embarrassing, to report a key loss, knowing that it will be reviewed, analyzed and evaluated by upper management. The idea is not to "headhunt" but to understand the problems and take whatever action is necessary to prevent a pattern of losses from developing.

At the beginning of each year, everybody complains that the quotas are too high. It's the natural thing to do and I did it too when I was a rep. However, when the year's over and all the numbers are in, management looks pretty smart. During my entire career, I can remember only one year when we ever came in short of quota. I don't mean that every individual made his or hers, but the cumulative numbers were always there.

Historically, 65 to 75 percent of IBM's people go over the top each year. Five to 10 percent usually break the bank. Of those who don't make 100 percent of their quota, only a few are in trouble. Most make it the next year and do O.K. Under 4 percent of IBM's marketing people are asked to leave involuntarily each year, and unsatisfactory sales performance is only one of the causes.

Throughout the year, extra commissions are offered over and above the quota program. These bonuses are initiated by headquarters management, usually in cooperation with the engineering/manufacturing divisions. They are used to help kick off a new product, enhance an existing program or gain momentum during a soft quarter. They certainly help energize the salespeople and, at the same time, put something extra into their wallets and pocketbooks.

When the subject of commissions has come up in a discussion with people outside IBM, I've often been asked: "Doesn't your program put a lot of pressure on your reps? To expect a company rep to earn 50 percent of income in commissions is rather unusual." It's true. However, the program applies pressure on *everybody*, not just the rep. But it's the kind of pressure that makes people work harder, and it is hoped, smarter. Making people reach is a positive thing. When an incentive program is working properly, it helps propel a person at a healthy pace throughout the year.

It's wonderful when you have motivations and incentives on your side. It makes you stretch. Having run five miles a day for the past twelve years, I know the truth in the old French saying: "One can go a long way after one is tired." I'd add: "But only when one is motivated."

THE PAYOFF

Just as a company cannot strive for excellence without putting pressure on itself, it cannot expect its people to be self-starters, innovators and company-minded unless it is generous in its appreciation of them. IBM demands a lot from its people, and understands the need to openly demonstrate its appreciation for those who work to achieve excellence. There's a broad range of appreciation, from a night on the town given to a rep by a marketing manager, to several thousands of dollars handed out by the head of a division.

Awards and rewards are distributed by every level of line management throughout the company. The higher the manager's position, the more money he has budgeted for this purpose.

Earlier, I mentioned the administrative person who received a wheelbarrowful of money for doing an exceptional job. When I was vice-president of the Data Processing Division, I praised one of the top marketing reps in front of an audience of several hundred of our people. Warren Hume, the division president, was very impressed with what I had to say about this person. He pulled me aside to find out a little more about him. Then Warren grabbed the microphone and announced, "You've just heard a story about an outstanding performance by an outstanding person." Turning to the rep, he continued, "When you return to your office, waiting for you will be a check for five thousand dollars!" The whole thing was impromptu, and it brought down the house. A president's award isn't usually a spur-of-the-moment thing. It's usually decided upon after reviewing recommendations submitted by all the branch and regional offices in his jurisdiction. It might, for example, be in recognition of what IBM calls a significant win—that's when a new account is acquired, or a competitive win-back is achieved, or a new application breakthrough occurs.

Serious about encouraging its people to feed it with suggestions, IBM is happy to give significant cash awards for those that are implemented. Awards have been given for ideas that improved the administrative process, enhanced products and reduced costs on the manufacturing floor. Ideas that pay off may be for such things as a new packaging technique that better protects a product, or a simplified process to more efficiently process an order.

A formalized corporate suggestion program exists, and a special department reviews each employee's submission, before sending it to the facility that will consider its practicability and dollar value. If the suggestion is adopted, the individual receives up to 25 percent of the accrued savings during the first two years of its use. The money involved can be tremendous—as high as six figures.

One of the first big-money ideas came from an employee in San Jose. He suggested the use of a wave soldering machine instead of hand soldering for logic card assembly. The company listened and cut a twenty-five-minute operation down to three seconds. He received a $100,000 bonus.

A service rep in Minneapolis saved the company over $1 million with his suggestion that a clip be added to the electronic 75 typewriter. His idea relieved wear on the rocker and earned him $100,000.

A contract specialist, also from Minneapolis, suggested an audit and control procedure that earned her $100,000.

An associate cost engineer from IBM Canada saved the company $70 million in two years with his suggested change in producing the serial number identifications that appear on every product. His idea was simple enough: stop stamping, start labeling. It made him a lot of money.

The IBM Suggestion Plan has been good for both the company and the employees who submitted useful ideas. The numbers are truly impressive: The company saved $300 million between 1975 and 1984, thanks to the suggestions of its employees, and it paid $60 million in awards to those who had the ideas. This just doesn't happen. IBM actively encourages its employees to get involved, to realize that their ideas count and will be respected. A twenty-two-page booklet, "Your Ideas Have Value," that describes the company's Suggestion

Plan is circulated throughout the company. In his introduction to its most recent edition, IBM CEO John Akers wrote: "Today, one of our business goals is to be the most efficient in everything we do. Another goal is to achieve the highest quality for our products. To meet those goals, we will need imaginative and cost-saving ideas more than ever before. I encourage you, therefore, to look for better ways to run the business—and to submit your suggestions."

It's no wonder that IBM has what may be the world's most active suggestion box. Incidentally, every suggestion is acknowledged. If the idea is rejected, the participant receives an explanatory letter. No one is ever made to feel that his or her idea is foolish or not taken seriously. The ideas *may be* important; the participant's feelings *are* important.

Another innovative program I recall was the Eagle Award, given to marketing reps who set new sales records in their division. The "best of the best" were thus honored—less than one hundred people who attained new highs in performance. Besides the attention and publicity accompanying so significant an award, the winners received a check for $5,000 and a beautiful trophy.

Two of IBM's most prestigious recognition programs are the Corporate Technical Award and the new IBM Fellows. In 1984, IBM recognized the contributions of 259 technical professionals, including seventy-nine who shared a record $2.7 million in awards. The largest award—$1.78 million—went to two teams, comprising forty-eight employees, who worked to bring about the success of the IBM Personal Computer and the 3880 Direct Access Storage Device. Also, five new IBM Fellows were named, bringing to eighty-eight the number appointed since 1963. Chosen for their accomplishments in engineering, programming and science, IBM Fellows are free to pursue their own projects for a five-year period. The title is retained for life.

AWARDS YOU CAN'T PUT IN THE BANK

Money isn't the only thing that motivates people. Almost anything that bolsters self-esteem can work. I don't mean that compliments or titles or certificates will satisfy a person who can't pay his bills—not for long, it won't—but it's a wonderful adjunct to a decent money package.

Each time an IBM rep achieves his annual quota, he becomes a member of the Hundred Percent Club. He doesn't have to brag about his results; his membership in the club is well publicized throughout the company. Among his peers he's recognized as a high achiever.

There's no doubt in my mind that a survey of new reps would show that their first goal, after being assigned a territory, is not to make "a lot of money" but to achieve membership in the Hundred Percent Club. A rep who has failed to make it for three years probably won't get a chance to go for it in the fourth.

The top 10 percent of successful salespeople are elevated to the Golden Circle and their achievement is acknowledged throughout the entire organization, worldwide. They and their spouses are invited to a convention in a place such as Bermuda or Hawaii, and given full VIP treatment. Their celebrity status becomes known throughout the company and industry. At this meeting, it's not unusual to hear the spouse say, "You better bring me back here next year."

Honoring those who do superior work is not only motivation for them to continue their high-level performance but also a strong incentive for others. A company can't be *too* appreciative of its high achievers. Organizations that take them for granted don't deserve to keep them.

IS IT ALL WORTHWHILE?

It takes a great deal of thought, lots of trial and error, and many man-hours to come up with the pay package for our marketing people. There are certainly easier ways to do it—straight salary or maybe a salary with a token incentive. But what IBM is doing must be O.K.

For one thing, the company doesn't want to lose good people because of money. Its jobs should be the best-paying in the industry. More than that, actually: they should be the best-paying in any industry—for comparable work. Regular surveys indicate that IBM stays ahead of both its direct competitors and other industries. It's obvious even without the surveys, because so very few IBMers ever leave for other opportunities.

It's rare when the company doesn't exceed its objectives—which are never understated. IBM's growth has been one of the most dramatic ever, and everyone knows that well-motivated people are responsible.

I'm convinced that every facet of the compensation package works. At times, it seems difficult to implement because there is a package tailor-made for every individual. Even so, it's worth it. It works because the company is not trying to nickel-and-dime anyone, only to reward people for a job well done. Compensation and motivation serve to enhance marketing as a professional career.

10

THE ENTREPRENEURIAL SPIRIT

Good people need room to develop. They have to find their own voice . . . each IBMer is a businessperson working within the framework of the company structure.

The same entrepreneurial spirit that makes new proprietary business ventures happen is necessary in the corporate establishment, as well. It isn't needed only when a business is being formulated. No matter how big or how old the corporation is, if it's going to respond to change and continually grow, it must keep alive the original spirit that transformed someone's idea and dream into the reality of a business.

Sadly, for too many companies, the daring and the enthusiasm generated during their beginnings seem impossible to sustain. Overburdened and stifled by the bureaucracy they created, many mature organizations move with the agility of an obese, arthritic giant. They're not as excited by adventure as they used to be. What turns them on is the idea of a safe, comfortable place to rest. Unfortunately for them, they have to be alert and alive just to survive, which is no easy feat in today's competitive world. These companies are usually led by decisionmakers who have lost some of their intuitiveness, and don't trust what's left of it. They don't want to make a move unless they are absolutely, positively certain that they've covered their backsides. They demand more and more facts on which to base their decisions, finally settling only for what they are convinced is a sure thing. But the less adventurous they become, the more difficult it is for them to discern even the safest path. It all boils down to too much emphasis on minimizing the risk rather than maximizing the opportunity. In time, the planning and decisionmaking processes take on a life of their own, engendering open-ended exercises that eventually self-destruct. I have no idea how much corporate time and money are wasted on plans that never had a chance of getting off the drawing board, but it's a crime against employees and stockholders who depend on dynamic leadership. Those leaders who have lost the entrepreneurial spirit should step aside, making room for those who desperately want to express theirs. Of course, people in power rarely step aside voluntarily. That's why IBM's policy of having officers relinquish certain jobs at age sixty is so effective. It gives the people at the top a marvelous opportunity to do some deep self-analysis; to examine their motives for wanting to stay in a position that may require the derring-do of a young, hungry, highly motivated entrepreneur.

Risk-takers are important not only at the top of the organization, but throughout all levels of the company. It's difficult to develop a nurturing environment for corporate entrepreneurialism if the spirit is missing at the top. Happily for those of us who came to IBM with the need to do more than simply make a living, we found a place that welcomed people with ideas, who were willing to argue with the managers, administrators and executives to get their ideas into motion. People like these cause problems, create turmoil and confound the conservatives who want peace and serenity in their organization. But they build companies; and it took a lot of them to build an IBM.

GREATNESS IS ENDURING

From the beginning, Tom Watson, Sr., knew that you couldn't develop corporate entrepreneurs if you encumbered your employees with an enervating bureaucratic structure. Watson was no theorist, but he knew intuitively that an overgrown bureaucracy strangles creativity and the spirit needed to take chances. His solution was to construct his company in such a way that no employee would have to deal with a giant structure, no matter how big it might grow. He succeeded. When I joined the company, it was a $250 million business and it didn't "feel" big. If I had been employed by a company a fraction of the size of IBM, I would probably have had to deal with a much bigger bureaucracy. Even today, a new employee coming into IBM—now a $50 billion corporation—finds himself in a small-business atmosphere. In part, this is true because the company never allows its branches to get too big; and, regardless of any function, a manager supervises about ten to twelve people, rarely more. This way, no one gets lost. A budding entrepreneur is quickly recognized and encouraged. The manager not only is expected to nurture this type of person but is evaluated on the success of the nurturing. The result is a working environment charged with excitement, creative energy, and commitment.

Any company that is experiencing the doldrums, or suffers from negativism, tension, frustration and unrest, should take a hard, long look at companies like IBM. That doesn't mean there are no disappointments or frustrations in IBM, but its overriding attitude is one of dynamic optimism: If you're the best, anything is possible. And you can be the best if you're willing to make a total commitment to that end.

THE CORPORATE REP

When I was president of the Data Processing Division, we came up each year with a different theme for the sales force. In 1969, the theme was *entrepreneurship*. Some people strongly objected: "We should avoid this subject. It might encourage some of our best people to leave IBM and start their own businesses." Others felt that it made no sense to talk about entrepreneurship in a publicly owned corporation, because the dictionary definition excluded anyone who was not risking his own money and did not have a proprietary interest in the business. I disagreed with the worriers at IBM, and with colleagues who couldn't see beyond Webster's definition.

Of course, the IBM rep does not take the same financial risks an independent agent takes—that is, he's assured a substantial part of his potential income, his expenses are covered and he's the recipient of a number of company benefits. On the other hand, the corporate rep has responsibilities and obligations, and is held accountable in a way that the independent is not. Being self-employed, the independent agent may lose a customer, or twenty, and can't be fired. Both invest their time in a career, and both take their share of risks.

That IBM reps receive at least half of their income in commissions—a high number for a corporate salesperson—attracts the kind of rep the company wants: an ambitious person with an entrepreneurial spirit. But that person is also expected to give the kind of service IBM's customers have a right to expect. The entire training program, starting with the first day, encourages reps to be creative, innovative and industrious.

Everything possible is done to eliminate bureaucratic obstacles that might stand in their way. The time clock everyone was required to punch was eliminated in the 1950s. Until the 1960s, every rep was required to submit a weekly work plan. There was a real celebration when that ended. I never thought it made sense for our reps to report into the office every morning, before their first call; no matter how it was rationalized, it was simply a way for a sales manager to make sure that his people were awake and ready for work. I'd tell my people: "You were hired because we believed you could do the job. Nobody's going to coddle you. But if you're not producing, I'm going to take a hard look to see what's wrong. I'll monitor your performance, and when you do well, you'll be applauded and rewarded. The truth is, you'll probably see less of me when you're doing a good job. It's when you're not performing well that I'll be around, trying to find out why."

Good people need room to develop. They have to find their own voice. Their growth will be stunted if they're too tightly supervised. They have to find their own style—a comfortable natural delivery. But an operating system that's rooted in suspicion and insecurity is certain to squeeze the spontaneity out of their performance. My advice to good people who find themselves fighting a losing battle for the right to personal expression is *run for your life!* Enthusiastic, bright, creative people turn sour under dull, self-conscious management that's protected by a bureaucratic system with no sensibility at all.

To promote the entrepreneurial spirit, especially throughout the sales and marketing divisions, IBM's management must take its share of risks. The company must give its salespeople a sense of territorial proprietorship. They need to be granted as much authority and responsibility as they can handle, as quickly as possible. That means getting out of the way of their decisionmaking, once the power is delegated. The corporate entrepreneur, like the independent, needs the freedom to experiment. He will make his share of mistakes and learn how to deal with them. If he is successful, the benefit to the company is immeasurable. He adds to the creative flow that energizes the entrepreneurial corporation.

In a sense, each IBMer is a business person working within the framework of the company structure. As reps gain experience, they are more and more on their own. At the same time, they enjoy the benefit of having the company's wide spectrum of support and services. One of the real tests is how creatively they can utilize everything available to them. In this respect, the corporate entrepreneur has a decided edge over the independent. The success of our rep hinges on teamwork and his ability to marshal the talent and expertise of a variety of specialists. His job is very much like that of a general manager with an abundance of resources. He must be wisely selective in the use of these resources and coordinate them with the needs of the customer. How well he meshes the available expertise to the problems he's dealing with will be a measure of his own ingenuity.

In order for the "spirit" to permeate the entire organization, everyone must share the same set of objectives. All must work together, that's true, but at the same time they must have a very strong sense of their individual involvement and contribution. A professional baseball team might be a good analogy: Nine entrepreneurs take the field, each covering his own territory, each with his own special expertise—independent performers, each dependent on the rest for the best results. There might be better analogies: a Dixieland band, maybe; a half-dozen free spirits. . . . You get the point.

In IBM's marketing format, each rep has his own business base, made up of a block of accounts that he inherited when he took over the territory, and perhaps a list of prospective accounts that he will try to sell. It's his patch. What he earns depends on how profitably he manages the business. The rep has a business to manage for IBM, but so do the marketing managers, the branch managers, the regional managers. As a rule, the closer they are to the customer, the further they are from bureaucracy.

It's pleasant when people who work together in an office do so in harmony. If they don't get along, if they pull in different directions or have problems communicating, the quality of their work life will suffer. In addition, how well they understand one another and how well they work together can have a direct bearing on their paychecks. To get their job done properly, and have the commissions rolling in, they must all march to the same drummer. This calls for a bottoms-up input and a tops-down plan, with everyone working toward the same goal.

CAREER PATHS FOR CORPORATE REPS

The motto of most ambitious employees, whatever their position, is "I'll move up or move on." That's compatible with the attitude of many success-driven companies, which say to their people, "You'll move up or you're out." The assumption is that people who work hard and strive for excellence will in time outgrow their position and be elevated. If they're not, they will become bored and feel wasted.

Promotions usually mean an immediate salary increase and greater earning potential. That's very important to most ambitious people. But salespeople are in a special situation. They don't have to move up to make more. At least, those who work for IBM don't. Plenty of IBM reps earn more money than line managers do, and I think that's the way it should be. I'm delighted when 10 to 15 percent of the sales force earn more than their bosses.

A professional sales force is vital to the success of a marketing organization. IBM is truly aware of that, and as you have read in these pages, it does everything possible to translate that awareness into concrete satisfaction for the reps. They are treated as heroes by everyone in the company—all the way up to the chairman of the board.

Although most of IBM's top-level management people started off in sales, selling skills aren't a surefire indicator that a person will make a terrific manager. While it's imperative to conduct an ongoing talent search for potential managers, it's also important to keep the vast majority of salespeople in their territories, and happy. Customers don't usually like it when they lose their rep. Not every salesperson wants to be a branch manager or a division president, but everyone wants as much recognition and job satisfaction as possible. So to build into the salesperson's career a theme of progression, the marketing rep, who started off as a trainee, can become an account rep, an advisory rep, a senior marketing rep, a consultant. Each of these titles is recognition of the salesperson's growth, professionalism and value of the company. But they are more than just titles; each of them carries a more lucrative reward system. IBM believes that a successful sales career is in itself a significant achievement—an entrepreneurial achievement— that mustn't be taken for granted.

THE CORPORATE BEAUTY CONTEST

The successful entrepreneur is by nature a talented, creative person. He or she has qualities that can enhance any company, if they are recognized, nurtured and exercised. Too many of the people running businesses today don't understand the importance of ferreting out the talent in their work force. Many times, management misunderstands this type of person. They are often difficult to read, and management therefore builds fences around them to squelch the creativity each company needs so badly. *Uncover the talent in your organization before you drive it away.* When people in your company spend their off-hours acting in community theater, or taking art classes, but do only what's expected of them on the job, don't you wonder if you're providing them with the opportunity they need to express their talents from nine to five?

Creativity and other characteristics of the latent entrepreneur will emerge anytime they're given the opportunity to do so. So when IBM finds talented people it moves them around, to broaden their point of view. Management tries to discover just which position in the organization will allow that talent to flourish. A person who has had an engineering assignment might be transferred to a product planning position; or someone is moved from finance to personnel. The idea is to bring talent and need together, to cross-pollinate whenever possible, to make sure that creative people are dealt with creatively in the company.

Although many corporate entrepreneurs work best alone, their work with others affords insights into their managerial and organizational abilities. When these people come to IBM management's attention, they are frequently assigned to task forces where they can be informally observed and evaluated. As corporate vice-president of marketing, I often invited five to ten field reps to spend two or three days on a task force assignment. We evaluated their reactions to confidential marketing information, and asked for input on such things as sales plan policies, marketing practices and product development. From this group I could easily find people ready for management positions.

Marketing people who have high management potential are often given key staff assignments lasting from one to three years. They are rotated between line and staff positions. This gives them the broadest possible exposure, to test their creativity and management skills in a variety of environments and situations. In these people identified and groomed for executive positions, the entrepreneurial spirit must burn brightly, if they are to run the corporation someday.

And as far as I'm concerned, field people are entrepreneurs. Whether they are branch managers, regional managers or division presidents, they are compensated, by and large, according to their bottom line, like the independent business owner. They have no guarantees. Each has his career on the line, all the time. Their performance is evaluated thoroughly;

each paycheck is based on productivity. Continual poor results will bring down the corporate entrepreneur as quickly as it will bring down the business owner—probably more quickly.

TURNING 'EM LOOSE

IBM's interest in corporate entrepreneuring is more than simply developing an adventurous attitude or spirit, though the importance of that is certainly recognized. And it certainly isn't an exercise in semantics—trying to embrace "entrepreneuring" because it's one of the hottest business buzzwords of the decade. IBMers never lose sight of the fact that their company is the product of one man's daring. IBM grew to its present size because of Tom Watson's ability to impart his entrepreneurial spirit to the tens of thousands of people who joined him. In the 1980s, some innovative programs were initiated to explore and test different types of corporate entrepreneuring. What's developed has been quite exciting. A number of independent, self-contained "businesses" have been established within the company. These units don't function as divisions of IBM, and they don't need to interact with any other part of the company or rely on any of its resources—except for money and talent. What makes them so different from any other part of IBM is that they are not subject to the company's strategic planning and review processes. No five-year plans for them. No rigid rules or inflexible policies. A freewheeling management style is encouraged, and their autonomous boards are free to make decisions beyond what is typically permitted by the company. In short, all organizational roadblocks have been eliminated. The units are, of course, expected to abide by IBM's ethics and dedication to quality.

The people who operate these Independent Business Units come from all over IBM and are headed by key executives and officers. They are asked to develop new products and establish them in the proper marketplace. What's wanted is that they go into areas in need of special care and nurturing to grow. The hope is that after a period of maturing, the new business will be integrated into the corporate mainstream.

In 1985, there were fourteen Independent Business Units within IBM. One is Manufacturing Systems Products in Boca Raton, Florida, a unit in the field of robotics. Another is IBM Instruments Inc., in Danbury, Connecticut, a manufacturer of measuring devices. IBM Information Services, in Milford, Connecticut, *is* leading the company's extensive effort to develop its own computer software and is aggressively acquiring new programs from outsiders. If the Milford operation were a separate company, it would rank in the Fortune 500.

Perhaps the best example of an IBM "business within a business"—the supersuccess story—is a little unit that was activated in 1980. Ten engineers were brought together under the leadership of Philip Estridge to start a new business. Four years later, this entrepreneurial unit of less than a dozen people had grown to a $5 billion division of IBM, Entry Systems, employing ten thousand people in Boca Raton, Florida, and Austin, Texas. That's how the IBM PC began.

At the first meeting, the eleven were told, "We want an IBM Personal Computer. We're already late, so you'll have to hurry. Do whatever you feel is necessary to get it done." They were given the freedom to buy components from the outside, if they thought that was the way to go—to negotiate whatever terms and conditions made sense to them. Even pricing and distribution were left to their discretion. It worked. The IBM Personal Computer is here to stay, a major contributor to the industry.

The eleven people who began Entry Systems were experienced IBMers with proven track records. They were high achievers. But more than that, they were true entrepreneurs, who didn't hesitate to put their careers on the line when a challenging opportunity was presented. The real story, though, is that a huge corporation with a managerial organization that's bigger than some governments is able to *develop and nurture such entrepreneurs.* It has nothing to do with sales, profit, size or the kind of business one is in. It has everything to do with spirit, caring and trying your best to understand the people you work with.

THE ROYAL DISSENTERS

The management of a company has to have its share of internal critics or else it has a tendency to get self-indulgent, fat and sloppy. Like most of us, I like to have things go my way, but I can't stand to work in a world of yes-men. They create an atmosphere that can lull you to sleep. I like people who care enough about what's going on to speak up when they don't like what they see. Of course, there are critics and there are *critics*, but even the worst of them are more stimulating than the best of the yes-men. The critic who has the most negative effect on me is the constant complainer—the cynic who gripes about everything but never offers a suggestion to help ward off the gloom and doom he forever forecasts. This guy isn't just a pain in the backside; he deadens one's responses to him. People turn him off; they don't listen to him. And a concern of his that may deserve some serious attention gets shrugged off. Another type of critic is the loyal dissenter. He's pretty good at spotting trouble, or seeing a weakness in a program or plan, but he hates to rock the boat; so he keeps any solutions he may have to himself. Finally, there's the kind of complainer every organization needs: the *royal* dissenter. He or she offers not only a well-thought-out criticism but also a considered approach to dealing with the problem.

I have always encouraged my people to question, to probe, to express their concerns—to criticize. "And when you do," I've told them, "try to be logical and calm; maintain your poise. Never be afraid of taking a stand. At the same time, be constructive; not abrasive and cynical. Don't turn every minor issue into a major one. When you decide to take me on, make sure that you have your facts straight, and be prepared to stand up for what you believe. Most of all, think in terms of a *solution.*"

The more responsibility you carry, the more important it is for you to get your people to think in terms of what they would do if they were in your shoes. You want them to develop a proprietary attitude about the company. The last thing you want to do is inhibit them from expressing their criticisms. Don't chase them to the nearest bar, where they can commiserate, over drinks, about how bad things are.

Every company needs its royal dissenters. Like the corporate entrepreneurs, they are risk-takers. They're willing to stick their necks out and challenge the status quo. They'll do it again and again when they are convinced that they're right. They write letters to top management, and fill the suggestion boxes. These people believe that they have the right ideas, and they want to convey them. They don't care whom they're talking to. It could be one of their peers, or the chairman of the board. They're not afraid to stand up in a meeting and challenge a speaker; but when they do, they do it in a constructive way. They are those "wild ducks" of business that Tom Watson, Jr., talks about. Their tenacious persistence—and guts—help keep a company young and exciting. In *In Search of Excellence,* they are singled out as the most important key to sustained innovative success in the excellent companies. Happily, IBM has always had its share of people who refused to fly in formation.

KNOWING HOW FAR TO LET OUT THE REINS

I've heard people say, "A good manager allows his people to fail." This school of thought says that once you give responsibility to a subordinate, it becomes his project, and you must stay out of his way—even when you know that he's on the wrong track! I don't buy it. It's not my style to think: "I know this guy is blowing it, but I have to allow him the luxury of fouling up." You have to use common sense! Depending upon the size of the project, its failure could turn out to be too expensive for the organization. You needn't yank the rug from under the employee. Instead of taking away responsibility, assume the role of mentor. Guide him into making the necessary corrections that will get him back on track, and then get out of his way. Remember that you turned over the project to him in the first place because you identified him as a person with the entrepreneurial spirit. You don't want to kill that.

In part, your success with these people will be determined by your ability to know how far to let out the reins and when to pull them in; in knowing how to nurture creativity and at the same time avoid a predictable head-on collision with failure. Taking risks, as far as I'm concerned, is taking *calculated risks*, not foolish ones. Although many checks can be built into the system to cushion the downside of a new venture (I talked about them earlier), nothing is more important than the care that goes into the selection of the risk-taker, the person with the idea or the dream who is willing to put his career on the line.

By the time anyone at IBM makes it to the executive suite, he's had more than his share of exposure to pressure situations. He's in a position to take risks, and is decisive and capable of acting on his convictions. Businesses that fail to develop entrepreneurs don't allow their lower and middle management to make tough decisions. They feel safer with consensus decisions; more comfortable with bureaucratic committees. In that type of company, an individual who climbs to a top managerial position has little or no risk-taking experience. He will not be an innovative or a daring leader.

During my thirty-four-year career with IBM, many tough touch-and-go decisions were made. At least five involved risks of tremendous magnitude. If the decisions were wrong, there would have been disastrous consequences for the company. Not one of the decisions was made because the company was "in trouble," nor were they reactions to sudden or unexpected forces. They were put into motion and implemented in the best of times for IBM, because the entrepreneurial spirit burns brightly anytime—if you have the kind of people who press for innovation and change, even when they'd never be faulted for relaxing and enjoying the present comfort. The five decisions I'm referring to have been mentioned earlier, but I'll run them by you in the context of this discussion: (1) IBM's switch from the punch-card system to stored programming; (2) the development and introduction of System/360, IBM's $5 billion gamble; (3) "unbundling"—breaking down the prices of our products into their various components; (4) when IBM consolidated our three marketing divisions from a product-set approach into two customer-set organizations; (5) adopting alternative distribution systems into the marketing program.

While all these moves proved to be successful, at the time of its conception and implementation each involved risk taking of the highest order. Because they were initiated when it would have been easier for IBM to play its cards close to the vest, sitting tight, doing nothing, they were truly important acts of corporate entrepreneurialism. They won't be the last of IBM's bold, creative moves. You can bet on it.

SOME FINAL THOUGHTS

In the Introduction, I suggested that any company of any size could emulate IBM's way. That's because the *way* IBM operates isn't expensive, nor is it exclusive. It deals, more than anything else, with people, their behavior and their values.

The company has grown to its great size, with incredible speed, because of its insatiable appetite to be the very best. That's its secret weapon. Of course, IBM makes useful products, but it's the quest for excellence that attracts and nurtures high achievers: young people whose ambitions are compatible with IBM's. The continual influx of this bright new talent keeps the company youthful, vibrant and light on its feet. But age is not a primary factor, since almost all of IBM's employees spend their entire professional career with the company, and stay on until retirement. Besides, whatever their age, IBM people are youthful, spirited and adventuresome.

I hope that *Fortune* magazine's annual survey for the past three years accurately reflects the business community's attitude about IBM. If IBM *is* America's most respected company, it's a good sign. Just as our children need honorable heroes for role models, so do the rest of us, including those who run corporate America. As far as I'm concerned, IBM does embody those traits and characteristics that are usually attributed to the American hero: honesty, intelligence, courage, strength, thoughtfulness and gentleness. The "I" in IBM could stand for Integrity.

Although the company operates in the high-tech world of lightning-fast communication, it tries to project a voice that is soft, calm and friendly—not frantic or threatening or jargon-laden.

I wish all companies would talk to their people about such things as behavior and ethics, as IBM does. It didn't embarrass IBM to circulate this statement to its 400,000 employees:

You are responsible for your actions, and this responsibility will not always be an easy one. The next time you have an ethical dilemma, you might try this test. Ask yourself: If the full glare of examination by associates, friends, even family, were to focus on your decision, would you remain comfortable with it? If you think you would, it probably is the right decision.

The three basic beliefs that guide every IBM action can be shared with anyone who's smart enough to grab on to them: *You must respect the dignity and rights of the individual. You must give the best possible service to the customer. You must pursue all tasks with the objective of accomplishing them in a superior way.* There it is, direct and uncomplicated. No one needs an MBA or a Ph.D. to understand those three statements; nor does it take a Fortune 500 company to implement them.

All of us, including IBM, will be better off when this becomes the standard operating procedure for all U.S. businesses. The sooner the better.

APPENDIX: EXCERPTS FROM IBM'S "BUSINESS CONDUCT GUIDELINES"

(a booklet given every IBM employee)

O ur company has an enviable reputation. People generally think of us as competent, successful and ethical. These three qualities are related. Our adherence to strict ethical standards has contributed, in a very direct way, to both the professionalism of our company and our success in the marketplace. Over the years, we have emphasized again and again that every employee is expected to act in accordance with the highest standards of ethics. This is still true today. And it will be true tomorrow.

*　*　*

Business today is being called upon as never before to explain its actions, provide reasons for its decisions and speak out clearly on where it stands on ethical behavior. . . . it [is] essential in this time of questioning and testing that everyone—employees and their families, customers and competitors, friends as well as critics—know just where IBM stands on basic ethical issues. . . . If there is a single, overriding message in these guidelines, it is that IBM expects every employee to act, in every instance, according to the highest standards of business conduct. Ultimately, in every business decision—as in personal ones—the responsibility is yours.

* * *

We depend on you to do the right thing; right for both you and the company. It is no exaggeration to say that IBM's reputation is in your hands.

* * *

First, there is the law. It must be obeyed. But the law is the minimum. You must act ethically.

* * *

Fair competition. The dictionary puts it very simply: Compete—To contend with another for acknowledgment, for a prize, for a profit.
Eth-i-cal. Dealing with morals or the principles of morality; pertaining to right and wrong in conduct. These simple definitions describe what IBM requires of those who represent it in the marketplace. It asks them to compete—vigorously, energetically, untiringly. But it also insists they compete ethically, honestly and fairly, in accordance with basic principles of morality. Clearly, there are situations that individual IBM employees confront only in business, and for those IBM provides detailed guidelines. But IBM employees who deal directly with customers must be guided first by the knowledge that ethics and morality are the same at work as at home. There is no special, less restrictive set of ethics for business, no easier "marketplace morality."

* * *

From the very beginning, IBM has relied on one thing above all to sell its products: Excellence. It always has been IBM's policy to provide the best possible products and services to customers, and to sell on the merits of our own products and services—not by disparaging competitors, or their products and services. In short, sell IBM. Disparaging remarks include not only false statements, but also information which is misleading or simply unfair. Even factually correct material can be disparaging if it's derogatory and irrelevant to the particular sales situation. This includes casting doubt on a competitor's capabilities or making unfair comparisons. Subtle hints or innuendos are wrong, too. For instance, asking customer or prospect what they've heard about the competitor's maintenance service. If your objective is to focus the prospect's attention on a known problem, don't do it.

* * *

As a matter of practice, if a competitor already has a firm order from a customer for an application, we don't market IBM products or services for that application before the competitor has installed others. However, this is a complicated subject. For example, it is often difficult to determine whether a firm order actually exists. Letters of intent, free trials, conditional agreements and the like usually are not firm orders. Unconditional contracts are. Generally speaking, if a firm order does not exist, an IBM marketing representative may sell. When a situation is unclear or if there is any doubt, seek advice from your business practices or legal function.

* * *

You should also be sensitive to how you use information about other companies, which often includes information about individuals. Those other companies and individuals are rightly concerned about their reputations and privacy. Adverse information of no business use should not even be retained in your files. And what information you do retain should be treated with discretion.

* * *

Don't boast. IBM should not try to get business by trading on its size or success or its position in the industry. That means no boasting to customers about how much money we spend on research or product development, or how many systems engineers we have available throughout the company to work with customers. It is all right to talk about the quality of IBM's products or services. Resources and people represent a commitment to the customer that, for example, an area education facility is staffed and equipped to provide the customer's education requirements. That's not boasting bigness; it's relevant to that particular customer's needs.

* * *

Don't make misrepresentations to anyone you deal with. If you believe the other person may have misunderstood you, correct any misunderstanding you find exists. Honesty is integral to ethical behavior, and trustworthiness is essential for good, lasting relationships.

* * *

Everyone you do business with is entitled to fair and even-handed treatment. This is true whether you are buying, selling or performing in any other capacity for IBM. . . . You must treat all suppliers fairly. In deciding among competing suppliers, weigh all the facts impartially, whether you are in purchasing, a branch office or some other part of the business, and whether you are buying millions of parts or a single, small repair job. Whether or not you directly influence decisions involving business transactions, you must avoid doing anything that might create the appearance that a customer or a supplier has "a friend at IBM" who exerts special influence on its behalf.

* * *

Seeking reciprocity is contrary to IBM policy and in some cases may even be unlawful. You may not do business with a supplier of goods or of services (a bank, for example) on condition that it agrees to use IBM products or services. Do not tell a prospective customer that IBM deserves the business because of our own purchases from his or her organization. This does not mean we cannot be supplied by an IBM customer. It does mean that IBM's decision to use a supplier must be independent of that supplier's decision to use IBM products or services.

* * *

It is IBM practice not to disclose, discuss or sell IBM products before their announcement. For IBM to reveal anything about unannounced products—whether equipment, programs, or services—to a prospect or customer could be viewed by a competitor as unfair. In addition, pre-announcement disclosure could reach other customers and impact sales of IBM's existing product line, or jeopardize IBM copyright or patent positions. Besides, it is always possible for technical difficulties during product development to result in cancellation or postponement of the new product.

Nondisclosure also means that an IBM representative may not attempt to delay a customer decision to order competitive equipment by hinting that a new IBM product is under development. (There are exceptions to the nondisclosure rule, as in the case of national interest, or when a user works with IBM to develop new products, programs, or services. For such cases, there are careful procedures which must be closely followed.)

Index

A Short Guide
to College Writing

W9-BRE-928

Sylvan Barnet was born in Brooklyn, New York, and educated at Erasmus Hall High School, New York University (BA), and Harvard University (MA, PhD). For a while he was a semiprofessional magician, but when he found that he could fool all of the people all of the time the work became boring, and so he became a college professor. He taught composition and English literature at Tufts University for thirty years, published scholarly articles on Shakespeare, and is the author and coauthor of several books about the art of writing.

Pat Bellanca was born in East Hanover, New Jersey; she holds degrees in English from Wellesley College (BA) and Rutgers University (MA, PhD). She teaches in the Expository Writing Program at Harvard College and is Director of Writing Programs at the Harvard Extension School, the university's open-enrollment evening division. Her research interests include composition studies and Gothic fiction, fields that are not unrelated.

Marcia Stubbs was born in Newark, New Jersey, where she was drum majorette of Weequahic High School's band, and she was educated at Stanford University and the University of Michigan. She has taught at Tufts University, Harvard University, and Wellesley College, where she has directed the Writing Program. In addition to annotations on students' compositions, she has written poems and verse translations, and she is the coauthor of several books on writing.

A Short Guide to College Writing

SECOND EDITION

Sylvan Barnet
Tufts University

Pat Bellanca
Harvard University

Marcia Stubbs
Wellesley College

PENGUIN ACADEMICS

PEARSON
Longman

New York   San Francisco   Boston
London   Toronto   Sydney   Tokyo   Singapore   Madrid
Mexico City   Munich   Paris   Cape Town   Hong Kong   Montreal

Senior Vice President and Publisher: Joseph Opiela
Senior Sponsoring Editor: Virginia L. Blanford
Senior Marketing Manager: Wendy Albert
Production Manager: Donna DeBenedictis
Project Coordination, Text Design, and Electronic Page Makeup:
  Sunflower Publishing Services
Senior Cover Design Manager/Designer: Nancy Danahy
Cover Photo: © Image Bank/Getty Images, Inc.
Photo Researcher: Sunflower Publishing Services
Senior Manufacturing Buyer: Dennis J. Para
Printer and Binder: R.R. Donnelley & Sons Company, Harrisonburg
Cover Printer: Phoenix Color Corporation

For permission to use copyrighted material, grateful acknowledgment is made
to the copyright holders on page 354, which are hereby made part of this
copyright page.

Library of Congress Cataloging-in-Publication Data

Barnet, Sylvan.
  A short guide to college writing / Sylvan Barnet, Pat Bellanca, Marcia
Stubbs.
      p. cm.—(Penguin academics)
  Includes index.
  ISBN 0-321-22469-8
    1. English language—Rhetoric—Handbooks, manuals, etc. 2. Report
writing—Handbooks, manuals, etc. I. Bellanca, Pat. II. Stubbs, Marcia.
III. Title. IV. Series.

PE1408.B4315 2004
808'.032—dc22   2004044563

Please visit us at http://www.ablongman.com.

ISBN 0-321-22469-8

    4 5 6 7 8 9 10—DOH—07 06 05

Contents

Preface

A Short Guide to College Writing, Second Edition, offers students practical advice on writing successful college essays from the beginning of the process to the end. The student can turn to this book for advice about choosing a topic, developing a thesis, constructing a paragraph, documenting a source, using a semicolon. The instructor can suggest chapters or passages that the student should consult in generating ideas, revising a draft, editing a revision, or preparing final copy. As in the first edition of this book, we emphasize analysis, argument, and research because skill in these matters is central to college writing—whether the student is writing a brief essay for a required first-year composition course, a longer essay for an art history course, or even a term paper for a political science seminar.

When students write essays, most of what they write sets forth a thesis and its support, which is to say that their writing advances a point of view, explains ideas, and lets readers see how the writers arrived at them. Because they want to be believed, writers must present their ideas and evidence persuasively and cite and document their sources accurately. In this edition of *A Short Guide to College Writing*, we provide even more help in these critical areas. Chapter 8, "Persuading Readers," has been expanded to include a small casebook on file-sharing—an area where many students have strong opinions. A new chapter, "Writing the Research Essay," includes sample student essays—one using the MLA style, the other using the APA style. We have also added material on responsibly evaluating, using, and documenting electronic sources. In Chapter 9, we have expanded our discussion of summary, paraphrase, quotation, and synthesis, and we have amplified the discussion of plagiarism. Finally, we have added a section on rhetorical analysis of the Gettysburg Address, which widens our study of prose style.

A Short Guide to College Writing, Second Edition, offers practical and accessible advice on all matters that concern student writers. The book will be useful not only to students in first-year composition courses but also to those in writing-intensive and writing-across-the-curriculum courses—courses that focus on a particular academic topic. We therefore omit writing assignments and extended readings. Where there is too much, the saying goes, something is missing. This book, we hope, offers just enough.

Acknowledgments

We thank the following reviewers of the first and second editions for their suggestions: Alan Baragona, Virginia Military Institute; Kerry L. Ceszyk, University of Wyoming; Bruce Closser, Andrews University; Shawn Fullmer, Fort Lewis College; Gloria Gitlin, Baylor University; Lisa Justine Hernandez, St. Edwards University; Cheryl Hindrichs, The Ohio State University; J. Paul Johnson, Winona State University; Mary M. Juzwik, University of Wisconsin, Madison; Erika Kreger, San Jose State University; Joan Livingstone-Weber, Western Illinois University; Craig N. Owens, Indiana University; Amy Pawl, Washington University; Chere L. Peguesse, Valdosta State University; Roxanne Pisiak, SUNY–Morrisville; Rachana Sachdev, Susquehanna University; Mary Sauer, IUPUI, Indianapolis; Julianne Seenan, Bellevue Community College; and Von Underwood, Cameron University.

We are grateful to our colleagues at Pearson Longman—editors Lynn Huddon and Ginny Blanford, production manager Donna DeBenedictis, and marketing manager Wendy Albert—and our production editor, Kevin Bradley, at Sunflower Publishing Services for their collaboration on this edition.

Finally, we thank the following friends and colleagues for their advice and support: Marilyn Brown, Patricia A. Cahill, Jody Clineff, Michael Curley, Nancy Sommers, Kerry Walk, and Wini Wood.

SYLVAN BARNET
PAT BELLANCA
MARCIA STUBBS

A Short Guide
to College Writing

PART ONE

THE WRITING PROCESS

The Balloon of the Mind

Hands, do what you're bid:

Bring the balloon of the mind

That bellies and drags in the wind

Into its narrow shed.

—William Butler Yeats

CHAPTER ONE

DEVELOPING IDEAS

All there is to writing is having ideas. To
learn to write is to learn to have ideas.

—*Robert Frost*

Starting

How to Write: Writing as a Physical Act

"One takes a piece of paper," William Carlos Williams wrote, "anything,
the flat of a shingle, slate, cardboard and with anything handy to the purpose begins to put down the words after the desired expression in mind."
Good advice, from a writer who produced novels, plays, articles, book
reviews, an autobiography, a voluminous correspondence, and more than
twenty-five books of poetry, while raising a family, enjoying a wide circle of friends, and practicing medicine in Rutherford, New Jersey. Not the
last word on writing (we have approximately 30,000 of our own to add),
but where we would like to begin: "One takes a piece of paper . . .
and . . . begins to put down the words. . . ."

Some Ideas About Ideas: Strategies for Invention

When asked to write an essay for a college course, students often have
one of two complaints: "I have nothing to say," or "I have the ideas but
I don't know how to express them." When we face a blank page, words
and ideas may elude us. We must actively seek them out. Since classical
times the term "invention," from the Latin *invenere* ("to come upon," or

"to find"), has been used to describe the active search for ideas. Invention includes such activities as asking and answering questions, listing, clustering, and freewriting. In the following pages we'll briefly describe several invention strategies. All of these strategies have one step in common: starting to write by writing.

Asking Questions and Answering Them

One of the first things journalists learn to do in getting a story is to ask six questions:

- Who?
- What?
- When?
- Where?
- Why?
- How?

The questions that journalists àsk are appropriate to their task: to report who did what to whom, and so on. Learning to write academic essays is largely learning to ask—and to answer—questions appropriate to academic disciplines.

Asking questions can be a useful strategy early in the writing process, especially for students who feel they don't have much to say about the material they've been asked to write about. That material, most often, will be a text of some kind: a written text (perhaps a treaty, or a judicial opinion, or a speech, or a poem), or some other object of interpretation (a film, painting, music video, even food on a plate). The first step in developing ideas about a text is to look closely at it. Asking questions and answering them is one way to focus your attention; it's also a way to begin finding things to say. Unexpected answers often emerge as soon as you raise a question.

In analyzing a visual text, for example, an art history student might ask and answer certain basic questions:

- When, where, and by whom was the work made?
- Where would the work originally have been seen? (Almost certainly *not* in a museum.)
- What purpose did the work serve?

Dorothea Lange, *Migrant Mother, Nipomo, California*, 1936. Gelatin-silver print. © Corbis.

- In what condition has the work survived?
- For whom was the work made?
- From what materials was it made?

Then, depending on the work, the student might pose more detailed questions. If, say, the work is a photograph (for example, Dorothea Lange's *Migrant Mother*, shown above), the following questions might be appropriate:

- What is the focus of the composition?
- What is the apparent distance between the viewer and the subjects?
- What is the mother's facial expression?
- How are the figures arranged?
- What's surprising or strange about the image?
- How might the subject have felt about being photographed?

A student in a sociology seminar writing a review of research on a topic would ask other kinds of questions about each study under review:

- What major question is posed in this study?
- What is its chief method of investigation?

- What mode of observation was employed, and is the mode limited in some way?
- How is the sample of observations defined, and is the sample representative?

A student in a literature class writing an analysis or exposition of a poem (for example, the Yeats poem on p. 1) would ask yet other kinds of questions:

- What is the poem about?
- What does the balloon represent?
- What is the speaker's tone?
- What does his tone reveal about his attitude toward the poem's subject?
- What makes this attitude complicated, tricky to pin down?

Students in all disciplines—art history, social science, and literature are given here only as examples—learn what questions matter by listening to lectures, participating in class discussions, and reading assigned books and articles. The questions differ from discipline to discipline, but the process—of asking and answering the questions that matter—is common to all of them.

Listing   Like asking questions and answering them, **listing** is a way to generate ideas; it can also help you pin down ideas that seem formless or vague. Listing is an especially useful strategy when you are making a comparison—of two figures in a photograph, for example, or two characters in a story, or two positions on an issue. Start writing by listing the similarities, and then list the differences. Or, start writing both lists at once, making brief entries, as they occur to you, in parallel columns.

Listing can help you generate and develop ideas; it can also help you to find a **topic** to write about. Suppose, for example, you have been assigned to write an essay on a form of popular culture that interests you. You can begin simply by listing some of the first forms of popular culture that occur to you as you think about the subject:

Popular Culture

```
movies, sci-fi, sci-fi movies?
TV movies, detective serials
```

```
soap operas (why are they called operas? Why soap
  operas?)
music videos
cop shows—Law and Order, CSI
male/female detectives
the blues
```

But having written "the blues" above, you begin to think of the words to a song:

When a woman takes the blues
She tucks her head and cries
But when a man catches the blues
He catches a freight and rides

By the time you have written these lyrics out from memory, you have pretty much decided that you'll write on the blues. You're interested in the blues and already know something about them; you have some CDs at hand; and an idea for an essay is beginning to form:

He catches a freight and rides . . .

Why all this talk of traveling? (It's worth remembering that an unanswered question is an essay topic in disguise.) You begin to search your memory, perhaps you listen to some music, maybe take some notes. The blues are full of travel, you find, but of different kinds. You begin, once again, to make a list, to jot down words or phrases:

```
disappointed lover        back to the South
travel to a job           life is a trip
from the South            jail
fantasy travel
```

Your new list provides more than a topic; you are now several steps closer to a draft of an essay that you think you may be able to write, on the meaning of travel in the blues.

Clustering Although it takes a different visual form, **clustering** is similar to listing. Sometimes ideas don't seem to line up vertically, one after another. Instead, they seem to form a cluster, with one idea or word related to a group of several others. It may be useful then to start by putting a key word or phrase (let's stay with "Travel in the Blues") in a circle in the center of a page, and then jotting down other words as they occur, encircling them and connecting them appropriately. A map or cluster might look like the diagram shown here.

If you start writing by putting down words that occur to you in a map or cluster, it may help you to visualize the relationship between ideas. The visualization may also prompt still other ideas and the connections between them.

Freewriting   One reason students have trouble getting words down on paper is that they mistakenly believe they must draft, revise, and edit their work simultaneously. In fact, however, these processes are separate, and the attempt to do them all at once can be paralyzing. **Freewriting** can help students who feel that they have ideas, but don't know how to get them on paper, because the strategy enables them to forget the rules for a while and just start writing.

To begin the process of freewriting, all you need to do is put your hands on a keyboard or pick up a pen or pencil and *start writing*. Forget about crafting the perfect introductory paragraph; don't worry about grammar or spelling or punctuation. If you can't think of the right word, write something close to it, or leave a blank space and move on. If you find yourself going in a direction you hadn't anticipated, keep writing anyway. Maybe there's something worth thinking about down the road— you won't know until you get there. If, for example, you're writing about why you disagree with one argument in the passage, a point on which you agree with the author may occur to you. Fine. Write it down now, while you're thinking of it. You can organize your points of agreement and disagreement later. Even if what you're thinking is something along the lines of "I hate this poem" (or photograph or whatever), put the thought down on paper and keep going. Why do you hate the poem? Is it confusing? Why? Does it appear to say two different things? What are they? Even an apparently unpromising line of thought can produce ideas. But if you reach what appears to be a dead end, simply move on, or start again someplace else. You are writing to discover what you think, and it's a good idea to work as quickly as you can. (Take Satchel Paige's advice: Don't look back; something might be gaining on you.)

Focusing

What to Write About: Subject, Topic, Thesis

So far, we've discussed several strategies for discovering and generating ideas. But to write a successful college essay, it's not enough simply to choose a **subject** and to have ideas about it; the next step is to begin to give those ideas some focus. To do so, you must narrow your area of interest to a **topic** within the subject, a process you may already have begun as you followed one or more of the above invention strategies. And you must state your idea about that topic in the form of a **thesis,** an argument, a *point.*

Finding a Topic   Any assignment requires you to narrow the subject so that you can treat it thoroughly in the allotted space and time. Therefore you write not on political primaries (a subject), but on a specific proposal to abolish them (a topic); not on penguins (a subject), but on the male penguin's role in hatching (a topic). A good general rule in finding a topic is to follow your inclinations: Focus on something about the subject that interests you.

Suppose that your assignment for a religion course is to read the Book of Ruth in the Hebrew Bible and to write an essay of 500 to 1000 words on it. If you start with a topic like "The Book of Ruth: A Charming Tale," you're in trouble. The topic is much too vague. In writing about it you'll find yourself hopping around from one place in the book to another, and in desperation saying things like "The Book of Ruth is probably one of the most charming tales in all literature," when you haven't read all literature, and couldn't define *charm* precisely, if your life depended on it.

What to do? Focus on something that interested you, or surprised you, or confused you about the book. (If you read the book with pencil in hand, taking some notes, underlining some passages, putting question marks at others, you'll have some good clues to start with.) The book is named after Ruth, but perhaps you find Naomi the more interesting character. If so, you might jot down: "Although the Book of Ruth is named after Ruth, I find the character of Naomi more interesting."

Stuck again? Ask yourself some questions. *Why* do you find her more interesting? To answer that question, reread the book, focusing your attention on all the passages in which Naomi acts or speaks or is spoken of by others. Ruth's actions, you may find, are always clearly motivated by her love for Naomi. But Naomi's actions are more complex, more puzzling. If you're puzzled, trust your feeling—*there is something puzzling there. What* motivated Naomi? Convert your question to "Naomi's Motivation" and you have a topic.

"Naomi's Motivation" is a topic in literary criticism, but if your special interest is, for example, economics, or sociology, or law, your topic might be one of these:

Economic Motivation in the Book of Ruth

Attitudes Toward Intermarriage in the Book of Ruth

The Status of Women in the Book of Ruth

Any one of these topics might be managed in 500 to 1000 words. But remember, you were assigned to write on the Book of Ruth. Suppress the impulse to put everything you know about economics or intermarriage or the status of women through the ages in between two thin slices, an opening sentence and a concluding sentence, on the Book of Ruth.

Let's take another example. Suppose that in a course on modern revolutionary movements you're assigned a research essay on any subject covered by the readings or lectures. You're interested in Mexican history, and after a preliminary search you decide to focus on the Revolution of 1910 or some events leading up to it. Depending on what is available in your library, or what you find in an Internet search, you might narrow your topic to one of these:

Mexican Bandits—The First Twentieth-Century Revolutionists

The Exploits of Joaquin Murieta and Tiburcio Vasquez—Romantic Legend and Fact

In short, it is not enough to have a subject (the Book of Ruth, revolutions); you must concentrate your vision on a topic, a significant part of the field, just as a landscape painter or photographer selects a portion of the landscape and then focuses on it. Your interests are your most trustworthy guides to the portion of the landscape on which to focus.

Developing a Tentative Thesis   As you think about your topic and information relating to it, try to formulate a **tentative thesis.** This *tentative* thesis is a working hypothesis, a proposition to be proved, disproved, or revised in light of information you discover. It ought to be a statement about which intelligent people *might disagree.* Readers won't bother to finish reading an essay if its thesis is an obvious truth, such as: "George Washington owned slaves," or "more men than women attend major league baseball games." There's no particular reason to argue a point that everyone would agree on. The two theses just specified can of course be supported with evidence: the number of slaves Washington owned, or the number of men and women who attend major league games. Nevertheless, the theses themselves remain unarguable and uninteresting. They need to be developed, most likely after additional reading and thinking, into more debatable statements: "although Washington owned slaves, some evidence indicates that he believed slavery was an evil institution"; "the number of women who attend major league games has in the past decade slightly increased, probably because. . . ."

Your tentative thesis, which usually can be stated in a sentence or two, will help you to maintain your focus, to keep in mind the points that you must support with evidence: quotations, facts, statistics, reasons, descriptions, and illustrative anecdotes. But be prepared to modify your tentative thesis, perhaps more than once, and perhaps substantially. Your first draft might, for example, contain this tentative thesis:

> Naomi's character is more interesting than Ruth's because her behavior is more complicated.

That tentative thesis might become a revised thesis at a later stage:

> Although Naomi's actions suggest her concern for her daughter-in-law, they also reveal self-interest.

Note that both the tentative thesis and the revised thesis are *arguable.* One can imagine a reader *dis*agreeing with either statement. "No," such a reader might say, "Ruth's behavior is *not* more complicated than Naomi's." Or: "I disagree—Naomi *is* concerned about her daughter-in-law; she's not self-interested at all." Once you begin amassing evidence to support your arguments, you may find to your surprise that the evidence supports a different thesis. Your best ideas on a topic may turn out to be radically different from the ideas with which you began. As we pointed out earlier, writing is not simply a way to express ideas you already have, it is also a way to discover new ones.

Let's look at another example: An early draft of an essay about Charlotte Perkins Gilman's "The Yellow Wallpaper," a late nineteenth-century short story about a woman who goes mad, might present the thesis that the story is about "the oppression of women." But a classroom discussion of the story and a minimal amount of library or Internet research would soon reveal that many, many readers have reached the conclusion that the story is in some way about the oppression of women. Because almost everyone would agree with this point, it is no longer arguable. A stronger thesis, developed through careful attention to the text, might specify the nature of the "oppression" and its particular results. One might note that the narrator has just had a baby and that the husband (perhaps as a consequence) treats his wife as if she were a child. A new thesis might then emerge: "The inherent conflict between the needs of the narrator's child and the expectations of her husband precipitates her eventual decline into madness." This point is more arguable and therefore more interesting than the idea that the story is about the oppression of women; one can imagine readers who might disagree with it by attributing the narrator's madness to other causes.

Although essays based on substantial analysis or research almost always include an explicit thesis sentence in the finished essay, short essays based on personal experience often do not. An essay recounting a writer's experience of racism, for example, or conveying the particular atmosphere of a neighborhood, is likely to have a central idea or focus, a thesis idea, rather than a thesis sentence. But whether stated or implied, the thesis idea must be developed (explained, supported, or proved) by evidence presented in the body of the essay. The kind of evidence will vary, of course, not only with your topic but also with your audience and purpose.

Developing Ideas

What constitutes evidence, and where does it come from? Writers explain, support, and develop their ideas with material derived from the reading, thinking, note-taking, questioning, and remembering that are part of the writing process from beginning to end. Materials for developing an essay on Naomi's motivation will be passages from the Book of Ruth, quotations that the writer introduces and explains. Similarly, materials for an essay on the blues will be quotations from a selection of lyrics. Materials for developing an essay on Dorothea Lange's photograph will include a detailed description of the figures, a discussion of their relation to each other, and perhaps some information about the photographer (p. 5) herself. In all of these instances, in fact, imagining a reader helps a writer develop ideas.

Thinking About Audience and Purpose

Thinking about your audience, about what you want your readers to understand and believe, is central to the revision process, which we discuss in Chapter 2. But thinking about audience and purpose can be helpful at earlier stages of writing too, when you are trying to develop an idea and to work up evidence to support it. If you are uncertain how to begin, or if, on the other hand, you are overwhelmed by the materials you have unearthed and don't know how to sort them out, try asking yourself these questions:

- Who are my readers?
- What do they need to know?
- What do I want them to believe?
- Why should they care about what I have to say?

When you ask, "Who is my reader?" the obvious answer—the teacher who assigned the essay—is, paradoxically, the least helpful. To learn to write well, you'll have to force that fact out of your mind, pretend it isn't true, or you're likely to feel defeated from the beginning. Write instead for someone who understands your material less well than you. Remember: *When you write, you are the teacher.* It's probably easier to assume the role of the teacher if you imagine your reader to be someone in your class—that is, someone intelligent and reasonably well informed who shares some of your interests but who does not happen to be you, and who therefore does not see the material in precisely the way you do. That reader can't know your thoughts unless you organize them and explain them clearly and thoroughly.

A RULE FOR WRITERS

In imagining your audience, assume that your reader is your classmate, not your instructor.

Writing academic essays usually requires examining and evaluating texts and other evidence beyond your personal experience or previous knowledge. Nevertheless, you still must trust your own ideas. Trusting your own ideas does not, of course, mean being satisfied with the first thought that pops into your head. Rather, it means respecting your ideas enough to examine them thoughtfully; it means testing, refining, and sometimes changing them. But it is always your reading of a text, your conduct of an experiment, your understanding of an issue that your essay attempts to communicate. If it does so, your reader will care—because you've brought new ideas, new insights, to the topic at hand.

Writing the Draft

If you have used one or more of the invention strategies we discuss above, and if you've begun to develop a focus on a topic within your larger subject, you should at this point have some sense of what your essay will be about. Now is the time to start writing the draft. How to begin?

1. Sit down and start writing. If you have the ideas but don't know how to express them, start writing anyway. Resist the temptation to check your e-mail, to make a cup of soup, to call your mother. Now is *not* the time to do your laundry or to make your bed. Sit down and start putting one word after another.

2. Start with something easy. Start anywhere. Start with what comes to mind first. For example, you might start by summarizing the passage you're responding to or by sketching any one of your ideas about it. *Don't think you must start with an introductory paragraph*; you can write an introduction later, once your ideas have become better defined. It doesn't matter where you begin, only that you do begin. Start anywhere and keep going.

3. Try freewriting. Just write. Pick up pen, grap a pencil, or put your hands on the keyboard, think about the material you've chosen to write about, and write what you're thinking. Don't worry about spelling or punctuation or grammar; don't censor yourself. No one but you will see what you've written. Your goal here is simply to put words on paper; you can evaluate them later.

4. Plan to stop writing. Give yourself a time limit. If you tend to procrastinate, try keeping your first sessions short. Promise yourself that you'll stop working after, say, twenty minutes, and *keep that promise*. If at the start you limit your writing sessions, you accomplish two things. You reduce anxiety: The thought of working at your desk for twenty minutes is not nearly as daunting as the thought of writing four or five pages. And after twenty minutes you'll have *something* down on paper. You can gradually increase the length of the sessions—to an hour, or three, or whatever is reasonable, given the assignment and your schedule.

5. Revise later. After a few false starts and probably more than one session, your ideas will begin to take form on the page. But at this early stage, don't expect them to appear in final form, beautifully organized and in polished sentences. Ideas rarely exist that way in one's mind. In fact, until we put them into words, ideas are usually only rough impressions or images, not clear thoughts at all. (As E. M. Forster wrote, "How do I know what I think until I see what I say?") Once you do get some ideas down on paper, you can begin to see which ones must be developed or deleted, where connections need to be made, where examples need to be added. At this stage, you may be close to having a first draft. Whether or not you like what you've written, take a rest from it. Do something else: Make your bed, or if you like, just climb into it.

CHAPTER TWO

DRAFTING AND REVISING

I have never thought of myself as a good writer. Anyone who wants reassurance of that should read one of my first drafts. But I'm one of the world's great revisers.

—*James Michener*

Reading Drafts

In Chapter 1, we focused on how to have ideas and how to get them down on paper. From the start of a project, the writer is almost simultaneously both inventing ideas and refining them. But we also advised that, particularly at the start, it's best to suspend critical judgment until you have begun to capture your thoughts, however roughly expressed, on paper. In this chapter, we will focus on ways to improve and refine rough drafts. We want to begin by making what may seem like an obvious point: To improve the draft you have written, *you must first read it.* Moreover, you must try to read it objectively and critically.

Imagining Your Audience and Asking Questions

To read your draft objectively, to make sure that you have said what you intended to say, put it aside for a day, or at least for a couple of hours. Then read it through, as if you were not the writer, but someone reading if for the first time. As you read, try to imagine the questions such a reader might want to ask you to understand what you meant. Then, read your draft again, asking yourself the following questions:

1. Does the draft present an idea? Does it have a focus or make a unified point?
2. Is the idea or are the ideas clearly supported? Is there convincing evidence? Are there sufficient specific details?
3. Is the material effectively organized?

There are many other questions you might ask, and we'll suggest some before we're done. But let's start with these.

1. Does the draft present an idea? Does it have a focus or make a unified point? Let's first consider the rare case: If on reading your draft objectively, you find that it doesn't present an idea, a point to develop, then there's probably no reason to tinker with it. It may be better to start again, using the invention techniques we discussed earlier. (Rereading the assignment is probably a good idea too.)

Almost surely, however, you will find some interesting material in your draft but you won't yet be sure what it adds up to. The chances are that some extraneous material is getting in your way—some false starts, needless repetition, or interesting but irrelevant information. Some pruning is probably in order.

Picasso said that in painting a picture he advanced by a series of destructions. A story about a sculptor makes a similar point. When asked how he had made such a lifelike image of an elephant from a block of wood, the sculptor answered, "Well, I just knocked off everything that didn't look like elephant." Often, revising a draft begins with similar "destruction." Having identified your main point, don't be afraid to hack away competing material until you can see that point clearly in its bold outline. Of course, you must have a lot of stuff on paper to begin with (at the start, nothing succeeds like excess). But often you must remove some of it before you can see that you have in fact roughly formulated the main point you want to make, and even produced some evidence to support it.

2. Is the idea or are the ideas clearly supported? Is there convincing evidence? Are there sufficient specific details? Writers are always reluctant to delete. Students with an assignment to write 500 or 1000 words by a deadline are, understandably, among the most reluctant. But, almost certainly, once you have settled on the focus of your essay, you will be adding material as well as deleting it. It isn't enough simply to state a point; you must also prove or demonstrate it.

If you argue, for example, that smoking should be banned in all public places, including parks and outdoor cafes, you must offer reasons for your position and also meet possible objections with counterarguments. If you are arguing that in Plato's *Apology* Socrates' definition of truth goes beyond mere correspondence to fact, you will need to summarize relevant passages of the *Apology* and introduce quotations illuminating Socrates' definition. Almost all drafts need the addition of specific details and examples to support and clarify generalizations.

3. Is the material effectively organized? As you prune away the irrelevancies and add the specific details and examples that will clarify and strengthen your point, as your draft begins more and more to "look like an elephant," ask yourself if the parts of your draft are arranged in the best order.

- If you have given two examples, or stated three reasons, with which one is it best to begin?
- Are paragraphs presented in a reasonable sequence?
- Will the relationship of one point to the next be clear to your reader?
- Does the evidence in each paragraph support the point of that paragraph? (The same evidence may be more appropriate to a different paragraph.)
- Does your opening paragraph provide the reader with a focus? Or, if the paragraph performs some other important function, such as getting the reader's attention, does the essay provide the reader with a focus soon enough?

In general, when working on the organization of drafts, follow two rules:

- Put together what belongs together.
- Put yourself in the position of your reader; make it as easy as possible for the reader to follow you.

Peer Review: The Benefits of Having a Real Audience

Occasionally a writing assignment will specify the reader you should address. More often, your reader must be imagined. We usually suggest imagining someone in your class who has not thought about your topic or considered the specific evidence you intend to examine.

In many writing classes, students routinely break up into small groups to read and discuss each other's work. **Peer review,** as this practice is commonly called, is useful in several ways.

Peer review gives the writer a real audience, readers who can point to what puzzles or pleases them, who ask questions and make suggestions, who may often disagree (with the writer or with each other), and who frequently, though not willfully, misread. Though writers don't necessarily like everything they hear, reading and discussing their work with others almost always gives them a fresh perspective on their work. (Having your intentions misread, because your writing isn't clear enough, can be particularly stimulating.)

Moreover, when students write drafts that will be commented on, they are doing what professional writers do. Like journalists, scholars, engineers, lawyers—anyone whose work is ordinarily reviewed many times, by friends and spouses, by colleagues, and by editors, before the work is published—students who write drafts for peer review know they will have a chance to discuss their writing with their colleagues (other students) before submitting a final version for evaluation. Writers accustomed to writing for a real audience are able, to some extent, to internalize the demands of a real audience. Even as they work on early drafts, they are sensitive to what needs to be added, or deleted, or clarified. Students who discuss their work with other students derive similar benefits. They are likely to write and revise with more confidence, and more energy.

The writer whose work is being reviewed is not the sole beneficiary. When students regularly serve as readers for each other, they become better readers of their own work, and consequently better revisers. *Learning to write is in large measure learning to read.*

Peer review in the classroom takes many forms; we'll look in a moment at an example as we trace a student's essay that is revised largely as a result of peer review. But even if peer review is not part of your writing class, you may want to work with a friend or another student in the class, reading each other's drafts.

When you work on your essay with your classmates or your friends, good manners and academic practice require that you thank them for their help, that you **document** their contributions. You can offer a sentence or two of general thanks at the end of the essay—something like this:

```
I'd like to thank the members of my peer revision
group, Rebecca Sharp and Isabella Thorpe, for help-
```

```
ing me to clarify the main idea of my essay and for
suggesting ways to edit my sentences.
```

Or you can thank your peer reviewers for their specific contributions by inserting a footnote or endnote at the end of the sentence that contains an idea or words you wish to acknowledge, and then writing a sentence like this:

```
Kevin Doughten drew my attention to the narrator's
play on words here; I wish to thank him for helping
me develop this point.
```

From Assignment to Essay: A Case History

On September 12, Suki Hudson was given the following assignment:

> Write an essay (roughly 500 words) defining racism or narrating an experience in which you were either the victim or the perpetrator of a racist incident. Your essay should offer a thesis supported by evidence from your experience. Bring a first draft with two copies to class on September 16 for peer review. Revised essay due September 26.

Suki kept no record of her first thoughts and jottings on the topic, but what follows is an early attempt to get something down on paper. Because it was far from the finished essay she would write, not yet even a first draft, we label it a Zero Draft:

```
Zero Draft. Sept. 13
```

```
     It was a warm sunny day in the playground. My
three-year-old brother and other children were play-
ing gaily until one of the boys' mothers interrupted.
She called her son, whispered something, and when he
went back to the playground he excluded my brother
from playing together. I didn't know what to call the
incident, but my heart ached as I watched my little
brother enviously looked at the other kids. I immedi-
ately left the playground with him, and the play-
ground has never been the same since that day.
```

At that point, having reached the end of the anecdote, Suki stopped. What she had written was not yet an essay, and it was far short of the suggested 500 words, but it was a start, which is all she had hoped to accomplish on this first try.

Later she read what she had written, and asked a friend to read it and see if he had any suggestions. It was a frustrating conversation. The friend didn't understand why Suki thought this was a "racist incident." Why did Suki leave the playground? Why hadn't she just asked the boy's mother for an explanation? The questions took her by surprise; she felt annoyed, then miserable. So she changed the subject.

But "the subject" didn't go away. Still later, she wrote the following account of the conversation in her journal:

Sept. 13

> I asked J to read my paper and he thought I was being paranoid. Why didn't I just ask the boy's mother what was the matter? But I could not have even thought of going up to the woman to question her motives. It was beyond my control if she wanted to be ignorant and cruel to a different race. (Or was it really my ignorance to walk away from a simple explanation?)

The following day, looking over what she had written, it occurred to her to try adding the journal entry to the anecdote. Maybe in a concluding paragraph she could explain why what happened in the playground was obviously a racist incident.

Here is the conclusion:

Sept. 14

> Most people in modern society don't recognize the more subtle cases of racism. People feel if they are not assaulting physically they are not violating the law, and as long as they are living according to the law, racism is not committed. However, the law or the constitution does not protect the human heart from getting hurt, and without a doubt the most critical racist action could be committed by close friends or their loved ones.

But having written that last line Suki was struck by something odd about it. The woman in the playground was not a loved one, nor was she a close friend. Still, it was true that racist acts can be committed by friends, and even if the acts are undramatic, they should be recognized as racist acts. At this point, she thought that she had a thesis for her essay, but she also realized that she had begun to recall a different experience. Starting again, she wrote the following account:

```
In Korea, I had a very close friend whose father was
Chinese. Although her mother was a Korean woman,
they were treated as foreign people in town, and
they were singled out on many occasions. Her father
died when she was little but everyone in town knew
she was a half Chinese. Her mother ran a Chinese
restaurant, and they lived very quietly. My family
knew her mother well and I was close friends with
the girl and for many years I was the only friend
she ever had. However, as I entered junior high
school my new group of friends didn't approve of her
background, and I drifted away from her. She was a
very quiet, shy person and although I stopped call-
ing or visiting her, she always remembered me on
holidays to send presents. After graduating from
junior high school she went to Taiwan to live with
her grandparents, whom she had never met. I gath-
ered she could not stand the isolation any longer
at her age. Many years later I realized how cruel I
have been to her, and I tried to locate her without
success.
```

The following day Suki combined the two drafts (hoping to come closer to the 500 words), added a new concluding paragraph, and (rather disgusted with the whole assignment) typed up her first draft to hand in the next day. She photocopied it, as instructed, for peer review in class.

Peer review in the classroom takes many forms. Ordinarily, the instructor distributes some questions to be answered by both the writer and the readers. Typically the writer is asked to speak first, explaining how far along he or she is in writing the essay, and what help readers might give. The writer might also be asked, "What are you most pleased with in your writing so far?"

Readers are then asked to respond. Instructions may vary, depending on the particular assignment, but the questions distributed in Suki's class, shown here, are fairly typical.

Questions for Peer Review   Writing 125R

Read each draft once, quickly. Then read it again, with the following questions in mind:

1. What is the essay's topic? Is it one of the assigned topics, or a variation from it? Does the draft show promise of fulfilling the assignment?

2. Looking at the essay as a whole, what thesis (main idea) is stated or implied? If stated, where is it stated? If implied, try to state it in your own words.

3. Looking at each paragraph separately:
   - What is the basic point (the topic sentence or idea)? How does the paragraph relate to the essay's main idea or to the previous paragraph?
   - Is each sentence clearly related to the previous sentence?
   - Is the paragraph adequately developed? Are there sufficient specific details or examples?
   - Is the transition from one paragraph to the next clear?

4. Look again at the introductory paragraph. Does it focus your attention on the main point of the essay? If not, does it effectively serve some other purpose? Does the opening sentence interest you in the essay? Do you want to keep reading?

5. Is the conclusion clear? Is the last sentence satisfying?

6. Does the essay have a title? Is it interesting? Informative?

7. What is the greatest strength of the essay? What is its main weakness?

8. What is the most important piece of advice you would offer on this essay?

First Draft   What follows is first the draft Suki gave the two members of her group, and then a summary of the group's discussion. Before reading her draft aloud (the procedure the instructor recommended for this session), Suki explained how she had happened to narrate two experiences and asked which narrative she should keep, or if she could keep both.

First Draft

S. Hudson

Sept. 16

1   It was a warm sunny day in the playground. My three-year-old brother and other children were playing gaily until one of the boys' mothers interrupted. She called her son to whisper something and when he went back to the playground he excluded my brother from playing together. I didn't know what to call the incident, but my heart ached as I watched my little brother enviously looked at other kids. I immediately left the playground with him, and the playground has never been the same since that day.

2   A friend of mine said I was being paranoid. It would have been appropriate to ask the boy's mother what was the matter, or if she had anything to do with the kids excluding my brother from playing. But I could not have even thought of going up to the woman to question her motives. It was beyond my control if she wanted to be ignorant and cruel to a different race, or perhaps my ignorance to walk away from a simple explanation.

3   Most people in modern society recognize only the dramatic instances of racism, and on a daily basis people don't recognize the more subtle cases of racism. People feel if they are not assaulting physically they are not violating the law, and as long as they are living according to the law, the racism is not committed. However, the law or the constitution does not protect the human heart from getting hurt, and without a doubt the most critical racist action could be committed by close friends or their loved ones.

4   In Korea, I had a very close friend whose father was Chinese. Although her mother was a Korean woman they were treated as foreign people in town, and they were singled out on many occasions. Her father died when she was little, but everyone in town knew she was a half Chinese. Her mother ran a Chinese restaurant,

and they lived very quietly. My family knew her mother
well and I was close friends with the girl and for
many years I was the only friend she ever had.
However, as I entered junior high school my new group
of friends didn't approve of her background and I
drifted away from her. She was a very quiet, shy
person, and although I stopped calling or visiting
her, she always remembered me on holidays to send
presents. After graduating from junior high school she
went to Taiwan to live with her grandparents whom she
had never met. I gathered she could not stand the
isolation any longer at her age. Many years later, I
realized how cruel I have been to her, and I tried to
locate her without success.

5   She was a victim in a homogeneous society, and
had to experience the pain she did not deserve. It is
part of human nature to resent the unknown, and
sometimes people become racist to cover their fears or
ignorance.

Summary of Peer Group Discussion

1. The group immediately understood why the friend (in the second
paragraph) had difficulty understanding that the first incident was racist.
It might well have been racist, but, they pointed out, Suki had said
nothing about the racial mix at the playground. It does become clear by
the fourth paragraph that the writer and her brother are Korean, but we
don't get this information early enough, and we know nothing of the race
of the woman who whispers to her son. Suki had neglected to say—
because it was so perfectly obvious to her—that she and her brother were
Korean; the mother, the other child, in fact all others in the playground,
were caucasian.

A RULE FOR WRITERS

Keep your readers in mind as you revise.

2. Suki's readers confirmed her uneasiness about the third paragraph.
They found it confusing for several reasons: (a) Suki had written "peo-

ple don't recognize the more subtle cases of racism." Did she mean that the mother didn't recognize her action as racist, or that Suki didn't? (b) In the first paragraph Suki had written "I didn't know what to call the incident." But then the second paragraph is contradictory. There she seems to accuse the mother of being "cruel to a different race." (c) And the last sentence of the third paragraph, they agreed, in which Suki writes of racist acts "committed by close friends," did not tie in at all with the first part of the essay, although it did serve to introduce the second anecdote.

3. Her group was enthusiastic, though, about Suki's telling of the two stories and advised her to keep both. Both were accounts of more or less subtle acts of racism. One student thought that they should appear in chronological order: first the Korean story and then the more recent story, set in the playground. But both readers were sure that she could find some way to put them together.

4. They were less sure what the essay's thesis was, or whether it even had one. One student proposed this:

> Subtle racist acts can be as destructive as dramatic instances (implied in paragraph 3).

The other proposed combining two points:

> It is part of human nature to resent the unknown

and

> . . . sometimes people become racist to cover their fears or ignorance (from the final paragraph).

All three members of Suki's group (Suki included) thought that the ideas in the essay were supported by the narratives. But the draft didn't yet hang together: Suki would have to work on the way the separate parts connected.

5. One member of the group then pointed out that the second paragraph could be deleted. The friend mentioned in it (who called Suki "paranoid") had been important to Suki's thinking about her first draft, but served no useful purpose in the draft they were looking at, and other details in that paragraph were murky.

6. On the other hand, the first paragraph probably needed additional details about the setting, the people involved, what each did. How does a three-year-old know he's been excluded from a play group? What happened? What did the other children do? What did he do? And, as the group had seen at once, some details were needed to establish the racist nature of the incident. They also reminded Suki that her essay needed a title.

7. Finally, some small details of grammar. Suki's English is excellent, although English is her second language. But the other two in her group, being native speakers of English, were able to catch the slightly odd diction in

> she always remembered me on holidays to send presents

and the error in

> my heart ached as I watched my little brother enviously looked at other kids.

Suki asked if the past tense was right in

> I realized how cruel I have been to her

and the others supplied

> I realized how cruel I had been to her

(though they could not explain the difference).

Final Version Several days later Suki consulted her notes and resumed work on her draft, and by September 25, the night before it was due, she was able to print the final version, which now included a title. (See pp. 28–30 for final version.)

Suki Hudson

Ms. Cahill

Writing 125R

September 20, 2004

Two Sides of a Story

1   It was a warm sunny day in the playground. My three-year-old brother and two other small boys were playing together in the sandbox. My brother was very happy, digging in the sand with a shovel one of the other boys had brought, when one of the mothers sitting on a bench across from me called to her son. She bent over and whispered something to him, and he went right over to my brother and pulled the shovel out of his hand. He pushed my brother aside and moved to the other side of the sandbox. The other boy followed him, and they continued to play. My heart ached as I watched my little brother enviously looking at the other kids. I didn't fully understand what had happened. I looked across at the mother, but she turned her head away. Then I picked up my brother and immediately left the playground with him.

2   I thought the woman was extremely rude and cruel, but I didn't think then that she was behaving in a racist way. We had only recently come here from Korea, and although I had been told that there was much

racism in America, I thought that meant that it was hard for some people, like blacks, to find jobs or go to good schools. In some places there were street gangs and violence. But I didn't understand that there could be subtle acts of racism too. I was aware, though, in the playground that my brother and I were the only Koreans, the only nonwhites. When the woman turned her face away from me it felt like a sharp slap, but I was ignorant about her motives. I only guessed that she told her child not to play with my brother, and I knew that the playground was never the same since that day.

3   That incident was several months ago. When I started to think about it again recently, I thought also of another time when I was ignorant of racism.

4   In Korea, I had a very close friend whose father was Chinese. Although her mother was a Korean woman they were treated as foreign people in town, and they were singled out on many occasions. Her father died when she was little, but everyone in town knew she was half Chinese. Her mother ran a Chinese restaurant, and they lived very quietly. My family knew her mother well and I was close friends with the girl, and for many years I was the only friend she ever had. However, as I entered junior high school my new group of friends didn't approve of her background and I drifted away from her.

She was a very quiet, shy person, and although I stopped calling or visiting her, she always remembered to send me presents on holidays. After graduating from junior high school, she went to Taiwan to live with her grandparents, whom she had never met. I gathered she could not stand the isolation any longer at her age. Many years later, I realized how cruel I had been to her, and I tried to locate her without success.

5   She was a victim in a homogeneous society, and had to experience pain she did not deserve. There was no law to protect her from that, just as there was no law to protect my little brother. Perhaps the woman in the playground did not realize how cruel she was being. She probably didn't think of herself as a racist, and maybe she acted the way I did in Korea, without thinking why. It isn't only the dramatic acts that are racist, and maybe it isn't only cruel people who commit racist acts. It is part of human nature to fear the unknown, and sometimes people become racist to cover their fears, or ignorance.

Acknowledgments

I would like to thank Ann Weston and Tory Chang for helping me to develop my main point, and to organize and edit my essay.

CHAPTER THREE

SHAPING PARAGRAPHS

Paragraph Form and Substance

It is commonly said that a good paragraph is

- *unified* (it makes one point, or it indicates where one unit of a topic begins and ends);
- *organized* (the point or unit is developed according to some pattern); and
- *coherent* (the pattern of development, sentence by sentence, is clear to the reader).

In this chapter, we will say these things too. But first we feel obliged to issue this warning: You can learn to write a unified, organized, coherent paragraph that no one in his or her right mind would choose to read. Here is an example:

> Charles Darwin's great accomplishments in the field of natural science resulted from many factors. While innate qualities and characteristics played a large part in leading him to his discoveries, various environmental circumstances and events were decisive factors as well. Darwin himself considered his voyage on the Beagle the most decisive event of his life, precisely because this was to him an educational experience similar to if not more valuable than that of college, in that it determined his whole career and taught him of the world as well.

Notice that the paragraph is unified, organized, and coherent. It has a **topic sentence** (the first sentence, which briefly states the main idea of the paragraph). It uses **transitional devices** ("while," "as well," "Darwin himself") and, as is often helpful, it **repeats key words.** But notice also that it is wordy, vague, and inflated ("in the field of," "many factors," "qualities and characteristics," "circumstances and events," "precisely because," "educational experience," "similar to if not more valuable than"). It is, in short, thin and boring. To whom does it teach what?

Consider, by contrast, these paragraphs from another essay on Darwin:

> Charles Darwin's youth was unmarked by signs of genius. Born in 1809 into the well-to-do Darwin and Wedgwood clans (his mother was a Wedgwood, and Darwin himself was to marry another), he led a secure and carefree childhood, happy with his family, indifferent to books, responsive to nature. The son and grandson of impressively successful physicians, he eventually tried medical training himself, but found the studies dull and surgery (before anesthesia) too ghastly even to watch. So, for want of anything better, he followed the advice of his awesome father (6' 2", 336 pounds, domineering in temperament) and studied for the ministry, taking his B.A. at Christ's College, Cambridge, in 1831.
>
> Then a remarkable turn of events saved Darwin from a country parsonage. His science teacher at Cambridge, John Stevens Henslow, arranged for Darwin the invitation to be naturalist on H.M.S. *Beagle* during a long voyage of exploration. Despite his father's initial reluctance, Darwin got the position, and at the end of 1831 left England for a five-year voyage around the globe that turned out to be not only a crucial experience for Darwin himself, but a passage of consequence for the whole world.
>
> —*Philip Appleman*

Notice how full of life these paragraphs are, compared to the paragraph that begins by asserting that "Charles Darwin's great accomplishments in the field of natural science resulted from many factors." These far more interesting paragraphs are filled with specific details, facts, and names that combine to convey ideas. We finish reading them with a sense of having learned something worth knowing, from someone fully engaged not only with the topic, but also with conveying it to someone else.

The one indispensable quality of a good paragraph is **substance.** A paragraph may

- define a term,
- describe a person or a place,

- make a comparison,
- tell an anecdote,
- summarize an opinion,
- draw a conclusion.

It may do almost anything provided that it holds the readers' attention by telling them something they want or need to know, or are reminded of with pleasure.

But even a substantial paragraph does not guarantee that you'll hold the attention of your readers, because readers, like writers, are often lazy and impatient. If readers find that they must work too hard to understand you, if they are confused by what you write, they can and will stop reading. The art of writing is in large part the art of keeping your readers' goodwill while you teach them what you want them to learn. Now, experienced writers can usually tell what makes a satisfactory unit, and their paragraphs do not always exactly follow the principles we are going to suggest. But we think that if you follow these principles you will develop a sense of paragraphing. Or, to put it another way, you will improve your sense of how to develop an idea.

The Shape of a Paragraph

The shape of a paragraph—the way in which its idea is set forth—will largely depend not only on the content but also on the position of the paragraph in the essay.

- The **content** of a paragraph explaining something may move from cause to effect, or from effect to cause; the content of a paragraph arguing a point may move from evidence to conclusion, or from conclusion to evidence.
- The **position** of the paragraph, its place in the essay as a whole, will also determine its shape. An opening paragraph will in one way or another lead into the topic (its main point may therefore come at the end). A middle paragraph should follow easily from the preceding paragraph, and it should also lead into the next paragraph—so a middle paragraph might begin with a transitional sentence (a sentence that begins with a "Furthermore" or a "Nevertheless") and announce its main point in the second sentence. Or even in its last sentence.

We will discuss such matters in detail in the following pages. But here we can say that when you revise a draft, you want to make certain not only that each paragraph is clear in itself but also that it fits neatly into your essay.

Paragraph Unity: Topic Sentences, Topic Ideas

The idea developed in each paragraph often appears, briefly stated, as a topic sentence. Topic sentences are most useful, and are therefore especially common, in paragraphs that offer arguments; they are much less useful, and therefore less common, in narrative and descriptive paragraphs.

The topic sentence usually is the first sentence in the paragraph—or the second, if the first sentence is transitional—because writers usually want their readers to know from the start where the paragraph is going. Sometimes, though, you may not wish to forecast what is to come; you may prefer to put your topic sentence at the end of the paragraph, summarizing the points that earlier sentences have made, or drawing a generalization based on the earlier details. Even if you do not include a topic sentence anywhere in the paragraph, the paragraph should have a **topic idea,** an idea that holds the sentences together.

Examples of Topic Sentences at Beginning and at End, and of Topic Ideas

1. The following paragraph, from an essay in which a professor of physiology compares Darwin and Freud, begins with a topic sentence.

> To begin with, Darwin and Freud were both multifaceted geniuses with many talents in common. Both were great observers, attuned to perceiving in familiar phenomena a significance that had escaped almost everyone else. Searching with insatiable curiosity for underlying explanations, both did far more than discover new facts or solve circumscribed problems, such as the structure of DNA: they synthesized knowledge from a wide range of fields and created new conceptual frameworks, large parts of which are still accepted today. Both were prolific writers and forceful communicators who eventually converted many or most of their contemporaries to their positions.
>
> —*Jared Diamond*

The first sentence announces the topic the rest of the paragraph will develop, the talents Darwin and Freud had in common. Each sentence that follows this topic sentence develops or amplifies it by considering one of the talents the two men shared. The second sentence concerns their powers of observation. The third sentence concerns their curiosity about "underlying explanations" and their ability to create "new conceptual frameworks." Note also the logical order of subtopics in the paragraph: The discussion moves from *observation*, to *analysis* and *synthesis*, to *communication*.

2. The next paragraph has its topic sentence at the end:

If we try to recall Boris Karloff's face as the monster in the film of *Frankenstein* (1931), most of us probably think of the seams holding the pieces together, and if we cannot recall other details we assume that the face evokes horror. But when we actually look at a picture of the face rather than recall a memory of it, we are perhaps chiefly impressed by the high, steep forehead (a feature often associated with intelligence), by the darkness surrounding the eyes (often associated with physical or spiritual weariness), and by the gaunt cheeks and the thin lips slightly turned down at the corners (associated with deprivation or restraint). The monster's face is of course in some ways shocking, but probably our chief impression as we look at it is that this is not the face of one who causes suffering but of one who himself is heroically undergoing suffering.

—*Sylvia Rodriguez*

When the topic sentence is at the end, the paragraph usually develops from the particular to the general, the topic sentence serving to generalize or summarize the information that precedes it. Such a topic sentence can be especially effective in presenting an argument: The reader hears, considers, and accepts the evidence before the writer explicitly states the argument, and if the writer has effectively presented the evidence, the reader willingly accepts the conclusion.

3. The next paragraph has no topic sentence:

A few years ago when you mentioned Walt Disney at a respectable party— or anyway this is how it was in California, where I was then—the standard response was a headshake and a groan. Intellectuals spoke of how he butchered the classics—from *Pinocchio* to *Winnie the Pooh*, how his wildlife pictures were sadistic and coy, how the World's Fair sculptures of hippopotamuses were a national if not international disgrace. A few crazies disagreed, and since crazies are always the people to watch, it began to be admitted that the early Pluto movies had a considerable measure of *je ne sais quoi*, that the background animation in *Snow White* was "quite extraordinary," that *Fantasia* did indeed have *one* great sequence (then it became two; now everyone says three, though there's fierce disagreement on exactly which three).

—*John Gardner*

The topic idea here is, roughly, "Intellectuals used to scorn Disney, but recently they have been praising him." Such a sentence could easily begin the paragraph, but it is not necessary because even without it the reader has no difficulty following the discussion. The first two sentences talk about Disney's earlier reputation; then the sentence about the "crazies" introduces the contrary view and the rest of the paragraph illustrates the growing popularity of this contrary view. The paragraph develops its point so clearly and consistently (it is essentially a narrative, in chronological order) that the reader, unlike the reader of a complex analytic paragraph, does not need the help of a topic sentence either at the beginning, to prepare for what follows, or at the end, to pull the whole together.

Unity in Paragraphs

Although we emphasize **unity** in paragraphs, don't assume that every development or refinement or alteration of your thought requires a new paragraph. Such an assumption would lead to an essay consisting entirely of one-sentence paragraphs. A good paragraph may, for instance,

- ask a question *and* answer it, or
- describe an effect *and* then explain the cause, or
- set forth details *and* then offer a generalization.

Indeed, if the question or the effect or the details can be set forth in a sentence or two, and the answer or the cause or the generalization can be set forth in a sentence or two, the two halves of the topic should be pulled together into a single paragraph. Only if, for example, the question is long and complex and the answer equally long or longer, will you need two or more paragraphs.

Let's consider three paragraphs from an essay on ballooning. In the essay from which the following paragraphs are taken, the writer has already explained that ballooning was born in late eighteenth-century France and that almost from its start there were two types of balloons, gas and hot air. Notice that in the paragraphs printed below:

- the first is on gas,
- the second is chiefly on hot air (but it helpfully makes comparisons with gas),
- and the third is on the length of flights of both gas and hot-air balloons.

In other words, each paragraph is about one thing—gas balloons, hot-air balloons, length of flight—but each paragraph also builds on what the reader has learned in the previous paragraphs. That the third paragraph is about the flights of gas *and* of hot-air balloons does not mean that it lacks unity; it is a unified discussion of flight lengths.

> Gas balloons swim around in air like a sleeping fish in water, because they weigh about the same as the fluid they're in. A good, big, trans-Atlantic balloon will have 2,000 pounds of vehicle, including gas bag and pilot, taking up about 30 cubic feet (as big as a refrigerator), plus 300 pounds of a "nothing" stuff called helium, which fills 30,000 cubic feet (as big as three houses). Air to fill this 30,000 cubic feet would also weigh 2,300 pounds, so the balloon system averages the same as air, floating in it as part of the wind.
>
> Hot-air balloons use the same size bag filled with hot air instead of helium, kept hot by a boot-sized blowtorch riding just over the pilot's head. Hot air is light, but not as light as helium, so you can't carry as much equipment in a hot-air balloon. You also can't fly as long or as far. Helium will carry a balloon for days (three and a half days is the record), until a lot of gas has leaked out. But a hot-air balloon cools down in minutes, like a house as soon as its heat source runs out of fuel; and today's best fuel (heat-for-weight), propane, lasts only several hours.
>
> A good hot-air flight goes a hundred miles, yet the gas record is 1,897 miles, set by a German in 1914 with the junk (by today's standards) they had then. Unmanned scientific gas balloons have flown half a million miles, staying up more than a year. Japan bombed Oregon in World War II with balloons. Two hot-air balloonists, Tracy Barnes and Malcolm Forbes, have made what they called transcontinental flights, but each was the sum of dozens of end-to-end hops, trailed by pick-up trucks, like throwing a frisbee from Hollywood to Atlantic City.
>
> *—David Royce*

Because Royce's paragraphs are unified, the reader is able to proceed from point to point without stumbling and without confusion. By contrast, the following paragraph, from a book on athletic coaching, lacks unity, and the effect is disconcerting.

> Leadership qualities are a prerequisite for achievement in coaching. A leader is one who is respected for what he says and does, and who is admired by his team. The coach gains respect by giving respect, and by possessing knowledge and skills associated with the sport. There are many "successful" coaches who are domineering, forceful leaders, gaining

power more through fear and even hate than through respect. These military-type men are primarily from the old school of thought, and many younger coaches are achieving their goals through more humanistic approaches.

Something is wrong here. The first half of the paragraph tells us that "a leader is one who is respected for what he says and does," but the second half of the paragraph contradicts that assertion, telling us that "many" leaders hold their position "more through fear and even hate than through respect." The trouble is *not* that the writer is talking about two kinds of leaders; a moment ago we saw that a writer can in one paragraph talk about two kinds of balloons. The trouble here is that we need a unifying idea if these two points are to be given in one paragraph. The idea might be: There are two kinds of leaders, those who are respected and those who are feared. This idea might be developed along these lines:

> Leadership qualities are a prerequisite for achievement in coaching, but these qualities can be of two radically different kinds. One kind of leader is respected and admired by his team for what he says and does. The coach gains respect by giving respect, and by possessing knowledge and skills associated with the sport. The other kind of coach is a domineering, forceful leader, gaining power more through fear than through respect. These military-type men are primarily from the old school of thought, whereas most of the younger coaches achieve their goals through the more humane approaches of the first type.

Organization in Paragraphs

A paragraph needs more than a unified point; it needs a reasonable **organization** or sequence. Exactly how the parts of a paragraph will fit together depends on what the paragraph is doing.

- If it is *describing* a place, it may move from a general view to the significant details—or from immediately striking details to some less obvious but perhaps more important ones. It may move from near to far, or from far to near, or from the past to the present.

- If it is *explaining*, it may move from cause to effect, or from effect to cause, or from past to present; or it may offer an example.

- If it is *arguing*, it may move from evidence to conclusion, or from a conclusion to supporting evidence; or it may offer one piece of evidence—for instance, an anecdote that illustrates the argument.

- If it is *narrating*, it will likely move chronologically.

- If a paragraph is *classifying* (dividing a subject into its parts), it may begin by enumerating the parts and go on to study each, perhaps in climactic order. Here is an example from a student essay on masks:

> The chief reasons people wear masks are these: to have fun, to protect themselves, to disguise themselves, and to achieve a new identity. At Halloween, children wear masks for fun; they may, of course, also think they are disguising themselves, but chiefly their motive is to experience the joy of saying "boo" to someone. As for protection, soldiers wore masks in ancient times against swords and battle-axes, in more recent times against poison gas. Masked bank robbers illustrate the third reason, disguise, and though of course this disguise is a sort of protection, a robber's reason for wearing a mask is fairly distinct from a soldier's. All of these reasons so far are easily understood, but we may have more trouble grasping the reason that people use masks in order to achieve a new identity. In some religious rituals, masks may be worn to frighten away evil spirits, or they may be disguises so that the evil spirits will not know who the wearer is. But most religious masks are worn with the idea that the wearer achieves a new identity, a union with supernatural powers, and thus in effect the wearer becomes--really becomes, not merely pretends to be--a new person.

Notice that the first sentence offers four reasons for wearing masks. The rest of the paragraph amplifies these reasons, one by one, and in the order indicated in the first sentence. Since the writer regards the last reason as the most interesting and the most difficult to grasp, she discusses it at the greatest length, giving it about as much space as she gives to the first three reasons altogether.

The way in which a paragraph is organized, then, will depend on the writer's purpose. Almost always, one purpose is to make something clear to a reader, which means that the writer must present information in an orderly way. Writers use several common methods to organize a paragraph and to keep things clear:

1. General to particular (topic sentence usually at the beginning)
2. Particular to general (topic sentence usually at the end)

3. Enumeration of parts or details or reasons (probably in climactic order)
4. Question and answer
5. Cause and effect
6. Comparison and contrast
7. Analogy
8. Chronology
9. Spatial order (e.g., near to far, or right to left)

The only rule that can cover all paragraphs is this: Readers must never feel that they are wandering in a maze as they follow the writer to the end of the paragraph.

Coherence in Paragraphs

In addition to having a unified point and a reasonable organization, a good paragraph is **coherent**—that is, the connections between ideas in the paragraph are clear. Coherence can often be achieved by inserting the right transitional words or by taking care to repeat key words.

Transitions

Richard Wagner, commenting on his work as a composer of operas, said, "The art of composition is the art of transition," for his art moved from note to note, measure to measure, scene to scene. **Transitions** establish connections between ideas; they alert readers to what will follow. Here are some of the most common transitional words and phrases, categorized by their function:

1. **Amplification or likeness:** similarly, likewise, and, also, again, second, third, in addition, furthermore, moreover, finally
2. **Emphasis:** chiefly, equally, indeed, even more important
3. **Contrast or concession:** but, on the contrary, on the other hand, by contrast, of course, however, still, doubtless, no doubt, nevertheless, granted that, conversely, although, admittedly
4. **Example:** for example, for instance, as an example, specifically, consider as an illustration, that is, such as, like
5. **Consequence or cause and effect:** thus, so, then, it follows, as a result, therefore, hence

6. **Restatement:** in short, that is, in effect, in other words
7. **Place:** in the foreground, further back, in the distance
8. **Time:** afterward, next, then, as soon as, later, until, when, finally, last, at last
9. **Conclusion:** finally, therefore, thus, to sum up

Consider the following paragraph:

> Folklorists are just beginning to look at Africa. A great quantity of folk-lore materials has been gathered from African countries in the past century and published by missionaries, travelers, administrators, linguists, and anthropologists incidentally to their main pursuits. No fieldworker has devoted himself exclusively or even largely to the recording and analysis of folklore materials, according to a committee of the African Studies Association reporting in 1966 on the state of research in the African arts. Yet Africa is the continent supreme for traditional cultures that nurture folklore. Why this neglect?
>
> —*Richard M. Dorson*

The reader gets the point, but the second sentence seems to contradict the first: The first sentence tells us that folklorists are just beginning to look at Africa, but the next tells us that lots of folklore has been collected. An "although" between these sentences would clarify the author's point, especially if the third sentence were hooked on to the second, thus:

> Folklorists are just beginning to look at Africa. Although a great quantity of folklore materials has been gathered from African countries in the past century by missionaries, travelers, administrators, linguists, and anthropologists incidentally to their main pursuits, no fieldworker has devoted himself . . .

But this revision gives us an uncomfortably long second sentence. Further revision would help. The real point of the original passage, though it is smothered, is that *although* many people have incidentally collected folklore materials in Africa, *professional* folklorists have not been active there. The contrast ought to be sharpened:

> Folklorists are just beginning to look at Africa. True, missionaries, travelers, administrators, linguists, and anthropologists have collected a quantity of folklore materials incidentally to their main pursuits, but folklorists have lagged behind. No fieldworker . . .

In this revision the words that clarify are the small but important words "true" and "but." The original paragraph is like a jigsaw puzzle that's missing some tiny but necessary pieces.

Repetition

Coherence is also achieved through the **repetition** of key words. When you repeat words or phrases, or when you provide clear substitutes, such as pronouns and demonstrative adjectives, you are helping the reader to keep step with your developing thoughts. Grammatical constructions too can be repeated, the repetitions or parallels linking the sentences or ideas. In the following example, notice how the repetitions provide continuity.

> In the movement from the miraculous prose of Toni Morrison to the screen, the story of *Beloved* has lost some of its breadth, complexity, and imaginative range. But its central messages—historical and human—have been sustained and, in some ways, enhanced by the gifts of the innovative Jonathan Demme and his associates and by the talent and commitment of the actors. We see in the film the wounds of slavery, inflicted and then self-inflicted through resistance—or, rather, we see the memories of these wounds as they still disturb the free. We see the resources of an African-American community for defining those wounds, for quarreling about them, and for healing them. The story of trauma and recovery is distinctive, but it is told so as to invite others in, into the haunted house at 124 Bluestone and into Baby Sugg's clearing in the woods.
>
> —*Natalie Zemon Davis*

Notice not only the exact repetitions ("wounds," "we see," "them") but also the slight variations, such as "inflicted," and "self-inflicted"; and the parallel construction of the last phrases of the last sentence ("into the haunted house [. . .] into Baby Sugg's clearing"), which brings a sense of closure to the paragraph.

Linking Paragraphs Together

Since each paragraph in an essay generally develops a single idea, a single, new aspect of the main point of the essay, as one paragraph follows another, readers should feel they are getting somewhere, smoothly and without stumbling. As you move from one paragraph to the next, from one step in the development of your main idea to the next, you probably can keep your readers with you if you link the beginning of each new paragraph to the end of the paragraph that precedes it. Often a single transitional word (such as those listed on pp. 40–41) will suffice; sometimes repeating key terms will help connect a sequence of paragraphs together and make your essay, as many writers put it, "flow."

Consider the movement of ideas in the following essay written in response to an assignment that asked students to analyze a family photograph.

Cheryl Lee

Writing 125

Ms. Medina

April 1, 2004

The Story Behind the Gestures

1   At the close of my graduation ceremony, my entire family gathered together to immortalize the special moment on film. No one escaped the flash of my mother's camera because she was determined to document every minute of the occasion at every possible angle. My mother made sure that she took pictures of me with my hat on, with my hat off, holding the bouquet, sitting, standing, and in countless other positions. By the time this family picture was taken, my smile was intact, frozen on my face. This is not to say that my smile was anything less than genuine, for it truly was a smile of thankfulness and joy. It is just that after posing for so many pictures, what initially began as a spontaneous reaction became a frozen expression.

2   The viewer should, however, consider not so much the frozen expressions of those in the photograph, but rather the fact that the picture is posed. A posed

Cheryl Lee, *The Story Behind the Gestures: A Family Photograph.* Reprinted by permission of the author, Cheryl Lee Rim.

picture supposedly shows only what the people in the picture want the viewer to see--in this case, their happiness. But ironically the photograph reveals much more about its subjects than the viewer first imagines. The photograph speaks of relationships and personalities. It speaks about the more intimate details that first seem invisible but that become undeniable through the study of gestures.

3   In the photograph, the most prominent and symbolic of gestures is the use and position of the arms. Both my father and mother place an arm around me and in turn around each other. Their encircling arms, however, do more than just show affection; they unify the three

figures into a close huddle that leads the viewer's eye directly to them as opposed to the background or the periphery. The slightly bended arms that rest at their sides act as arrows that not only reinforce the three figures as the focal point but also exclude the fourth figure, my brother, from sharing the spotlight. Unlike the other members of the family whose arms and hands are intertwined, Edwin stands with both hands down in front of him, latching onto no one. The lack of physical contact between the huddled figures and Edwin is again emphasized as he positions himself away from the viewer's eye as he stands in the periphery.

4   Edwin's position in the photograph is indicative of him as a person, for he always seems to isolate himself from the spotlight, from being the center of attention. Thus, it is his decision to escape public scrutiny, not the force of my parents' arms that drives him to the side. His quiet, humble nature directs him away from even being the focal point of a picture and leads him towards establishing his own individuality and independence in privacy. His long hair and his "hand-me-down" clothes are all an expression of his simply being himself. The reason behind his physical independence is the emotional independence that he already possesses at the age of sixteen. He stands alone because he can stand alone.

5   While Edwin stands apart from the other three figures, I stand enclosed and protected. The lock of arms as well as the bouquet restrain me; they dissuade me from breaking away in favor of independence. Although my mother wants me to achieve the same kind of independence that Edwin has achieved, she works to delay the time when I actually will move away to the periphery. Perhaps my being the only daughter, the only other female in the family, has something to do with my mother's desire to keep me close and dependent as long as possible. Her arm reaches out with bouquet in hand as if to shield me from the world's unpleasantness. Even though my father also holds onto me with an encircling arm, it is my mother's firm grip that alone persuades me to stay within the boundary of their protective arms.

6   Her grip, which proves more powerful than my father's hold, restrains not only me but also my father. In the picture, he falls victim to the same outstretched hand, the same touch of the bouquet. Yet this time, my mother's bouquet does more than just restrain; it seems to push my father back "into line" or into his so-called place. The picture illustrates this exertion of influence well, for my mother in real life does indeed assume the role of the dominant figure. Although my father remains the head of the

household in title, it is my mother around whom the household revolves; she oversees the insignificant details as well as the major ones. But my father doesn't mind at all. Like me, he also enjoys the protection her restraining arm offers. It is because of our mutual dependence on my mother that my father and I seem to draw closer. This dependence in turn strengthens both of our relationships with my mother.

7   At the time the picture was taken, I seriously doubt that my mother realized the significance of her position in the picture or the import of her gestures. All of us in fact seem too blinded by the festivity of the occasion to realize that this photograph would show more than just a happy family at a daughter's graduation. The family photograph would inevitably become a telling portrait of each member of the family. It would, in a sense, leave us vulnerable to the speculative eyes of the viewer, who in carefully examining the photograph would recognize the secrets hidden in each frozen expression.

A few observations on these paragraphs may be useful. First, notice that each paragraph in the sequence examines a different aspect of the photograph and introduces a new point into the discussion. The first paragraph gives background information (the photograph was taken at Lee's graduation); the second paragraph states the writer's point—that studying the gestures of her family members enables us to understand their "personalities and relationships." Each succeeding paragraph treats one of these gestures (paragraph 2, for example, considers the encircling

arms) or one of the personalities or relationships. Paragraph 4 focuses on the writer's brother Edwin; paragraph 5 focuses on Lee's relationship to her mother; paragraph 6 focuses on her mother and father. We might think that symmetry requires that each family member get a single paragraph, but given the complexity of their relationships to each other, and given the mother's dominance in the family, it makes sense that things don't break down so neatly and that Lee devotes two paragraphs to her mother.

Second, notice how Lee makes the essay cohere. Although she uses some transitional words ("however" at the beginning of the second paragraph; "while" at the beginning of the fifth paragraph), she establishes coherence in this essay primarily by repeating the key terms of her discussion. The first sentence of each new paragraph picks up a word or phrase from the last sentence of the paragraph preceding it. The phrase "frozen expressions" links the end of the first paragraph to the beginning of the second; "gesture" links the second paragraph to the third; "position" links the third to the fourth; "stand" links the fourth to the fifth; and so on. These links are hardly noticeable on a first reading, but because Lee uses transitions and repetition effectively, the writing flows, and the reader never stumbles.

Paragraph Length

Although a paragraph can contain any number of sentences, two is probably too few, and ten might be too many. It is not a matter, however, of counting sentences; paragraphs are coherent blocks, substantial units of your essay, and the spaces between them are brief resting-places allowing the reader to take in what you have said. One double-spaced, word-processed page of writing (approximately 250 words) is about as much as the reader can take before requiring a slight break. On the other hand, a single page with half a dozen paragraphs is probably faulty because the reader is too often interrupted with needless pauses and because the page has too few *developed* ideas: An assertion is made, and then another, and another. These assertions are unconvincing because they are not supported with detail.

The Use and Abuse of Short Paragraphs

A short paragraph can be effective when it summarizes a highly detailed previous paragraph or group of paragraphs, or when it serves as a transition between two complicated paragraphs, but unless you are sure that the reader needs a break, avoid thin paragraphs. A paragraph that is

nothing but a transition can usually be altered into a transitional phrase or clause or sentence that starts the next paragraph. But of course there are times when a short paragraph is exactly right. Notice the effect of the two-sentence paragraph between two longer paragraphs:

> After I returned to prison, I took a long look at myself and, for the first time in my life, admitted that I was wrong, that I had gone astray—astray not so much from the white man's law as from being human, civilized— for I could not approve the act of rape. Even though I had some insight into my own motivations, I did not feel justified. I lost my self-respect. My pride as a man dissolved and my whole fragile moral structure seemed to collapse, completely shattered.
>
> That is why I started to write. To save myself.
>
> I realized that no one could save me but myself. The prison authorities were both uninterested and unable to help me. I had to seek out the truth and unravel the snarled web of my motivations. I had to find out who I am and what I want to be, what type of man I should be, and what I could do to become the best of which I was capable. I understood that what had happened to me had also happened to countless other blacks and it would happen to many, many more.
>
> —*Eldridge Cleaver*

If the content of the second paragraph were less momentous, it would hardly merit a paragraph. Here the brevity contributes to the enormous impact; those two simple sentences, set off by themselves, seem equal in weight, so to speak, to the longer paragraphs that precede and follow. They are the hinges on which the door turns.

When used for emphasis, short paragraphs can be effective.

Often, though, short paragraphs (like the one directly above) leave readers feeling unsatisfied, even annoyed. Consider these two consecutive paragraphs from a draft of a student's essay on Leonardo da Vinci's *Mona Lisa:*

> Leonardo's "Mona Lisa," painted about 1502, has caused many people to wonder about the lady's expression. Different viewers see different things.
>
> The explanation of the puzzle is chiefly in the mysterious expression that Leonardo conveys. The mouth and the eyes are especially important.

Sometimes you can improve a sequence of short paragraphs merely by joining one paragraph to the next. But unsatisfactory short paragraphs

Leonardo da Vinci, *Mona Lisa*. © Alinari/Art Resource.

usually cannot be repaired so simply: The source of the problem is usually not that sentences have been needlessly separated from each other, but that generalizations have not been supported by details, or that claims haven't been supported by evidence. Here is the student's revision, strengthening the two thin paragraphs of the draft.

Leonardo's "Mona Lisa," painted about 1502, has caused many people to wonder about the lady's expression. Doubtless she is remarkably lifelike but exactly what experience of life, what mood, does she reveal? Is she sad, or gently mocking, or uncertain or self-satisfied, or lost in daydreams? Why are we never satisfied when we try to name her emotion?

Part of the uncertainty may of course be due to the subject as a whole. What can we make out of the combination of this smiling woman and that utterly unpopulated landscape? But surely a large part of the explanation lies in the way that Leonardo painted the

```
face's two most expressive features, the eyes and the
mouth. He slightly obscured the corners of these, so
that we cannot precisely characterize them: although on
one viewing we may see them one way, on another viewing
we may see them slightly differently. If today we think
she looks detached, tomorrow we may think she looks
slightly threatening.
```

This revision is not simply a padded version of the earlier paragraphs; it is a necessary clarification of them, for without the details the generalizations mean almost nothing to a reader.

Introductory Paragraphs

As the poet Byron said, at the beginning of a long part of a long poem, "Nothing so difficult as a beginning." Almost all writers find that the first paragraphs in their drafts are false starts. As we suggest in Chapter 1, we think you shouldn't worry too much about the opening paragraph of your draft; you'll almost surely want to revise your opening later anyway.

When writing a first draft, you merely need something to break the ice. But in your finished paper the opening cannot be mere throat-clearing. The opening should be interesting. Here are some common *un*interesting openings to avoid:

1. A dictionary definition ("Webster says . . .").

2. A restatement of your title. The title is (let's assume) "Anarchism and the Marx Brothers," and the first sentence says, "This essay will study the anarchic acts of the Marx Brothers." True, the sentence announces the topic of the essay, but it gives no information about the topic beyond what the title already offers, and it provides no information about you either—that is, no sense of your response to the topic, such as might be present in, say, "The Marx Brothers are funny, but one often has the feeling that under the fun the violence has serious implications."

3. A broad generalization, such as "Ever since the beginning of time, human beings have been violent." Again, such a sentence may be fine if it helps you to start drafting, but it should not remain in your final version: It's dull—and it tells your readers almost nothing about the essay they're about to read. (Our example, after all, could begin anything from an analysis of *The Matrix* to a term paper on Liberia.) To put it another way, the ever-since-the-beginning-of-time opening

lacks substance—and if your opening lacks substance, it will not matter what you say next. You've already lost your reader's attention.

What is left? What *is* a good way for a final version to begin? Your introductory paragraph will be at least moderately interesting if it gives information, and it will be pleasing if the information provides focus—that is, if it lets the reader know exactly what your topic is, and where you will be going. Remember, when you write, *you* are the teacher; it won't do to begin with a vague statement:

```
George Orwell says he shot the elephant because . . .
```

We need some information, identifying the text you are writing about:

```
George Orwell, in "Shooting an Elephant," says he
shot the elephant because . . .
```

Even better is,

```
In "Shooting an Elephant," George Orwell sets forth
his reflections on his service as a policeman in
Burma. He suggests that he once shot an elephant
because . . . but his final paragraph suggests that
we must look for additional reasons.
```

Why is this opening better? Because it begins to suggest why the essay is worth reading. It points to a contradiction in the Orwell piece, a problem worth examining: Orwell says one thing, but that thing may not be entirely true.

Compare, for example, the opening sentences from three essays written by students on Anne Moody's *Coming of Age in Mississippi*. The book is the autobiography of an African-American woman, covering her early years with her sharecropper parents, her schooling, and finally her work in the civil rights movement.

```
The environment that surrounds a person from an early
age tends to be a major factor in determining their
character.
```

This is an all-purpose sentence that serves no specific purpose well; it could conceivably begin an essay on almost any topic: a study of the moral development of children, an analysis of the film *Seabiscuit*, a biog-

raphy of Napoleon. Notice also the faulty reference of the pronoun (the plural "their" refers to the singular "a person"), the weaseling of "tends to be a major factor," and the vagueness of "early age" and "environment" and "character." These all warn us that the writer will waste our time.

> It is unfortunate but true that racial or color prej-
> udice shows itself early in the life of a child.

Less pretentious than the first example, but it labors the obvious, sounds annoyingly preachy, and still doesn't say much about the topic at hand.

> Anne Moody's autobiography, Coming of Age in Missis-
> sippi, vividly illustrates how she discovered her
> identity as an African-American.

Surely this is the best of the three openings. Informative and focused, it identifies the book's theme and method, and it offers an evaluation. The essayist has been considerate of her readers: If we are interested in women's autobiographies or life in the South, we will read on. If we aren't, we are grateful to her for letting us off the bus at the first stop.

Let's look now not simply at an opening sentence but at an entire first paragraph, the opening paragraph of an analytic essay. Notice how the student provides the reader with the necessary information about the book she is discussing (the diary of a man whose son is brain-damaged) and also focuses the reader's attention on the essay's topic (the quality that distinguishes this diary from others).

> Josh Greenfeld's diary, A Place for Noah,
> records the attempts of a smart, thoughtful man to
> reconcile himself to his son's autism, a severe men-
> tal and physical disorder. Most diaries function as
> havens for secret thoughts, and Greenfeld's diary
> does frequently supply a voice to his darkest fears
> about who will ultimately care for Noah. It provides,
> too, an intimate glimpse of a family striving to
> remain a coherent unit despite their tragedy. But
> beyond affording such urgent and personal revela-
> tions, A Place for Noah, in chronicling the isolation
> of the Greenfelds, reveals how inadequate and inef-
> fectual our medical and educational systems are in

> responding to families victimized by catastrophic
> illness.

This example is engaging, in part because it indicates why a reader might be interested in reading the essay it begins: Greenfeld's book is more than just a diary; it also explores the consquences of a problem—catastrophic illness—that can affect anyone.

Of course you can provide interest and focus by other, more indirect means, among them the following:

- A quotation
- An anecdote or other short narrative
- An interesting fact (a statistic, for instance, showing the reader that you know something about your topic)
- A definition of an important term—but not merely one derived from a dictionary
- A question—but an interesting one, such as "Why do we call some words obscene?"
- A glance at a view different from your own
- An assertion that a problem exists

Many excellent opening paragraphs do not use any of these devices, and you need not use any of them if they feel forced. But in your reading you may observe that these devices are used widely. Here is an example of the second device, **an anecdote,** that makes an effective, indeed an unnerving, introduction to an essay on aging.

> There is an old American folk tale about a wooden bowl. It seems that Grandmother, with her trembling hands, was guilty of occasionally breaking a dish. Her daughter angrily gave her a wooden bowl, and told her that she must eat out of it from now on. The young granddaughter, observing this, asked her mother why Grandmother must eat from a wooden bowl when the rest of the family was given china plates. "Because she is old!" answered her mother. The child thought for a moment and then told her mother, "You must save the wooden bowl when Grandma dies." Her mother asked why, and the child replied, "For when you are old."
> —*Sharon R. Curtin*

The third strategy, **an interesting detail,** shows the reader that you know something about your topic and that you are worth reading. We have already seen (p. 32) a rather quiet example of this device, in a para-

graph about Charles Darwin, which began "Charles Darwin's youth was unmarked by signs of genius." Here is a more obvious example, from a student essay on blue jeans:

> That blue jeans or denims are not found only in Texas is not surprising if we recall that jeans are named for Genoa (Gene), where the cloth was first made, and that denim is cloth <u>de Nîmes</u>, that is, from Nîmes, a city in France.

(Such information is to be had by spending about thirty seconds with a dictionary.)

The fourth strategy, **a definition,** is fairly common in analytic essays; the essayist first clears the ground by specifying the topic. Here is the beginning of a student's essay on bilingual education.

> Let's begin by defining "bilingual education." As commonly used today, the term does <u>not</u> mean teaching students a language other than English. Almost everyone would agree that foreign-language instruction should be available, and that it is desirable for Americans to be fluent not only in English but also in some other language. Nor does "bilingual education" mean offering courses in English as a second language to students whose native language is, for example, Chinese, or Spanish or Navajo or Aleut. Again, almost everyone would agree that such instruction should be offered where economically possible. Rather, it means offering instruction in such courses as mathematics, history, and science <u>in the student's native language</u>, while also offering courses in English as a second language. Programs vary in details, but the idea is that the non-native speaker should be spared the trauma of total immersion in English until he or she has completed several years of studying English as a second language. During this period, instruction in other subjects is given in the student's native language.
>
> --Tina Bakka

The fifth strategy, **a question,** is briefly illustrated by the opening paragraph of an essay about whether it is sometimes permissible for doctors to lie to their patients.

Should doctors ever lie to benefit their patients—to speed recovery or to conceal the approach of death? In medicine as in law, government, and other lines of work, the requirements of honesty often seem dwarfed by greater needs: the need to shelter from brutal news or to uphold a promise of secrecy; to expose corruption or to promote the public interest.

—*Sissela Bok*

The sixth strategy, **a glance at the opposition,** is especially effective if the opposing view is well established, but while you state it, you should manage to convey your distrust of it. Here is an example:

One often hears, correctly, that there is a world food crisis, and one almost as often hears that not enough food is produced to feed the world's entire population. The wealthier countries, it is said, jeopardize their own chances for survival when they attempt to subsidize all of the poorer countries in which the masses are starving. Often the lifeboat analogy is offered: There is room in the boat for only X people, and to take in $X+1$ is to overload the boat and to invite the destruction of all. But is it true that the world cannot and does not produce enough food to save the whole population from starving?

—*V. Nagarajan*

The seventh strategy, **the assertion that a problem exists,** is common in essays that make proposals. The following example is the first paragraph of a grant proposal written by biomedical engineers seeking government funding for their research project, a new method for treating liver cancer. Notice that the paragraph does not offer the authors' proposal; it simply points out that there is an unsolved problem, and the reader infers that the proposal will offer the solution.

Liver cancer, especially metastatic colorectal cancer, is a significant and increasing health concern. In the United States, half of the 157,000 new cases of colorectal cancer will develop metastases in the liver. These metastases will lead to over 17,000 deaths annually. And while not as significant a health risk as colorectal metastasis, hepatocellular carcinoma is being diagnosed with increasing frequency. The current standard of practice for treating liver cancer is surgical resection, but only 10% of patients are eligible for this procedure. (Circumstances limiting eligibility include the tumor location, the number of lobes affected by the cancer, the patient's general poor health, and cirrhosis.) Moreover, fewer than 20% of those patients who undergo resection survive for three years without recurrence. Transplantation is an alternative to resection, but this technique is not appropriate for metastatic disease or for larger cancers, and the shortage of liver grafts limits the usefulness of this technique. Systemic chemotherapy has been shown to have a therapeutic effect on metastases, but it has also been shown to have no effect on long-term survival rates.

—Michael Curley and Patrick Hamilton

Clearly, there is no one way to write an opening paragraph, but we want to add that you cannot go wrong in beginning your essay—especially if it's an analytic essay written for a course in the humanities—with a paragraph that includes **a statement of your thesis.** A common version of this kind of paragraph follows this pattern:

- It offers some background (if you're writing about a novel, for example, you'll give the author and title as well as relevant information about the novel's plot).

- It suggests the problem the essay will address (in the paragraph below, the problem is implied: In *Frankenstein* similar characters meet very different fates; how can we account for the difference?).

- It ends with a sentence that states the main point, or thesis, of the essay.

In Frankenstein, Mary Shelley frames the novel with narratives of two similar characters who meet markedly different fates. Frankenstein, the medical researcher, and Walton, the explorer, are both passionately determined to push forward the boundaries of human knowledge. But while Walton's ambition to explore unknown regions of the earth is directed by reason and purpose, Frankenstein's ambition to create life is unfocussed and misguided. This difference in the nature of their ambitions determines their fates. Walton's controlled ambition leads him to abandon his goal in order to save the lives of his crew members. When we last see him, he is heading toward home and safety. Frankenstein's unchecked ambition leads to his own death and the self-destruction of his creature.

Concluding Paragraphs

Concluding paragraphs, like opening paragraphs, are especially difficult if only because they are so conspicuous. Fortunately, you are not always obliged to write one. Descriptive essays, for example, may end merely with a final paragraph, not with a paragraph that draws a conclusion. In an expository essay explaining a process or mechanism, you may simply stop when you have finished.

But if you do have to write a concluding paragraph, say something interesting. It is not of the slightest interest to say "Thus we see . . ." and then echo your title and first paragraph. There is some justification for a summary at the end of a long essay because the reader may have half forgotten some of the ideas presented thirty pages earlier, but an essay that can easily be held in the mind needs something more. A good concluding paragraph rounds out the previous discussion. Such a paragraph may offer a few sentences that summarize (it should not begin with the obvious dull phrase, "in summary"); but it will probably also draw an inference that has not previously been expressed. To draw such an inference is not to introduce an entirely new idea—the end of an essay is hardly the place for that. Rather it is to see the previous material in a fresh perspective, to take the discussion perhaps one step further.

Because all writers have to find out what they think about any given topic, and have to find the strategies appropriate for presenting these thoughts to a particular audience, we hesitate to offer a do-it-yourself kit for final paragraphs, but the following simple devices often work:

- End with a quotation, especially a quotation that amplifies or varies a quotation used in the opening paragraph.

- End with some idea or detail from the beginning of the essay and thus bring it full circle.

- End with a new (but related) point, one that takes your discussion a step further.

- End with an allusion, say to a historical or mythological figure or event, putting your topic in a larger framework.

- End with a glance at the readers—not with a demand that they mount the barricades, but with a suggestion that the next move is theirs.

If you adopt any of these devices, do so quietly; the aim is not to write a grand finale, but to complete or round out a discussion.

All essayists will have to find their own ways of ending each essay; the five strategies we have suggested are common, but they are not for you if you don't find them useful. And so, rather than ending this section with rules about how to end essays, we suggest how not to end them: Don't merely summarize, don't say "in conclusion," don't introduce a totally new point, and don't apologize.

CHECKLIST FOR REVISING PARAGRAPHS

☐ Does the paragraph *say* anything? Does it have substance? (See pp. 31–33.)

☐ Does the paragraph have a topic sentence? If so, is it in the best place? If the paragraph doesn't have a topic sentence, might one improve the paragraph? Or does the paragraph have a clear topic idea? (See pp. 34–36.)

☐ If the paragraph is an opening paragraph, is it interesting enough to attract and to hold a reader's attention? (See pp. 51–57.) If it is a later paragraph, does it easily evolve out of the previous paragraph and lead into the next paragraph? (See pp. 42–48.)

☐ Does the paragraph contain some principle of development—for instance, from cause to effect or from general to particular? What is the purpose of the paragraph? Does the paragraph fulfill the purpose? (See pp. 38–40.)

☐ Does each sentence clearly follow from the preceding sentence? Have you provided transitional words or cues to guide your reader? Would it be useful to repeat certain key words, for clarity? (See pp. 40–42.)

☐ Is the closing paragraph effective, or is it an unnecessary restatement of the obvious? (See pp. 58–59.)

CHAPTER FOUR

REVISING FOR CONCISENESS

> Excess is the common substitute for
> energy.
>
> —*Marianne Moore*

Writers who want to keep the attention and confidence of their audience revise for conciseness. The general rule is to say everything relevant in as few words as possible. The conclusion of the Supreme Court's decision in *Brown v. the Board of Education of Topeka,* for example—"Separate educational facilities are inherently unequal"—says it all in six words.

The writers of the following sentences bore us because they don't make every word count.

```
     There are two pine trees which grow behind this
house.
     On his left shoulder is a small figure standing.
He is about the size of the doctor's head.
     The judge is seated behind the bench and he is
wearing a judicial robe.
```

Compare those three sentences with these revisions:

```
     Two pine trees grow behind this house.
     On his left shoulder stands a small figure, about
the size of the doctor's head.
     The judge, wearing a robe, sits behind the bench.
```

The time to begin revising for conciseness is when you think you have an acceptable draft in hand—something that pretty much covers your topic and comes reasonably close to saying what you believe about it. As you go over your draft, study each sentence to see what can be deleted without loss of meaning. Read each paragraph, preferably aloud, to see if each sentence supports the topic sentence or idea and clarifies the point you are making. Leave in the concrete details and examples that support your ideas, but cut out all the deadwood that chokes them:

- Extra words
- Empty or pretentious phrases
- Weak qualifiers
- Redundancies
- Negative constructions
- Wordy uses of the verb *to be*
- Other extra verbs and verb phrases

Instant Prose

Here are some examples of Instant Prose from students' essays:

```
Frequently a chapter title in a book reveals to the
reader the main point that the author desires to
bring out during the course of the chapter.
```

We could try revising this, cutting the twenty-seven words down to seven:

```
A chapter's title often reveals its thesis.
```

But why bother? Unless the title is an exception, is the point worth making?

```
The two poems are basically similar in many ways, yet
they have their significant differences.
```

True, all poems are both similar to and different from other poems. Start over with your next sentence, perhaps something like:

```
The two poems, superficially similar in rough
paraphrase, are strikingly different in diction.
```

> Although the essay is simple in plot, the
> theme encompasses many vital concepts of emotional
> makeup.
> Following a transcendental vein, the nostalgia in
> the poem takes on a spiritual quality.
> Cassell only presents a particular situation con-
> cerning the issue, and with clear descriptions and a
> certain style sets up an interesting article.

These examples fall into the category of Unadulterated Instant Prose. Not even the writers of these sentences now know what they mean.

Writing Instant Prose is an acquired habit, like smoking cigarettes; fortunately it's easier to kick. It often begins in high school, sometimes earlier, when the victim is assigned a ten-page paper, or is told that a paragraph *must* contain at least three sentences, or that a thesis is stated in the introduction to an essay, elaborated in the body, and repeated in the conclusion. If the instructions appear arbitrary, and the student is bored or intimidated by them, the response is likely to be meaningless and mechanical.

Such students have forgotten the true purpose of writing—the discovery and communication of ideas, attitudes, and judgments. They concentrate instead on the word count: stuffing sentences, padding paragraphs, repeating points, and adding flourishes. Rewarded by a satisfactory grade, they repeat the performance, and in time, through practice, develop some fluency in spilling out words without thought or commitment, and almost without effort. Such students may enter college feeling somehow inauthentic, perhaps even aware that they don't really mean what they write—a sure symptom of habitual use of, or addiction to, Instant Prose.

How to Avoid Instant Prose

1. Trust yourself. Writing Instant Prose is not only a habit; it's also a form of alienation. If you habitually resort to Instant Prose, you probably don't think of what you write as your own but as something you produce on demand for someone else, most likely that unreasonable authority, the teacher, whose mysterious whims and insatiable appetite for words must somehow be satisfied. Breaking the habit begins with recognizing it. It means learning to respect your ideas and experiences, and determining that when you write, you'll write what you mean. This involves taking some risks, of course; habits offer some security or they would have no grip on us. Moreover, we all have moments when we doubt that our ideas are worth taking seriously. Keep writing honestly anyway. The self-doubts will pass; accomplishing something—writing one clear sentence—can help make them pass.

2. Learn to recognize Instant Prose Additives in your writing and in what you read. And you *will* find them in what you read—in textbooks and in academic journals, notoriously. Here's an example from a recent book on contemporary theater:

> One of the principal and most persistent sources of error that tends to bedevil a considerable proportion of contemporary literary analysis is the assumption that the writer's creative process is a wholly conscious and purposive type of activity.

Notice all the extra stuff in the sentence: "principal and most persistent," "tends to bedevil," "considerable proportion," "type of activity." Cleared of deadwood the sentence might read:

> The assumption that the writer's creative process is wholly conscious bedevils much contemporary criticism.

3. Acquire two things: a new habit, Revising for Conciseness; and what Isaac Singer calls "the writer's best friend," a wastebasket.

Extra Words and Empty Words

Delete extra words; replace vague, empty, or pretentious words and phrases with specific and direct language. Notice how, in the examples provided, the following words crop up: *significant, situation, involving, effect.* These words have legitimate uses but are often no more than Instant Prose Additives. Delete them whenever you can. Similar words to watch out for: *aspect, basically, facet, factor, fundamental, manner, nature, type, ultimate, utilization, viable, virtually, vital.* If they make your writing sound good, don't hesitate—cross them out at once.

Wordy

However, it must be remembered that Ruth's marriage could have positive effects on Naomi's situation.

Concise

Ruth's marriage, however, will also provide security for Naomi.

In the revision, the unnecessary "it must be remembered that" has been struck out. For the vague words "positive effects" and "situation," specific words have been substituted. The revision, though briefer, says more.

Wordy

In high school, where I had the opportunity for three years of working with the student government, I realized how significantly a person's enthusiasm could be destroyed merely by the attitudes of his superiors.

Concise

In high school, during three years on the student council, I saw students' enthusiasm destroyed by insecure teachers and cynical administrators.

Again, the revised sentence gives more information in fewer words. How?

Wordy

It creates a better motivation of learning when students can design their own programs involving education. This way students' interests can be focused on.

Concise

Motivation improves when students design their own programs, focused on their own interests.

Weak Intensifiers

Words like *very, quite, rather, completely, definitely,* and *so* can usually be struck from a sentence without loss. Paradoxically, sentences are often more emphatic without intensifiers. Try reading the following sentences both with and without the bracketed words:

At that time I was [very] idealistic.

We found the proposal [quite] feasible.

The scene was [extremely] typical.

The death scene is [truly] grotesque.

Always avoid using intensifiers with *unique.* Either something is unique—the only one of its kind—or it is not. It can't be very, quite, so, pretty, or fairly unique.

Circumlocutions

Roundabout or long-winded ways of saying things weaken your prose and tire your reader. Notice how each circumlocution in the first column is matched by a concise expression in the second.

I came to the realization that	I realized that
She is of the opinion that	She thinks that
The quotation is supportive of	The quotation supports
Concerning the matter of	About
During the course of	During
For the period of a week	For a week
In the event that	If
In the process of	During, while
Regardless of the fact that	Although
Due to the fact that	Because
For the simple reason that	Because
The fact that	That
Inasmuch as	Since
If the case was such that	If
It is often the case that	Often
In all cases	Always
I made contact with	I called, saw, phoned, wrote
At that point in time	Then
At this point in time	Now

Now revise this sentence:

> These movies have a large degree of popularity for the simple reason that they give the viewers insight in many cases.

Wordy Beginnings

Vague words and phrases sometimes clog the beginnings of sentences. They're like elaborate windups before the pitch.

Wordy

By analyzing carefully the last lines in this stanza, you find the connections between the loose ends of the poem.

Concise

The last lines of the stanza connect the loose ends of the poem.

Wordy

What the cartoonist is illustrating and trying to get across is the greed of the oil producers.

Concise

The cartoon illustrates the greed of the oil producers.

Wordy

In opposition to the situation of the younger son is that of the elder who remained in his father's house, working hard and handling his inheritance wisely.

Concise

The elder son, by contrast, remained in his father's house, worked hard, and handled his inheritance wisely.

Notice that when the deadwood is cleared from the beginning of the sentence, the subject appears early, and the main verb appears close to it:

The last lines . . . connect. . . .

The cartoon illustrates. . . .

The elder son . . . remained. . . .

Locating the right noun for the subject, and the right verb for the predicate, is the key to revising sentences with wordy beginnings.

Empty Conclusions

Often a sentence that begins well has an empty conclusion. The words go on but the sentence seems to stand still; if it's not revised, it requires another sentence to explain it.

Empty

"Those Winter Sundays" is composed so that a reader can feel what the poet was saying. (How is it composed? What is he saying?)

Informative

"Those Winter Sundays" describes the speaker's anger as a child, and his remorse as an adult.

Empty

In both Orwell's and Baldwin's essays the feeling of white supremacy is very important. (Why is white supremacy important?)

Informative

Both Orwell and Baldwin trace the insidious consequences of white supremacy.

Wordy Uses of the Verbs To Be, To Have, *and* To Make

Notice that in the preceding unrevised sentences a form of the verb *to be* introduces the empty conclusion: *"was* saying," *"is* very important." In each revision, the right verb added and generated substance. In the following sentences, substitutions for the verb *to be* both invigorate and shorten otherwise substantial sentences. (The wordy expressions are italicized, and so are the revisions.)

Wordy

The scene *is taking place* at night, in front of the capitol building.

Concise

The scene *takes place* at night, in front of the capitol building.

Wordy

In this shoeshining and early rising *there are indications* of church attendance.

Concise

The early rising and shoeshining *indicate* church attendance.

Wordy

The words "flashing," "rushing," "plunging," and "tossing" *are suggestive of* excitement.

Concise

The words "flashing," "rushing," "plunging," and "tossing" *suggest* excitement.

A RULE FOR WRITERS

Whenever you can, replace a form of the verb *to be* with a stronger verb.

To Be	**Strong Verb**
and a participle (*is taking*)	*takes*
and a noun (*are indications*)	*indicate*
and an adjective (*are suggestive*)	*suggest*

In the following example, substitutions for the verbs *to have* and *to make* shorten and enliven the sentence.

Wordy

The Friar *has knowledge* that Juliet is alive.

Concise

The Friar *knows* that Juliet is alive.

Wordy

The stanzas *make a vivid contrast* between Heaven and Hell.

Concise

The stanzas *vividly contrast* Heaven and Hell.

Like all rules, this one has exceptions. We don't list them here; you'll discover them by listening to your sentences.

Redundancy

Redundancy refers to unnecessary repetition in the expression of ideas. "Future plans," after all, are only plans, and "to glide smoothly" or "to scurry rapidly" is only to glide or to scurry. Unlike repetition, which often provides emphasis or coherence (for example, "government of the people, by the people, for the people"), redundancy can always be eliminated.

Redundant

Any student could randomly sit anywhere. (If the students could sit anywhere, the seating was random.)

Concise

Students could sit anywhere.

Students chose their seats at random.

Redundant

In the orthodox Cuban culture, the surface of the female role seemed degrading. [Perhaps this sentence means what it says. More probably "surface" and "seemed" are redundant.]

Concise

In the orthodox Cuban culture, the female role seemed degrading.

In the orthodox Cuban culture, the female role was superficially degrading.

Redundant

In "Araby" the boy feels alienated emotionally from his family.

Concise

In "Araby" the boy feels alienated from his family.

What words can be crossed out of the following phrases?

throughout the entire article

her attitude of indifference

a conservative type suit

his own personal opinion

elements common to both of them

emotions and feelings

shared together

alleged suspect

Many phrases in common use are redundant. For example, there is no need to write "blare noisily," since the meaning of the adverb "noisily" is conveyed in the verb "blare." Watch for phrases like these when you revise:

round in shape	resulting effect
tall in stature	prove conclusively
must necessarily	connected together
basic fundamentals	very unique
true fact	very universal
free gift	the reason why is because

Negative Constructions

Negative constructions are often wordy and sometimes pretentious.

Wordy

Housing for married students is *not unworthy of* consideration.

Concise

Housing for married students is worth considering.

Better

The trustees should earmark funds for married students' housing. [Probably what the author meant.]

"See what I mean? You're never sure just where you stand with them." © The
New Yorker Collection 1971. Al Rossi from Cartoonbank.com. All Rights Reserved.

The Golden Rule of writing is "Write for others as you would have them
write for you," not "Write for others in a manner not unreasonably dis-
similar to the manner in which you would have them write for you."

Extra Sentences, Extra Clauses: Subordination

Sentences are sometimes wordy because ideas are given more elaborate
grammatical constructions than they need. When revising, try to reduce
these constructions. Two sentences, for example, may be reduced to one,
or a clause may be reduced to a phrase.

Wordy

The Book of Ruth was probably written in the fifth century B.C. It was
a time when women were considered the property of men.

Concise

The Book of Ruth was probably written in the fifth century B.C., when women were considered the property of men.

Wordy

The first group was the largest. This group was seated in the center of the dining hall.

Concise

The first group, the largest, was seated in the center of the dining hall.

Who, Which, That

Watch for clauses beginning with *who, which,* and *that.*

Wordy

George Orwell is the pen name of Eric Blair, *who was* an English writer.

Concise

George Orwell is the pen name of Eric Blair, an English writer.

Wordy

They are seated at a table *which* is covered with a patched and tattered cloth.

Concise

They are seated at a table covered with a patched and tattered cloth.

Wordy

There is one feature *that is* grossly out of proportion.

Concise

One feature is grossly out of proportion.

For further discussion of *which* clauses, see "A Writer's Glossary" in Chapter 12 (p. 299).

It Is, This Is, There Are

Watch for sentences and clauses beginning with *it is, this is, there are* (again, wordy uses of the verb *to be*). These expressions often lead to a *which* or a *that,* but even when they don't they may be wordy.

Wordy

This is a quotation from Black Elk's autobiography *which* discloses his prophetic powers.

Concise

This quotation from Black Elk's autobiography discloses his prophetic powers.

Wordy

It is frequently considered *that Hamlet* is Shakespeare's most puzzling play.

Concise

Hamlet is frequently considered Shakespeare's most puzzling play.

Wordy

In Notman's photograph of Buffalo Bill and Sitting Bull *there are* definite contrasts between the two figures.

Concise

Notman's photograph of Buffalo Bill and Sitting Bull contrasts the two figures.

Some Concluding Remarks About Conciseness

We spoke earlier about how students succumb to Instant Prose and acquire other wordy habits—by writing what they think the teacher has asked for. We haven't forgotten that instructors assign papers of a certain length in college too. But the length given is not an arbitrary limit that must be reached—the instructor who asks for a ten-page paper is probably trying to tell you that it's likely to take you ten pages to develop your ideas on the topic at hand. Such, apparently, was the intention of William Randolph Hearst, the newspaper publisher, who cabled an astronomer, "Is there life on Mars? Cable reply 1000 words." The astronomer's reply was, "Nobody knows," repeated 500 times.

What do you do when you've been asked to produce a ten-page paper and after diligent writing and revising you find you've said everything relevant to your topic in seven and a half pages? Our advice is, hand it in. We can't remember ever counting the words or pages of a substantial, interesting essay; we assume that our colleagues elsewhere are equally reasonable and equally overworked. If we're wrong, tell us about it—in writing, and in the fewest possible words.

CHECKLIST FOR REVISING FOR CONCISENESS

☐ Does every word count? Can any words or phrases be cut without loss of meaning?

☐ Are there any empty or pretentious words such as *situation, factor, virtually, significant,* and *utilize?* (See pp. 63–63.)

☐ Do intensifiers such as *very, truly,* and *rather* weaken your sentences? (See p. 64.)

☐ Are there any roundabout or long-winded locutions? Do you say, for example, *at that point in time* when you mean *then,* or *for the simple reason that* when you mean *because?* (See pp. 64–65, 68–69.)

☐ Do sentences get off to a fast start? Can you cut any sentences that open with "it is . . . that"? (See pp. 65–66.)

☐ Can you replace forms of the verbs *to be, to have,* and *to make* with precise and active verbs? (See pp. 67–68.)

☐ Are there any redundancies or negative constructions? (See pp. 68–70.)

☐ Can any sentences be combined using subordination? (See pp. 70–71.)

CHAPTER FIVE

REVISING FOR CLARITY

Here's to plain speaking and clear understanding.

—*Sidney Greenstreet, in* The Maltese Falcon

Clarity

First, read the following two examples:

> We have seen new realities created by the advance of physics. But this chain of creation can be traced back far beyond the starting point of physics. One of the most primitive concepts is that of an object. The concepts of a tree, a horse, any material body, are creations gained on the basis of experience, though the impressions from which they arise are primitive in comparison with the world of physical phenomena. A cat teasing a mouse also creates, by thought, its own primitive reality. The fact that the cat reacts in a similar way toward any mouse it meets shows that it forms concepts and theories which are its guide through its own world of sense impressions.
>
> —*Albert Einstein and Leopold Infeld*

> Skills constitute the manipulative techniques of human goal attainment and control in relation to the physical world, so far as artifacts or machines especially designed as tools do not yet supplement them. Truly human skills are guided by organized and codified ***knowledge*** of both

the things to be manipulated and the human capacities that are used to manipulate them. Such knowledge is an aspect of cultural-level symbolic processes, and, like other aspects to be discussed presently, requires the capacities of the human central nervous system, particularly the brain. This organic system is clearly essential to all of the symbolic processes; as we well know, the human brain is far superior to the brain of any other species.

—Talcott Parsons

Why is the first passage easier to understand than the second?

Both passages discuss the relationship between the brain and the physical world it attempts to understand. The first passage, by Einstein and Infeld, is, if anything, more complex both in what it asserts and in what it suggests than the second, by Parsons. Both passages explain that the brain organizes sense impressions. But Einstein and Infeld further explain that the history of physics can be understood as an extension of the simplest sort of organization, such as we all make in distinguishing a tree from a horse, or such as even a cat makes in teasing a mouse. Parsons only promises that "other aspects" will "be discussed presently." How many of us are eager for those next pages?

Good writing is clear, not because it presents simple ideas but because it presents ideas in the simplest form the subject permits. A clear analysis doesn't falsely reduce a complex problem to a simple one; it breaks it down into its simple, comprehensible parts and discusses them, one by one. A clear paragraph explains one of these parts coherently, and in language as simple and as particular as the reader's understanding requires and the context allows. Where Parsons writes of "organized and codified *knowledge* of . . . the things to be manipulated," Einstein and Infeld write simply of the concept of an object. And even "object," a simple but general word, is further clarified by the specific, familiar examples, "tree" and "horse." Parsons writes of "the manipulative techniques of . . . goal attainment and control in relation to the physical world, so far as artifacts or machines especially designed as tools do not yet supplement them." Einstein and Infeld show us a cat teasing a mouse.

Notice also the clear organization of Einstein and Infeld's paragraph. The first sentence, clearly transitional, refers to the advance of physics traced in the preceding pages. The next sentence, introduced by "But," reverses our direction: We are now going to look not at an advance, but at primitive beginnings. And the following sentences, to the end of the paragraph, fulfill that promise. We move back to primitive human concepts, clarified by examples, and finally to the still more primitive example of the cat. Parson's paragraph is also organized, but the route is much more difficult to follow.

Why do people write obscurely? It's difficult to write clearly.[1] Authorities may be obscure not because they want to tax you with unnecessary problem, but because they don't know how to avoid them. If you have ever tried to install a computer upgrade by following the "easy instructions," you know that the simplest kind of expository writing, giving instructions, can foil the writers most eager for your goodwill (that is, those who want you to use their products). Few instructions, unfortunately, are as unambiguous as "Go to jail. Go directly to jail. Do not pass Go. Do not collect $200."

You can, though, learn to write clearly, by learning to recognize common sources of obscurity in writing and by consciously revising your own work. We offer, to begin with, three general rules:

- Use the simplest, most exact, most specific language your subject allows.

- Put together what belongs together, in the essay, in the paragraph, and in the sentence.

- Keep your reader in mind, particularly when you revise.

Now for more specific advice, and examples—the cats and mice of revising for clarity.

Clarity and Exactness: Using the Right Word

Denotation

Be sure the word you choose has the right explicit meaning, or *denotation.* Did you mean *sarcastic* or *ironic? Fatalistic* or *pessimistic? Disinterested* or *uninterested? Biannual* or *semiannual? Enforce* or *reinforce? Use* or *usage?* If you're not sure, check the dictionary. You'll find some of the most commonly misused words discussed in "A Writer's Glossary," Chapter 12, pages 278–301. Here are examples of a few others:

> Daru faces a dilemma between his humane feelings and his conceptions of justice. [Strictly speaking, a dilemma requires a choice between two equally unattractive alternatives. "Conflict" would be a better word here.]

> However, as time dragged on, exercising seemed to lose its charisma. [What is charisma? Why is it inexact here?]

[1]Our first draft of this sentence read "Writing clearly is difficult." Can you see why we changed it?

"I'm not quite clear on this, Fulton. Are you moaning about your prerequisites, your requisites, or perquisites?" © The New Yorker Collection 1976. Mischa Richter from Cartoonbank.com. All Rights Reserved.

When I run, I don't allow myself to stop until I have reached my destiny. [What is the difference between *destiny* and *goal?*]

Connotation

Be sure the word you choose has the right *connotation* (association, implication). As Mark Twain said, the difference between the right word and the almost right word is the difference between lightning and the lightning bug.

Boston politics has always upheld the reputation of being especially crooked. [*Upheld* inappropriately suggests that Boston has proudly maintained its reputation. *Has always had* would be appropriate here, but pale. *Deserved* would, in this context, be ironic, implying—accurately—the writer's scorn.)

This book, unlike many other novels, lacks tedious descriptive passages. ["Lacks" implies a deficiency. How would you revise the sentence?]

New Orleans, notorious for its good jazz and good food. . . . [Is *notorious* the right word here, or *famous?*]

Sunday, Feb. 9. Another lingering day at Wellesley. [In this entry from a student's journal, "lingering" strikes us as right. What does "lingering" imply about Sundays at Wellesley that "long" would not?]

Because words have connotations, most writing—even when it pretends to be objective—conveys attitudes as well as facts. Consider, for example, this passage by Jessica Mitford, describing part of the procedure used for embalming:

> A long, hollow needle attached to a tube . . . is jabbed into the abdomen, poked around the entrails and chest cavity, the contents of which are pumped out. . . .

Here, as almost always, the writer's *purpose* in large measure determines the choice of words. Probably the sentence accurately describes part of the procedure, but it also, of course, records Mitford's contempt for the procedure. Suppose she wanted to be more respectful—suppose, for example, she were an undertaker writing an explanatory pamphlet. Instead of the needle being "jabbed" it would be "inserted," and instead of being "poked around the entrails" it would be "guided around the viscera," and the contents would not be "pumped out" but would be "drained." Mitford's words would be the wrong words for an undertaker explaining embalming to apprentices or to the general public, but, given her purpose, they are exactly the right ones because they clearly convey her attitude.

Notice, too, that many words have social, political, or sexist overtones. What is implied by the distinction? Consider the differences in *connotation* in each of the following series:

underdeveloped nations, developing nations, emerging nations

preference, bias, prejudice

upbringing, conditioning, brainwashing

intelligence gathering, espionage, spying

antiabortion, pro-life; pro-abortion, pro-choice

Avoiding Sexist Language

Traditionally, the pronouns *he* and *his* have been used as generic pronouns when both men and women are implied: "A historian must consider the context of *his* source." But contemporary writers avoid the generic use of male pronouns, because such usage is sexist (our example excludes women historians from the discussion), and because it can be misleading and unclear (the example may suggest that there are no women historians, or that women historians do something different from the men). They commonly turn to three remedies in their writing:

- Using both male and female pronouns: "A historian must consider the context of *his* or *her* source."
- Substituting the plural form: "*Historians* must consider the context of *their* source."
- Eliminating the pronoun: "Historians must consider a source's context."

Note: Writers and speakers sometimes attempt to correct sexist language by using a plural pronoun with a singular subject: "A *historian* must consider *their* source's context." But this approach produces ungrammatical sentences: The pronoun doesn't agree with its antecedent. (For more on agreement, see p. 99.) Writers also sometimes use such constructions as "his/her," "him/her," or "s/he": "A historian must consider his/her source." While not incorrect, we think that this approach produces ugly sentences, and we recommend that you use one of the three remedies above.

Likewise, avoid using "man" and "mankind" generically:

Man's need for approval. . . .

Substitute gender-neutral terms for gender-specific terms whenever possible—unless, of course, your sentence refers specifically to one gender. The sentence above could thus be revised:

Humanity's need for approval. . . .

Our need for approval. . . .

Here are more examples of gender-specific or sexist terms, with possible replacements:

Sexist Term	Gender-Neutral Term
chairman	chairperson, chair, head
manpower	personnel
layman	layperson
stewardess	flight attendant

Sexist Term	Gender-Neutral Term
freshman	first-year student
mailman	mail carrier
poetess	poet

Quotation Marks as Apologies

When you have used words with exact meanings (denotations) and appropriate associations (connotations) for your purpose, don't apologize for them by putting quotation marks around them. If the words *copped a plea*, *ripped off*, or *kids* suit your purpose better than *plea-bargained*, *stolen*, or *children*, use them. If they are inappropriate, don't put them in quotation marks; find the right words.

Being Specific

When writing descriptions, catch the richness, complexity, and uniqueness of things. Suppose, for example, you are describing a scene from your childhood, a setting you loved. There was, in particular, a certain tree . . . and you write: "Near the water there was a big tree that was

© Bill Griffith. Reprinted with special permission of King Features Syndicate.

rather impressive." Most of us would produce something like that sentence. Here is the sentence Ernesto Galarza wrote in *Barrio Boy:*

> On the edge of the pond, at the far side, there was an enormous walnut tree, standing like an open umbrella whose ribs extended halfway across the still water of the pool.

We probably could not have come up with the metaphor of the umbrella because we wouldn't have seen the similarity. (As Aristotle observed, the gift for making metaphors distinguishes the poet from the rest of us.) But we can all train ourselves to be accurate observers and reporters. For "the water" (general) we can specify "pond"; for "near" we can say how near, "on the edge of the pond," and add the specific location, "at the far side"; for "tree" we can give the species, "walnut tree"; and for "big" we can provide a picture, its branches "extended halfway across" the pond: It was, in fact, "enormous."

Galarza does not need to add limply, as we did, that the tree "was rather impressive." The tree he describes *is* impressive. That he accurately remembered it persuades us that he was impressed, without his having to tell us he was. For writing descriptions, a good general rule is: Show, don't tell.

Be as specific as you can be in all forms of exposition too. Take the time, when you revise, to find the exact word to replace vague phrases or clichés. In the following examples we have to guess or invent what the writer means.

Vague

The clown's part in *Othello* is very small.

Specific

The clown appears in only two scenes in *Othello.*

The clown in *Othello* speaks only thirty lines. [Notice the substitution of the verb *appears* or *speaks* for the frequently debilitating *is.* And in place of the weak intensifier *very* we have specific details to tell us how small the role is.]

Vague

He feels uncomfortable at the whole situation. [Many feelings are uncomfortable. Which one does he feel? What's the situation?]

Specific

He feels guilty for having distrusted his father.

Vague Cliché

Then she criticized students for living in an ivory tower. [Did she criticize them for being detached or for being secluded? For social irresponsibility or studiousness?]

Specific

Then she criticized students for being socially irresponsible.

Using Examples

In addition to exact words and specific details, illustrative examples make for clear writing. Einstein and Infeld, in the passage quoted on page 74, use as an example of a primitive concept a cat teasing not only its first mouse but also "any mouse it meets." Here is another passage from *Barrio Boy*; like the paragraph from Einstein and Infeld, this paragraph clarifies and develops its topic through examples:

> In Jalco people spoke in two languages—Spanish and with gestures. These signs were made with the face or hands or a combination of both. If you bent one arm and tapped the elbow with the other hand, it meant "He is stingy." When you sawed one arm across the other you were saying that someone you knew played the fiddle terribly. To say that a man was a tippler you made a set of cow's horns with the little finger and the thumb of one hand, bending the three middle fingers to the palm and pointing the thumb at your mouth. And if you wanted to indicate, without saying so for the sake of politeness, that a mutual acquaintance was daffy, you tapped three times on your forehead with your middle finger.
>
> —*Ernesto Galarza*

Now look at a student's paragraph, here printed in the left column, from an essay whose thesis is that rage can be a useful mechanism for effecting change. Then compare the left-hand paragraph with the same paragraph, revised, at the right. Note the specific ways, sentence by sentence, the student revised for clarity.

In my high school we had little say in the learning processes that were used. The subjects that we were required to take were irrelevant. One had to take them to earn enough points to	In my high school we had little say about our curriculum. We were required, for example, to choose either American or European History to earn enough points for graduation. We wanted, but were at

graduate. Some of the teachers were sympathetic to our problem. They would tell us about when they were young, how they tried to oppose their school system. But when they were young it was a long time ago, for most of them. The principal would call assemblies to speak on the subject. They were entitled "The Value of an Education" or "Get a Good Education to Have a Bright Future." The titles were not inviting. They had nothing to do with our plight. Most students never came to any agreements with the principal because most of his thoughts and views seemed old and outdated.

first refused, the option of Black History. Some of our teachers were sympathetic with us; one told me about her fight opposing the penmanship course required in her school. Nor was the principal totally indifferent--he called assemblies. I remember one talk he gave called "The Value of an Education in Today's World," and another, "Get a Good Education to Have a Bright Future." I don't recall hearing about a Black History course in either talk. Once, he invited a group of us to meet with him in his office, but we didn't reach any agreement. He solemnly showed us an American History text (not the one we used) that had a whole chapter devoted to Black History.

Jargon and Technical Language

Most dictionaries give three meanings for *jargon:* technical language, meaningless language, and inflated or pretentious language.

The members of almost every profession or trade—indeed, almost all people who share any specialized interest—use the jargon of their field. And this is certainly true of members of academic disciplines. In fact, learning a new discipline involves learning a new vocabulary, a new set of technical terms. Art historians talk of *cubism, iconography,* and *formalism;* Freudians talk of *cathect, libido,* and the *oral phase;* film critics and theorists talk of *anamorphic lenses, optical printers,* and *silent speed.*

Untitled, 1949. Willem de Kooning, American (b. 1904). Black enamel. © 2004 The Willem de Kooning Foundation/Artists Rights Society (ARS), New York.

Properly used, technical language communicates information concisely and clearly, and it can create a comfortable bond between speakers, or between the writer and the reader.

For example, in the following sentences, concerned with twentieth-century art from a museum publication, the writer reasonably assumes that her readers—most likely people who are interested in and knowledgeable about art—will be able to make sense of such technical terms as "biomorphic," "calligraphic," "gesture," and "Abstract Expressionism":

> In Willem de Kooning's biomorphic black enamel drawing . . . drawn for a member of the Julliard String Quartet, the artist has abandoned the idea of a central organizing form. Black calligraphic shapes whip across the surface of the paper. There is a sense of gesture, an essential feature of Abstract Expressionism.

On the other hand, jargon sometimes *is* inflated and pretentious. Consider, for example, the following sentence by an art historian writing on American Indian baskets made for whites in the early twentieth century:

DILBERT reprinted by permission of United Feature Syndicate, Inc.

Native curios were privileged in bourgeois parlor decoration as metonymic representations of the premodern, their significations enhanced by hand-made production and utilitarian function, two aspects of the premodern also valorized in the contemporary American Arts and Crafts Movement.

This sentence does communicate information to specialists. In fact, much academic prose sounds an awful lot like the quoted sentence. Nevertheless, we believe that such language doesn't communicate clearly and efficiently. One problem with the sentence is that the level of abstraction is very high. Unlike the term "biomorphic," which means "evoking images of biological organisms," or the term "calligraphic," which here describes figures that recall the curves and loops of handwriting, the terms "premodern," "significations," and "valorized" don't call to mind specific, concrete things. The other problem with such language is that it is inflated, or more complicated than it needs to be. Consider the following paraphrase of the sentence on baskets:

Middle-class whites valued native curios and displayed them in their parlors. Because these objects were handmade and because they had been used in daily life, they stood for a pre-industrial world, a world celebrated also in the contemporary American Arts and Crafts Movement.

In general, it's best to use plain English—or, at least, the plainest English possible. After all, in an essay you wouldn't speak of a "preliminary overall strategizing concept" when "plan" would do. Don't use abstract, inflated language simply in order to sound impressive. On the other hand, do use the specialized terms of your field if you have come to know what they mean, and if they are the best way to make your point, and if you are fairly confident that your imagined reader is familiar with them. If it's your hunch that your reader does not know the terms, you'll have to define them.

Clichés

Clichés (literally, in French, molds from which type is cast) are trite expressions, mechanically reproduced. Since they are available without thought, they are great Instant Prose Additives (see pp. 61–63). Writers who use Clichés are usually surprised to be criticized: They find the phrases attractive and may even think them exact. (Phrases become clichés precisely because they have wide appeal and therefore wide use.) But clichés, by their very nature, cannot communicate the uniqueness of your thoughts. Furthermore, because they come instantly to mind, they tend to block the specific detail or exact expression that will let the reader know what precisely is in your mind. In revising, when you strike out a cliché, you force yourself to do the work of writing clearly. How many clichés can you spot in the following example?

> Finally, the long awaited day arrived. Up bright and early. . . . She peered at me with suspicion; then a faint smile crossed her face.

Here are some other worn-out phrases to avoid:

first and foremost	time honored
the acid test	bustled to and fro
fatal flaw	short but sweet
budding genius	few and far between
slowly but surely	D-day arrived
little did I know	sigh of relief
the big moment	last but not least

In attempting to avoid clichés, however, don't go to the other extreme of wildly original, super-vivid writing—"'Well then, say something to her,' he roared, his whole countenance gnarled in rage." It's better to

write, "he said." (Anyone who intends to write dialogue should memorize Ring Lardner's intentionally funny line, "'Shut up!' he explained.")

Metaphors and Mixed Metaphors

Ordinary speech abounds with metaphors. We speak or write of the *foot of a mountain*, the *germ of an idea*, the *root of a problem*. Metaphors so deeply embedded in the language that they no longer evoke pictures in our minds are called **dead metaphors.** Usually they offer us, as writers, no problems: We need neither seek them nor avoid them; they are simply there. (Notice, for example, "embedded" two sentences back.) Such metaphors become problems, however, when we unwittingly call them back to life, as Howard Nemerov observes: "That these metaphors may be not dead but only sleeping, or that they may arise from the grave and walk in our sentences, is something that has troubled everyone who has ever tried to write plain expository prose."

Dead metaphors are most likely to haunt us when they are embodied in clichés. Since we use clichés without attention to what they literally say or point to, we are unlikely to be aware of the dead metaphors buried in them. But when we attach one cliché to another, we may raise the metaphors from the grave. The result is likely to be a **mixed metaphor;** the effect is almost always absurd.

Water seeks its own level whichever way you want to slice it.

Traditional liberal education has run out of gas and educational soup kitchens are moving into the vacuum.

The low ebb has been reached and hopefully it's turned the corner.

Her energy, drained through a stream of red tape, led only to closed doors.

As comedian Joe E. Lewis observed, "Show me a man who builds castles in the air and I'll show you a crazy architect."

Fresh metaphors, on the other hand, imaginatively combine accurate observations. They are not prefabricated ideas; they are a means of discovering or inventing new ideas. They enlarge thought and enliven prose. Here are two examples from students' journals:

```
    I have some sort of sporadic restlessness in me,
like the pen on a polygraph machine. It moves along in
curves, then suddenly shoots up, blowing a bubble in my
throat, making my chest taut, forcing me to move
around. It becomes almost unbearable and then suddenly
it will plunge, leaving something that feels like a
smooth orange wave.
    Time is like wrapping papers. It wraps memories,
decorates them with sentiment. No matter (almost)
what's inside, it's remembered as a beautiful piece of
past time. That's why I even miss my high school years,
which were filled with tiredness, boredom, confusion.
```

And here is a passage from an essay in which a student analyzes the style of a story he found boring:

```
Every sentence yawns, stretches, shifts from side to
side, and then quietly dozes off.
```

Experiment with metaphors, let them surface in the early drafts of your essays and in your journals, and by all means, introduce original and accurate comparisons in your essays. But leave the mixed metaphors to politicians and comedians.

Euphemisms

Euphemisms are words substituted for other words thought to be offensive. In deodorant advertisements there are no *armpits*, only *underarms*, which may *perspire*, but not *sweat*, and even then they don't *smell*. A parent reading a report card is likely to learn not that his child got an F in conduct but that she "experiences difficulty exercising self-control: (a) verbally (b) physically." And where do old people go? To Sun City, "a retirement community for senior citizens."

We do not advise you to write or speak discourteously; we do advise you, though, to use euphemisms sparingly, when tact recommends them. It's customary in a condolence letter to avoid the word *death*, and, depending both on your own feelings and those of the bereaved, you may wish to follow that custom. But there's no reason on earth to write "Hamlet passes on." You should be aware, moreover, that some people find euphemisms themselves offensive. Margaret Kuhn, for instance, argues that the word *old* is preferable to *senior*. "Old," she says "is the right word. . . . I think we should wear our gray hair, wrinkles, and crumbling joints as badges of distinction. After all, we worked damn hard to get them."

When revising, replace needless euphemisms with plain words.

Passive or Active Voice?

Verbs appear in either the active or passive voice. In the active voice, the subject acts on the object: "I wrote the review." ("I" is the subject.) In the passive voice, the subject receives the action: "The review was written by me." (Here, "the review" is the subject.) In general prefer the active voice. The passive voice is often vague and sentences using it are needlessly wordy.

Consider the following passage, the opening paragraph of an analytic essay on the classical aspects of a library at a women's college:

> A person walking by Margaret Clapp Library (1908–1913) is struck by its classical design. The symmetry of the façade is established by the regularly spaced columns of the Ionic order on the first story of the building and by pilasters on the second level. In the center of the lower tier are two bronze doors: On the left door a relief is seen, depicting Sapientia (Wisdom), and on the right is seen the image of Caritas (Charity). The Greco-Roman tradition is furthered by the two bronze statues on either side of the entrance. On the left is Vesta (goddess of the hearth) and on the right Minerva (goddess of wisdom). Through the use of classical architecture and Greco-Roman images, an image is conveyed—one which Wellesley College hopes to create in its women.

Although the paragraph is richly informative, it is sluggish, chiefly because the writer keeps using the passive voice: "A person . . . is struck by"; "symmetry is established by"; "a relief is seen"; "on the right is seen"; "tradition is furthered by"; "an image is conveyed."

Converting some or all of these expressions into the active voice greatly improves the passage:

> The most striking feature of the Margaret Clapp Library is its classical design. Regularly spaced columns of the Ionic order on the first story, and pilasters on the second, establish the symmetry of the façade. In the center of the lower tier are two bronze doors: On the left door a relief depicts Sapientia (Wisdom), and on the right Caritas (Charity). A bronze statue on each side of the entrance (Vesta, goddess of the hearth, on the left, and Minerva, goddess of wisdom, on the right) furthers the Greco-Roman tradition. Wellesley College hopes, through the use of classical architecture and Greco-Roman sculpture, to inspire in its students particular ideals.

There are, however, times when the passive is appropriate: (1) when the doer is obvious ("Bush was elected president in 2000"), (2) when the doer is unknown ("The picture was stolen between midnight and 1:00 A.M."), and (3) when the doer is unimportant ("Unexposed film should be kept in a light-proof container").

When revising, consider each sentence in which you have used the passive voice. If the passive suits your meaning, retain it; if it obscures your meaning, change it. More often than not, the passive voice obscures meaning.

Passive Voice

The revolver given Daru by the gendarme *is left* in the desk drawer. [Left by whom? The passive voice here obscures the point.]

Active Voice

Daru leaves the gendarme's revolver in the desk drawer.

Passive Voice

Daru serves tea and the Arab *is offered* some. [Confusing shift from the active voice "serves" to the passive voice "is offered."]

Active Voice

Daru serves tea and *offers* the Arab some.

Finally, avoid what has been called the Academic Passive: "In this essay it has been argued that. . . ." This cumbersome form used to be

"And remember—no more subjunctives where the correct mood is indicative."

common in academic writing (to convey scientific objectivity) but "I have argued" is usually preferable to such stuffiness.

The Writer's "I"

It is seldom necessary in writing an essay (even on a personal experience) to repeat "I think that" or "in my opinion." Your reader knows that what you write is your opinion. Nor is it necessary, if you've done your job well, to apologize. "After reading the story over several times I'm not really sure what it is about, but . . ." Write about something you are reasonably sure of. Occasionally, though, when there is a real problem in the text, for example the probable date of the Book of Ruth, it is not only permissible to disclose doubts and to reveal tentative conclusions; it may be necessary to do so.

Note also that there is no reason to avoid the pronoun *I* when you are in fact writing about yourself. Attempts to avoid *I* ("this writer," "we," expressions in the passive voice such as "it has been said above" and "it was seen") are noticeably awkward and distracting. And sometimes you may want to focus on your subjective response to a topic in order to clarify a point. The following opening paragraph of a movie review provides an example:

> I take the chance of writing about Bergman's *Persona* so long after its showing because this seems to me a movie there's no hurry about. It will be with us a long time, just as it has been on my mind for a long time. Right now, when I am perhaps still under its spell, it seems to me Bergman's masterpiece, but I can't imagine ever thinking it less than one of the great movies. This of course is opinion; what I know for certain is that *Persona* is also one of the most difficult movies I will ever see; and I am afraid that in this case there is a direct connection between difficulty and value. It isn't only that *Persona* is no harder than it has to be; its peculiar haunting power, its spell, and its value come directly from the fact that it's so hard to get a firm grasp on.
>
> —*Robert Garis*

Students who have been taught not to begin sentences with *I* often produce sentences that are eerily passive even when the verbs are in the active voice. For example:

```
Two reasons are important to my active participation
    in dance.
The name of the program that I enrolled in is the
    Health Careers Summer Program.
An eager curiosity overcame my previous feeling of
    fear to make me feel better.
```

But doesn't it make more sense to say:

```
I dance for two reasons.
I enrolled in the Health Careers Summer Program.
My curiosity aroused, I was no longer afraid.
```

> **A RULE FOR WRITERS**
>
> Make the agent of the action the subject of the sentence.

Clarity and Coherence

Writing a coherent essay is hard work; it requires mastery of a subject and skill in presenting it; it always takes a lot of time. Writing a coherent paragraph often takes more fussing and patching than you expect, but once you have the hang of it, it's relatively easy and pleasant. Writing a coherent sentence requires only that you stay awake until you get to the end of it.

We all do nod off sometimes, even over our own prose. But if you make it a practice to read your work over several times, at least once aloud, you give yourself a chance to spot the incoherent sentence before your reader does, and to revise it. Once you see that a sentence is incoherent, it's usually easy to recast it.

Cats Are Dogs

Looking at a picture of a woman, a man once said to the painter Henri Matisse, "That woman's arm is too long." "That's not a woman," Matisse replied, "it's a painting."

In some sentences a form of the verb *to be* mistakenly asserts that one thing is in a class with another. Is a picture a woman? Are cats dogs? Students did write the following sentences:

Incoherent

X. J. Kennedy's poem "Nothing in Heaven Functions as It Ought" is a contrast between Heaven and Hell.

As soon as you ask yourself the question "Is a poem a contrast?" you have, by bringing the two words close together, isolated the problem. A poem may be a sonnet, an epic, an ode—but not a contrast. The writer was trying to say what the poem does, not what it is.

Coherent

X. J. Kennedy's poem "Nothing in Heaven Functions as It Ought" contrasts Heaven and Hell.

Incoherent

Besides, he tells himself, a matchmaker is an old Jewish custom. [Is a matchmaker a custom?]

Coherent

Besides, he tells himself, consulting a matchmaker is an old Jewish custom.

Incoherent

Ruth's devotion to Naomi is rewarded by marrying Boaz. [Does devotion marry Boaz?]

Coherent

Ruth's marriage to Boaz rewards her devotion to Naomi.

Incoherent

He demonstrates many human frailties, such as the influence of others' opinions upon one's actions. [Is influence a frailty? How might this sentence be revised?]

Items in a Series

If you were given a shopping list that mentioned apples, fruit, and pears, you would be puzzled and possibly irritated by the inclusion of "fruit." Don't puzzle or irritate your reader with a **false series** of this sort. Analyze sentences containing items in a series to be sure that the items are of the same order of generality. For example:

False series

His job exposed him to the "dirty work" of the British and to the evils of imperialism. ["The 'dirty work' of the British" is a *specific* example of the more *general* "evils of imperialism." The false series makes the sentence incoherent.]

Revised

His job, by exposing him to the "dirty work" of the British, brought him to understand the evils of imperialism.

In the following sentence, which item in the series makes the sentence incoherent?

Why should one man, no matter how important, be exempt from investigation, arrest, trial, and law-enforcing tactics?

Modifiers

A modifier should appear close to the word it modifies (that is, describes or qualifies). Three kinds of faulty modifiers are common: misplaced, squinting, and dangling.

Misplaced Modifiers   A modifier that seems to modify the wrong word is called a **misplaced modifier.** Such faulty connections are often unintentionally funny. The judo parlor that advertised "For $20 learn basic methods of protecting yourself from an experienced instructor" probably attracted more amused readers than paying customers.

Misplaced

Orwell shot the elephant under pressured circumstances. [Orwell was under pressure, not the elephant. Reposition modifier.]

Revised

Orwell, under pressure, shot the elephant.

Misplaced

Orwell lost his individual right to protect the elephant as part of the imperialistic system. [The elephant was not part of the system; Orwell was.]

Revised

As part of the imperialistic system, Orwell lost his right to protect the elephant.

Misplaced

Amos Wilder has been called back to teach at the Divinity School after ten years retirement due to a colleague's illness. [Did Wilder retire for ten years because a colleague was ill? Revise the sentence.]

Sometimes other parts of sentences are misplaced:

Misplaced

We learn from the examples of our parents who we are. [The sentence appears to say we are our parents.]

Revised

We learn who we are from the examples of our parents.

Misplaced

It is up to the students to revise the scheme, not the administrators. [We all know you can't revise administrators. Revise the sentence.]

Squinting Modifiers If a modifier is ambiguous—that is, if it can be applied equally to more than one term—it is sometimes called a **squinting modifier:** It seems to look forward as well as backward.

Squinting

Being with Jennifer more and more enrages me. [Is the writer spending more time with Jennifer, or is she more enraged? Probably more enraged.]

Revised

Being with Jennifer enrages me more and more.

Squinting

Writing clearly is difficult. [Is this sentence about "writing" or about "writing clearly"?]

Revised

It is clearly difficult to write.

Revised

It is difficult to write clearly.

Squinting

Students only may use this elevator. [Does "only" modify students? If so, no one else may use the elevator. Or does it modify elevator? If so, students may use no other elevator.]

Revised

Only students may use this elevator.

Students may use only this elevator.

Note: The word *only* often squints, seeming to look in two directions. In general, put *only* immediately before the word or phrase it modifies. Often it appears too early in the sentence. (See "A Writer's Glossary" in Chapter 12, p. 292.)

Dangling Modifiers If a modifier refers to a term that appears nowhere in the sentence, you have what is called a **dangling modifier.**

Dangling

Being small, his ear scraped against the belt when his father stumbled. [The writer meant that the boy was small, not the ear. But the boy is not in the sentence.]

Revised

Because the boy was small, his ear scraped against the belt when his father stumbled.

Being small, the boy scraped his ear against the belt when his father stumbled.

Dangling

A meticulously organized person, his suitcase could be tucked under an airplane seat. [How would you revise the sentence?]

A RULE FOR WRITERS

When you revise sentences, put together what belongs together.

Reference of Pronouns

A pronoun is used in place of a noun. Because the noun usually precedes the pronoun, the noun to which the pronoun refers is called the *antecedent* (Latin: "going before"). For example:

antecedent   pronoun

When *Sheriff Johnson* was on a horse, *he* was a big man.

But the pronoun can also precede the noun:

pronoun   noun

When *he* was on a horse, *Sheriff Johnson* was a big man.

The word *antecedent* can be used here too. In short, the antecedent is the word or group of words referred to by a pronoun.

Whenever possible, make sure that a pronoun has a clear reference. Sometimes it isn't possible: *It* is commonly used with an unspecified reference, as in "It's hot today," and "Hurry up please, it's time"; and there can be no reference for interrogative pronouns: "What's bothering you?" and "Who's on first?" But otherwise always be sure that you've made clear what noun the pronoun is standing for.

Vague Reference of Pronouns

Vague

Apparently, they fight physically and it can become rather brutal. ["It" doubtless refers to "fight," but "fight" in this sentence is the verb, not an antecedent noun.]

Clear

Their fights are apparently physical, and sometimes brutal.

Vague

I was born in Colón, the second largest city in the Republic of Panama. Despite this, Colón is still an undeveloped town. ["This" has no specific antecedent. It appears to refer to the writer's having been born in Colón.]

Clear

Although Colón, where I was born, is the second largest city in Panama, it remains undeveloped. (For more on *this*, see also "A Writer's Glossary," in Chapter 12, p. 297.)

Shift in Pronouns   This common error is easily corrected.

In many instances the child was expected to follow the profession of your father. [Expected to follow the profession of whose father, "yours" or "his"?]

Having a tutor, you can get constant personal encouragement and advice that will help me budget my time. [If "you" have a tutor, will that help "me"?]

Ambiguous Reference of Pronouns   A pronoun normally refers to the first appropriate noun or pronoun preceding it. Same-sex pronouns and nouns, like dogs, often get into scraps.

Ambiguous

Her mother died when she was eighteen. [Who was eighteen, the mother or the daughter?]

Clear

Her mother died when Mabel was eighteen.

Her mother died at the age of eighteen. [Note the absence of ambiguity in "His mother died when he was eighteen."]

Ambiguous

Daru learns that he must take an Arab to jail against his will. [Both Daru and the Arab are male. The writer of the sentence meant that Daru learns he must act against his will.]

Clear

Daru learns that he must, against his will, take an Arab to jail.

Agreement

Noun and Pronoun Everyone knows that a singular noun requires a singular pronoun, and a plural noun requires a plural pronoun, but writers sometimes slip.

Faulty

singular   plural

A dog can easily tell if people are afraid of *them.*

Correct

singular   singular

A dog can easily tell if people are afraid of *it.*

Faulty

   singular   plural

Every student feels that Wellesley expects *them* to do their best.

Correct

   singular   singular

Every student feels that Wellesley expects *her* to do her best.

Each, everybody, nobody, no one, and *none* are especially troublesome. See the entries on these words in "A Writer's Glossary" in Chapter 12.

Subject and Verb A singular subject requires a singular verb, a plural subject a plural verb.

Faulty

     plural   singular

Horror *films* bring to light a subconscious fear and *shows* a character who succeeds in coping with it.

Correct

     plural   plural

Horror films bring to light a subconscious fear and *show* a character who succeeds in coping with it.

The student who wrote "shows" instead of "show" thought that the subject of the verb was "fear," but the subject really is "Horror films," a plural.

Faulty

The manager, as well as the pitcher and the catcher, were fined.

Correct

The manager, as well as the pitcher and the catcher, was fined.

If the sentence had been "The manager and the pitcher . . . ," the subject would have been plural and the required verb would be *were:*

The manager and the pitcher were fined.

But in the sentence as it was given, "as well as" (like *in addition to, with,* and *together with*) does *not* add a subject to a subject and thereby make a plural subject. "As well as" merely indicates that what is said about the manager applies to the pitcher and the catcher.

Three Additional Points

1. A collective noun—that is, a noun that is singular in form but that denotes a collection of individuals, such as *mob, audience, jury*—normally takes a *singular* verb:

Correct

The mob is at the gate.

Correct

An audience of children *is* easily bored. [The subject is "an audience," *not* "children."]

Correct

The jury is seated.

But when the emphasis is on the individuals within the group—for instance when you are calling attention to a division within the group—you can use a plural verb:

The jury disagree.

Still, because this sounds a bit odd, it is probably better to recast the sentence:

The jurors disagree.

2. Sometimes a sentence that is grammatically correct may nevertheless sound awkward:

One of its most noticeable features is the lounges.

Because the subject is "one"—*not* "features"—the verb must be singular, "is," but "is" sounds odd when it precedes the plural "lounges." The solution: **Revise the sentence.**

Among the most noticeable features are the lounges.

3. When a singular and a plural subject are joined by *or,* *either . . . or,* **or** *neither . . . nor,* **use a verb that agrees in number with the subject closest to the verb.** Examples:

Correct

Either the teacher *or the students are* mistaken.

Correct

Either the students *or the teacher is* mistaken.

The first version uses "are" because the verb is nearer to "students" (plural) than to "teacher" (singular); the second uses "is" because the verb is nearer to "teacher" than to "students."

Repetition and Variation

Sometimes repetition can help clarify or emphasize a point; sometimes repetition is simply unnecessary and dull. Here are five general rules on the subject.

1. Don't be afraid to repeat a word if it is the best word. The following paragraph repeats "joyful," "book," "moments," and "in its"; notice also "joyful" and "joy." Repetition, a device necessary for continuity and clarity, holds the paragraph together.

> *The Brothers Karamozov* is a joyful book. Readers who know what it is about may find this an intolerably whimsical statement. It does have moments of joy, but they are only moments; the rest is greed, lust, squalor, unredeemed suffering, and sometimes terrifying darkness. But the book is joyful in another sense: in its energy and curiosity, in its formal inventiveness, in the mastery of its writing. And therefore, finally, in its vision.
>
> *—Richard Pevear*

2. Use pronouns, when their reference is clear, as substitutes for nouns. Notice Pevear's use of pronouns; notice also that in the second and third sentences, he substitutes "it" for "book," and then uses "the book" again in the fourth sentence. Substitutions that neither confuse nor distract keep a paragraph from becoming dull.

3. Do not, however, confuse the substitutions we have just spoken of with the fault called Elegant Variation. A groundless fear of repetition sometimes leads students to write first, for example, of "Dostoevesky," then of "the writer," then of "our author." Such variations strike the reader as silly. They can, moreover, be confusing because they can suggest that the student is referring to different writers.

4. Don't repeat a word if it is being used in two different senses.

Confusing

My theme focuses on the theme of the book. [The first "theme" means "essay"; the second means "underlying idea" or "motif."]

Clear

My essay focuses on the theme of the book.

Confusing

Caesar's character is complex. The comic characters, however, are simple. [The first "character" means "personality"; the second means "persons" or "figures in the play."]

Clear

Caesar is complex; the comic characters, however, are simple.

5. Eliminate words repeated unnecessarily. The use of words like *surely, in all probability, it is noteworthy* may become habitual. If they don't help the reader to follow your thoughts, they are Instant Prose Additives. Cross them out.

In general, when you revise, decide if a word should be repeated, varied, or eliminated by testing sentences and paragraphs for both sound and sense.

Clarity and Sentence Structure: Parallelism

Use parallels to clarify relationships. Few of us are likely to compose such deathless parallels as "I came, I saw, I conquered," or "of the people, by the people, for the people," but we can see to it that coordinate expressions correspond in their grammatical form. Consider the following sentence and the revision:

Awkward

He liked drawing and to paint.

Parallel

He liked to draw and to paint.

He liked drawing and painting.

In the first version, "drawing" (a gerund) and "to paint" (an infinitive) are not grammatically parallel. The difference in grammatical form blurs the writer's point that there is a similarity between the two activities; the resulting sentence is fuzzy and awkward.

In the following examples, the parallel construction is italicized.

Awkward

The dormitory rules needed revision, a smoking area was a necessity, and a generally more active role for the school in social affairs were all significant to her.

Parallel

She recommended that the school *revise* its dormitory rules, *provide* a smoking area, and *organize* more social activities.

Awkward

Most Chinese parents disapprove of interracial dating or they just do not permit it.

Parallel

Most Chinese parents *disapprove* of interracial dating, and many *forbid* it.

In parallel constructions, be sure to check the consistency of articles, prepositions, and conjunctions. For example:

Awkward

He wrote papers on a play by Shakespeare, a novel of Dickens, and a story by Oates.

Parallel

He wrote papers on a play by Shakespeare, a novel by Dickens, and a story by Oates.

The shift from "by" to "of" and back to "by" serves no purpose and is merely distracting.

To sum up:

> A pupil once asked Arthur Schnabel (the noted pianist) whether it was better to play in time or to play as one feels; his characteristic mordant reply was another question: "Why not feel in time?"
>
> —*David Hamilton*

CHECKLIST FOR REVISING FOR CLARITY

☐ Is word choice precise and specific? While writing the draft, did you feel that a particular word was close to what you meant, but not quite right? If so, replace that word with the *right* word. (See pp. 76–78.)

☐ Do you offer concrete examples where necessary? (See pp. 82–83.)

☐ Are technical terms used appropriately and helpfully? Can any jargon be replaced with plain English? (See pp. 83–86.)

☐ Does your prose include any dead or mixed metaphors, or clichés? (See pp. 87–88.)

☐ Have you put together what belongs together? Do modifiers appear close to, and refer clearly to, the words they modify? (See pp. 95–97.)

☐ Have you eliminated sexist language? Have you replaced such words as "mankind" and "poetess" with gender-neutral terms, and eliminated the generic "he," "him," and "his"? (See pp. 78–80.)

☐ Have you replaced passive verbs with active verbs where appropriate? (See pp. 89–91.)

☐ Do pronouns have clear references, and do they agree in number with the nouns to which they refer? (See pp. 97–99.)

☐ Does the structure of your sentence reflect the structure of your thought? Are parallel ideas in parallel constructions? (See pp. 102–04.)

CHAPTER SIX
WRITING WITH STYLE

The friends that have it I do wrong
When ever I remake a song,
Should know what issue is at stake:
It is myself that I remake.
                    —*William Butler Yeats*

Academic Styles, Academic Audiences

When you write an essay for a course, you are learning how people working in that academic discipline express themselves. To communicate with other people in the discipline, you must adapt your voice to the conventions of the discipline and to the audience's expectations about writing within that discipline. Some disciplines (literature, for example) frown on passive verbs. But in lab reports in the sciences passive verbs are often acceptable, in part because they help focus the reader's attention on the experiment rather than on the person who conducted it, and thereby help to establish authority.

To make matters even more complicated, the conventions are changing, and they vary to some degree from class to class, and instructor to instructor. For example, one literature instructor might accept an essay containing the word "we" (as in "we see here the author's fascination with landscape"); another might object to its use, arguing that the "we" falsely implies that all readers—regardless of race, class, gender, and so on—read all texts in the same way.

These differences frustrate some students. To these students, writing an essay becomes a game of figuring out What the Instructor Wants. (For what it's worth, such students can frustrate instructors a bit too.) It may help both students and instructors to keep in mind that there isn't one *right* style—and that the differences among styles are a matter of disciplinary convention and (to some degree) theoretical approach, not arbitrary and inscrutable personal taste.

It is impossible to list here all the different conventions you'll encounter in college. You don't need to learn them all anyway. You simply need to be alert to the ways in which people talk to each other in the disciplines within which you're writing, and do your best to follow the conventions you observe. We illustrate a few of these differences below.

Here is the first paragraph of an article from an issue of the *Cambridge Journal of Economics:*

> In this paper I shall develop a framework which may be used to examine several alternative theories of the rate of interest. The four most widely accepted approaches are the Neoclassical Loanable Funds, Keynes's Liquidity Preference, Neoclassical Synthesis ISLM, and Basil Moore's Horizontalist (or endogenous money). I will use the framework developed here to present a fifth: an integration of liquidity preference theory with an endogenous money approach. I first briefly set forth the primary alternative approaches, then develop an analytical framework based on an asset or stock approach and use it to discuss several theories of the interest rate: those advanced by Keynes, by Moore, by neoclassical theory and the monetarists, by Kregel, and by Tobin. Finally, I shall use the framework to reconcile liquidity preference theory with an endogenous money approach.
>
> *—L. Randall Wray*

Note the use of the pronoun "I," the direct statement of what the writer will do ("In this paper I shall develop a framework . . ."); and the listing of the steps of his procedure ("I first briefly set forth," and so on). A literary critic would be unlikely to present his or her ideas so methodically, as the next example suggests.

Here is the first paragraph of a chapter from a study of Bram Stoker's *Dracula*, in which a literary critic analyzes the novel in its social and political context.

> "In obedience to the law as it then stood, he was buried in the centre of a *quadrivium*, or conflux of four roads (in this case four streets), with a stake

driven through his heart. And over him drives for ever the uproar of unresting London!" No, not *Dracula* (1897), but the closing lines of a much earlier nineteenth-century work, Thomas De Quincey's bleakly ironic essay "On Murder Considered as One of the Fine Arts" (1854). De Quincey is describing how in 1812 the London populace dealt with the body of one of its prize exhibits, a particularly grisly serial killer who had escaped the gallows by hanging himself in his cell in the dead of night. Yet it is difficult for us to read this gleefully chilling passage today without thinking of Bram Stoker's classic vampire novel. The quirky Christian symbolism, the mandatory staking down of the monster to keep it from roaming abroad, the sense of busily self-absorbed London unaware of its proximity to a murderous presence that haunts its most densely populated byways: together these features seem virtually to define a basic iconography for the vampire Gothic as it achieved canonical status in *Dracula*.

—*David Glover*

Note the absence of the pronoun "I" and the presence of the pronoun "we." Note also the playfulness of the style (the reference to a "gleefully chilling passage" and the "staking down of the monster"), the specificity of the language, and the variety in punctuation and sentence structure.

Here is the opening paragraph of a chemistry student's study of the enzyme calf alkaline phosphatase.

```
Enzymes, protein molecules that catalyze reactions, are
crucial for many biochemical reactions. This research
project studies the actions of the enzyme calf alkaline
phosphatase on the substrate p-nitrophenyl phosphate.
The focus of this research project is the relation of
alkaline phosphatase denaturation to temperature. Heat
denaturation has been well documented in major biology
and chemistry texts, but few textbooks mention how
extreme cold affects enzyme structure and function.
This study will examine how alkaline phosphatase
responds to both high and low temperatures.
                                    --Hilary Suzawa
```

Note the absence of personal pronouns (the "*research project* studies"), the orderly and careful presentation of information (including the brief definition of the word "enzymes" in the first sentence), and the clear statement of purpose. (You might compare this writer's first sentence with Glover's—deliberately misleading—opening.)

Defining Style

As we suggest above, style in academic writing is partly a matter of disciplinary conventions. But style also reflects the individual writer's mind, his or her values and sensibility. Style is not simply a flower here and some gilding there; it pervades the whole work. Van Gogh's style, or Walt Disney's, let us say, consists in part of features recurring throughout a single work and from one work to the next: angular or curved lines, hard or soft edges, strong or gentle contrasts, and so on. Pictures of a seated woman by each of the two artists are utterly different, and if we have seen a few works by each, we can readily identify who did which one. Artists leave their fingerprints, so to speak, all over their work. Writers leave their voiceprints.

Although the word *style* comes from the Latin *stilus* and originally referred to a Roman writing instrument, even in Roman times *stilus* had acquired a figurative sense, referring not only to the instrument but also to the writer's choice of words and arrangement of words into sentences. But is it simply the choice and arrangement of words we comment on when we speak of a writer's style, or are we also commenting on the writer's mind? Don't we feel that a piece of writing, whether it's on Civil War photographs or on genetics and intelligence, is also about the writer? The writing, after all, sets forth the writer's views of a chosen topic. It sets forth perceptions and responses to something the writer has thought about. The writer has, from the start, from the choice of a topic, revealed that he or she found it worth thinking about. The essay, in attempting to persuade us to think as the writer does, reveals not only how and what the writer thinks, but also what he or she values. As E. B. White has noted, "no writer long remains incognito."

When we write about things "out there," our writing always reveals the form and likeness of our minds, just as every work of art reveals the creator as well as the ostensible subject. A portrait painting, for example, is not only about the sitter, it is also about the artist's perceptions of the sitter; hence the saying that every portrait is a self-portrait. Even photographs are as much about the photographer as they are about the subject. Richard Avedon said of his portraits of famous people, "They are all pictures of me, of the way I feel about the people I photograph." A student's essay similarly, if it is written truly, is not exclusively about "*La Causa* and the New Chicana"; it is also about the perceptions and responses of the writer to both racism and sexism.

Style and Tone

Suppose we take a page of handwriting, or even a signature. We need not believe that graphology is an exact science to believe that the shape of the ink-lines on paper (apart from the meaning of the words) often tells us something about the writer. We look at a large, ornate signature, and we sense that the writer is confident; we look at a tiny signature written with the finest of pens, and we wonder why anyone is so self-effacing.

More surely than handwriting, the writer's style reveals, among other things, an attitude toward the self, toward the reader, and toward the subject. The writer's attitudes are reflected in what is usually called *tone*. It is difficult to separate style from tone but we can try. Most discussions of style concentrate on what might be thought of as ornament: figurative language ("a sea of troubles"), inversion ("A leader he is not"), repetition and parallelism ("government of the people, by the people, for the people"), balance and antithesis ("It was the best of times, it was the worst of times"). Indeed, for centuries style has been called "the dress of thought," implying that the thought is something separate from the expression; the thought, in this view, is dressed up in stylistic devices. But in most of the writing that we read with interest and pleasure, the stylistic devices are not ornamental but integral. When we talk about wit, sincerity, tentativeness, self-assurance, aggressiveness, objectivity, and so forth, we can say we are talking about style, but we should recognize that style now is not a matter of ornamental devices that dress up some idea, but part of the idea itself. And "the idea itself" includes the writer's unified yet appropriately varied tone of voice.

To take a brief example: The famous English translation of Caesar's report of a victory,

> I came, I saw, I conquered,

might be paraphrased thus:

> After getting to the scene of the battle, I studied the situation. Then I devised a strategy that won the battle.

But this paraphrase loses much of Caesar's message; the brevity and the parallelism of the famous version, as well as the alliteration (*came, conquered*), convey tight-lipped self-assurance—convey, that is, the tone that reveals Caesar to us. And this tone is a large part of Caesar's message. Caesar is really telling us not only about what he did, but also about what sort of person he is. He is perceptive, decisive, and effective. The three actions, Caesar in effect tells us, are (for a man like Caesar) one. (The Latin original is even more tight-lipped and more unified by alliteration: *veni, vidi, vici.*)

Let's look now at a longer example, the opening sentence of Lewis Thomas's essay "On Natural Death":

> There are so many new books about dying that there are now special shelves set aside for them in bookstores, along with the health, diet and home-repair paperbacks and the sex manuals.

This sentence could have ended where the comma is placed: The words after "bookstores" are, it might seem, not important. One can scarcely argue that by specifying some kinds of "special shelves" Thomas clarifies an otherwise difficult or obscure concept. What, then, do these additional words do? They tell us nothing about death and almost nothing about bookshops, but they tell us a great deal about Thomas's *attitude* toward the new books on death. He suggests that such books are faddish and perhaps (like "the sex manuals") vulgar. After all, if he had merely wanted to call up a fairly concrete image of a well-stocked bookstore, he could have said "along with books on politics and the environment," or some such thing. His next sentence runs:

> Some of them are so packed with detailed information and step-by-step instructions for performing the function you'd think this was a new sort of skill which all of us are now required to learn.

Why "you'd think" instead of, say, "one might believe"? Thomas uses a colloquial form, and a very simple verb, because he wants to convey to us his commonsense, homely, down-to-earth view that these books are a bit pretentious—a pretentiousness conveyed in his use of the words "performing the function," words that might come from the books themselves. In short, when we read Thomas's paragraph we are learning as much about Thomas as we are about books on dying. We are hearing a voice, perceiving an attitude, and we want to keep reading, not only because we are interested in death but also because Thomas has managed to make us interested in Thomas, a thoughtful but unpretentious fellow.

Now listen to a short paragraph from John Szarkowski's *Looking at Photographs*. Szarkowski is writing about one of Alexander Gardner's photographs of a dead Confederate sharpshooter.

© Bettman/Corbis.

> Among the pictures that Gardner made himself is the one reproduced here. Like many Civil War photographs, it showed that the dead of both sides looked very much the same. The pictures of earlier wars had not made this clear.

Try, in a word or two, to characterize the tone (the attitude, as we sense it in the inflection of the voice) of the first sentence. Next, the tone of the second, and then of the third. Suppose the second and third sentences had been written thus:

> It showed that the dead of both sides looked very much the same. This is made clear in Civil War photographs, but not in pictures of earlier wars.

How has the tone changed? What word can you find to characterize the tone of the whole, as Szarkowski wrote it?

Acquiring Style

In the preceding pages we said that your writing reveals not only where you stand (your thesis) and how you think (the structure of your argument), but also who you are and how you take yourself (your tone). To follow our argument to its limit, we might say that everything in this book—including rules on the comma (the place in a sentence where you breathe)—is about style. We do. What more is there to say?

Clarity and Texture

Let's look first at a distinction Aristotle makes between two parts of style: that which gives clarity and that which gives texture. Exact words, concrete illustrations of abstractions, conventional punctuation, and so forth—matters we treat in some detail in the chapters on revising and editing—make for clarity. On the whole, this part of style is inconspicuous when present; when absent, the effect ranges from mildly distracting to ruinous. Clarity is the foundation of style. It can be achieved by anyone willing to make the effort.

Among the things that give texture, or individuality, are effective repetition, variety in sentence structure, wordplay, and so forth. This second group of devices, on the whole more noticeable, makes the reader aware of the writer's particular voice. These devices can be learned too, but seldom by effort alone. In fact, playfulness helps here more than doggedness. Students who work at this part of style usually enjoy hanging around words. At the same time, they're likely to feel that when they put words on paper, even in a casual letter to a friend, they're putting themselves on the line. Serious, as most people are about games they really care about, but not solemn, they'll come to recognize the rules of play in John Holmes's advice to young poets: "You must believe that your feelings and your words for your feelings are important. . . . That they are unique is a fact; that you believe they are unique is necessary."

A Repertory of Styles

We now look at a second distinction: between style as the reader perceives it from the written word and style as the writer experiences it. The first is static: It's fixed in writing or print; we can point to it, discuss it, analyze it. The second, the writer's experience of his or her own style, changes as the writer changes. In his essay "Why I Write" George Orwell said, "I find that by the time you have perfected any style of writing, you have always outgrown it." An exaggeration that deposits a truth. The essay comes to this conclusion, however: "Looking back through my work, I see that it is invariably where I lacked a political purpose that I wrote lifeless books and was betrayed into purple passages, sentences without meaning, decorative adjectives and humbug generally." A suggestion surely, that through trial and error, and with maturity, a writer comes to a sense of self, a true style, not static and not constantly changing, but achieved.

As an undergraduate you may seldom know what purpose, in Orwell's sense, you will have. You may be inclined toward some subjects and against others, you may have decided on a career—many times. But if your education is worth anything like the money and time invested in it, your ideas and feelings will change more rapidly in the next few years than ever before in your memory, and perhaps more than they ever will again. Make use of the confusion you're in. Reach out for new experiences to assimilate; make whatever connections you can from your reading to your inner life, reaching back into your past and forward into your future. And keep writing.

To keep pace with your changing ideas—and here is our main point— you'll need to acquire not one style, but a repertory of styles, a store of writing habits on which you can draw as the need arises.

Originality and Imitation

We conclude with a paradox: One starts to acquire an individual style by studying and imitating the style of others. The paradox isn't limited to writing. Stylists in all fields begin as apprentices. The young ball player imitates the movements of Nomar Garciaparra; the chess player hangs around the park or club watching the old pros, then finds a book that probably recommends beginning with Ruy Lopez's opening. When Michelangelo was an apprentice he copied works by his predecessors; when Millet was young he copied works by Michelangelo; when Van Gogh was young he copied works by Millet. The would-be writer may be lucky enough to have a teacher, one he can imitate; more likely he will, in W. H. Auden's words, "serve his apprenticeship in the library."

PART TWO

COLLEGE WRITING

CHAPTER SEVEN

ANALYZING TEXTS

Look at the drawing below by Pieter Brueghel the Elder, titled *The Painter and the Connoisseur* (done about 1565), and then jot down your responses to the questions that follow.

Albertina, Wien.

Analyzing a Drawing

1. One figure is given considerably more space than the other. What may be implied by this fact?

2. What is the painter doing (besides painting)?

3. What is the connoisseur doing?

4. What does the face of each figure tell you about each man's character? The figures are physically close; are they mentally close? How do you know?

Now consider this brief discussion of the drawing.

> The painter, standing in front of the connoisseur and given more than two-thirds of the space, dominates this picture. His hand holds the brush with which he creates, while the connoisseur's hand awkwardly fumbles for money in his purse. The connoisseur apparently is pleased with the picture he is looking at, for he is buying it, but his parted lips give him a stupid expression and his eyeglasses imply defective vision. In contrast, the painter looks away from the picture and fixes his eyes on the model (reality) or, more likely, on empty space, his determined expression suggesting that he possesses an imaginative vision beyond his painting and perhaps even beyond earthly reality.

The author of this paragraph uses *analysis* to interpret the drawing, to discover its meaning. The paragraph doesn't simply tell us that the picture shows two people close together—that would be a *description*, not an analysis. This analytic paragraph separates the parts of the picture, pointing out that the two figures form a contrast. It explains why one figure gets much more space than the other, and it explains what the contrasting gestures and facial expressions imply. The writer of the comment has "read" or interpreted the drawing by examining how the parts function—that is, how they relate to the whole.

Analyzing Texts

Much of academic reading and writing is analytical. You read of the causes of a revolution, of the effects of inflation, or of the relative importance of heredity and environment; you write about the meaning of a short story, the causes and effects of poverty, the strengths and weaknesses of some proposed legislative action. And much of this reading and writing is based on the analysis of *texts*. As we note in Chapter 1, the word "text" derives from the Latin for "woven" (as in textile), and it has come to refer not only to words stitched together into sentences (whether novels or letters or advertisements), but also to all kinds of objects of interpretation: films, paintings, music videos, even food on a plate.

For that reason, much of our discussion in this chapter focuses on textual analysis. Of course writing an analysis of a drawing differs from writing an analysis of a poem (or, for that matter, from an analysis of a legislative proposal or an argument about the causes of inflation). Nevertheless, we believe that there are important similarities between these processes. In all cases, the reader must be able to envision the object under scrutiny, so the writer must summarize it or describe it precisely. In all cases, the writer must be able to explain what the text *means*, so the writer must pay close attention to its details, to its parts—to how they work, to what they imply or suggest, to their relationship to each other and to the whole.

It is worth keeping in mind, though, that when academic writers write analytically, their purpose is to persuade the reader to see things *their* way: to understand the poem the way they do; to reach their conclusion about the causes of poverty; to adopt their position on the proposed legislative action. The analysis helps the writer to make a larger point: It provides the evidence for the argument. In Chapter 8, "Persuading Readers," we discuss argument in more detail. But for now, we'll focus on analysis and how it differs from summary and paraphrase.

Analysis Versus Summary and Paraphrase

Before we talk more about analysis, we should see how it differs from summary and paraphrase. A **summary** is a brief version of what a text adds up to. A film reviewer may summarize the plot of a film in a sentence or two, and a book reviewer may in a short paragraph summarize the plot of a novel or the argument of a book advocating reform of our welfare system. Similarly, a student may find that it is useful to summarize a text that will be later analyzed in an essay.

The Gettysburg Address: Summary, Paraphrase, Analysis

Summarizing

For convenience, we will focus on a piece of writing that you are probably familiar with, Lincoln's Gettysburg Address. And let's assume that your first-year composition instructor has asked you to analyze this text. Your analytic essay will be devoted chiefly to showing how the writing works. (Analysis, you will recall, is essentially the examination of the relationships of parts, showing how they function.) In this instance, you will probably show

- How the speech is organized (you may find that the basic pattern is birth, death, rebirth).
- How certain words set forth profound reverberations.
- How the metaphors are related.

We will look at such things in a moment. Here is Lincoln's text:

The Gettysburg Address

Fourscore and seven years ago our fathers brought forth on this continent a new nation, conceived in liberty and dedicated to the proposition that all men are created equal. Now we are engaged in a great civil war, testing whether that nation or any nation so conceived and so dedicated can long endure. We are met on a great battlefield of that war. We have come to dedicate a portion of that field as a final resting-place for those who here gave their lives that that nation might live. It is altogether fitting and proper that we should do this. But in a larger sense, we cannot dedicate, we cannot consecrate, we cannot hallow this ground. The brave men, living and dead who struggled here have consecrated it far above our poor power to add or detract. The world will little note nor long remember what we say here, but it can never forget what they did here. It is for us the living rather to be dedicated here to the unfinished work which they who fought here have thus far so nobly advanced. It is rather for us to be here dedicated to the great task remaining before us—that from these honored dead we take increased devotion to that cause for which they gave the last full measure of devotion—that we here highly resolve that these dead shall not have died in vain, that this nation under God shall have a new birth of freedom, and that government of the people, by the people, for the people shall not perish from the earth.

You may want to begin your analytic essay with a summary of the text. Here, as a sample, is a student's summary:

```
Although we have come to dedicate a portion of the
battlefield at Gettysburg to the memory of those who
died here, our real task is to dedicate ourselves to
the preservation of the nation for which they died--a
nation in which the people govern themselves.
```

In writing an essay, you might therefore as a lead-in to your analysis say (as the student did) something like this:

```
In 1863 Lincoln was invited to speak briefly at the
dedication of a cemetery at Gettysburg, Pennsylvania.
His essential point is that although we have come to
dedicate a portion of the battlefield at Gettysburg
to the memory of those who died, our real task is
to dedicate ourselves to the preservation of the
nation--for which they died--a nation in which the
people govern themselves.
```

Or, you might choose to announce a bit more obviously that you are offering a summary, along these lines:

```
Before we look at the ways in which Lincoln uses
metaphor in the Gettysburg Address, a brief summary
may be useful: Lincoln's essential point is that
although we have come to dedicate a portion of the
battlefield at Gettysburg to the memory of those who
died in an effort to preserve the Union, our real
task is to dedicate ourselves to the preservation of
the nation for which they died--a nation in which the
people govern themselves.
```

Paraphrasing

A **paraphrase** is something entirely different. Whereas a summary is much briefer than the original, a paraphrase is usually as long or longer because it is a restatement, a sort of translation into the same language. Thus, in the first sentence of the Gettysburg Address, Lincoln's "four score and seven years ago" would be paraphrased as "eighty-seven years ago." (It happens that in this case the paraphrase—three words—is actually shorter than the original—six words—but usually a paraphrase is at least as long as the original.) Let's look again at the first sentence of the Gettysburg Address:

```
Four score and seven years ago our fathers brought
forth on this continent, a new nation, conceived in
Liberty, and dedicated to the proposition that all
men are created equal.
```

Here is a student's paraphrase:

> Eighty-seven years ago (i.e., in 1776, the year of the American Revolution) our ancestors introduced to North America a new country; this country was brought into existence ("conceived") by the male framers of the Constitution who saw Liberty as the mother of the new nation, and it was set apart or specially marked ("dedicated") as a nation in which all human beings are regarded as equal.

Briefly, a paraphrase has two key features:

- It is as long as the original, and usually longer.
- It is usually designed to help a reader—or writer—understand a dense text.

Why paraphrase? First, a paraphrase can help clarify a difficult or obscure passage for your reader. Second, the act of paraphrasing can help you as the writer, by forcing you to slow down your reading and making you think carefully about each word. Careful reading is the first step in analytic thinking.

CAUTION

In your own essays, do not paraphrase a source simply in order to avoid summarizing it or to avoid quoting it directly. If you merely restate a lucid source, changing words but in essence proceeding phrase by phrase, offering synonyms, you are **plagiarizing,** even if you begin saying something like "Jiménez has pointed out that. . . ." Why is such material plagiarism? Because all of the ideas and all of the structure of the thought, as well as some of the words, are someone else's. True, by acknowledging Jiménez ("Jiménez has pointed out") you are informing the reader that the ideas are not yours, but this acknowledgment does not tell the reader that you are using Jiménez's sentences, substituting some words. For additional information on plagiarism, see "Acknowledging Sources" (pp. 205–11).

In an analytic essay you should include a paraphrase only rarely, only when you think your readers may need some help in grasping the meaning of the text. If you simply want to remind your readers of the gist of a text you are responding to, it is better to summarize it rather than to paraphrase it. If you want them to see the text that you are analyzing, to experience it directly, quote the passage word for word, in quotation marks if it is short or set off and indented in block-quotation format if it is long.

Analyzing

An **analysis** of the Gettysburg Address—an attempt to show how it works, how it achieves its special effects—will not simply paraphrase the text but will make such points as these:

- "Four score and seven years" evokes the Bible, which in Psalm 90 speaks of human life as "three score years and ten"; Lincoln thus begins the speech by solemnly introducing a holy context.

- "Four score and seven" is not the only evocation of the Bible; Lincoln also uses "dedicate" (in the Bible the word commonly means "set aside for a divine purpose"), "consecrate," "hallow" (to make holy), "devotion" (this word contains the word "vow"), "under God"— words appropriate to the creation of a cemetery, and words suggesting that the dead soldiers were sacrifices to a divine purpose.

- The address moves from the past (the first sentence refers to the Revolution in 1776) to the present (for instance "now we are met," "we are engaged," "we cannot") and then to the future ("shall have a new birth," "shall not perish").

- A metaphor of birth begins the speech ("conceived" in the first sentence), and another ends the speech ("new birth" in the last sentence); somewhat fainter images of birth are also present in "brought forth" and "create."

- Alliteration (the repetition of initial sounds) helps to bind words together ("*f*our score . . . *f*athers . . . *f*orth; *n*ew *n*ation"), and moves the language from ordinary prose toward the more highly textured language of poetry.

- Triads also elevate the language beyond ordinary prose ("we cannot dedicate, we cannot consecrate, we cannot hallow," "of the people, by the people, for the people").

Observations such as these give a reader a sense not merely of the ideas of the address—that would be a paraphrase—but a sense of how the elements in the address work to create effects and meanings.

Paraphrasing for Clarity

Many works of literature include words whose meanings differ from their present meanings, and much academic writing uses technical words that are not familiar to outsiders. As we note in Chapter 5 in our discussion of clarity, almost all of us use some technical language that seems like jargon to outsiders. Baseball uses words such as *double-play, bunt, shutout,* and *perfect game,* but these words mean nothing to many native speakers of English—all those millions of people for whom baseball is not the national pastime. Art historians talk of *museology* and *commodity fashion systems.* Economists, sociologists, psychologists, and indeed all professionals regularly use words that are unfamiliar to most of us. And, because you will be reading their writings, you will be encountering the special language of their particular disciplines.

Here is an example, from a book written by a professor of art history:

> Art history is one of a network of interrelated professions whose overall function has been to fabricate a historical past that could be placed under systematic observation for use in the present. As with its allied fields—art criticism, aesthetic philosophy, art practice, connoisseurship, the art market, museology, tourism, commodity fashion systems, and the heritage industry—the art historical discipline incorporated an amalgam of analytic protocols, and epistemological technologies, of diverse ages and origins.
>
> —*Donald Preziosi*

Some of these words may be new to you—perhaps "connoisseurship," "museology," "protocols," "epistemological." Some may be familiar, but perhaps you are not entirely sure of their meanings ("fabricate," "aesthetic philosophy," "commodity fashion systems," "amalgam"). You realize that if you are going to get anything out of Preziosi's essay, and perhaps respond to one of his arguments, you had better make sure that you know what he is talking about. So, with a dictionary in hand if necessary, you think about the meaning of each word and paraphrase these sentences. Here is one student's paraphrase:

```
The study of the history of art is one of a group of
closely connected specialized occupations whose pur-
pose is to construct a view of the past that can be
set up for methodical study by those who live now. As
with related areas of study--the evaluation of art,
the study of beauty ("aesthetic philosophy"), the
business of making works of art ("art practice"), the
study of the authenticity and dating of works of art
("connoisseurship"), the art business (i.e. dealers
and auction houses), the running of museums, the
tourist industry, the business of selling fashion,
the business of running institutions devoted to the
past (for instance Williamsburg, Virginia)--the study
of the history of art is built on a combination of
```

```
methods of analysis, speculating, and setting forth
ideas in words. These methods are procedures for
transmitting information and applied science con-
cerned with the nature of knowledge. The combination
draws on the old and new, from here and from there.
```

When the student was asked to summarize Preziosi's paragraph, she came up with this sentence:

```
The field of art history is part of a network that
includes such things as art criticism, museums, the art
market, and the tourist industry; it uses a variety of
intellectual tools.
```

Again, the paraphrase was intended merely for the student's own sake. If she were writing for an audience with little knowledge of contemporary views of art history, she might have used the paraphrase in her essay, with a lead-in such as "Preziosi's first few sentences are highly packed, and a paraphrase may therefore help to clarify some of the terms. According to Preziosi, the field of art history. . . ."

> **NOTE**
>
> For advice on how to cite a paraphrase and an explanation of the difference between an acceptable and unacceptable paraphrase, see pages 206–09.

Paraphrasing and Summarizing Literary Texts

Paraphrase is especially useful in essays analyzing literature, where the meanings of words are often multiple. Let's look at a short work of literature, Shakespeare's Sonnet 116:

Let me not to the marriage of true minds
Admit impediments. Love is not love
Which alters when it alteration finds,
Or bends with the remover to remove.   4
O no, it is an ever-fixèd mark
That looks on tempests and is never shaken.
It is the star to every wandering bark
Whose worth's unknown, although his height be taken.   8
Love's not time's fool, though rosy lips and cheeks
Within his bending sickle's compass come;

Love alters not with his brief hours and weeks,
But bears it out even to the edge of doom.   12
If this be error and upon me proved,
I never writ, nor no man ever loved.

Shakespeare wrote this sonnet four hundred years ago, so it is not surprising that some of his words and phrases are not immediately clear. A student offered this paraphrase of the first six lines:

```
May I never concede ("admit") that obstacles can
alter the spiritual union of faithful ("true") minds.
Love cannot be considered true love if it changes
when it encounters change (for instance, when it sees
the beloved's loss of physical beauty, or when it
sees the beloved's economic circumstances change), or
if it withdraws or deviates or turns away when the
other party withdraws ("remove[s]") love. Certainly
not; love is a permanent-standing thing ("ever-fixed
mark"), like a landmark or beacon, that observes dis-
turbances but is itself undisturbed ("never shaken").
```

Try your hand at paraphrasing the rest of the sonnet. (In line 7 "bark" means "ship"; in line 8 "height" means "altitude"; in line 9 "Time's fool" is "plaything (i.e., victim) of Time"; in line 10 "his" is "Time's"; and in line 12 "edge of doom" is the "brink of Doomsday (Judgment Day)."

A summary of the first six lines would be notably different in content and length from a paraphrase. A student might write something like this:

```
I will never grant that true love changes when it
sees some sort of change in the beloved.
```

A RULE FOR WRITERS

Remember that a **summary** is often useful in an analytical or argumentative essay that responds to another argument because the summary reminds readers of the main points of a text. A **paraphrase** is useful if the original is particularly dense, either because it is highly metaphoric or because it is written in highly technical or obsolete language. An **analysis** is an examination of how the parts relate to the whole—for example, how certain words suggest an objective speaker, and how lengthy sentences suggest a highly educated speaker—or conversely, how lengthy sentences consisting of simple clauses linked by "and . . . and . . . and" may suggest a simple speaker.

Classifying and Thinking

Analysis (literally a separating into parts) is not only the source of much writing that seeks to explain but also a way of thinking, a way of arriving at conclusions (generalizations), a way of discovering meaning. Much of what we normally mean by analysis requires classifying ideas or things into categories and thinking about how the categories relate to each other. Writers who analyze texts must, of course, classify their observations. The student who analyzed the Gettysburg Address (p. 123) noted that Lincoln's language often evokes the Bible. Other kinds of analysis require classifying things or ideas as well.

When you think about choosing courses, for example, you classify the courses by subject matter, or by degree of difficulty ("Since I'm taking two hard courses, I ought to look for an easy one"), or by the hour at which they are offered, or by the degree to which they interest you, or by their merit as determined through the grapevine.

When you classify, you establish categories by breaking down the curriculum into parts, and by then putting into each category courses that significantly resemble each other but that are not identical. We need categories: We simply cannot get through life treating every object as unique.

Examples of Classifying

Suppose you were asked to write an essay putting forth your ideas about punishment for killers. You would need to distinguish between those killers whose actions are premeditated and those killers whose actions are not. And in the first category you might make further distinctions:

1. Professional killers who carefully contrive a death
2. Killers who are irrational except in their ability to contrive a death
3. Robbers who contrive a property crime and who kill only when they believe that killing is necessary in order to commit that crime

You can hardly talk usefully about capital punishment or imprisonment without making some such analysis of killers. You have, then, taken killers and *classified* them, for the sake of educating yourself and those persons with whom you discuss the topic. Unless you agree with the "Off with their heads" attitude of the mad Queen of Hearts you will be satisfied with your conclusion only after you have tested it by dividing your topic into parts, each clearly distinguished from the others, and then showed how they are related.

Here's another example: If you think about examinations, you may find that they can serve several purposes. They may test knowledge, intelligence, or skill in taking examinations; or they may stimulate learning. Therefore, if you wish to discuss what constitutes a good examination, you must decide what purpose an examination *should* serve. Possibly you will decide that in a particular course an examination should chiefly stimulate learning, but that it should also test the ability to reason. To arrive at a reasonable conclusion, a conclusion worth sharing and, if need be, defending, you must first recognize and sort out the several possibilities.

Often the keenest analytical thinking considers not only what parts are in the whole, but also what is *not* there—what is missing in relation to a larger context that we can imagine. For example, if we analyze the female characters in the best-known fairy tales, we will find that most are either sleeping beauties or wicked stepmothers. These categories are general: "Sleeping beauties" includes all passive women valued only for their appearance, and "wicked stepmothers" includes Cinderella's cruel older sisters. (Fairy godmothers form another category, because they are not human beings.) Analysis helps us to discover the almost total absence of resourceful, productive women in the typical fairy tale. You might begin a thoughtful essay with a general statement to this effect and then support the statement—your thesis—with an analysis of "Cinderella," "Little Red Riding Hood," and "Snow White."

Cause and Effect

Analytical reasoning moving from cause to effect is also often expected in academic discussions, which are much given to questions such as the following:

> What part did the Bay of Pigs attack on Cuba play in the Cuban missile crisis of 1962?
>
> What is the function of Mrs. Linde in Ibsen's *A Doll's House?*
>
> How does the death penalty affect jury verdicts?
>
> Why do people enjoy horror movies?
>
> What are the effects of billboard advertising?

Let's look at the first eight paragraphs of an essay, by the architect and scholar Dolores Hayden, that addresses the last question on the list, arguing from cause to effect.

Dolores Hayden

Advertisements, Pornography, and Public Space

1 Americans need to look more consciously at the ways in which the public domain is misused for spatial displays of gender stereotypes: These appear in outdoor advertising, and to a lesser extent in commercial displays, architectural decoration, and public sculpture. While the commercial tone and violence of the American city is often criticized, there is little analysis of the routine way that crude stereotypes appear in public, urban spaces as the staple themes of commercial art. Most Americans are accustomed to seeing giant females in various states of undress smiling and caressing products such as whiskey, food, and records. Male models also sell goods, but they are usually active and clothed—recent ad campaigns aimed at gay men seem to be the first major exception. Several geographers have established that men are most often shown doing active things, posed in the great outdoors; women are shown in reflective postures responding to male demands in interior spaces. As the nineteenth-century sexual double standard is preserved by the urban advertising, many twentieth-century urban men behave as if good women are at home while bad ones adorn the billboards and travel on their own in urban space; at the same time, many urban women are encouraged to think of emotionlessness, war-mongering, and sexual inexhaustibility as natural to the Marlboro cowboy, war heroes' statues, and every other male adult.

2 This double standard is the result of advertising practices, graphic design, and urban design. Sanctioned by the zoning laws, billboards are approved by the same urban planning boards who will not permit child care centers or mother-in-law apartments in many residential districts. But the problem with billboards is not only aesthetic degradation. By presenting gender stereotypes in the form of nonverbal body language, fifty feet long and thirty feet high, billboards turn the public space of the city into a stage set for a drama starring enticing women and stern men.

3 Let us observe outdoor advertising and other urban design phenomena with similar effects, as they are experienced by two women

on an urban commuting trip along the Sunset Strip in Los Angeles in June 1981. Standing on a street corner, the two women are waiting for a bus to go to work. The bus arrives, bearing a placard on the side advertising a local nightclub. It shows strippers doing their act, their headless bodies naked from neck to crotch except for a few blue sequins. The two women get on the bus and find seats for the ride along Sunset Boulevard. They look out the windows. As the bus pulls away, their heads appear incongruously above the voluptuous cardboard female bodies displayed on the side. They ride through a district of record company headquarters and film offices, one of the most prosperous in L.A.

4   Their first views reveal rows of billboards. Silent Marlboro man rides the range; husky, khaki-clad Camel man stares at green hills; gigantic, uniformed professional athletes catch passes and hit home runs on behalf of booze. These are the male images. Then, on a billboard for whiskey, a horizontal blonde in a backless black velvet dress, slit to the thigh, invites men to "Try on a little Black Velvet." Next, a billboard shows a well-known actress, reclining with legs spread, who notes that avocados are only sixteen calories a slice. "Would this body lie to you?" she asks coyly, emphasizing that the body language which communicates blatant sexual availability is only meant to bring attention to her thin figure. Bo Derek offers a pastoral contrast garbed in nothing but a few bits of fur and leather, as she swings on a vine of green leaves, promoting *Tarzan, the Ape Man.*

5   Next the bus riders pass a club called the Body Shop that advertises "live, nude girls." Two reclining, realistic nudes, one in blue tones in front of a moonlight cityscape, one in orange sunshine tones, stretch their thirty-foot bodies along the sidewalk. This is the same neighborhood where a billboard advertising a Rolling Stones' record album called "Black and Blue" made news ten years ago. A manacled, spread-legged woman with torn clothes proclaimed "I'm Black and Blue from the Rolling Stones—and I love it!" Members of a group called Women Against Violence Against Women (WAVAW) arrived with cans of spray paint and climbed the scaffolding to make small, uneven letters of protest: "This is a crime against women." Demonstrations and boycotts eventually succeeded in achieving the removal of that image, but not in eliminating the graphic design problem. "Black and Blue" has been replaced by James Bond in a tuxedo, pistol in hand, viewed through the spread legs and buttocks of a giant woman in a bathing suit and improbably high heels, captioned "For Your Eyes Only."

6   When the two women get off the bus in Hollywood, they experience more gender stereotypes as pedestrians. First, they walk past a department store. In the windows mannequins suggest the prevailing ideals of sartorial elegance. The male torsos lean forward, as if they are about to clinch a deal. The female torsos, pin-headed, tip backward and sideways, at odd angles, as if they are about to be pushed over onto a bed. The themes of gender advertisements are trumpeted here in the mannequins' body language as well as on billboards. Next, the women pass an apartment building. Two neoclassical caryatids support the entablature over the front door. Their breasts are bared, their heads carry the load. They recall the architecture of the Erechtheum on the Acropolis in Athens, dating from the 5th century B.C., where the sculptured stone forms of female slaves were used as support for a porch in place of traditional columns and capitals. This is an ancient image of servitude.

7   After the neo-classical apartment house, the commuters approach a construction site. Here they are subject to an activity traditionally called "running the gauntlet," but referred to as "girl watching" by urban sociologist William H. Whyte. Twelve workers stop whatever they are doing, whistle, and yell: "Hey, baby!" The women put their heads down, and walk faster, tense with anger. The construction workers take delight in causing exactly this response: "You're cute when you're mad!" Whyte regards this type of behavior as charming, pedestrian fun in "Street Life," where he even takes pleasure in tracing its historic antecedents, but he has never been whistled at, hooted at, and had the dimensions of his body parts analyzed out loud on a public street.[1]

8   Finally, these women get to the office building where they work. It has two statues out front of women. Their bronze breasts culminate in erect nipples. After they pass this last erotic public display of women's flesh, sanctioned as fine art, they walk in the door to begin the day's work. Their journey has taken them through an urban landscape filled with images of men as sexual aggressors and women as submissive sexual objects.

Now let's analyze these paragraphs. In the first paragraph Hayden introduces the question her essay will address: "How do billboards and

---

[1] William H. Whyte, "Street Life," *Urban Open Spaces* (Summer 1980); for a more detailed critique of hassling: Lindsy Van Gelder, "The International Language of Street Hassling," *Ms.* 9 (May 1981), 15–20, and letters about this article, *Ms.* (September 1981); and Cheryl Benard and Edith Schlaffer, "The Man in the Street: Why He Harasses," *Ms.* 9 (May 1981), 18–19.

other outdoor representations of male and female bodies perpetuate gender stereotypes?" (our paraphrase). She points out that there has been "little analysis" of this problem, thus suggesting that it is worth investigating. In the last sentence of the second paragraph, she states an argument: "billboards turn the public space of the city into a stage set for a drama starring enticing women and stern men." Paragraphs 4 through 8 discuss the "causes." We note Hayden classifies these images fairly methodically: paragraphs 4 and 5 focus on billboards representing women as "available"; paragraph 6 focuses first on mannequins that represent women as vulnerable, and then on architectural elements that represent women as subservient; paragraph 8 focuses on bronze statues of female torsos.

In the next (and last) three paragraphs of the essay, Hayden discusses the effects of these representations: "women guard themselves," "men assume that ogling is part of normal public life," and the "sexual double standard" is maintained "in a brutal and vulgar way."

9   The transient quality of male and female interaction in public streets makes the behavior provoked by billboards and their public design images particularly difficult to attack. Psychologist Erving Goffman has analyzed both print ads and billboards as *Gender Advertisements* because art directors use exaggerated body language to suggest that consumers buy not products but images of masculinity or femininity.[2] If passers-by are driving at fifty miles per hour, these gender cues cannot be subtle. In *Ways of Seeing*, art historian John Berger describes the cumulative problem that gender stereotypes in advertising create for woman as "split consciousness."[3] While many women guard themselves, some men assume that ogling is part of normal public life. Women are always wary, watching men watch them, and wondering if and when something is going to happen to them.

10   Urban residents also encounter even more explicit sexual images in urban space. Tawdry strip clubs, X-rated films, "adult" bookstores and sex shops are not uncommon sights. Pornographic video arcades are the next wave to come. Pornography is a bigger, more profitable industry in the United States than all legitimate film and record business combined.[4] It spills over into soft-porn, quasi-porn, and taste-

[2]Erving Goffman, *Gender Advertisements* (New York: Harper Colphon, 1976), pp. 24–27; Nancy Henley, *Body Politics: Power, Sex, and Nonverbal Communication* (Englewood Cliffs, NJ: Prentice-Hall, 1977), p. 30; Marianne Wex, *Let's Take Back Our Space* (Berlin: Movimento Druck, 1979).
[3]John Berger et al., *Ways of Seeing* (Harmondsworth, England: BBC and Penguin, 1972), pp. 45–64.
[4]Tom Hayden, *The American Future: New Visions Beyond Old Frontiers* (Boston: South End Press, 1980), p. 15.

less public imagery everywhere. In the midst of this sex-exploitation, if one sees a real prostitute, there is mild surprise. Yet soliciting is still a crime. Of course, the male customer of an adult prostitute is almost never arrested, but the graphic designer, the urban designer, and the urban planner never come under suspicion for their contributions to a commercial public landscape that preserves the sexual double standard in a brutal and vulgar way.

11 Feminist Laura Shapiro calls our society a "rape culture."[5] Adrienne Rich has written of "a world masculinity made unfit for women or men."[6] But surely most Americans do not consciously, deliberately accept public space given over to commercial exploitation, violence and harassment of women. Indeed, the success of the "Moral Majority" displays how a few activists were able to tap public concern effectively about commercialized sexuality, albeit in a narrow, antihumanist way. In contrast, the example of the Women's Christian Temperance Union under Frances Willard's leadership, and the parks movement under Olmsted's,[7] show religious idealism, love of nature, and concern for female safety can be activated into dynamic urban reform movements that enlarge domestic values into urban values, instead of diminishing them into domestic pieties.

Analysis and Description

Analysis differs from description, as we note on page 118, but passages of description are commonly used in essays to support analysis of visual texts. In the essay "Advertisements, Pornography, and Public Space," for example, Dolores Hayden asks and answers the question "What are the effects of representations of women in public space?"; as she answers this question, she presents us with brief but vivid descriptions of billboards, mannequins, and architectural elements. Hayden's essay is primarily analytical; reading it, we share the writer's thoughts, but these thoughts are not the random and fleeting notions of reverie. The thoughts have been organized for us; the effects of billboards and other images on both women and men have been classified and presented to us in an orderly and coherent account made vivid by passages of description. Even if we have never seen the advertisement for the James Bond film or the Rolling Stones album, we can visualize these images because Hayden has made

---

[5]Laura Shapiro, "Violence: The Most Obscene Fantasy," in Jo Freeman, ed., *Women: A Feminist Perspective*, 2nd ed. (Palo Alto, CA: Mayfield, 1979), pp. 469–73.
[6]Ibid., p. 469.
[7]Frederick Law Olmsted (1822–1903) was an American landscape architect. Among his notable works are Central Park in Manhattan and Prospect Park in Brooklyn.

them present to us. Through these passages, we share at least imaginatively in the experiences that gave rise to her thinking. And through description, if the communication between writer and reader has been successful, we are persuaded to share the writer's opinions.

Description at Work in the Analytic Essay

Hayden uses description in her essay to support her analysis of the effects of certain kinds of representations of women—the kind of analysis that might be written for a course in sociology or popular culture.

But because description is not analysis, if you are asked to analyze a painting for your art history class or an advertisement for your media studies class, it won't be enough simply to describe the thing in detail. It may be useful, then, to make some distinctions between the two processes, *description* and *analysis*. Hayden *describes* a billboard when she says, "a horizontal blonde in a backless black velvet dress, slit to the thigh, invites men to 'Try on a little Black Velvet' "; she *describes* mannequins in a department store window: "The female torsos, pin-headed, tip backward and sideways, at odd angles." She reports what any viewer might see if he or she looked closely enough. These statements don't offer evaluations, although Hayden's diction and tone—the words "slit" and "pin-headed," for example—do begin to shape our responses to these images. But when Hayden goes on to say that those mannequins look "as if they are about to be pushed over onto a bed" she is making an *inference*, she's telling her readers what the image *implies* or *suggests*; she is *analyzing*. Likewise, she *describes* the caryatids (columns in the shape of females) on the front door of an apartment building when she says,

> Their breasts are bared, their heads carry the load.

But she's *analyzing* when she says,

> They recall the architecture of the Erechtheum on the Acropolis in Athens, dating from the 5th century B.C., where the sculptured stone forms of female slaves were used as support for a porch in place of traditional columns and capitals. This is an ancient image of servitude.

She's comparing (a common analytic procedure) the modern caryatids to those on the Acropolis, and she's offering an evaluation, a judgment: The caryatids at the entrance of the modern building present an "image of servitude." In another sense, she's explaining how the caryatids function. She not only answers the question "what do these images mean?" she explains *how* they mean.

Comparing

> If you want to really see something, look at
> something else.
>
> —*Howard Nemerov*

We began this chapter with a brief analysis of a Brueghel drawing. We *compared* Brueghel's handling of the two figures: the amount of space each figure occupied, their activities, their facial expressions, the directions of their gaze; we thereby arrived at an interpretation of the *meaning* of Brueghel's drawing. We might say that the drawing invites the comparison, and in so doing communicates Brueghel's understanding of the artist's vision, or of the value of art.

Writers, too, often use comparisons to explain a concept or idea or to arrive at a judgment or conclusion. As in drawing or painting, the point of a comparison in writing is not simply to list similarities or differences, but to explain something, to illuminate what the similarities and differences add up to. What the comparison—or analysis—adds up to is sometimes referred to as a *synthesis*, literally, a combining of separate elements to form a coherent whole.

Notice George Orwell's technique in the following paragraph, from an essay titled "England, Your England," written during World War II. Orwell clarifies our understanding of one kind of military march, the Nazi goose-step, by calling attention to how it differs from the march used by English soldiers. Notice, too, the point of his comparison, which he makes clear in his second sentence, and which resonates throughout the comparison.

One rapid but fairly sure guide to the social atmosphere of a country is the parade-step of its army. A military parade is really a kind of ritual dance, something like a ballet, expressing a certain philosophy of life. The goose-step, for instance, is one of the most horrible sights in the world, far more terrifying than a dive-bomber. It is simply an affirmation of naked power; contained in it, quite consciously and intentionally, is the vision of a boot crashing down on a face. Its ugliness is part of its essence, for what it is saying is "Yes, I *am* ugly, and you daren't laugh at me," like the bully who makes faces at his victim. Why is the goose-step not used in England? There are, heaven knows, plenty of army officers who would be only too glad to introduce some such thing. It is not used because the people in the street would laugh. Beyond a certain point, military display is only possible in countries where the common people dare not laugh at the army. The Italians adopted the goose-step at about the time when Italy passed definitely under German control, and, as one would expect, they do it less well than the Germans. The Vichy government, if it survives, is bound to introduce a stiffer parade-ground discipline into what is left of the French army. In the British army the drill is rigid and complicated, full of memories of the eighteenth century, but without definite swagger; the march is merely a formalised walk. It belongs to a society which is ruled by the sword, no doubt, but a sword which must never be taken out of the scabbard.

—*George Orwell*

Organizing Short Comparisons

An essay may be devoted entirely to a comparison, say of two kinds of tribal organization. But such essays are relatively rare. More often, an essay includes only a paragraph or two of comparison—for example, explaining something unfamiliar by comparing it to something familiar. Let's spend a moment discussing how to organize a paragraph that makes a comparison—though the same principles can be applied to entire essays.

The first part may announce the topic, the next part may discuss one of the two items being compared, and the last part may discuss the other. We can call this method *lumping*, because it presents one item in a lump, and then the other in another lump. Thus Orwell says all that he wishes to say about the goose-step in one lump, and then says what he wishes to say about the British parade-step in another lump. But in making a comparison a writer may use a different method, which we'll call *splitting*. The discussion of the two items may run throughout the paragraph, the writer perhaps devoting alternate sentences to each.

Because almost all writing is designed to help the reader see what the writer has in mind, it may be especially useful here to illustrate this second structure, splitting, with a discussion of visible distinctions. The following comparison of a Japanese statue of a Buddha with a Chinese statue of a bodhisattva (a slightly lower spiritual being, dedicated to saving humankind) treats the Buddha first, and then the bodhisattva.

The Buddha, recognizable by a cranial bump that indicates a sort of supermind, sits erect and austere in the lotus position (legs crossed, each foot with the sole upward on the opposing thigh), in full control of his body. The carved folds of his garments, in keeping with the erect posture, are severe, forming a highly disciplined pattern that is an outward expression of his remote, constrained, austere inner nature. The bodhisattva, on the other hand, sits in a languid, sensuous posture known as "royal ease," the head pensively tilted downward, one knee elevated, one leg hanging down. He is accessible, relaxed, and compassionate.

The structure is, simply this:

The Buddha (posture, folds of garments, inner nature)

The bodhisattva (posture, folds of garments, inner nature)

If, however, the writer had wished to split rather than to lump, she would have compared an aspect of the Buddha with an aspect of the bodhisattva, then another aspect of the Buddha with another aspect of the

Shaka, the Historical Buddha, Japan, Heian period, late 10th–early 11th century; cherry with polychrome and gold; single woodblock construction; 83 cm (height of figure); 72.5 cm (height of hairline).

Guanyin, China, Jin Dynasty, 12th century; wood with traces of polychrome and gold, 141 × 88 × 88 cm.

bodhisattva, and so on, perhaps ending with a synthesis to clarify the point of the comparison. The paragraph might have read like this:

> The Buddha, recognizable by a cranial bump that indicates a sort of supermind, sits erect and austere, in the lotus position (legs crossed, each foot with the sole upward on the opposing thigh), in full control of his body. In contrast, the bodhisattva sits in a languid, sensuous posture known as "royal ease," the head pensively tilted downward, one knee elevated, one leg hanging down. The carved folds of the Buddha's garments, in keeping with his erect posture, are severe, forming a highly disciplined pattern, whereas the bodhisattva's garments hang naturalistically. Both figures are spiritual but the Buddha is remote, constrained, and austere; the bodhisattva is accessible, relaxed, and compassionate.

In effect the structure is this:

The Buddha (posture)

The bodhisattva (posture)

The Buddha (garments)

The bodhisattva (garments)

The Buddha and the bodhisattva (synthesis)

Whether in any given piece of writing you should compare by lumping or by splitting will depend largely on your purpose and on the complexity of the material. We can't even offer the rule that splitting is good for brief, relatively obvious comparisons, lumping for longer, more complex ones, though such a rule usually works. We can, however, give some advice:

1. If you split, reread your draft with two points in mind:
   - *Imagine your reader,* and ask yourself if it is likely that this reader can keep up with the back-and-forth movement. Make sure (perhaps by a summary sentence at the end) that the larger picture is not obscured by the zigzagging.
   - *Don't leave any loose ends.* Make sure that if you call attention to points 1, 2, and 3 in X, you mention all of them (not just 1 and 2) in Y.
2. If you lump, do not simply comment first on X and then on Y.
   - *Let your reader know where you are going,* probably by means of an introductory sentence.

- *Don't be afraid in the second half to remind your reader of the first half.* It is legitimate, and even desirable, to relate the second half of the comparison to the first half. A comparison organized by lumping will not break into two separate halves if the second half develops by reminding the reader how it differs from the first half.

Longer Comparisons

Now let's think about a comparison that extends through two or three paragraphs. If you are comparing the indoor play (for instance, board games or play with toys) and the sports of girls with those of boys, you can, for example, devote one paragraph to the indoor play of girls, a second paragraph to the sports of girls, a third to the indoor play of boys, and a fourth to the sports of boys. If you are thinking in terms of comparing girls and boys, such an organization uses lumps, girls first and then boys (with a transition such as "Boys on the other hand . . ."). But you might split, writing four paragraphs along these lines:

> Indoor play of girls
>
> Indoor play of boys
>
> Sports of girls
>
> Sports of boys

Or you might organize the material into two paragraphs:

> Play and sports of girls
>
> Play and sports of boys

There is no rule, except that the organization and the point of the comparison be clear.

Consider these paragraphs from an essay by Sheila Tobias on the fear of mathematics. The writer's thesis in the essay is that although this fear is more commonly found in females than in males, biology seems not to be the cause. After discussing some findings (for example, that girls compute better than boys in elementary school, and that many girls tend to lose interest in mathematics in junior high school), the writer turns her attention away from the schoolhouse. Notice that whether a paragraph is chiefly about boys or chiefly about girls, the writer keeps us in mind of the overall point: reasons why more females than males fear math.

> Not all the skills that are necessary for learning mathematics are learned in school. Measuring, computing, and manipulating objects that have dimensions and dynamic properties of their own are part of the everyday

life of children. Children who miss out on these experiences may not be well primed for math in school.

Feminists have complained for a long time that playing with dolls is one way of convincing impressionable little girls that they may only be mothers or housewives—or, as in the case of the Barbie doll, "pinup girls"—when they grow up. But doll-playing may have even more serious consequences for little girls than that. Do girls find out about gravity and distance and shapes and sizes playing with dolls? Probably not.

A curious boy, if his parents are tolerant, will have taken apart a number of household and play objects by the time he is ten, and, if his parents are lucky, he may even have put them back together again. In all of this he is learning things that will be useful in physics and math. Taking parts out that have to go back in requires some examination of form. Building something that stays up or at least stays put for some time involves working with structure.

Sports is another source of math-related concepts for children which tends to favor boys. Getting to first base on a not very well hit grounder is a lesson in time, speed, and distance. Intercepting a football thrown through the air requires some rapid intuitive eye calculations based on the ball's direction, speed, and trajectory. Since physics is partly concerned with velocities, trajectories, and collisions of objects, much of the math taught to prepare a student for physics deals with relationships and formulas that can be used to express motion and acceleration.

The first paragraph offers a generalization about "children," that is, about boys and girls. The second paragraph discusses the play of girls with dolls, but discusses it in a context of its relevance, really irrelevance, to mathematics. The third paragraph discusses the household play of boys, again in the context of mathematics. The fourth paragraph discusses the outdoor sports of boys, but notice that girls are not forgotten, for its first sentence is "Sports is another source of math-related concepts for children which tends to favor boys." In short, even when there is a sort of seesaw structure, boys on one end and girls on the other, we never lose sight of the thesis that comprises both halves of the comparison.

Ways of Organizing an Essay Devoted to a Comparison

What happens if you want to organize a comparison or contrast that runs through an entire essay, say a comparison between two political campaigns, or between the characters in two novels. Remember, first of all, that you are writing a comparison not merely as an exercise but in order to make a significant point—let's say, to demonstrate the superiority of *X* to *Y.*

Probably your first thought, after making some jottings, will be to lump rather than to split—that is, to discuss one half of the comparison and then to go on to the second half. We'll discuss this useful method of organization in a moment, but here we want to point out that many instructors and textbooks disapprove of such an organization, arguing that the essay too often breaks into two parts and that the second part involves a good deal of repetition of categories set up in the first part. They prefer splitting. Let's say you are comparing the narrator of *Huckleberry Finn* with the narrator of *The Catcher in the Rye*, in order to show that despite superficial similarities, they are very different, and that the difference is partly the difference between the nineteenth century and the twentieth. An organization often recommended is something like this:

1. First similarity (the narrator and his quest)
   a. Huck
   b. Holden
2. Second similarity (the corrupt world surrounding the narrator)
   a. Society in *Huckleberry Finn*
   b. Society in *The Catcher in the Rye*
3. First difference (degree to which the narrator fulfills his quest and escapes from society)
   a. Huck's plan to "light out" to the frontier
   b. Holden's breakdown

And so on, for as many additional differences as seem relevant. Here is another way of splitting and organizing a comparison:

1. First point: the narrator and his quest
   a. Similarities between Huck and Holden
   b. Differences between Huck and Holden
2. Second point: the corrupt world
   a. Similarities between the worlds in *Huck* and *The Catcher*
   b. Differences between the worlds in *Huck* and *The Catcher*
3. Third point: degree of success
   a. Similarities between Huck and Holden
   b. Differences between Huck and Holden

But a comparison need not employ either of these methods of splitting. There is even the danger that an essay employing either of them may not come into focus until the essayist stands back from the seven-layer cake and announces, in the concluding paragraph, that the odd layers taste better. In your preparatory thinking you may want to make comparisons in pairs, but you must come to some conclusions about what these add up to before writing the final version. The final version should not duplicate the thought processes; rather, it should be organized so as to make the point clearly and effectively.

The point of the essay is not to list pairs of similarities or differences, but to illuminate a topic by making thoughtful comparisons. Although in a long essay you cannot postpone until page 30 a discussion of the second half of the comparison, in an essay of, say, fewer than ten pages, nothing is wrong with setting forth half of the comparison and then, in the light of what you've already said, discussing the second half. True, an essay that uses lumping will break into two unrelated parts if the second half makes no use of the first or fails to modify it; but the essay will hang together if the second half looks back to the first half and calls attention to differences that the new material reveals.

The danger of organizing the essay into two unrelated lumps can be avoided if in formulating your thesis you remember that the point of a comparison is to call attention to the unique features of something by holding it up against something similar but significantly different. If the differences are great and apparent, a comparison is a waste of effort. ("Blueberries are different from elephants. Blueberries do not have trunks. And elephants do not grow on bushes.") Indeed, a comparison between essentially and evidently unlike things can only obscure, for by making the comparison the writer implies there are significant similarities, and readers can only wonder why they do not see them. The essays that do break into two halves are essays that make *un*instructive comparisons: The first half tells the reader five things about baseball, the second half tells the reader five unrelated things about football.

CHECKLIST FOR REVISING COMPARISONS

☐ Is the point of the comparison—your reason for making it—clear? (See p. 135.)

☐ Do you cover all significant similarities and differences? (See p. 138.)

☐ Is the comparison readable—that is, is it clear and yet not tediously mechanical? (See p. 138.)

☐ Is lumping or splitting the best way to make this comparison? (See pp. 136–41.)

☐ If you are offering a value judgment, is it fair? Have you overlooked weaknesses in your preferred subject, and strengths in your less preferred subject?

Process Analysis

Popular writing offers many examples of the form of writing known as **process analysis.** Newspaper articles explain how to acquire a home aquarium or how to "detail" your car to improve its resale value; magazine articles explain how to begin a program of weight training or how to make a safe exit in an airplane emergency. The requirements a writer must follow when preparing such an article, sometimes called a **directive process analysis,** can be simply stated:

• Know the material thoroughly.

• Keep your audience in mind.

• Set forth the steps clearly, usually in chronological order.

• Define unfamiliar terms.

In addition, if writers want to express their pleasure in the process or their sense of its utility or value, in the introductory paragraph or in the conclusion they should keep such comments brief, they must not interrupt the explanation of the process, and they must not gush.

Explaining a process is common in academic writing too, though usually the explanation is of how something happens or has happened, and it is thus sometimes called an **informative process analysis.** The writer's purpose is for the reader to understand the process, not to perform it. You may find yourself reading or writing about a successful election strategy or a botched military campaign. In an exam you may be explaining your plan to solve a mathematical problem, or you may be explaining how the imagery works in a Shakespearean sonnet. You might write an essay on the camera techniques Hitchcock used in a sequence, or a term paper based on your research in marine biology. Once again, you will need to keep your reader in mind, to organize your explanation clearly and logically, and, of course, to write with expert knowledge of your subject.

The essay below reports on a lecture that was, from the evidence, an entertaining example of an *informative process analysis.*

Anne Hebald Mandelbaum

It's the Portly Penguin That Gets the Girl, French Biologist Claims

1   The penguin is a feathered and flippered bird who looks as if he's on his way to a formal banquet. With his stiff, kneeless strut and natural dinner jacket, he moves like Charlie Chaplin in his heyday dressed like Cary Grant in his.

2   But beneath the surface of his tuxedo is a gallant bird indeed. Not only does he fast for 65 days at a time, sleep standing up, and forsake all others in a lifetime of monogamy, but the male penguin also guards, watches over, and even hatches the egg.

3   We owe much of our current knowledge of the life and loves of the king and emperor penguins to—*bien sûr*—a Frenchman. Twenty-eight-year-old Yvon Le Maho is a biophysiologist from Lyons who visited the University last week to discuss his discoveries and to praise the penguin. He had just returned from 14 months in Antarctica, where he went to measure, to photograph, to weigh, to take blood and urine samples of, to perform autopsies on—in short, to study the penguin.

4   Although his original intent had been to investigate the penguin's long fasts, Monsieur Le Maho was soon fascinated by the amatory aspect of the penguin. Copulating in April, the female produces the egg in May and then heads out to sea, leaving her mate behind to incubate the egg. The males huddle together, standing upright and protecting the 500-gram (or 1.1-pound) egg with their feet for 65 days. During this time, they neither eat nor stray: each steadfastly stands guard over his egg, protecting it from the temperatures which dip as low as −40 degrees and from the winds which whip the Antarctic wilds with gusts of 200 miles an hour.

5   For 65 days and 65 nights, the males patiently huddle over the eggs, never lying down, never letting up. Then, every year on July 14th—Bastille Day, the national holiday of France—the eggs hatch and thousands of penguin chicks are born. M. Le Maho told his amused and enthusiastic audience at the Biological Laboratories.

6   The very day the chicks are born—or, at the latest, the following day—the female penguins return to land from their two-and-a-half month fishing expedition. They clamber out of the water and toboggan along the snow-covered beaches toward the rookery and their mates. At this moment, the males begin to emit the penguin equivalent of wild, welcoming cheers—"*comme le cri de trompette,*" M. Le Maho later told the *Gazette* in an interview—"like the clarion call of the trumpet."

7   And, amid the clamorous thundering of 12,000 penguins, the female recognizes the individual cry of her mate. When she does, she begins to cry to him. The male then recognizes *her* song, lifts the newborn chick into his feathered arms, and makes a beeline for the female. Each singing, each crying, the males and females rush toward each other, slipping and sliding on the ice as they go, guided all the while by the single voice each instinctively knows.

8   The excitement soon wears thin for the male, however, who hasn't had a bite to eat in more than two months. He has done his duty and done it unflaggingly, but even penguins cannot live by duty alone. He must have food, and quickly.

9   Having presented his mate with their newborn, the male abruptly departs, heading out to sea in search of fish. The female, who has just returned from her sea-going sabbatical, has swallowed vast quantities of fish for herself and her chick. Much of what she has eaten she has not digested. Instead, this undigested food becomes penguin baby food. She regurgitates it, all soft and paplike, from her storage throat right into her chick's mouth. The chicks feed in this manner until December, when they first learn to find food on their own.

10   The penguins' reproductive life begins at age five, and the birds live about 25 years. Their fasting interests M. Le Maho because of its close similarities with fasting in human beings. And although many migratory birds also fast, their small size and indeed their flight make it almost impossible to study them closely. With the less-mobile and non-flying penguin, however, the scientist has a relatively accessible population to study. With no damage to the health of the penguin, M. Le Maho told the *Gazette*, a physiobiologist can extract blood from the flipper and sample the urine.

11   "All fasting problems are the same between man and the penguin," M. Le Maho said. "The penguin uses glucose in the brain, experiences ketosis as does man, and accomplishes gluconeogenesis, too." Ketosis is the build-up of partially burned fatty acids in the blood, usually as a result of starvation; gluconeogenesis is the mak-

ing of sugar from non-sugar chemicals, such as amino acids. "The penguin can tell us a great deal about how our own bodies react to fasting conditions," M. Le Maho said.

12   He will return to Antarctica, M. Le Maho said, with the French government-sponsored *Expéditions Polaires Françaises* next December. There he will study the growth of the penguin chick, both inside the egg and after birth; will continue to study their mating, and to examine the penguin's blood sugar during fasting.

13   During the question-and-answer period following his talk, M. Le Maho was asked what the female penguin looks for in a mate. Responding, M. Le Maho drew himself up to his full five-foot-nine and said, "*La grandeur.*"

Explaining an Analysis

As we have suggested, the writer of an analytical essay arrives at a thesis by asking questions and answering them, by separating the topic into parts and by seeing—often through the use of lists and scratch outlines—how those parts relate. Or, we might say, analytic writing presupposes detective work: The writer looks over the evidence, finds some clues, pursues the trail from one place to the next, and makes the arrest. Elementary? Perhaps.

You may recall that Sherlock Holmes customarily searches for evidence, finds it, and then—and this is important—explains it to his listener, usually Dr. Watson. When you write an analytic essay, you are Holmes, and your reader is Watson. Even when as a writer, after preliminary thinking you have solved a problem—that is, focused on a topic and formulated a thesis—you are, as we have said before, not yet done. It is, alas, not enough simply to present the results of your analytical thinking to a reader who, like Dr. Watson, will surely want to know "How in the world did you deduce that?" And like Holmes, writers are often impatient; we long to say with him "I have no time for trifles." But the real reason for our impatience is, as Holmes is quick to acknowledge, that "It was easier to know it than to explain why I know it." But explaining to readers why or how, presenting both the reasoning that led to a thesis and the evidence that supports the reasoning, is the writer's job.

In your preliminary detective work (that is, in reading, taking notes, musing, jotting down some thoughts, and writing rough drafts) some insights (perhaps including your thesis) may come swiftly, apparently spontaneously, and in random order. You may be unaware that you have been thinking analytically at all. In preparing your essay for your reader, however, you become aware, in part because *you must become aware.* To replace your reader's natural suspicion with respect for your analysis, you must explain your reasoning in an orderly and interesting fashion, and you must present your evidence.

CHAPTER EIGHT

PERSUADING READERS

To persuade readers is to convince them of the merit of your point of view, whether you're arguing against censorship, or for capital punishment, or in favor of a particular interpretation of a short story. To be persuasive, you must present *reasonable arguments*, supported with *evidence*. In academic essays, the distinction between argument and analysis is often blurry. In the preceding chapter, for example, Dolores Hayden's analytic essay ("Advertisements, Pornography, and Public Space") does more than assert that certain kinds of images appear in certain places. It sets forth an **argument:** we ought not to allow public space to be given over to the harassment of women. The writer supports that argument with **evidence,** a report of images that she has observed, images that she subjects to careful **analysis.** In Chapter 10, "Writing the Research Essay," we'll examine an essay in which the writer uses **analysis** and **argument** in roughly equal proportion. In this chapter, after a brief comment on persuasion by emotional appeal, we'll focus on the elements of argument: on the distinction between claims and evidence, on the importance of defining terms and of avoiding fallacies, and on the use of wit in persuasive writing.

Emotional Appeals

It is often said that good argumentative writing appeals only to reason and logic (Greek: *logos*), never to emotion (*pathos*), and that any sort of emotional appeal is illegitimate, irrelevant, fallacious. Logic textbooks may even stigmatize with Latin labels the various sorts of emotional appeal—for instance, *argumentum ad populam* (appeal to the prejudices of the mob, as in "Come on, we all know that schools don't teach any-thing anymore") and *argumentum ad misericoridam* (appeal to pity, as in "No one can blame this poor kid for stabbing a classmate because his mother was often institutionalized and his father beat him").

True, appeals to emotion may get in the way of the facts of the case; they may blind the audience by stimulating tears. When an emotional argument confuses the issue or shifts attention away from the facts of the issue, we can reasonably speak of the fallacy of emotional appeal. But no fallacy is involved when an emotional appeal heightens the facts, bring-ing them home to the audience rather than masking them. If we are talk-ing about legislation that would govern police actions, it is legitimate to show a photograph of the battered, bloodied face of a victim of alleged police brutality. Of course such a photograph cannot tell if the subject threatened the officer with a gun or repeatedly resisted an order to sur-render. But it can tell us that the victim was severely beaten and (like a comparable description in words) evoke in us emotions that may prop-erly enter into our decision about what sorts of limitations on police actions are appropriate. Similarly, an animal rights activist who is argu-ing that calves are cruelly confined might reasonably tell us the size of the pen in which the beast—unable to turn around or even to lie down—is kept. Others may argue that calves don't much care about turning around or have no right to turn around, but the verbal description, which unquestionably makes an emotional appeal, can hardly be called falla-cious or irrelevant.

In appealing to emotions, then:

• Do not falsify (especially by oversimplifying) the issue.

• Do not distract attention from the facts of the case.

For the most part, you should focus on the facts and concentrate on offer-ing reasons (essentially, statements linked with "because"), but you may also legitimately bring the facts home to your readers by seeking to induce in them the appropriate emotions. Your words will be fallacious only if you stimulate emotions that are not rightly connected with the facts of the case.

Making Reasonable Arguments

Persuasive writing that offers evidence and relies chiefly on reasoning rather than on appeals to the emotions is usually called *argument*. What distinguishes argument from exposition is this: Whereas both consist of statements, in argument some statements are offered as *reasons* for other statements. Another way of characterizing argument is that argument assumes there is or may be substantial disagreement between informed readers. To overcome this disagreement, the writer of an argument offers reasons that seek to convince by their validity. Here, for example, is C. S. Lewis arguing against vivisection, the experimentation on live animals for scientific research:

> A rational discussion of this subject begins by inquiring whether pain is, or is not, an evil. If it is not, then the case against vivisection falls. But then so does the case for vivisection. If it is not defended on the ground that it reduces human suffering, on what ground can it be defended? And if pain is not an evil, why should human suffering be reduced? We must therefore assume as a basis for the whole discussion that pain is an evil, otherwise there is nothing to be discussed.
>
> Now if pain is an evil then the infliction of pain, considered in itself, must clearly be an evil act. But there are such things as necessary evils. Some acts which would be bad, simply in themselves, may be excusable and even laudable when they are necessary means to a greater good. In saying that the infliction of pain, simply in itself, is bad, we are not saying that pain ought never to be inflicted. Most of us think that it can rightly be inflicted for a good purpose—as in dentistry or just and reformatory punishment. The point is that it always requires justification. On the man whom we find inflicting pain rests the burden of showing why an act which in itself would be simply bad is, in those particular circumstances, good. If we find a man giving pleasure it is for us to prove (if we criticize him) that his action is wrong. But if we find a man inflicting pain it is for him to prove that his action is right. If he cannot, he is a wicked man.

And here is Supreme Court Justice Louis Brandeis, concluding his justly famous argument that government may not use evidence illegally obtained by wiretapping:

> Decency, security and liberty alike demand that government officials shall be subjected to the same rules of conduct that are commands to the citizen. In a government of laws, existence of the government will be imperiled if it fails to observe the law scrupulously. Our Government is the potent, the omnipresent teacher. For good or for ill, it teaches the whole people by its example. Crime is contagious. If the Government becomes a lawbreaker, it breeds contempt for law; it invites every man to become a law unto himself; it invites anarchy. To declare that in the administra-

tion of the criminal law the end justifies the means—to declare that the Government may commit crimes in order to secure the conviction of a private criminal—would bring terrible retribution. Against that pernicious doctrine this Court should resolutely set its face.

Notice here that Brandeis's reasoning is highlighted by his forceful style. Note the resonant use of parallel constructions ("Decency, security and liberty," "For good or for ill," "it breeds . . . it invites," "To declare . . . to declare") and the variation between long and short sentences. Note too the wit in his comparisons: Government is a teacher, crime is like a disease.

Claims and Evidence

Evidence is what a writer offers in support of a **claim**—an assertion, usually that something is true, or right, or good. Evidence usually comes in the form of examples, testimony, and statistics.

Three Kinds of Claims: Claims of Fact, Value, and Policy

We can usually distinguish between two kinds of claims, claims of fact and claims of value, and we can sometimes distinguish these from a third kind of claim, claims of policy.

Claims of Fact

Claims of fact assert that something is or was or will be. They include, for instance, arguments about cause and effect, correlation, probability, and states of affairs. The following examples can be considered claims of fact:

Vanilla is the most popular flavor of ice cream in the United States.

Pornography stimulates violence against women.

Pornography has the potential of leading to violence.

Pornography serves a useful social purpose because it offers a harmless release of impulses that might otherwise be released in such activities as molestation or rape.

Capital punishment reduces crime.

Capital punishment does not reduce crime.

Diversity in a college benefits all students.

Racial integration of the armed forces was achieved with very little conflict during the Korean War.

To support a claim of this sort, you must provide evidence. Such evidence might, for instance, be testimony (for instance, your own experience, or statements by men who have said that pornography stimulated them to violence), or it might be statistics (gathered from a report in a scholarly journal). Even if the claim has to do with the future—let's say the claim that gun control will not reduce crime—you try to offer evidence. For example, you might gather information about the experiences of other countries, or even of certain states, that have adopted strict regulations concerning the sale of guns.

Claims of Value

Claims of value concern what is right or wrong, good or bad, better or worse than something else:

Country music deserves to be taken seriously.

Rock is better than country music.

Capital punishment is barbaric.

Euthanasia is immoral.

Some claims of value may be mere expressions of taste: "Vanilla is better than chocolate." It is hard to imagine how one could go about supporting such a claim—or refuting it. One probably can do no better than reply with the Latin proverb, *"De gustibus non est disputandum."* (There is no disputing about tastes.) Notice, however, that the claim that vanilla is better than chocolate is quite different from the claim that most Americans prefer vanilla to chocolate. The last statement is a claim of fact, not of value, and it can be proved or disproved with evidence—for example, with information provided by the makers of ice cream.

Claims of value that go beyond the mere expression of taste—for instance, claims of morality or claims of artistic value—are usually supported by appeals to standards. ("The Patriot Act is bad *because* governments should not restrict the rights of individuals," or "Hip-hop music is good *because* it is complex."). In supporting claims of value, writers usually appeal to standards that they believe are acceptable to their readers. Here are some examples:

Sex-education programs in schools are inappropriate *because* aspects of moral education should properly be given only by parents.

Sex-education programs in schools are appropriate *because* society has a duty to provide what most parents obviously are reluctant to provide.

Doctors should be permitted to end a patient's life if the patient makes such a request, *because* each of us should be free to make the decisions that most concern us.

Euthanasia is unacceptable *because* only God can give or take life.

In arguing a claim of value, be sure you have clearly in your mind the standards that you believe support the claim. You may find it appropriate to explain *why* you hold these standards, and *how* adherence to these standards will be of benefit.

Claims of Policy

Claims of policy assert that a policy, law, or custom should be initiated or altered or dropped. Such claims usually are characterized by words like "should," "must," and "ought."

Children should be allowed to vote, if they wish to.

A course in minority cultures ought to be required.

The federal tax on gasoline must be raised.

In defending an unfamiliar claim of policy, you may want to begin by pointing out that there is a problem that is usually overlooked. For instance, if you urgently believe that children should have the right to vote—a view almost never expressed—you'll probably first have to convince your audience that there really is an arguable issue here, an issue concerning children's rights, an issue that deserves serious thought.

In defending a claim of policy you will probably find yourself providing information, just as you would do in support of a claim of fact. For instance, if your topic is children and the vote, you might point out that until 1920 women could not vote in the United States, the usual arguments being that they were mentally unfit and that they would vote the way their men told them to vote. Experience has proved that these low estimates of the capabilities of the disenfranchised were absurd.

But in defending a claim of policy you will probably have to consider values as well as facts. Thus, in arguing for an increase in the gasoline tax, you might want not only to provide factual information about how much money a five-cents-per-gallon tax would raise, but also to argue that such an increase is *fairer* than an alternative such as reducing social security benefits.

Three Kinds of Evidence: Examples, Testimony, Statistics

Writers of arguments seek to persuade by offering evidence. There are three chief forms of evidence used in argument:

- Examples
- Testimony, the citation of authorities
- Statistics

We'll briefly consider each of these.

Examples

The word *example* is from the Latin *exemplum*, which means "something taken out." An example is the sort of thing, taken from among many similar things, that one selects and holds up for view, perhaps after saying "For example," or "For instance."

Three categories of examples are especially common in written arguments:

- Real examples
- Invented instances
- Analogies

Real examples are actual instances that have occurred. If, say, we are arguing that gun control won't work, we point to those states that have adopted gun control laws and that nevertheless have had no reduction in crimes using guns. Or, if we want to support the assertion that a woman can be a capable head of state, we may find ourselves pointing to women who actually served as heads of state, such as Golda Meir and Indira Ghandi (prime ministers of Israel and India) and to Margaret Thatcher (prime minister of England).

The advantage of using real examples is, clearly, that they are real. Of course, an opponent might stubbornly respond that Golda Meir, Indira Gandhi, and Margaret Thatcher for some reason or other could not function as the head of state in *our* country. Someone might argue, for instance, that the case of Golda Meir proves nothing, since the role of women in Israeli society is different from the role of women in the United States (a country in which a majority of the citizens are Christians). And another person might argue that much of Mrs. Gandhi's power came from the fact that she was the daughter of Nehru, an immensely popular Indian statesman. Even the most compelling real example inevitably will in some ways be special or particular, and in the eyes of some readers may not seem to be a fair example.

Consider, for instance, a student who is arguing that peer review should be part of a writing course. The student points out that he or she found it of great help in high school. An opponent argues that things in college are different—college students should be able to help themselves, even highly gifted college students are not competent to offer college-level instruction, and so on. Still, as the feebleness of these objections (and the objections against Meir and Gandhi) indicates, real examples can be very compelling.

Invented instances are exempt from the charge that, because of some detail or other, they are not relevant as evidence. Suppose, for example, you are arguing against capital punishment, on the grounds that if an innocent person is executed, there is no way of even attempting to rectify the injustice. If you point to the case of X, you may be met with the reply that X was not in fact innocent. Rather than get tangled up in the guilt or innocence of a particular person, it may be better to argue that we can suppose—we can imagine—an innocent person convicted and executed, and we can imagine that evidence later proves the person's innocence.

Invented instances have the advantage of presenting an issue clearly, free from all of the distracting particularities and irrelevancies that are bound up with any real instance. But invented instances have the disadvantage of being invented, and they may seem remote from the real issues being argued.

Analogies are comparisons pointing out several resemblances between two rather different things. For instance, one might assert that a government is like a ship, and in times of stress—if the ship is to weather the storm—the authority of the captain must not be questioned.

But don't confuse an analogy with proof. An analogy is an extended comparison between two things; it can be useful in exposition, for it explains the unfamiliar by means of the familiar: "A government is like a ship, and just as a ship has a captain and a crew, so a government has . . ."; "Writing an essay is like building a house; just as an architect must begin with a plan, so the writer must. . . ." Such comparisons can be useful, helping to clarify what otherwise might be obscure, but their usefulness goes only so far. Everything is what it is, and not another thing. A government is not a ship, and what is true of a captain's power need not be true of a president's power; and a writer is not an architect. Some of what is true about ships may be roughly true of governments, and some of what is true about architects may be true of writers, but there are differences too. Consider the following analogy between a lighthouse and the death penalty:

> The death penalty is a warning, just like a lighthouse throwing its beams out to sea. We hear about shipwrecks, but we do not hear about the ships the lighthouse guides safely on their way. We do not have proof of the number of ships it saves, but we do not tear the lighthouse down.
>
> —*J. Edgar Hoover*

How convincing is Hoover's analogy as an argument, that is, as a reason for retaining the death penalty?

Testimony

Testimony, or the citation of authorities, is rooted in our awareness that some people are recognized as experts. In our daily lives we constantly turn to experts for guidance: We look up the spelling of a word in the dictionary, we watch weather forecasts on television, we take an ailing cat to the vet for a checkup. Similarly, when we wish to become informed about controversial matters, we often turn to experts, first to help educate ourselves, and then to help convince others.

Don't forget that *you* are an authority on many things. For example, today's newspaper includes an article about the cutback in funding for the teaching of the arts in elementary and secondary schools. Art educators are responding that the arts are not a frill, and that in fact the arts provide the analytical thinking, teamwork, motivation, and self-discipline that most people agree are needed to reinvigorate American schools. If you have been involved in the arts in school—for instance, if you studied painting or learned to play a musical instrument—you are in a position to evaluate these claims. Similarly, if you have studied in a bilingual educational program, your own testimony will be invaluable in any discussion of the merits of bilingual programs.

There are at least two reasons for offering testimony in an argument. The obvious one is that expert opinion carries some weight with any audience; the less obvious one is that a change of voice (if the testimony is not your own) in an essay may afford the reader a bit of pleasure. No matter how engaging your own voice may be, a fresh voice—whether that of

Thomas Jefferson, Ruth Bader Ginsburg, or Alice Walker—may provide a refreshing change of tone.

But, of course, there are dangers: The chief danger is that the words of authorities may be taken out of context or otherwise distorted, and the second is that the authorities may not be authorities on the present topic. Quite rightly we are concerned with what Jefferson said, but it is not clear that his words can be fairly applied, on one side or the other, to such an issue as abortion. Quite rightly we are concerned with what Einstein said, but it is not clear that his eminence as a physicist constitutes him an authority on, say, world peace. In a moment, when we discuss errors in reasoning, we'll have more to say about the proper and improper use of authorities.

Statistics

Statistics, another important form of evidence, are especially useful in arguments concerning social issues. If we want to argue for raising the driving age, we will probably do some research in the library and will offer statistics about the number of accidents caused by people in certain age groups.

But a word of caution: The significance of statistics may be difficult to assess. For instance, opponents of gun control legislation have pointed out, in support of the argument that such laws are ineffectual, that homicides in Florida *increased* after Florida adopted gun control laws. Supporters of gun control laws cried "Foul," arguing that in the years after adopting these laws Miami became (for reasons having nothing to do with the laws) the cocaine capital of the United States, and the rise in homicide was chiefly a reflection of murders involved in the drug trade. That is, a significant change in the population has made a comparison of the figures meaningless. This objection seems plausible, and probably the statistics therefore should carry little weight.

A Note on Definition in the Persuasive Essay

To argue a point or to explain an idea, writers frequently need to provide definitions. Defining the terms of an argument is one of the persuasive writer's most useful strategies: A writer making an argument for or against abortion would be likely at some point in the essay to define the term "life."

The words may be *specialized* or unfamiliar to the writer's intended audience—for example, the words "venture capitalist" or "enterprise zones." Or, a writer might define a word that the audience may think it knows but that (in the writer's opinion) the audience may misunderstand. For instance, you might argue that the words "guerrilla" and "terrorist" are not synonyms, and then go on to define each word, showing the differences between them.

In addition to defining a word because it is specialized ("venture capitalist"), or because we want to distinguish it from another word ("guerrilla" and "terrorist"), we may define a word because the word has many meanings, and we want to make sure that readers take the word in a particular way. A word like "ability," for example, may require defining in a discussion of the Scholastic Aptitude Test. To argue that the SAT does or does not measure "academic ability," the writer and reader need, in a sense, to agree on a specific meaning for "ability." This kind of definition, where the writer specifies or stipulates a meaning ("By *ability* I mean . . ."), is called a **stipulative definition.**

The word *stipulate*, by the way, comes from a Latin word meaning "to bargain." Explaining a word's *etymology*, its history or its origin, as we have just done, is often an aid in definition.

In short, when defining a word or term, writers have many options, and they need to take into account both their own purposes in writing and their readers' needs.

Definition at Work

In the following brief essay student Lena Flora defines the term *political correctness.*

The Plight of the Politically Correct

Political correctness is a style of language, an attitude, and a standard of ethics that people have now been struggling with for years. Part of the reason for this struggle lies in the fact that no one is exactly sure what is and what is not politically correct. The phrase political correctness might be defined as "conformity to a body of liberal or radical opinion, especially on social matters." Political correctness also involves the avoidance of anything, even established vocabulary, that might be construed as discriminatory or pejorative. In effect, political correctness seems to mean taking every word in the English language, scrutinizing it for any way that it could possibly offend any one person, and using this criterion to ban its use in day-to-day speech. For example, I can no longer grow up and be a fireman, a policeman, a mailman, or a woman. I may not even be allowed to call myself female. Does this mean that I am fated to call myself testosteronally-challenged, or maybe x-chromosomally gifted? Am I a chauvinist pig if I like to be known as a woman, or if I refer to my daughter as my little girl? By some strict politically correct standards, yes. Also, political correctness forces me to refrain from using many adjectives I might use to describe myself. I am not Oriental, short, or near-sighted. Instead, I am an Asian-American, vertically-challenged, and distant-visually-challenged person of feminine gender. I certainly don't feel challenged in any of these areas, only in the area of speaking with political correctness.

How Much Evidence Is Enough?

If you allow yourself ample time to write your essay, you probably will turn up plenty of evidence to illustrate your arguments, such as examples drawn from your own experience and imagination, from your reading, and from your talks with others. Evidence will not only help to clarify and to support your assertions, but it will also provide a concreteness that will be welcome in a paper that might be on the whole fairly abstract. Your sense of your audience will have to guide you as you select your evidence. Generally speaking, a single example may not fully illuminate a difficult point, and so a second example, a clincher, may be desirable. If you offer a third or fourth example you probably are succumbing to a temptation to include something that tickles your fancy. If it is as good as you think it is, the reader probably will accept the unnecessary example and may even be grateful. But before you heap up examples, try to imagine yourself in your reader's place, and ask if the example is needed. If it is not needed, ask yourself if the reader will be glad to receive the overload.

One other point: On most questions, say on the value of bilingual education or on the need for rehabilitation programs in prisons, it's not possible to make a strictly logical case, in the sense of an absolutely airtight proof. Don't assume that it is your job to make an absolute proof. What you are expected to do is to offer a reasonable argument.

Two Kinds of Reasoning: Induction and Deduction

We have just said that you are expected to offer a reasonable argument, which means that your essay will probably demonstrate two kinds of thinking, inductive and deductive. **Induction** is the process of reasoning from particular to general, or drawing a conclusion about all members of a class from a study of some members of the class. Every elephant I have seen is grayish, so by induction (from Latin for "lead into," "lead up to") I conclude that all elephants are grayish. And here we get to what is called *logos*, reasoning, as opposed to *pathos*, emotion.

Here's another example: I have met ten graduates of Vassar College and all are females, so I conclude that all Vassar graduates are females. This conclusion, however, happens to be incorrect; Vassar originally admitted only women, but it now admits men. Induction is valid only if the sample is representative.

Because we can rarely be certain that a sample is representative, induced conclusions are usually open to doubt. Still, we live our lives largely by induction; we have dinner with a friend, we walk the dog, we write home for money—all because these actions have produced certain results in the past and we assume that actions of the same sort will produce results consistent with our earlier experience. Nelson Algren's excellent advice must have been arrived at inductively: "Never eat at a place called Mom's, and never play cards with a man called Doc." In developing our argument, we draw on experience—"Policy X has been successful in all ten instances where it was tried, so we can assume it will probably succeed here too"—but we must understand that we are not dealing with certainties.

Deduction (from Latin for "lead down from") is the process of reasoning from premises to a logical conclusion. Here is the classic example: "All men are mortal" (the major premise); "Socrates is a man" (the minor premise); "Therefore Socrates is mortal" (the conclusion). Such an argument, which takes two truths and joins them to produce a third truth, is called a *syllogism* (from Greek for "a reckoning together"). Deduction moves from a general statement to a specific application; it is, therefore, the opposite of induction, which moves from specific instances to a general conclusion.

Notice that if a premise of a syllogism is not true, one can reason logically and still come to false conclusion. Example: All teachers are members of a union; Jones is a teacher; Therefore Jones is a member of a union. Although the formal process of reasoning is correct here, the major premise is false—not all teachers are members of a union—and so the conclusion is worthless. (Jones may or may not be a member of a union.) In other words, "Garbage in, garbage out."

Let's now look at some common errors in thinking, whether inductive or deductive.

Avoiding Fallacies

Let's further examine writing reasonable arguments by considering some obvious errors in reasoning. In logic these errors are called **fallacies** (from a Latin verb meaning "to deceive"). As Tweedledee says in *Through the Looking-Glass*, "If it were so, it would be; but as it isn't, it ain't. That's logic."

To persuade readers to accept your opinions you must persuade them that you are reliable; if your argument includes fallacies, thoughtful readers will not take you seriously. More important, if your argument includes fallacies, you are misleading yourself. When you search your draft for fallacies, you are searching for ways to improve the quality of your thinking. Here are nine fallacies to avoid.

1. False authority. Don't try to borrow the prestige of authorities who are not authorities on the topic in question—for example, a heart surgeon speaking on politics. Similarly, some former authorities are no longer authorities, because the problems have changed or because later knowledge has superseded their views. Adam Smith, Jefferson, Eleanor Roosevelt, and Einstein remain persons of genius, but an attempt to use their opinions when you are examining modern issues—even in their fields—may be questioned. Remember the last words of John B. Sedgwick, a Union Army general at the Battle of Spotsylvania in 1864: "They couldn't hit an elephant at this dist—." In short, before you rely on an authority, ask yourself if the person in question *is* an authority on the topic. And don't let stereotypes influence your idea of who is an authority. Remember the Yiddish proverb: "A goat has a beard, but that doesn't make him a rabbi."

2. False quotation. If you do quote from an authority, don't misquote. For example, you may find someone who grants that "there are strong arguments in favor of abolishing the death penalty"; but if she goes on to argue that, on balance, the arguments in favor of retaining it seem stronger to her, it is dishonest to quote her words so as to imply that she favors abolishing it.

3. Suppression of evidence. Don't neglect evidence that is contrary to your own argument. You owe it to yourself and your reader to present all the relevant evidence. Be especially careful not to assume that every question is simply a matter of *either/or*. There may be some truth on both sides. Take the following thesis: "Grades encourage unwholesome competition, and should therefore be abolished." Even if the statement about the evil effect of grading is true, it may not be the whole truth, and therefore it may not follow that grades should be abolished. One might point out that grades do other things too: They may stimulate learning, and they may assist students by telling them how far they have progressed. One might nevertheless conclude, on balance, that the fault outweighs the benefits. But the argument will be more persuasive now that the benefits of grades have been considered.

Concede to the opposition what is due it, and then outscore the opposition. If you don't discuss the opposing evidence, your readers will keep wondering why you do not consider this point or that, and may consequently dismiss your argument. Confronting the opposition will almost surely strengthen your own argument. As Edmund Burke said 200 years ago, "He that wrestles with us strengthens our nerves, and sharpens our skill. Our antagonist is our helper."

4. Generalization from insufficient evidence. In rereading a draft of an argument that you have written, try to spot your own generalizations. Ask yourself if a reasonable reader is likely to agree that the generalization is based on an adequate sample.

A visitor to a college may sit in on three classes, each taught by a different instructor, and may find all three stimulating. That's a good sign, but can we generalize and say that the teaching at this college is excellent? Are three classes a sufficient sample? If all three are offered by the Biology Department, and if the Biology Department includes only five instructors, perhaps we can tentatively say that the teaching of biology at this institution is good. If the Biology Department contains twenty instructors, perhaps we can still say, though more tentatively, that this sample indicates that the teaching of biology is good. But what does the sample say about the teaching of other subjects at the college? It probably does say something—the institution may be much concerned with teaching across the board—but then again it may not say a great deal, since the Biology Department may be exceptionally concerned with good teaching.

5. The genetic fallacy. Don't assume that something can necessarily be explained in terms of its birth or origin, its genesis. "He wrote the novel to make money, so it can't be any good" is not a valid inference. The value of a novel does not depend on the author's motivations in writing it. Indeed, the value or worth of a novel needs to be established by reference to other criteria. Neither the highest nor the lowest motivations guarantee the quality of the product. Another example: "Capital punishment arose in days when people sought revenge, so now it ought to be abolished." Again an unconvincing argument: Capital punishment may have some current value; for example, it may serve as a deterrent to crime. But that's another argument, and it needs evidence if it is to be believed.

6. Begging the question and circular reasoning. Don't assume the truth of the point that you should prove. The term *begging the question* is a trifle odd. It means, in effect, "You, like a beggar, are asking me to grant you something at the outset."

Consider two examples: "The barbaric death penalty should be abolished"; "This senseless language requirement should be dropped." Both statements assume what they should prove—that the death penalty is barbaric and that the language requirement is senseless. You can of course make assertions such as these, but you must go on to prove them.

Circular reasoning is usually an extended form of begging the question. What ought to be proved is covertly assumed: "X is the best-qualified candidate for the office, because the most informed people say so." Who are the most informed people? Those who recognize X's superiority. Circular reasoning, then, normally includes intermediate steps absent from begging the question, but the two fallacies are so closely related that they can be considered one. Here's another example: "I feel sympathy for her because I identify with her." Despite the "because," no reason is really offered. What follows "because" is merely a restatement, in slightly

"*Look, maybe you're right, but for the sake of argument let's assume you're wrong and drop it.*" © The New Yorker Collection 1983. Robert Mankoff from Cartoonbank.com. All Rights Reserved.

different words, of what precedes; the shift of words, from "feel sympathy" to "identify with," has misled the writer into thinking she is giving a reason. Other examples: "Students are interested in courses when the subject matter and the method of presentation are interesting"; "There cannot be peace in the Middle East because the Jews and the Arabs will always fight." In each case, an assertion that ought to be proved is reasserted as a reason in support of the assertion.

7. *Post hoc ergo propter hoc* (Latin for "after this, therefore because of this"). Don't assume that because *X* precedes *Y, X* must cause *Y.* For example: "He went to college and came back a boozer; college corrupted him." He might have taken up liquor even if he had not gone to college. Another example: "When a fifty-five-mile-per-hour limit was imposed in 1974, after the Arab embargo on oil, the number of auto fatalities decreased sharply, from 55,000 deaths in 1973 to 46,000 in 1974, so it is evident that a fifty-five-mile-per-hour limit—still adhered to in some states—saves lives." Not quite. Because gasoline was expensive after the embargo, the number of miles traveled decreased. The number of fatalities *per mile* remained constant. The price of gas, not the speed limit, seems responsible for the decreased number of fatalities. Moreover, the national death rate has continued to fall. Why? Several factors are at work: seat-belt and child-restraint laws, campaigns against drunk driving, improved auto design, and improved roads. Medicine, too, may have improved so that today doctors can save accident victims who in 1974 would have died. In short, it probably is impossible to isolate the correlation between speed and safety.

8. *Argumentum ad hominem* (Latin for "argument toward the man"). Here the argument is directed toward the person rather than toward the issue. Don't shift from your topic to your opponent. A speaker argues in favor of legalizing abortions and her opponent, instead of facing the merits of the argument, attacks the character or the associations of the opponent: "When you were married, you had an extra-marital affair and became pregnant, didn't you?"

9. False assumption. Consider the Scot who argued that Shakespeare must have been a Scot. Asked for his evidence, he replied, "The ability of the man warrants the assumption." Or take a statement such as "She goes to Yale, so she must be rich." Possibly the statement is based on faulty induction (the writer knows four Yale students, and all four are rich) but more likely he is just passing on a cliché. The Yale student in question may be on a scholarship, may be struggling to earn the money, or may be backed by parents of modest means who for eighteen years have saved money for her college education. Other examples: "I haven't heard him complain about French 10, so he must be satisfied"; "She's a writer, so she must be well read." A little thought will show how weak such assertions are; they *may* be true, but they may not.

The errors we have discussed are common. In revising, try to spot them and eliminate or correct them. You have a point to make, and you should make it fairly. If it can be made only unfairly, you do an injustice not only to your reader but also to yourself; you should try to change your view of the topic. You don't want to be like the politician whose speech had a marginal note: "Argument weak; shout here."

Wit

In addition to using sound argument and other evidence, writers often use wit, especially irony, to persuade. In irony, the words convey a meaning somewhat different from what they explicitly say. Wry understatement is typical. Here, for instance, is Thoreau explaining why in *Walden*, his book about his two years in relative isolation at Walden Pond, he will talk chiefly about himself:

> In most books, the *I*, or first person, is omitted; in this it will be retained; that, in respect to egotism, is the main difference. We commonly do not remember that it is, after all, always the first person that is speaking. I should not talk so much about myself if there were anybody else whom I knew as well. Unfortunately, I am confined to this theme by the narrowness of my experience.

Notice the wry apology in Thoreau's justification for talking about himself: He does not know anyone else as well as he knows himself. Similarly, in "unfortunately" ("Unfortunately, I am confined to this theme by the narrowness of my experience") we again hear a wry voice. After all, Thoreau knows, as we know, that *no one* has experience so deep or broad that he or she knows others better than himself or herself. Thoreau's presentation of himself as someone who happens not to have had the luck of knowing others better than himself is engagingly clever.

Avoiding Sarcasm

Because writers must, among other things, persuade readers that they are humane, sarcasm has little place in persuasive writing. Although desk dictionaries usually define sarcasm as "bitter, caustic irony" or "a kind of satiric wit," if you think of a sarcastic comment that you have heard you will probably agree that "a crude, sneering remark" is a better definition. Lacking the wit of good satire and the carefully controlled mockery of irony, sarcasm usually relies on gross overstatement and intends simply to humiliate. *Sarcasm* is derived from a Greek word meaning "to tear flesh" or "to bite the lips in rage," altogether an unattractive business. Sarcasm is unfair, for it dismisses an opponent's arguments with ridicule rather than with reason; it is also unwise, for it turns the reader against the speaker or writer. Readers hesitate to ally themselves with a writer who apparently enjoys humiliating the opposition. A sarcastic remark can turn the hearers against the speaker and arouse sympathy for the victim. In short, sarcasm usually doesn't work.

Tone and Ethical Appeal

Although this chapter is chiefly about persuasion in the sense of rational discourse—the presentation of reasons in support of a thesis or conclusion—there are other forms of persuasion. We've already mentioned one of them: the *appeal to emotion*. The *appeal to force* is another: As Al Capone put it, "You can get a lot more done with a kind word and a gun, than with a kind word alone." But, in a sense, kind words themselves can

"Please forgive Edgar. He has no verbal skills." © The New Yorker Collection 1980. Lee Lorenz from Cartoonbank.com. All Rights Reserved.

do quite a lot. The writer's **tone,** or voice, matters. A moment ago we cautioned against the use of sarcasm, on the grounds that the satirist is perceived as an unattractive character, and this caution can now be put into a larger context, something that Aristotle called the **ethical appeal,** from *ethos,* the Greek work for "character." The ethical appeal is based on the idea that effective speakers and writers convey by their tone the suggestion that they are good people, specifically that they are

- informed
- intelligent
- benevolent
- honest

Because they are perceived as trustworthy, their words inspire confidence in their listeners and their readers. When we read an argument, we hear or sense a *voice* or *persona* behind the words, and our assent to the argument depends partly on the extent to which we trust this speaker, this voice, this character.

How can you inspire this trust? To begin with, you should indeed be informed, intelligent, benevolent, and honest. Still, possession of these qualities does not guarantee that you will convey them in your writing. You will have to revise your drafts so that these qualities become apparent to your audience—so that nothing in your essay causes your reader to doubt your knowledge, intelligence, good intentions, and integrity. A blunder in logic, a misleading quotation, a sarcastic remark—all such slips can cause readers to withdraw their trust from the writer.

Our general advice: When you argue, be courteous and be respectful of your topic, of your audience, and of the people who hold views you are arguing against. It's generally not persuasive to present as villains or fools all persons who hold views different from your own, especially if some of them are your readers. Recognize opposing views, assume they are held in good faith, state them fairly, and be temperate in arguing your own position: "If I understand their view correctly . . ."; "It seems reasonable to conclude that . . ."; "Perhaps, then, we can agree that. . . ."

Organizing an Argument

As we have said earlier, writers find out what they think partly by means of the act of putting words on paper. But in presenting arguments for their readers, writers rarely duplicate their own acts of discovery. To put it another way, the process of setting forth ideas, and supporting them, does not follow the productive but untidy, repetitive, often haphazard process of preliminary thinking. For instance, a point that did not strike us until the middle of the third draft may, in the final version, appear in the opening paragraph. Or an example that seemed useful early in our thinking may, in the process of revision, be omitted in favor of a stronger example. Through a series of revisions, large and small, we try to work out the best strategy for persuading our readers to accept our reasoning as sound, our conclusion as valid. Unfortunately, we find, an argument cannot be presented either as it occurs to us or all at once.

No simple formula governs the organization of all effective argumentative essays. An essay may begin by announcing its thesis and then set forth the supporting reasons. Or it may begin more casually, calling attention to specific cases, and then generalize from these cases. Probably it will then go on to reveal an underlying unity that brings the thesis into view, and from here it will offer detailed reasoning that supports the thesis.

As the writer of a persuasive essay, you almost always have to handle, in some sequence or other, the following matters:

- The context of the argument (for instance, an explanation of why the issue should be considered, or reconsidered)
- The thesis
- The evidence that supports the thesis
- The counterevidence
- The response to counterclaims and counterevidence (either a refutation or a concession that there *is* merit to the counterclaims but not as much as to the writer's thesis)
- Some sort of reaffirmation, perhaps that the topic needs attention or that the thesis advanced is the most plausible or the most workable or the most moral, or that the ball is now in the reader's court

Three methods of organizing arguments are fairly common, and one or another may suit an essay you're working on.

1. Begin with the context of the argument, then set forth the thesis statement and work from the simplest argument up to the most complex, taking account of opposing arguments as you set forth your own arguments. Such an arrangement will keep your reader with you, step by step.

2. After setting forth the context and your thesis, arrange the arguments in order of increasing strength. The danger in following this plan is that you may lose the reader from the start, because you begin with a weak argument. Avoid this problem by telling your reader that indeed the first argument is relatively weak (if it is terribly weak, it isn't an argument at all, so scrap it), but that you offer it for the sake of completeness or because it is often given, and that you will soon give the reader far stronger arguments. Face the opposition to this initial argument, grant that opposition as much as it deserves, and salvage what is left of the argument. Then proceed to the increasingly strong arguments, devoting at least one paragraph to each. Introduce each argument with an appropriate transition ("another reason," "even more important," "most convincing of all"). State it briefly, summarize the opposing view, and then demolish this opposition. With this organization, your discussion of each of your own arguments ends affirmatively.

3. After sketching the background and stating your thesis in an introductory paragraph, mass all of the opposing arguments, and then respond to them one by one. In short, when you (1) think you have done your initial thinking and your rethinking, (2) have, if appropriate, consulted some published sources, (3) have talked with friends and perhaps with experts, and (4) have moved from random notes and lists to fairly full drafts, you are not quite done. You still must (1) check what you hope is your last draft to see if you have found the best possible order for the arguments, (2) have given effective examples, and (3) have furnished transitions. In short, you must check to see that you have produced an argument that will strike a reasonable reader as courteous, clear, and concrete.

CHECKLIST FOR REVISING DRAFTS OF PERSUASIVE ESSAYS

- [ ] Are the terms clearly defined? (See pp. 157–59.)
- [ ] Is the thesis stated promptly and clearly? (See p. 169.)
- [ ] Are the assumptions likely to be shared by your readers? If not, are they reasonably argued rather than merely stated? (See pp. 163–65.)
- [ ] Are the facts verifiable? Is the evidence reliable? (No out-of-date statistics, no generalizations from insufficient evidence?) (See pp. 154–57.)
- [ ] Is the reasoning sound? (See pp. 161–65.)
- [ ] Are the authorities really authorities on this matter? (See pp. 161–62.)
- [ ] Are all of the substantial counterarguments recognized and effectively responded to? (See p. 162.)
- [ ] Does the essay make use, where appropriate, of concrete examples? (See pp. 154–55.)
- [ ] Is the organization effective? Does the essay begin in a compelling way, keep the thesis in view, and end interestingly? (See pp. 168–70.)
- [ ] Is the tone appropriate? (Avoid sarcasm. Present yourself as fair-minded, and assume that those who hold a view opposed to yours are also fair-minded.) (See pp. 166–67.)

Persuasion at Work: Two Writers Consider the Death Penalty

We present below two essays, the first arguing in favor of the death penalty, the second arguing against it. Following each essay, we offer a brief analysis of the writer's persuasive devices and strategies.

Edward Koch
Death and Justice: How Capital Punishment Affirms Life

Edward Koch, born in New York City, was mayor of New York from 1978 to 1989. This essay first appeared in the New Republic.

1   Last December a man named Robert Lee Willie, who had been convicted of raping and murdering an 18-year-old woman, was executed in the Louisiana state prison. In a statement issued several minutes before his death, Mr. Willie said: "Killing people is wrong. . . . It makes no difference whether it's citizens, countries, or governments. Killing is wrong." Two weeks later in South Carolina, an admitted killer named Joseph Carl Shaw was put to death for murdering two teenagers. In an appeal to the governor for clemency, Mr. Shaw wrote: "Killing is wrong when I did it. Killing is wrong when you do it. I hope you have the courage and moral strength to stop the killing."

2   It is a curiosity of modern life that we find ourselves being lectured on morality by cold-blooded killers. Mr. Willie previously had been convicted of aggravated rape, aggravated kidnapping, and the murders of a Louisiana deputy and a man from Missouri. Mr. Shaw committed another murder a week before the two for which he was executed, and admitted mutilating the body of the 14-year-old girl he killed. I can't help wondering what prompted these murderers to speak out against killing as they entered the death-house door. Did their newfound reverence for life stem from the realization that they were about to lose their own?

3   Life is indeed precious, and I believe the death penalty helps to affirm this fact. Had the death penalty been a real possibility in the minds of these murderers, they might well have stayed their hand. They might have shown moral awareness before their victims died, and not after. Consider the tragic death of Rosa Velez, who happened to be home when a man named Luis Vera burglarized her apartment in Brooklyn. "Yeah, I shot her," Vera admitted. "She knew me, and I knew I wouldn't go to the chair."

4   During my twenty-two years in public service, I have heard the pros and cons of capital punishment expressed with special intensity. As a district leader, councilman, congressman, and mayor, I have represented constituencies generally thought of as liberal. Because I support the death penalty for heinous crimes of murder, I have sometimes been the subject of emotional and outraged attacks by voters who find my position reprehensible or worse. I have listened to their ideas. I have weighed their objections carefully. I still support the death penalty. The reasons I maintain my position can be best understood by examining the arguments most frequently heard in opposition.

5   1. *The death penalty is "barbaric."* Sometimes opponents of capital punishment horrify with tales of lingering death on the gallows, of faulty electric chairs, or of agony in the gas chamber. Partly in response to such protests, several states such as North Carolina and Texas switched to execution by lethal injection. The condemned person is put to death painlessly, without ropes, voltage, bullets, or gas. Did this answer the objections of death penalty opponents? Of course not. On June 22, 1984, the *New York Times* published an editorial that sarcastically attacked the new "hygienic" method of death by injection, and stated that "execution can never be made humane through science." So it's not the method that really troubles opponents. It's the death itself they consider barbaric.

6   Admittedly, capital punishment is not a pleasant topic. However, one does not have to like the death penalty in order to support it any more than one must like radical surgery, radiation, or chemotherapy in order to find necessary these attempts at curing cancer. Ultimately we may learn how to cure cancer with a simple pill. Unfortunately, that day has not yet arrived. Today we are faced with the choice of letting the cancer spread or trying to cure it with the methods available, methods that one day will almost certainly be considered barbaric. But to give up and do nothing would be far more barbaric and would certainly delay the discovery of an eventual cure. The analogy between cancer and murder is imperfect, because murder is not the "disease" we are trying to cure. The disease is injustice. We may not like the death penalty, but it must be available to punish crimes of cold-blooded murder, cases in which any other form of punishment would be inadequate and, therefore, unjust. If we create a society in which injustice is not tolerated, incidents of murder—the most flagrant form of injustice—will diminish.

7   2. *No other major democracy uses the death penalty.* No other major democracy—in fact, few other countries of any description—

are plagued by a murder rate such as that in the United States. Fewer and fewer Americans can remember the days when unlocked doors were the norm and murder was a rare and terrible offense. In America the murder rate climbed 122 percent between 1963 and 1980. During that same period, the murder rate in New York City increased by almost 400 percent, and the statistics are even worse in many other cities. A study at M.I.T. showed that based on 1970 homicide rates a person who lived in a large American city ran a greater risk of being murdered than an American soldier in World War II ran of being killed in combat. It is not surprising that the laws of each country differ according to differing conditions and traditions. If other countries had our murder problem, the cry for capital punishment would be just as loud as it is here. And I daresay that any other major democracy where 75 percent of the people supported the death penalty would soon enact it into law.

8   3. *An innocent person might be executed by mistake.* Consider the work of Hugo Adam Bedau, one of the most implacable foes of capital punishment in this country. According to Mr. Bedau, it is "false sentimentality to argue that the death penalty should be abolished because of the abstract possibility that an innocent person might be executed." He cites a study of the 7,000 executions in this country from 1893 to 1971, and concludes that the record fails to show that such cases occur. The main point, however, is this. If government functioned only when the possibility of error didn't exist, government wouldn't function at all. Human life deserves special protection, and one of the best ways to guarantee that protection is to assure that convicted murderers do not kill again. Only the death penalty can accomplish this end. In a recent case in New Jersey, a man named Richard Biegenwald was freed from prison after serving 18 years for murder; since his release he has been convicted of committing four murders. A prisoner named Lemuel Smith, who, while serving four life sentences for murder (plus two life sentences for kidnapping and robbery) in New York's Green Haven Prison, lured a woman corrections officer into the chaplain's office and strangled her. He then mutilated and dismembered her body. An additional life sentence for Smith is meaningless. Because New York has no death penalty statute, Smith has effectively been given a license to kill.

9   But the problem of multiple murder is not confined to the nation's penitentiaries. In 1981, 91 police officers were killed in the line of duty in this country. Seven percent of those arrested in the cases that have been solved had a previous arrest for murder. In New York City

in 1976 and 1977, 85 persons arrested for homicide had a previous arrest for murder. Six of these individuals had two previous arrests for murder, and one had four previous murder arrests. During those two years the New York police were arresting for murder persons with a previous arrest for murder on the average of one every 8.5 days. This is not surprising when we learn that in 1975, for example, the median time served in Massachusetts for homicide was less than two and a half years. In 1976 a study sponsored by the Twentieth Century Fund found that the average time served in the United States for first-degree murder is ten years. The median time served may be considerably lower.

10   4. *Capital punishment cheapens the value of human life.* On the contrary, it can be easily demonstrated that the death penalty strengthens the value of human life. If the penalty for rape were lowered, clearly it would signal a lessened regard for the victims' suffering, humiliation, and personal integrity. It would cheapen their horrible experience, and expose them to an increased danger of recurrence. When we lower the penalty for murder, it signals a lessened regard for the value of the victim's life. Some critics of capital punishment, such as columnist Jimmy Breslin, have suggested that a life sentence is actually a harsher penalty for murder than death. This is sophistic nonsense. A few killers may decide not to appeal a death sentence, but the overwhelming majority make every effort to stay alive. It is by exacting the highest penalty for the taking of human life that we affirm the highest value of human life.

11   5. *The death penalty is applied in a discriminatory manner.* This factor no longer seems to be the problem it once was. The appeals process for a condemned prisoner is lengthy and painstaking. Every effort is made to see that the verdict and sentence were fairly arrived at. However, assertions of discrimination are not an argument for ending the death penalty but for extending it. It is not justice to exclude everyone from the penalty of the law if a few are found to be so favored. Justice requires that the law be applied equally to all.

12   6. *Thou shalt not kill.* The Bible is our greatest source of moral inspiration. Opponents of the death penalty frequently cite the sixth of the Ten Commandments in an attempt to prove that capital punishment is divinely proscribed. In the original Hebrew, however, the Sixth Commandment reads "Thou shalt not commit murder," and the Torah specifies capital punishment for a variety of offenses. The biblical viewpoint has been upheld by philosophers throughout history. The greatest thinkers of the nineteenth century—Kant, Locke,

Hobbes, Rousseau, Montesquieu, and Mill—agreed that natural law properly authorizes the sovereign to take life in order to vindicate justice. Only Jeremy Bentham was ambivalent. Washington, Jefferson, and Franklin endorsed it. Abraham Lincoln authorized executions for deserters in wartime. Alexis de Tocqueville, who expressed profound respect for American institutions, believed that the death penalty was indispensable to the support of social order. The United States Constitution, widely admired as one of the seminal achievements in the history of humanity, condemns cruel and inhuman punishment, but does not condemn capital punishment.

13   7. *The death penalty is state-sanctioned murder.* This is the defense with which Messrs. Willie and Shaw hoped to soften the resolve of those who sentenced them to death. By saying in effect, "You're no better than I am," the murderer seeks to bring his accusers down to his own level. It is also a popular argument among opponents of capital punishment, but a transparently false one. Simply put, the state has rights that the private individual does not. In a democracy, those rights are given to the state by the electorate. The execution of a lawfully condemned killer is no more an act of murder than is legal imprisonment an act of kidnapping. If an individual forces a neighbor to pay him money under threat of punishment, it's called extortion. If the state does it, it's called taxation. Rights and responsibilities surrendered by the individual are what give the state its power to govern. This contract is the foundation of civilization itself.

14   Everyone wants his or her rights, and will defend them jealously. Not everyone, however, wants responsibilities, especially the painful responsibilities that come with law enforcement. Twenty-one years ago a woman named Kitty Genovese was assaulted and murdered on a street in New York. Dozens of neighbors heard her cries for help but did nothing to assist her. They didn't even call the police. In such a climate the criminal understandably grows bolder. In the presence of moral cowardice, he lectures us on our supposed failings and tries to equate his crimes with our quest for justice.

15   The death of anyone—even a convicted killer—diminishes us all. But we are diminished even more by a justice system that fails to function. It is an illusion to let ourselves believe that doing away with capital punishment removes the murderer's deed from our conscience. The rights of society are paramount. When we protect guilty lives, we give up innocent lives in exchange. When opponents of capital punishment say to the state: "I will not let you kill in my name," they are

also saying to murderers: "You can kill in your *own* name as long as I have an excuse for not getting involved."

16   It is hard to imagine anything worse than being murdered while neighbors do nothing. But something worse exists. When those same neighbors shrink back from justly punishing the murderer, the victim dies twice.

An Analysis of Koch's Argument

Koch uses a range of devices to persuade readers to his point of view. In the first paragraph he uses two quotations by murderers, and thereby begins to establish his authority on the topic. He uses mild **irony** in the second paragraph when he writes, "It is a curiosity of modern life that we find ourselves being lectured on morality by cold-blooded killers." (Although retaining his composure, Koch conveys indignation that we can all share, for "we" are all subject to these lectures.) Koch cites another killer in the third paragraph, one who provides **evidence** for Koch's thesis by saying, in effect, that if the death penalty had been in place he might not have committed murder. In the fourth paragraph the writer presents himself as a man of honor ("During my twenty-two years in public service"—not "During my twenty-two years as a politician"), a man who has often been subject to "emotional and outraged attacks." So the speaker is himself a sort of victim, not a man who lashes out at others. (Writers of persuasive essays seek to present themselves as persons of good will, and, if possible, as persons who have been wronged by their opponents.)

Note, too, Koch's style. After giving us a sentence in which he tells of the trials he has undergone, he gives us three short sentences, each of six words, and each beginning with "I":

"I have listened to their ideas."

"I have weighed their objections carefully."

"I still support the death penalty."

Not quite Julius Caesar's *veni, vidi, vici*, but firm, concise, deliberate. What more can a reader want than a man who listens to his opponents and weighs their objections carefully?

Later paragraphs use, among other persuasive devices, an **analogy** (between cancer and murder in paragraph 6); **statistics** (in paragraphs 7 and 9); **authority** (in paragraph 8 he cites Hugo Bedau, "one of the most implacable foes of capital punishment in this country"); and a

hypothetical situation (in paragraph 7 he speculates, "If other countries had our murder problem . . ."). There is even, in paragraph 13, one touch of **wit:** "If an individual forces a neighbor to pay him money under threat of punishment, it's called extortion. If the state does it, it's called taxation."

Koch's statistics are impressive, though on further thought, we find them a bit puzzling. He tells us that in 1981, ninety-one police officers were killed in the line of duty, and that seven percent of those arrested in the cases that have been solved had already been arrested for a murder. Possibly only eighteen cases were solved; if so, a single person previously arrested for murder would give us Koch's seven percent. Another odd thing about this evidence: Koch says that seven percent had a "previous arrest for murder"—which is not at all the same as a previous conviction for murder. A person arrested for murder but acquitted is, in our system, not to be thought of as a murderer, only as a person wrongly accused of murder. The statistics do indeed lend weight to Koch's argument, but we think he could have been clearer and used them more effectively.

David Bruck
The Death Penalty

David Bruck, born in 1949, holds a law degree from the University of South Carolina. After serving four years as a public defender in South Carolina, he entered private practice in order to devote all of his efforts to defending inmates on death row. This essay was written as a direct response to the essay by Edward Koch, beginning on page 171.

1   Mayor Ed Koch contends that the death penalty "affirms life." By failing to execute murderers, he says, we "signal a lessened regard for the value of the victim's life." Koch suggests that people who oppose the death penalty are like Kitty Genovese's neighbors, who heard her cries for help but did nothing while an attacker stabbed her to death.

2   This is the standard "moral" defense of death as punishment: even if executions don't deter violent crime any more effectively than imprisonment, they are still required as the only means we have of doing justice in response to the worst of crimes.

3   Until recently, this "moral" argument had to be considered in the abstract, since no one was being executed in the United States. But the death penalty is back now, at least in the southern states, where every one of the more than 30 executions carried out over the last two years has taken place. Those of us who live in those states are getting to see the difference between the death penalty in theory, and what happens when you actually try to use it.

4   South Carolina resumed executing prisoners in January with the electrocution of Joseph Carl Shaw. Shaw was condemned to death for helping to murder two teenagers while he was serving as a military policeman at Fort Jackson, South Carolina. His crime, propelled by mental illness and PCP, was one of terrible brutality. It is Shaw's last words ("Killing was wrong when I did it. It is wrong when you do it. . . .") that so outraged Mayor Koch: he finds it "a curiosity of modern life that we are being lectured on morality by cold-blooded killers." And so it is.

5   But it was not "modern life" that brought this curiosity into being. It was capital punishment. The electric chair was J. C. Shaw's platform. (The mayor mistakenly writes that Shaw's statement came in the form of a plea to the governor for clemency: actually Shaw made it only seconds before his death, as he waited, shaved and strapped into the chair, for the switch to be thrown.) It was the chair that provided Shaw with celebrity and an opportunity to lecture us on right and wrong. What made this weird moral reversal even worse is that J. C. Shaw faced his own death with undeniable dignity and courage. And while Shaw died, the TV crews recorded another "curiosity" of the death penalty—the crowd gathered outside the death-house to cheer on the executioner. Whoops of elation greeted the announcement of Shaw's death. Waiting at the penitentiary gates for the appearance of the hearse bearing Shaw's remains, one demonstrator started yelling, "Where's the beef?"

6   For those who had to see the execution of J. C. Shaw, it wasn't easy to keep in mind that the purpose of the whole spectacle was to affirm life. It will be harder still when Florida executes a cop-killer named Alvin Ford. Ford has lost his mind during his years of death-row confinement, and now spends his days trembling, rocking back and forth, and muttering unintelligible prayers. This has led to litigation over whether Ford meets a centuries-old legal standard for mental competency. Since the Middle Ages, the Anglo-American legal system has generally prohibited the execution of anyone who is too mentally ill to understand what is about to be done to him and why. If Florida

wins its case, it will have earned the right to electrocute Ford in his present condition. If it loses, he will not be executed until the state has nursed him back to some semblance of mental health.

7   We can at least be thankful that this demoralizing spectacle involves a prisoner who is actually guilty of murder. But this may not always be so. The ordeal of Lenell Jeter—the young black engineer who recently served more than a year of a life sentence for a Texas armed robbery that he didn't commit—should remind us that the system is quite capable of making the very worst sort of mistake. That Jeter was eventually cleared is a fluke. If the robbery had occurred at 7 P.M. rather than 3 P.M., he'd have had no alibi, and would still be in prison today. And if someone had been killed in that robbery, Jeter probably would have been sentenced to death. We'd have seen the usual execution-day interviews with state officials and the victim's relatives, all complaining that Jeter's appeals took too long. And Jeter's last words from the gurney would have taken their place among the growing literature of death-house oration that so irritates the mayor.

8   Koch quoted Hugo Adam Bedau, a prominent abolitionist, to the effect that the record fails to establish that innocent defendants have been executed in the past. But this doesn't mean, as Koch implies, that it hasn't happened. All Bedau was saying was that doubts concerning executed prisoners' guilt are almost never resolved. Bedau is at work now on an effort to determine how many wrongful death sentences may have been imposed: his list of murder convictions since 1900 in which the state eventually *admitted* error is some 400 cases long. Of course, very few of these cases involved actual executions: the mistakes that Bedau documents were uncovered precisely because the prisoner was alive and able to fight for his vindication. The cases where someone is executed are the very cases in which we're least likely to learn that we got the wrong man.

9   I don't claim that executions of entirely innocent people will occur very often. But they will occur. And other sorts of mistakes already have. Roosevelt Green was executed in Georgia two days before J. C. Shaw. Green and an accomplice kidnapped a young woman. Green swore that his companion shot her to death after Green had left, and that he knew nothing about the murder. Green's claim was supported by a statement that his accomplice made to a witness after the crime. The jury never resolved whether Green was telling the truth, and when he tried to take a polygraph examination a few days before his scheduled execution, the state of Georgia refused to allow the examiner into the prison. As the pressure for symbolic retribution mounts,

the courts, like the public, are losing patience with such details. Green was electrocuted on January 9, while members of the Ku Klux Klan rallied outside the prison.

10   Then there is another sort of arbitrariness that happens all the time. Last October, Louisiana executed a man named Ernest Knighton. Knighton had killed a gas station owner during a robbery. Like any murder, this was a terrible crime. But it was not premeditated, and is the sort of crime that very rarely results in a death sentence. Why was Knighton electrocuted when almost everyone else who committed the same offense was not? Was it because he was black? Was it because his victim and all 12 members of the jury that sentenced him were white? Was it because Knighton's court-appointed lawyer presented no evidence on his behalf at his sentence hearing? Or maybe there's no reason except bad luck. One thing is clear: Ernest Knighton was picked out to die the way a fisherman takes a cricket out of a bait jar. No one cares which cricket gets impaled on the hook.

11   Not every prisoner executed recently was chosen that randomly. But many were. And having selected these men so casually, so blindly, the death penalty system asks us to accept that the purpose of killing each of them is to affirm the sanctity of human life.

12   The death penalty states are also learning that the death penalty is easier to advocate than it is to administer. In Florida, where executions have become almost routine, the governor reports that nearly a third of his time is spent reviewing the clemency requests of condemned prisoners. The Florida Supreme Court is hopelessly backlogged with death cases. Some have taken five years to decide, and the rest of the Court's work waits in line behind the death appeals. Florida's death row currently holds more than 230 prisoners. State officials are reportedly considering building a special "death prison" devoted entirely to the isolation and electrocution of the condemned. The state is also considering the creation of a special public defender unit that will do nothing else but handle death penalty appeals. The death penalty, in short, is spawning death agencies.

13   And what is Florida getting for all of this? The state went through almost all of 1983 without executing anyone: its rate of intentional homicide declined by 17 percent. Last year [1984] Florida executed eight people—the most of any state, and the sixth highest total for any year since Florida started electrocuting people back in 1924. Elsewhere in the U.S. last year, the homicide rate continued to decline. But in Florida, it actually rose by 5.1 percent.

14   But these are just the tiresome facts. The electric chair has been a centerpiece of each of Koch's recent political campaigns, and he

knows better than anyone how little the facts have to do with the public's support for capital punishment. What really fuels the death penalty is the justifiable frustration and rage of people who see that the government is not coping with violent crime. So what if the death penalty doesn't work? At least it gives us the satisfaction of knowing that we got one or two of the sons of bitches.

15   Perhaps we want retribution on the flesh and bone of a handful of convicted murderers so badly that we're willing to close our eyes to all of the demoralization and danger that come with it. A lot of politicians think so, and they may be right. But if they are, then let's at least look honestly at what we're doing. This lottery of death both comes from and encourages an attitude toward human life that is not reverent, but reckless.

16   And that is why the mayor is dead wrong when he confuses such fury with justice. He suggests that we trivialize murder unless we kill murderers. By that logic, we also trivialize rape unless we sodomize rapists. The sin of Kitty Genovese's neighbors wasn't that they failed to stab her attacker to death. Justice does demand that murderers be punished. And common sense demands that society be protected from them. But neither justice nor self-preservation demands that we kill men whom we have already imprisoned.

17   The electric chair in which J. C. Shaw died earlier this year was built in 1912 at the suggestion of South Carolina's governor at the time, Cole Blease. Governor Blease's other criminal justice initiative was an impassioned crusade in favor of lynch law. Any lesser response, the governor insisted, trivialized the loathsome crimes of interracial rape and murder. In 1912 a lot of people agreed with Governor Blease that a proper regard for justice required both lynching and the electric chair. Eventually we are going to learn that justice requires neither.

An Analysis of Bruck's Response to Koch

Although Bruck wrote this essay as a response to Koch's essay, he does not respond point-by-point to all of Koch's arguments. For instance, he does not take up Koch's **assumption** (paragraphs 3, 6) that the death penalty is a deterrent to would-be murderers. Or consider his response to Koch's argument that even if the death penalty is now administered in an almost random way, the proper thing to do is to administer it more justly—that is, more widely. Bruck does not discuss Koch's proposal; rather, he simply argues that because the penalty is administered in what seems to be a random way, it ought not to be administered at all. On the other hand, Bruck does vigorously challenge Koch's **claim** that the death penalty "affirms life." Bruck's fifth paragraph, which ends with a description of the crowd waiting at the penitentiary gates for the hearse bearing Shaw's remains, strikes us as especially effective.

Some additional comments may be useful. We find it odd that Bruck cites the case of Lenell Jeter in order to show that "the system is quite capable of making the very worst sort of mistake" (paragraph 7). Jeter was not executed, and in fact he was not even sentenced to execution. Jeter was sentenced to life imprisonment for an armed robbery that he didn't commit. But what does this case have to do with murderers and with capital punishment? It shows only that someone can be wrongly convicted of a crime—a point that no one would deny. What Bruck needs, if his case is to be strong, is an **example** of an innocent person who was not only convicted of murder but was also sentenced to death and who was in fact executed, but he offers no such example.

In paragraph 8 Bruck speaks of murder cases in which the state admitted error. He says that "very few . . . involved actual executions." Why doesn't he specify the number? We don't know why, but probably it is indeed so small a number that it would be unimpressive and thus would not strongly buttress his case. In paragraph 9 he grants that executions of "entirely innocent people" will not occur very often, but he insists "they will occur." This assertion may be true, but it would be more convincing if he could point to **examples** from the past, if he could offer **statistics**.

Bruck is careful to indicate that he is fully aware of the brutality of the murders he discusses; he thus **concedes to the opposition its due.** Thus, in paragraph 4 he says that a certain murder "was one of terrible brutality," and in paragraph 10, speaking of another murder, he says that "Like any murder, this was a terrible crime." Nothing in the essay suggests that he sentimentalizes murderers, is unsympathetic to their victims, or is soft on crime—unless one assumes, in a circular fashion, that anyone who opposes the death penalty is therefore soft on crime.

Paragraph 10 suggests that those who are executed are unfairly chosen from a pool of comparable candidates. Bruck says that Knighton may have been chosen because he was black and his victim was white, or because his lawyer was particularly unpersuasive, or perhaps simply because of bad luck. Bruck's point, then, is not that Knighton was necessarily the victim of racial prejudice, but that local conditions and chance seem to determine who gets executed. That's probably true, but it doesn't address Koch's objection. Koch, you'll recall, said that if capital punishment now is administered at random, the thing that needs reform is the way it is administered. Or put it this way: If capital punishment is indeed just, the fact that X is executed and Y (a comparable offender) is not executed does not mean that X is unjustly treated; it means that justice has not been done to Y (or to Y's victims).

The final paragraph seems to us to be effective rhetoric, though one can quarrel with some of the **logic**. By talking about "the electric chair in which J. C. Shaw died earlier this year," Bruck returns us to the early part of his essay (that is, to paragraph 4, in which Shaw was introduced), and thus he tends to wrap up his essay. That's nice. On the other hand, by telling us that the chair was built in 1912 at the suggestion of Governor Cole Blease, who led "an impassioned crusade in favor of lynch law," he is engaging in the **fallacy** that logicians call "poisoning the well" (an attempt to discredit a proposition by associating it with something unattractive). Whether Blease was a saint or a monster is of no relevance to the issue of whether capital punishment is just.

Persuasion at Work: Two Writers Consider Music File-Sharing

The following essays present opposing arguments on music file-sharing. We offer a brief analysis after each piece.

Gary Shapiro

Lasting Impression— Downloading Is Illegal

Gary Shapiro, an attorney, is President and Chief Executive Officer of the Consumer Electronics Association (CEA), a trade group, and the chair of the Home Recording Rights Coalition. His essay in favor of music file-sharing originally appeared in the online publication ZDNet US *on September 30, 2002.*

1   Hollywood, the music industry, select policy-makers, and now the Justice Department have adopted a new "copyspeak" that equates the downloading of files from the internet with "piracy," "stealing," and "shoplifting."

2   The pervasive theme of copyspeak is that downloading from the Internet is both illegal and immoral. It is neither. No doubt this era's rapid shift to digital technology is changing the rules of the game—there is little doubt that some use the benefits of technology to make and distribute unauthorized copies for personal financial gain in clear violation of copyright law.

3   But we've been down the road of technological advancement before. How we resolve this latest tension between copyright and technology will define our future ability to communicate, create and share information, education and entertainment. Indeed, if the play button becomes the pay button, our very ability to raise the world's standard of living and education will be jeopardized.

4   With each new technology, the fears of the music and motion picture industries have grown. Television and the VCR allegedly marked the end of movies. CDs and cassettes would cause harm from real-time transfers and one-at-a-time copies. Today's technologies make these fears seem almost quaint.

5   The growth of reproduction, storage, and transmission technology has terrified copyright owners—most notably the music and motion picture industries. With high-speed connectivity and the Internet, the perceived copyright theft is not buying a CD and making a copy for a friend; it's downloading from a stranger or making available thousands of copies with the touch of a keystroke.

6   Based on these and similar threats the content community has gone on a scorched earth campaign—attacking new recording and peer-to-peer technologies—using the Congress, media, and courts to challenge recording in the digital age.

7   As an industry that recognizes the legitimate concerns of copyright owners that exist in a digital world, consumer-electronics companies have been working for years with both the recording and motion picture industries on developing technological measures that meet the needs of both industries by protecting content at the source.

8   But despite these efforts, the copyright community has declared war on technology and is using lawsuits, legislatures, and clever copyspeak public relations to restrict the ability to sell and use new technologies. The downloading of a song to sample an artist's wares—behavior most Americans between 13 and 25 engage in regularly—has been likened to a criminal and immoral act. It's time to take a close, hard look at this characterization.

9   Downloading is not illegal. Fair use rights—the right of consumers to make copies of copyrighted materials for their personal use—are

guaranteed to consumers by statute, and applied judicially on a case-by-case basis. This means that, while some consumer practices ultimately could be adjudicated as either fair use or infringement, there is scant basis for challenging them as criminal activity, as copyspeak would now have it.

10   In copyspeak, there is no such thing as fair use "rights," rather fair use is only an affirmative defense to copyright infringement and therefore not a right. But various recognized "rights" may only be asserted as affirmative defenses in a lawsuit. For example, in a slander suit, one may assert the First Amendment right but only as an affirmative defense; this does not diminish the fact that the right exists.

11   Time after time, practices of individuals that were initially equated with "piracy" or "theft" have been shown to be neutral, even beneficial, to copyright owners, and have been accepted as fair use. Think of the VCR and the Supreme Court decision holding that its use to tape full movies is completely legal.

12   To make downloading immoral, you have to accept that copyrighted products are governed by the same moral and legal principles as real property, thus the recent and continuous reference by the copyright community to label downloading as stealing. But the fact is that real and intellectual property are different and are governed by different principles.

13   Downloading a copyrighted product does not diminish the product, as would be the case of taking and using tangible property such as a dress. At worst, it is depriving the copyright owner of a potential sale. The truth is, it may be causing a sale (through familiarity) or, even more likely, have no impact on the sale. My son often will become familiar with artists through downloading their music on the Internet and then will go out and buy the CD. Indeed, recent studies by independent organizations have shown this to be the case.

14   The comparison to real property fails for several other reasons. Real property is subject to ownership taxes. Real property lasts forever and can be owned forever. A copyright can be owned only for a limited period of time. Indeed, the United States Constitution declares this. More, copyright law must bow to the First Amendment, which expressly allows people to use a copyrighted product without the permission of the copyright owner. This concern contributes to the statutory and judicial concept of "fair use." The First Amendment includes not only the right to send but also the right to receive. Indeed, in 1984 the U.S. Supreme Court in declaring the VCR a legal product said

that it could be OK to copy an entire copyrighted product. So if the Supreme Court expressly held that VCR copying in the home for non-commercial purposes is a legal activity, how is it suddenly labeled as "piracy" because the device is a computer?

15 The music industry has made little effort to look at new business models or provide a viable and attractive alternative to the downloading services. Instead, they spend their time complaining they "cannot compete with free," referring to the free downloading the Internet allows. But the marketplace demonstrates you can compete with free. Purveyors of bottled water do it. America Online does it. Book retailers do it with libraries. Independent online music services say they can do it, if they can clear the rights.

16 The recording industry and motion picture industry need to look for technological solutions to their own problems. Blaming declining revenue on downloading ignores the economic conditions, multiple entertainment options and a dearth of quality major label artists facing consumers. Content providers would be served better by working with technology companies to deploy these solutions rather than suing teenagers and lobbying Congress to legislate unreasonable and consumer-unfriendly mandates.

An Analysis of Shapiro's Argument

Perhaps the first thing to note about Gary Shapiro's essay is that its author isn't exactly a disinterested party (people who write arguments generally aren't, of course). As President and CEO of the Consumer Electronics Association, he represents companies that, among other things, make the devices on which downloaded music may be played. He uses several strategies to persuade readers to his point of view and to present himself as reasonable and authoritative. He presents his **thesis** clearly and emphatically in paragraph 2: "The pervasive theme of copyspeak is that downloading from the Internet is both illegal and immoral. It is neither." He immediately **acknowledges that the counterargument** has some merit, thus presenting himself as a fair-minded thinker, someone we can trust. He notes that "there is little doubt that some use the benefits of technology to make and distribute unauthorized copies for personal financial gain in clear violation of copyright law." Then, in paragraph 3, he presents the alarming **claim**—a claim that he does not support with **evidence**—that "if the play button becomes the pay button, our very ability to raise the world's standard of living and education will be jeopardized." (His argument would be more compelling, we think, if he were to point to particular effects on education and economics.)

His **tone** combines mild scorn for his opponents, who indulge in what he calls "copyspeak," and a world-weary exasperation with their foolish claims: "we've been down [this] road . . . before." (In general, in writing an argument it is not a good idea to express scorn or impatience; your readers are more likely to be persuaded if they sense that you are well-meaning and thoughtful, not a wiseguy.) Wanting to set us straight, Shapiro advises us "to take a close hard look" at the idea that downloading—which, according to his **statistics**, "most Americans between 13 and 25 engage in regularly"—is criminal. A first step is **defining a key term** in his argument: "Fair use rights—the right of consumers to make copies of copyrighted materials for their personal use—are guaranteed to consumers by statute, and applied judicially on a case-by-case basis." He also presents **analogies.** He compares downloading music and taping movies on VCRs (which was declared legal by the Supreme Court in the Betamax case of 1984, in which the film industry sued Sony for making it possible for consumers to videotape movies). He also draws an analogy between real property and copyrighted intellectual property. The latter, he claims, is an analogy that "fails": downloading is justifiable precisely because copyrighted material is not analogous to real property, which can be owned forever.

In his response to Shapiro's argument, Cary Sherman will take particular issue with this definition of "fair use rights" and with the claims about property.

Cary Sherman

Perspective: Honest Talk About Downloads

Cary Sherman, a musician, songwriter, and attorney, is President of the Recording Industry Association of American (RIAA), a trade organization that represents record companies and related businesses. The RIAA is currently suing individuals who have downloaded music from the Internet, including a 12-year-old girl and a professor at Yale. This essay appeared in the online publication CNET News *on October 16, 2002.*

1   Last month, Consumer Electronics Association CEO Gary Shapiro took the debate over peer-to-peer file sharing to a new level. In brief,

he declared that downloading off the Web is neither illegal nor immoral.

2   This pronouncement—given in a speech at the Optical Storage Symposium and echoed in condensed fashion in a *commentary* on CNET's News.com—is breathtaking, both because it is so blatantly wrong and because the arguments Shapiro advances in an attempt to justify his conclusions are so transparently specious. Nonetheless, it deserves a response, because people need to know that Shapiro's proclamation, if not a deliberate and outright attempt to misinform, amounts at best to wishful thinking.

3   Certainly, there is nothing wrong with downloading per se. In fact, record companies and legitimate online music companies are aggressively promoting downloading as a fabulous way to get more music to more consumers. There is, however, a real problem with the unauthorized downloading of copyrighted material, both legally and morally.

4   "Despite the assertions of the Justice Department," Shapiro claims, "downloading is not illegal." Actually, it's not "the assertions of the Justice Department" that makes unauthorized downloading illegal. It's Title 17 of the United States Code, which prohibits the unauthorized reproduction, distribution, or digital transmission of copyrighted material.

5   It's also a long line of decisions interpreting that statutory provision, in court after court, in case after case. There is simply no doubt that copying and/or distributing copyrighted material on peer-to-peer file-sharing systems without the permission of the copyright holder is illegal, and Shapiro's preference that the law were otherwise does not make it so.

6   In an effort to overcome this rather problematic detail, Shapiro turns to the old standby, "fair use rights." While he doesn't explain exactly what these "rights" would permit, he makes it sound as if copyright owners are against fair use, and implies that fair use allows consumers to download anything they want. In fact, copyright owners rely on the fair use doctrine as much as (if not more than) anyone, because so much of what is created may be derivative of another's art.

7   So, we all respect and support fair use. But can fair use justify the uploading and downloading between anonymous strangers of entire copyrighted works of entertainment? No way.

8   That card has already been played in a number of file-sharing cases, and the courts have specifically rejected it. As U.S. District Court Judge Marvin E. Aspen ruled just last month in the Aimster case, the idea that "the ongoing, massive, and unauthorized distrib-

ution and copying of copyrighted works somehow constitutes 'personal use' is specious and unsupported."

9 Shapiro also turns to the other old standby, the Betamax case, to show that practices initially equated with "piracy" or "theft" have been accepted as fair use. But here again, he neglects to point out that the courts have already considered this claim several times in fact and repeatedly found that peer-to-peer file-sharing bears no resemblance to the facts or law in the Betamax case.

10 Perhaps realizing that the law as written and interpreted by the courts isn't really on his side, Shapiro devotes the heart of his speech to a passionate if poorly reasoned assault on the very notion of intellectual property. "To make downloading immoral," he says, "you have to accept that copyrighted products are governed by the same moral and legal principles as real property."

11 But the fact is that real and intellectual property are different and are governed by different principles. Downloading a copyrighted product does not diminish the product, as would be the case of taking and using tangible property such as a dress. At worst, it is depriving the copyright owner of a potential sale.

12 Though Shapiro apparently regards this as a key point, it is actually a distinction without a difference. Let's accept for the moment his assertion that "depriving the copyright owner of a potential sale" does not "diminish the product." In what way, then, is "taking and using tangible property such as a dress" any different? Whether you steal a dress from a store or steal a recording from an artist, you are harming the owner by depriving him or her of a potential sale.

13 To argue that the owner of the copyright can replace his intellectual property more cheaply or easily than the owner of the dress is to miss the point. Both owners have been deprived of something of value, and both are entitled to seek redress under the law.

14 Shapiro goes on to contend that it's unfair to compare intellectual property to real property, because unlike intellectual property, real property can be taxed and "can be owned forever." So? Intellectual property royalties can be (and are) taxed, and the fact that the property right isn't for forever makes it even more important that it be adequately protected during its term. Shapiro also argues that, unlike real property, "copyright law must bow to the First Amendment that expressly allows people to use a copyrighted product without the permission of the copyright owner."

15 Leaving aside the fact that the First Amendment "expressly" says no such thing (nor, as noted above, does the fair use doctrine permit free downloading), the fact is that real property rights are no more or

less unqualified than intellectual property rights. A peace officer can commandeer your car. A public-works agency can compel you to sell your land. A zoning board can make you tear down your treehouse.

16 At bottom, Shapiro seems to be saying that abstract concepts aren't as valuable or deserving of protection as tangible objects. (Plagiarists, take heart: Stealing other people's writings is OK with Shapiro, just as long as you don't steal the computer they wrote it on.) Whether or not he really believes this (and given the dependence of his member companies on patent, copyright, and trade-secret protection, it's hard to see how he could), his speech paints a portrait of artists as crybaby Luddites standing in the way of global prosperity.

17 What "the creative community" has done to warrant such scorn beyond trying to protect its rights is hard to fathom. The idea that artists want to put an end to downloading or even peer-to-peer file sharing is absurd. All they are asking is that people stop ripping them off.

18 And make no mistake about it, they are being ripped off, notwithstanding Shapiro's remarkable statement that despite illegal downloading, "music sales are holding their own." Perhaps he hasn't heard about the 10 percent decline in sales last year and the additional 10 percent drop in the first six months of this year. And he must have missed the stories on the layoffs, the cutbacks and all the labels and retail stores that have closed.

19 Stripped to its essence, Shapiro's attitude flies in the face of centuries of civil law and practice, as part of which civilized societies grant artists, authors, and other creative people the right to own and control the original work they produce, be they paintings, poems, songs, or any other form of literary or artistic expression. In the United States, copyright authority is woven into the national fabric. The founding fathers didn't like placing restrictions on the public, but they regarded this particular need with such urgency that they took the unique step of not only inserting it into Article I of the Constitution but also explaining why it was important ("To promote the Progress of Science and useful Arts").

20 Of course, in Shapiro's view, none of this matters, for the real culprits aren't consumers who want something for nothing or hardware manufacturers who don't mind encouraging them for the sake of their own sales. Rather, they're the antediluvian record and movie companies that fail to take advantage of the Internet and then "whine that they 'cannot compete with free.'" In Shapiro's twenty-first century marketplace, might evidently makes right. Instead of looking to the

law, he insists, "The recording industry and motion picture industry should stop complaining so much and consider a more flexible business model."

21   Well, our companies are already doing that, very aggressively in fact. And the increasing availability of music online—in a host of subscription and download services that offer more and more content, in a smorgasbord of different packages, at a variety of competitive price points—also rebuts his claim that the music industry has made little effort to look at new business models that take advantage of the new technologies.

22   But the fact that record companies are embracing new technologies and the Internet is really beside the point. In nutshell, what Shapiro is really saying is something like this: Despite what Congress and the courts say, digital stealing isn't really stealing, and therefore it isn't immoral. Moreover, despite what the U.S. Constitution says, intellectual property rights aren't really rights because intellectual property isn't really property. Therefore, even if music piracy really is stealing, copyright owners don't have a right to take reasonable steps to prevent it.

23   If that sounds like sophistry, it's because it is. Ironically, Shapiro accuses the copyright community of declaring "war on technology." But the only war being waged here is the rhetorical warfare that Shapiro has launched against artists and labels that simply want to protect their ability to continue in the business of creating music.

24   The last thing we need is more overheated and polarizing rhetoric. Shapiro would do well to drop the destructive diatribes and instead engage in some constructive dialogue. That's the only way we're going to figure out how to better serve consumers, creators, and technology companies alike in these challenging times.

An Analysis of Sherman's Response to Shapiro

Like Shapiro, Sherman is no disinterested participant in this debate. As president of the RIAA, he represents the recording industy, which claims to be losing a great deal of money because of illegal downloading. In paragraph 18 of his essay, Shapiro presents **statistics** to **support this claim** and to contest Shapiro's assertion that the recording industry is doing just fine. He notes a 10 percent decline in the sales of recorded music in 2001 and an additional 10 percent decline in the first half of 2002. He also presents **evidence from authority** to support his claim that Shapiro is simply *wrong*: unauthorized downloading is illegal because of "Title 17 of the United States Code, which prohibits the unauthorized reproduction, distribution, or digital transmission of copyrighted material," not because of "assertions of the Justice Department"—a phrase that now looks vague and imprecise.

The heart of Sherman's argument is his analysis of Shapiro's claims about music, property, and fair use rights. In paragraph 6, Sherman complains that Shapiro doesn't set out exactly what these rights are. Sherman himself doesn't **define** these rights either, except to say that they don't "justify the uploading and downloading between anonymous strangers of entire copyrighted works of entertainment." In paragraph 9, he calls into question Shapiro's analogy between home recording of films ("the Betamax case"), again by presenting **evidence from authority.** The courts, he says, have not found a similarity between downloading and home video recording. In paragraphs 12 and 13, Sherman asserts that stealing a dress and downloading a piece of music are, in fact, analogous (Shapiro had offered this **analogy,** only to dispute it).

Sherman's **tone** is by turns angry, sarcastic, witty, and reasonable. In our comment on Shapiro's essay, we cautioned against expressing scorn or impatience. On the other hand, if you are writing about something that strikes you as morally outrageous, of course you may convey anger, not sweet reasonableness. In paragraph 2, Sherman calls Shapiro's argument "specious" and says that if it isn't "a deliberate and outright attempt to misinform" then it's "at best . . . wishful thinking." Later, in paragraph 15, he uses sarcasm as he draws an analogy between downloading and plagiarism: "Plagiarists, take heart: Stealing other people's writings is OK with Shapiro, just as long as you don't steal the computer they wrote it [*sic*] on." Sherman turns to **wit** when he criticizes Shapiro's "portrait of artists as crybaby Luddites"[1] (the shift in diction, the informal "crybaby" modifying the word Luddite, a term from a very different level of usage, is funny). But he also presents himself as a reasonable person: in paragraph 3, he **acknowledges the counterargument** when he notes that "there is nothing wrong with downloading per se"; he does this again in paragraph 7 when he grants that "we all respect and support fair use," and again in the final sentence of the essay when he presents himself as interested in finding ways "to better serve consumers, creators, and technology companies."

. . .

---

[1]The Luddites were early nineteenth-century English textile workers who protested the effect of technological changes in the textile industry by destroying the new machines. The term refers pejoratively to people who are opposed to technological advances.

The music file-sharing controversy continues. To get a sense of the latest range of arguments articulated by lawyers, recording industry executives, consumers, and musicians, you can simply enter relevant keywords ("RIAA," "CEA," "music file-sharing," "music downloading") into an Internet search engine, where you'll find such online articles as Courtney Love's enraged critique of the music industry in a column for *Salon.com* and Janis Ian's carefully researched defense of file-sharing (it increases musicians' exposure, she says)—and countless other points of view, some well reasoned, some not.

As we have seen in the two preceding essays, offering airtight proof on a controversial matter may be an impossible proposition. Virginia Woolf put it this way: "When a subject is highly controversial . . . one cannot hope to tell the truth. One can only show how one came to hold whatever opinion one does hold."

CHAPTER NINE

USING SOURCES

Research is formalized curiosity. It is
poking and prying with a purpose.
—*Zora Neale Hurston*

Why Use Sources?

In preparing to write, academic writers use sources to enlarge and refine
their ideas. These sources can include facts, opinions, and the ideas of
others, recorded in print or in bytes, and in the form of books, articles,
lectures, reports, reviews, and interviews. Research essays—which are
also sometimes called "researched essays" or "documented essays"—are
based in part on such sources, and you'll write them in many of your college courses.

Even an essay that is primarily persuasive or analytical may be in part
based on research. For example, if you have been asked to write an essay
in which you state your position on the death penalty, you will probably
need to take into consideration the arguments of others who have written on the topic. If you've been asked to analyze a novel by Kate Chopin,
it may be useful to read what current literary critics have said about it.
If you don't consider any source, you risk taking a very uniformed position. Considering what others have said and developing your own position in relation to their ideas is central to academic writing.

Not everyone likes research, of course. There are hours spent reading
books and articles that prove to be contradictory or irrelevant. When the
project is large, you may feel that there isn't enough time to read all the
material that's available—or even to get your hands on it. Regardless of

the scope of the project, some of the books may be dull. The poet William
Butler Yeats, though an indefatigable worker on projects that interested
him, engagingly expressed an indifference to the obligation that confronts
every researcher: to look carefully at all the relevant evidence. Running
over the possible reasons why Jonathan Swift did not marry (that he had
syphilis, for instance, or that he feared he would transmit a hereditary
madness), Yeats says: "Mr. Shane Leslie thinks that Swift's relation to
Vanessa was not platonic, and that whenever his letters speak of a cup of
coffee they mean the sexual act; whether the letters seem to bear him out
I do not know, for those letters bore me."

Though research sometimes requires one to read boring things, those
who engage in it feel, at other times, an exhilaration, a sense of triumph
at becoming expert on something. When you know what others have said
about your topic, you are in a position to say: "Here is how other people
have thought about this question; their ideas are all very interesting, but
I see the matter differently: Let me tell you what *I* think."

In the paragraph below, the second paragraph of a research essay we
reprint in full in the next chapter, a student does just that, more or less.
In the essay, Beatrice Cody argues against interpretations of the Chopin's
The Awakening as a feminist political statement—the prevailing view.
Instead, she contends that the suicide of Chopin's protagonist, Edna Pontellier, "resulted from the torments of her individual psyche, her inability to cope with the patriarchal expectations, which most women in fact
were able to tolerate."

> It is difficult to say how Chopin wished The
> Awakening to be interpreted. Heroines who explore
> their own individuality (with varying degrees of suc-
> cess and failure) abound in her work (Shinn 358);
> Chopin herself, though married, was a rather nontra-
> ditional wife who smoked cigarettes, and, like Edna
> Pontellier, took walks by herself (Nissenbaum
> 333-34). One might think therefore that Chopin was
> making a political statement in The Awakening about
> the position of women in society based on her own
> rejection of that position. But aside from slim bio-
> graphical evidence and the assertions of some critics
> such as Larzer Ziff and Daniel S. Rankin that Chopin
> sympathized with Edna, we have no way of knowing
> whether she regarded this protagonist as a victim of
> sexist oppression or simply, to quote her family doc-

tor in the novel itself, as "a sensitive and highly
organized woman [. . . who] is especially peculiar"
(66). It is therefore necessary to explore the two
possibilities, using evidence from the novel to
determine whether Edna Pontellier's awakening is
political or peculiarly personal in nature.

Note the authority with which the student writes as she (respectfully) calls into question the conclusions of others who have written about the novel she's studied and researched. She has read enough to know that the biographical evidence supporting a feminist reading of *The Awakening* is "slim"; she has found enough evidence to say (persuasively, we think) that "It is. . .necessary to explore" the matter further. She knows a lot about her topic. She has become, over the course of several weeks, a kind of expert on it.

There can be great satisfaction in knowing enough about a topic to contribute to the store of knowledge and ideas about it. There can also be great satisfaction in simply learning to use the seemingly infinite resources now available to researchers—in print or electronic formats—as well as in learning to document and to acknowledge your research accurately and responsibly.

In this chapter we discuss

- how to find and evaluate sources, both print and electronic,
- how to take useful notes,
- how to use others' ideas to help you develop your own, and
- how to paraphrase, summarize, and quote the work of others, so that their words and ideas are distinct from yours.

What Is a Source?
Primary and Secondary Materials

Sources are usually divided into two categories, primary and secondary. A **primary source** is the real subject of study; a **secondary source** is a critical or historical account written about a primary source. For example, if you want to know whether Shakespeare's attitude toward Julius Caesar was highly traditional or highly original, or a little of each, you would read *Julius Caesar*, other Elizabethan writings about Caesar, and translations of Latin writings known to the Elizabethans. These are primary sources. In addition to these, you would read secondary sources such as modern books on Shakespeare and on Elizabethan attitudes toward Rome and toward monarchs.

Similarly, the primary material for an essay on Kate Chopin's *The Awakening* novel, is of course the novel itself; the secondary material consists of such things as biographies of Chopin and critical essays on the novel. But the line between these two kinds of sources is not always sharp. For example, if you are concerned with the degree to which *The Awakening* is autobiographical, primary materials include not only the novel and also Chopin's comments on her writing but perhaps also the comments of people who knew her. Thus the essays—based on interviews with Chopin—that two of her friends published in newspapers probably can be regarded as primary material because they were contemporary with the novel and because they give direct access to Chopin's views, while the writings of later commentators constitute secondary material.

Developing a Research Topic

Your instructor may assign a topic, in which case, you'll be saved some work. (On the other hand, you may find yourself spending a lot of time with material you don't find exciting. On yet another hand, you may become interested in something you'd otherwise never have known about.) More likely, you'll need to develop your own topic, a topic related to the subject of the course for which the research essay has been assigned. Some possibilities:

- Perhaps you've read Maxine Hong Kingston's *The Woman Warrior* (1976) for a Women's Studies course, and you have become interested in Confucian or Buddhist ideas that inform the narrative.

- Perhaps your government course has touched on the internment of Japanese-Americans during World War II, and you'd like to know more about what happened.

- Perhaps you've read Chopin's *The Awakening* for a literature course, and you're wondering what readers thought about the novel when it was first published.

Any of these interests could well become a topic for a research essay. But how do you find the relevant material?

Finding Sources

We can't give you a roadmap or a recipe for finding the sources you need. The number of possible topics is infinite, as is the number of sources. Research approaches vary widely. And the Internet—the vast interconnection of computer networks that has made an extraordinary amount of information available to researchers and everyone else—complicates things further. By its very nature, the Internet is constantly changing; guides to research on the Internet are generally out of date even before they appear in print.

Nevertheless, we do have some general suggestions. One good rule of thumb is to begin with what you already know, with what you already have at hand. For instance, the textbook for your government course may cite official documents on the relocation and internment of Japanese-Americans. Or your edition of Chopin's *The Awakening* may contain an introduction that references some critical essays on the novel; it's also likely to contain a selected bibliography, a list of books and articles about Chopin and her work. If you have already identified a few titles, you can go directly to your library's online catalog and begin your search there. (We'll have a bit more to say about online searches in a moment.)

If, however, you know very little about the topic, and haven't yet identified any possible sources (let's say you know nothing or almost nothing about Confucianism, but Maxine Hong Kingston's *The Woman Warrior* has made you want to learn about it), it's not a bad idea to begin with an encyclopedia—the *Encyclopaedia Britannica*, perhaps—which you'll find online through your library's e-resources Web page, and in hardcopy form in the library's reference area. In addition to providing basic information about your topic, encyclopedia articles usually include cross-references to other articles within the encyclopedia, as well as suggestions for further reading. These suggestions can help you begin to compose a list of secondary sources for your essay. And of course you need not limit yourself to one encyclopedia. There are hundreds of invaluable specialized encyclopedias, such as *Encyclopedia of Anthropology, Encyclopedia of Crime and Justice, Encyclopedia of Psychology, Encyclopedia of Religion* (a good place to go for an introduction to Confucianism), and *Kodansha Encyclopedia of Japan*. Several of them are certain to be available in your library's reference area or through your library's central information system.

The Library's Central Information System

All libraries used to work in more or less the same way. Each one had a card catalog, a set of hundreds of little drawers containing thousands (even millions) of alphabetically arranged three-by-five cards. When you wanted a book, you went to the card catalog and looked it up by title, author, or subject. Because books would of course differ from library to library, the cards would also of course differ, but the system in every library was pretty much the same.

In recent years, online catalogs have replaced card catalogs in college, university, and public libraries. And the on-line catalog constitutes only a tiny fraction of the information available to you through your institution's library. With the help of enormous databases such as JSTOR, Lex-isNexis, and Project Muse, you can search thousands of academic journals, newspapers, and magazines. From a computer terminal in your library (or from home via an Internet connection), you can access bibliographies and indexes, full-text versions of encyclopedias, dictionaries, and academic journals, the catalogs of *other* libraries—and much more.

Unlike card catalogs, each library's central information system is a bit different. Resources differ from one library to the next. And like the Internet itself, your library's central information system is changing every day. For these reasons, perhaps the best advice we can give you about learning to find books and articles in your library is to go to your college or university's research librarian and ask for help.

Using the Internet

As we've noted, the Internet can be a tremendous resource for researchers. But because anyone, anywhere, can post pretty much anything, the information available on the Internet can be difficult to evaluate. When you're working with secondary sources that have been published in journals or in book form, for the most part you're working with material that experts in that field have judged to be worth reading. Before it's published, an article in a journal such as *Society* or *College English*, for example, will have been read by a number of reviewers (most or all of them college professors in the field), as well as by members of an advisory board and several editors. If *Society* or *College English* is in your institution's library—and we bet it is—it's there in part because librarians have decided it is worth including in the serials collection. An article in one of these journals may have weaknesses, but several experts have thought it was pretty good.

Much of the information available on the Internet has not been similarly vetted. Advertisements coexist with course syllabi. By entering the relevant keyword into a search engine such as Google or Yahoo! you could (if you wanted to) access a chat group on Russell Crowe as easily as you could find photographs of people's pets. Or an interview with Jamaica Kincaid. Or the full text of *Romeo and Juliet*. Or an essay on your

"On the Internet, nobody knows you're a dog." © The New Yorker Collection 1993.
Peter Steiner from Cartoonbank.com. All Rights Reserved.

research topic, written by your professor—or by the person who sits next to you in your biology class.

How do you judge what may be worth considering? In part by using the analytic skills we discuss elsewhere in this book. The following checklist will help you focus your analysis.

CHECKLIST FOR EVALUATING WEB SITES

☐ Who produced the site (a teacher, a commercial entity, a student)?
☐ Who sponsored the site?
☐ For whom is the author writing? Who is the intended audience?

☐ Can you tell if the author of the document is an authority in the field? (Perhaps the document is linked to the author's home page.)

☐ Does he or she reference other critics or writers? Good ones?

☐ Is the text well written?

☐ Do arguments seem well supported, or is the document full of vague generalizations?

☐ When was the site created or last updated?

For more on this matter, we recommend (appropriately enough) that you consult documents available on the Web, such as "Evaluating Information Found on the Internet" (http://milton.mse.jhu.edu:8001/research/education/net.html). It *should* still be available—but that's the other problem with Internet sources: What's here today may be gone tomorrow.

Reading and Taking Notes on Secondary Sources

Almost all researchers—professionals as well as beginners—find that they end up with some notes that are irrelevant, and, on the other hand, find, when drafting the paper, that they vaguely remember certain material they now wish they had taken notes on. Especially in the early stages of a project, when the topic and thesis may still be relatively unfocused, it's hard to know what is noteworthy and what is not. You simply have to flounder a bit.

It may be helpful to skim an article or book all the way through the first time around without taking notes. By the time you reach the end, you may find it isn't noteworthy. Or you may find a useful summary near the end that will contain most of what you can get from the piece. Or you may find that, having a sense of the whole, you can now quickly reread the piece and take notes on the chief points that concern you.

Even if you follow this procedure, a certain amount of inefficiency is inevitable; therefore plenty of time should be allowed. And it's worth keeping in mind that different people really do work differently. We list here three strategies; we suspect that, over time, you'll develop your own.

• Take notes using four-by-six-inch cards, writing on one side only, because material on the back of a card is usually neglected when you come to write the paper. (Taking notes by hand offers several advantages—not least of which is that you don't need access to a computer to do it.)

> Verrett, pp. 152-154 ✓   botulism argument
>   search for substitute
>
> p.152 Industry and gov't approved nitrite as color
> fixer. Now shifting ground, saying it prevents
> botulism. Verrett points out "legal snag." New
> approval needed for new use.
> (Thus public hearing and unwanted attention)
>
> p.154 "... the industry--USDA-FDA coalition seems
> firm in its position that there is no substitute for
> nitrate, now or ever. Their posture is misdirected
> at defending nitrites, devising ways to keep it
> in food rather than ways to get it out." ✓
>
>   Verrett and Carper, Eating May Be Hazardous

- Take notes on your computer, keeping a separate file for each book or article. Material can be easily moved from one file to another as the organization of the essay begins to take shape.

- Don't take notes—or take very few notes. Photocopy secondary material you think you might use, if it is brief, and underline and annotate that material as you read and think about it. (Material from electronic sources can be downloaded and later printed out and annotated as well. In fact, it's advisable to download any information you access online. Online sources can disappear; but if you download or print the source, you'll be able to check it if necessary, and will be able produce it if there are any questions about your use of it.) The disadvantage here is obvious: This method uses a lot of paper. But there are two big advantages. Passages from the sources are transcribed (or, in the cases of downloaded material, moved) only once, into the draft itself, so there's less risk of mistakes and distortions. And the research—the collecting of information—can go very quickly. *A word of caution:* It's crucial that you think carefully about the material you're collecting and that you annotate it thoroughly. If you don't—that is, if you merely photocopy and mindlessly highlight vast areas—you'll find yourself with a pile of paper, and no idea of what to do with it.

A Guide to Note-Taking

1. Scan the work before you start taking notes. Before assiduously taking notes from the first paragraph onward, or highlighting long passages, try to get a sense of the author's thesis. You may find an early paragraph that states the thesis outright; you may also find a concluding paragraph that offers a summary of the evidence that supports the thesis. Having gained a general idea of the work, you can now take notes sparingly while you read the material carefully and critically.

2. Read critically. Read thoughtfully, continually asking yourself if the author supports assertions with adequate evidence. Be especially sure to ask what can be said *against* assertions that coincide with your own beliefs. The heart of critical thinking is a willingness to face objections to one's own beliefs.

3. Be sure to record the title and author of the source. If you're using notecards, specify the source in an abbreviated form in the upper left corner. If you're taking notes on your computer, make a separate file for each book or article, and use the author's name and the first significant word of the title to identify the file. If you're using photocopies or downloaded material, make sure that you also photocopy the bibliographic information—which usually appears in full on the title page of a book and often (but not always) appears on the first page of a journal article. (And be sure to make a record of the full span of the article, not just the pages that you have copied.)

4. Write summaries, not paraphrases (that is, write abridgments rather than restatements, which in fact may be as long as or longer than the original). As we note in our chapter on analyzing texts, there is rarely any point to paraphrasing. Generally speaking, either quote exactly (and put the passage in quotation marks, with a notation of the source, including the page number or numbers) or summarize, reducing a page or even an entire article or chapter of a book to a few sentences that can be written on a notecard, typed into your computer, or squeezed into the margin of a photocopied page. Even when you summarize, record your source (including the page numbers), so that you can give appropriate credit in your essay.

5. Quote sparingly. Of course in your summary you will sometimes quote a phrase or a sentence—putting it in quotation marks—but quote sparingly. You are not simply transcribing what you read; rather you are assimilating knowledge and you are thinking, and so for the most part your source should be chewed and digested rather than swallowed whole. Thinking now, while taking notes, will also help you later to avoid plagiarism. If, on the other hand, when you take notes you mindlessly copy material at length, later when you are writing the essay you may be tempted to copy it yet again, perhaps without giving credit. Likewise, if you simply photocopy pages from articles or books, and then merely underline some passages without annotating your reading, you probably will not be thinking; you will just be underlining. But if you make a terse summary you will be forced to think and to find your own words for the idea. Quote directly only those passages that are particularly effective, or crucial, or memorable. In your finished essay these quotations will provide authority and emphasis.

6. Quote accurately. After copying a quotation, check your transcription against the original, and correct any misquotation. Verify the page number also. If a quotation runs from the bottom of, say, page 306 to the top of 307, make a distinguishing mark (for instance two backslashes after the last word of the first page), so that if you later use only part of the quotation, you will know the page on which it appeared.

7. Use ellipses to indicate the omission of any words within a sentence. If the omitted words are at the end of the quoted sentence, put a period immediately at the point where you end the sentence, and then add three spaced periods.

```
If the . . . words are at the end of the quoted sen-
tence, put a period immediately at the point where
you end. . . .
```

8. Use square brackets to indicate your additions to the quotations. Here is an example:

```
Here is an [uninteresting] example.
```

9. *Do not* change even an occasional word when copying a passage, even if you think you will be later putting it into your own words. Notes of this sort may find their way into your essay, your reader will sense a style other than your own, and suspicions (and perhaps even charges) of plagiarism will follow. (For a detailed discussion of plagiarism, see below).

10. Comment on your notes. Consider it your obligation to *think* about the material as you take notes, evaluating it and using it as a stimulus to further thought. For example, you may want to say "Tyler seems to be generalizing from insufficient evidence," or "Corsa made the same point five years earlier"; but make certain that later you will be able to distinguish between these comments and the notes summarizing or quoting your source. A suggestion: Surround all comments recording your responses with double parentheses, thus: ((Is there evidence for this assertion?)).

11. Write a keyword on each card or at the beginning of each section of notes in your computer file. A brief key—for example "effect on infants' blood"—can help you to tell at a glance what is on the card or in the file.

Acknowledging Sources

Using Sources Without Plagiarizing

Your purpose as an academic writer is to develop *your own ideas* about the topic you are writing about. Secondary sources will help you shape and develop your thoughts about your topic, but your purpose is to develop an argument and an analysis that is your own. It is crucial, then, to be clear about the distinction between your words and ideas and those of your sources. Not to do so is to risk charges of **plagiarism.** To plagiarize is to use someone else's words or ideas without attributing them to a source; it is to pass off someone else's work as your own. It is, in short, theft. The institutional consequences of plagiarism vary from school to school, and from case to case. In the university where one of us teaches, students who are found guilty of plagiarism are, among other things, banned from the campus for a year. At other schools, students can be expelled permanently; at still others, they simply receive a failing grade for the course and are put on academic probation.

Respect for your readers and for your sources requires that you acknowledge your indebtedness for material when

- you quote directly from a work, or
- you paraphrase or summarize someone's words (the words of your paraphrase or summary are your own, but the ideas are not), or
- you use an idea that is not common knowledge.

Most commonly, the words, ideas, and information you'll cite in a research essay will come from printed and electronic sources. But you must also acknowledge the advice of peer editors and ideas that come from lectures and class discussions, unless your instructor tells you not to do so. (We explain how to format the citations for all these sources in Chapter 13.)

Let's suppose you are going to make use of William Bascom's comment on the earliest responses of Europeans to African art:

> The first examples of African art to gain public attention were the bronzes and ivories which were brought back to Europe after the sack of Benin by a British military expedition in 1897. The superb technology of the Benin bronzes won the praise of experts like Felix von Luschan who wrote in 1899, "Cellini himself could not have made better casts, nor anyone

else before or since to the present day." Moreover, their relatively realistic treatment of human features conformed to the prevailing European aesthetic standards. Because of their naturalism and technical excellence, it was at first maintained that they had been produced by Europeans— a view that was still current when the even more realistic bronze heads were discovered at Ife in 1912. The subsequent discovery of new evidence has caused the complete abandonment of this theory of European origins of the bronzes of Benin and Ife, both of which are cities in Nigeria.

> —*William Bascom,* African Art in Cultural Perspective
> *(New York: Norton, 1973), p. 4*

Acknowledging a Direct Quotation   A student wanting to use some or all of Bascom's words might write something like this:

```
According to William Bascom, when Europeans first
encountered Benin and Ife works of art in the late
nineteenth century, they thought that Europeans had
produced them, but the discovery of new evidence
"caused the complete abandonment of this theory of
European origins of the bronzes of Benin and Ife,
both of which are cities in Nigeria" (4).
```

In this example, the writer introduces Bascom with a signal phrase ("According to William Bascom "); then she summarizes several sentences from Bascom; then she uses quotation marks to indicate the passage that comes directly from Bascom's book. Note that the summary does not borrow Bascom's language; the words are all the writer's own. Note also that what appears inside the quotation marks is an exact transcription of Bascom's words: The writer has not changed any word endings, or omitted any words, or inserted any punctuation of her own. (The "4" inside parentheses at the end of the passage is the page reference. Again, we explain how to use the MLA system of parenthetic citation in Chapter 13.)

Acknowledging a Paraphrase or Summary   Summaries (abridgments) are usually superior to paraphrases (rewordings, of approximately the same length as the original) because summaries are briefer. As we explain in Chapter 7, "Analyzing Texts," when you are using secondary sources, you will for the most part be writing summaries, not paraphrases—unless the language of the source is especially complex. If Bascom's sentences had been obscure—for instance, if they used highly technical language—there would have been a reason to paraphrase them. In that case, the writer of the essay would explicitly have said she was paraphrasing Bascom, and she would have explained why.

Occasionally you may find that you cannot summarize a passage in your source and yet you don't want to quote it word for word—perhaps because it is too technical or because it is poorly written. In that case, you need to paraphrase the passage—that is, you need to put it into your own words. Even though you have put the idea into your own words, you must give credit to the source because the idea is not yours. *Both summaries and paraphrases must be acknowledged.* In both cases, the author must be identified by name, and the location of the source—a page reference if you are using a print source—must be given.

Here is an example of an **acceptable summary:**

```
William Bascom, in African Art, points out that the
first examples of African art brought to Europe--
Benin bronzes and ivories--were thought by Europeans
to be of European origin, because they were realistic
and well made, but evidence was later discovered that
caused this theory to be abandoned (4).
```

The summary is adequate, and the page reference indicates where the source is to be found. But if the writer had omitted the signal phrase "William Bascom, in *African Art,* points out that," the result would have been plagiarism. Not to give Bascom credit would be to plagiarize, even if the words are the writer's own. The offense is just as serious as not acknowledging a direct quotation.

The following paragraph is an example of an **unacceptable summary.** The writer uses too much of Bascom's language, and she follows his organization of the material: she has not turned the material into her own writing. And she gives Bascom no credit for his ideas.

```
The earliest examples of African art to become widely
known in Europe were bronzes and ivories that were
brought to Europe in 1897. These works were thought
to be of European origin, and one expert said that
Cellini could not have done better work. Their tech-
nical excellence, as well as their realism, fulfilled
the European standards of the day. The later discov-
ery of new evidence at Benin and Ife, both in Nige-
ria, refuted this belief.
```

Again, one problem here is that all the *ideas* are Bascom's—and his name appears neither in a signal phrase nor in a citation. Another problem is that the writer doesn't put the passage entirely into her own words. Rather, she simply substitutes one phrase for another, maintaining much of the structure and organization of Bascom's sentences. The writing is Bascom's, in a thin disguise. She substitutes

> "The earliest examples of African art"

for Bascom's

> "The first examples of African art";

she substitutes

> "to become widely known"

for

> "to gain public attention";

she substitutes

> "Their technical excellence, as well as their realism"

for

> "their naturalism and technical excellence."

The writer here is plagiarizing—perhaps without even knowing it. But it should be clear that neither the words nor the ideas in this passage are the writer's own. This form of plagiarism, where a writer simply substitutes his or her own phrases here and there but retains the form and content of the original passage, is one of the most common forms of plagiarism that writing instructors see. Much of it occurs, we believe, because students don't know it's wrong—and because they don't see their job as developing their *own* ideas in relation to their sources.

As we have noted, it is unlikely that a writer would paraphrase a passage that is as straightforward and as free of technical language as Bascom's: the main reason for paraphrasing is to clarify a text that might be confusing to a reader—a literary text, for example, or a particularly complex or technical piece of writing. In the following example, a passage that contains an **acceptable paraphrase** of a sentence from Darwin's *Origin of Species*, the student clarifies a key point in Darwin's argument:

> Before discussing the relationship between Darwin's
> observations of animal life and his views of the nature

```
of human society, it may be helpful to clarify the
meaning of a key sentence in The Origin of Species.
Darwin says, in Chapter 3,
      I should premise that I use the term Struggle for
      Existence in a large and metaphorical sense, includ-
      ing dependence of one being on another, and includ-
      ing (which is more important) not only the life of
      the individual, but success in leaving progeny.
In other words, Darwin notes that he wishes to say in
advance that his phrase "Struggle for Existence" is to
be understood in a figurative way to indicate not only
how the survival of a creature is dependent on other
creatures, but also to refer to the importance of pro-
ducing offspring.
```

The paraphrase clarifies the terms that might have been obscure in the original ("premise" means "say in advance"; "progeny" means "offspring"), and it is entirely in the student's own language. If the student had borrowed any of Darwin's phrases or significant words, the paraphrase would have been inadequate. Here is an example of an **unacceptable paraphrase** of Darwin's sentence:

```
In other words, Darwin says that he wants to posit
that he will use the term Struggle for Existence in a
grand and poetical way, to mean dependence of one
being on another, as well as--more significantly--its
success in leaving offspring.
```

Note that several phrases are lifted directly from the source (for example, "use the term Struggle for Existence" and "dependence of one being on another"); note also the cheesy substitution of "posit" for "premise" and "grand and poetical" for "large and metaphorical." The source (Darwin) is identified, and in a way, the problems *seem* minor: it's just a sentence, after all. But if there were a pattern of such problems in a student essay, if there were several such sentences, the student would be open to charges of plagiarism.

Acknowledging an Idea   Let's say you have read an essay in which Irving Kristol argues that journalists who pride themselves on being tireless critics of national policy are in fact irresponsible critics because they have no policy they prefer. If this strikes you as a new idea and you adopt it in an essay—even though you set it forth entirely in your own words and with examples not offered by Kristol—you must acknowledge your debt to Kristol. *Not to acknowledge such borrowing is plagiarism.* Your readers will not think the less of you for naming your source; rather, they will be grateful to you for telling them about an interesting writer.

Fair Use of Common Knowledge

If in doubt as to whether or not to give credit (either with formal documentation or merely in a phrase such as "Carol Gilligan says . . ."), give credit. But as you begin to read widely in your field or subject, you will develop a sense of what is considered common knowledge.

Unsurprising definitions in a dictionary can be considered common knowledge, and so there is no need to say "According to Webster, a novel is a long narrative in prose." (That's weak in three ways: It's unnecessary, it's uninteresting, and it's inexact since "Webster" appears in the titles of several dictionaries, some good and some bad.)

Similarly, the date of Freud's death can be considered common knowledge. Few can give it when asked, but it can be found out from innumerable sources, and no one need get the credit for providing you with the date. Again, if you simply *know*, from your reading of Freud, that Freud was interested in literature, you need not cite a specific source for an assertion to that effect, but if you know only because some commentator on Freud said so, and you have no idea whether the fact is well known or not, you should give credit to the source that gave you the information. Not to give credit—for ideas as well as for quoted words—is to plagiarize.

"But How Else Can I Put It?"

If you have just learned—say from an encyclopedia—something that you sense is common knowledge, you may wonder how to change into your own words the simple, clear words that this source uses in setting forth this simple fact. For example, if before writing an analysis of a photograph of Buffalo Bill and Sitting Bull, you look up these names in the *Encyclopaedia Britannica*, you will find this statement about Buffalo Bill (William F. Cody): "In 1883 Cody organized his first Wild West exhibition." You could not use this statement as your own, word for word, without feeling uneasy. But to put in quotation marks such a routine statement of what can be considered common knowledge, and to cite a source for it, seems pretentious. After all, the *Encyclopedia Americana* says much the same thing in the same routine way: "In 1883 . . . Cody organized Buffalo Bill's Wild West." It may be that the word "organized" is simply the most obvious and the best word, and perhaps you will end up using it. Certainly, to change "Cody organized" into "Cody presided over the organization of" or "Cody assembled" or some such thing in an effort to avoid plagiarizing would be to make a change for the worse and still to be guilty of plagiarism. What, then, can you do? You won't get yourself into this mess of wondering whether to change clear, simple wording into awkward wording if in the first place, when you take notes, you *summarize* your sources, thus: "1883: organized Wild West," or "first Wild West: 1883." Later (even if only thirty minutes later), when drafting your paper, if you turn this nugget—probably combined with others—into the best sentence you can, you will not be in danger of plagiarizing, even if the word "organized" turns up in your sentence.

Of course, even when dealing with material that can be considered common knowledge—and even when you have put it into your own words—you probably *will* cite your source if you are drawing more than just an occasional fact from a source. For instance, if your paragraph on Buffalo Bill uses half a dozen facts from a source, cite the source. You do this both to avoid charges of plagiarism and to protect yourself in case your source contains errors of fact.

CHAPTER TEN

WRITING THE RESEARCH ESSAY

When you use sources, you are not merely dumping on the table the contents of a shopping cart filled at the scholar's supermarket, the library. You are cooking a meal. You must have a point, an opinion, a thesis. You are working toward a conclusion, and your readers should always feel they are moving toward that conclusion rather than reading an anthology of commentary on the topic. You've become an expert on your topic; you now know what others have to say about it, but if you've been *thinking* about what the secondary sources have said about your primary material, it's likely that you've noticed contradictions and gaps, that you agree with some opinions and arguments (and disagree with others), that you've begun to develop your *own* ideas about your topic.

There remains the difficult job of writing the essay.

Writing the Essay

Beyond referring you to the rest of this book, we can offer only seven pieces of advice.

1. With a tentative thesis in mind, begin by rereading your notes and sorting them by topic. Put together what belongs together. Don't hesitate to reject interesting material that now seems irrelevant or redundant. After sorting, re-sorting, and rejecting, you will have a kind of first draft without writing a draft.

2. From your notes, make a first outline. Although you can't yet make a paragraph outline, you may find it useful to make a fairly full outline, indicating not only the sequence of points but also the quotations that you will use. In sketching the outline, of course you will be guided by your *thesis*. As you worked, you probably modified your tentative ideas in the light of what your further research produced, but by now you ought to have a relatively firm idea of what you want to say. Without a thesis you will have only the basis for a *report*, not a potential essay.

3. Transcribe or download quotations, even in the first draft, exactly as you want them to appear in the final version. Of course this takes some time, and the time will be wasted if, as may well turn out, you later see that the quotation is not really useful. (On the other hand, the time has not really been wasted, since it helped you ultimately to delete the unnecessary material.)

If at this early stage you just write a note reminding yourself to include the quotation—something like "here quote Jackson on undecided voters"—when you reread the draft you won't really know how the page sounds. You won't, for instance, know how much help your reader needs by way of a lead-in to the quotation, or how much discussion should follow. Only if you actually see the quotation are you in the position of your audience, and it's a good idea to try to imagine your audience, even at this early stage.

4. Include, right in the body of the draft, all of the relevant citations. This way, when you come to revise, you don't have to start hunting through your notes to find who said what, and where. You can, for the moment, enclose these citations within diagonal lines, or within double parentheses—anything to remind you that they will be your documentation.

5. Resist the urge to include every note in your essay. As we suggest in Chapter 1, writing is a way of discovering ideas. Consequently, as you write your first draft, your thesis will inevitably shift, and notes that initially seemed important will now seem irrelevant. Don't stuff them into the draft, even if you're concerned about meeting a page requirement: Readers know padding when they see it.

6. Resist the urge to do more research. As you draft, you may also see places where another piece of evidence, another reference to a source, or another example would be useful. And you may feel compelled to head back to the library. We think that for now you should resist that urge too: It may simply be procrastination in disguise. Continue writing this first draft if possible, and plan to incorporate new material in a later draft.

7. As you revise your draft, make sure that you do not merely tell the reader "A says ... B says ... C says...." Rather, by using a lead-in or signal phrase such as "A claims," "B provides evidence that," "according to C," "D concedes that," you help the reader to see the role of the quotation in your paper. Further, after quoting or summarizing a source, you should normally comment on it, thereby making clear the relation between your own ideas and those of the source.

CHECKLIST FOR REVISING DRAFTS
OF RESEARCH RSSAYS

☐ Is the tentative title informative and focused?

☐ Does the paper make a point, or does it just accumulate other people's ideas? (See pp. 194–96.)

☐ Does it reveal the thesis early? (See pp.11–12; 168–79)

☐ Are claims supported by evidence? (See pp. 154–57.)

☐ Are all the *words* and *ideas* of the sources accurately attributed? (See pp. 205–10.)

☐ Are quotations introduced adequately with signal phrases (such as "according to Ziff," or "Smith contends," or "Johnson points out") to indicate who is speaking? (See p. 213.)

☐ Are all of the long quotations necessary, or can some of them be effectively summarized? (See p. 206.)

☐ Are quotations discussed adequately? (See p. 204; see also Chapter 7, "Analyzing Texts.")

☐ Does the paper advance in orderly stages? Can your imagined reader easily follow your thinking? (See Chapter 2, "Drafting and Revising.")

☐ Is the documentation in the correct form? (See Chapter 13, "Documenting Sources.")

A Sample Research Essay (MLA Format)

We began this chapter with a paragraph from the following research essay, "Politics and Psychology in *The Awakening*." We noted that Beatrice Cody used her research to help her develop her *own* position on the novel. As you read her essay, be alert to the range of sources Cody has chosen, and to the range of ways in which she uses them: to establish the critical position she'll be arguing against, to give helpful background on Chopin's life, to provide information on the responses of Chopin's contemporaries to the novel, and so on.

Note: Cody uses the Modern Language Association (MLA) form of in-text citations, which are clarified by a list headed "Works Cited." We explain the MLA system in detail in Chapter 13, "Documenting Sources." In that chapter we also explain and illustrate the American Psychological Association (APA) form of in-text citations, and we offer information on several other systems of documentation.

Cody 1

Beatrice Cody
Ms. Bellanca
Writing 125
12 April 2004

Politics and Psychology in
The Awakening

Title announces focus and scope of essay.

1   At first glance, Kate Chopin's novel The Awakening (1899) poses no problem to the feminist reader. It is the story of Edna Pontellier, a woman living at the turn of the century who, partly through a half-realized summer romance, discovers that sensual love, art, and individuality mean more to her than marriage or motherhood. When she concludes that there can be no compromise between her awakened inner self and the stifling shell of her outer life as a wife and mother, she drowns herself. In such a summary, Edna appears to be yet another victim of the "Feminine Mystique" described by Betty Friedan in the 1950's, a mind-numbing malaise afflicting the typical American housewife whose husband and society expected her to care for family at the expense of personal freedom and fulfillment. However, it is possible that the events leading to Edna's tragic death were not caused solely by the expectations of a sexist society pre-dating Friedan's model, in which a wife was not only dutiful to but also the "property" of her husband (Culley 119),

Plot summary helps orient readers unfamiliar with novel.

Cody 2

Citation includes title because there are two works by Chopin on Works Cited list.

and a mother not only stayed home but also sacrificed even the "essential" for her children (Chopin Awakening 48).

Clear statement of thesis.

Perhaps Edna's suicide resulted from the torments of her individual psyche, her inability to cope with the patriarchal expectations, which most women in fact were able to tolerate.

Citation 2 includes name because author isn't cited in the sentence itself.

It is difficult to say how Chopin wished The Awakening to be interpreted. Heroines who explore their own individuality (with varying degrees of success and failure) abound in her work (Shinn 358); Chopin herself, though married, was a rather nontraditional wife who smoked cigarettes, and, like Edna Pontellier, took walks by herself (Nissenbaum 333-34). One might think

Sources are paraphrased here. Although the words of the sources aren't used, ideas must be acknowledged.

therefore that Chopin was making a political statement in The Awakening about the position of women in society based on her own rejection of that position. But aside from slim biographical evidence and the assertions of some critics such as Larzer Ziff and Daniel S. Rankin that Chopin sympathized with Edna, we have no way of knowing whether she regarded this protagonist as a victim of sexist oppression or simply, to quote her family doctor in the novel itself, as

Brackets around "who" indicate that word has been added.

"a sensitive and highly organized woman . . . [who] is especially peculiar" (66). It is therefore necessary to explore the two possibilities, using

Citation includes page number because title and author are clear from context.

evidence from the novel to determine
whether Edna Pontellier's awakening is
political or peculiarly personal in
nature.

3   It does not take a deeply feminist
awareness to detect the dominant,
controlling stance Edna's husband,
Leonce, assumes in their marriage.
Throughout the novel Chopin documents
the resulting injustices, both great and
small, which Edna endures. In one
instance Leonce comes home late at night
after Edna has fallen asleep, and, upon
visiting their sleeping children,
concludes that both of them are
feverish. He wakes Edna so that she may
check on them, despite her assertion
that the children are perfectly well.
He chides her for her "inattention" and
"habitual neglect of the children"
(7)--rather than respecting her ability
as their mother to judge the state of
their health or attending to them
himself--and reduces her to tears. She
defers to his judgment, looking at the
boys as he had asked, and, finding them
entirely healthy, goes out to the porch
where "an indescribable oppression
. . . filled her whole being with a
vague anguish" (8). Though in some ways
inconsequential, actions such as these
epitomize Leonce Pontellier's attitude
toward women and particularly toward
his wife. It is his belief that she has
a certain role and specific duties

. . . (three spaced periods) indicate that words have been omitted from sentence.

Cody 4

(those of a woman) which must be done well--according to his (a man's) standards. Although he would probably claim to love Edna, he does not seem to regard her as an autonomous individual; she is the mother of his children, the hostess of such "callers" as he deems appropriate (i.e., the ones who will bring him influence and esteem) (51) and essentially another decoration in his impeccably furnished house (50). When Edna's awakening leads her to abandon household chores in favor of painting, Chopin exposes Leonce's sexism:

Prose quota-
tions longer
than four
typed lines
are indented
one inch
from the left
margin and
double-
spaced.

> Mr. Pontellier had been a rather courteous husband so long as he met a certain tacit submissiveness in his wife. But her new and unexpected line of conduct completely bewildered him . . . her absolute disregard for her duties as a wife angered him. (57)

Block quota-
tions are not
enclosed
within quo-
tation
marks. Note
that the
period pre-
cedes the
parenthetic
citation in
a block
quotation.

4   It would seem from such evidence that Chopin intended The Awakening to depict the wrongs that women suffered at the hands of men in her society. Taking this cue from Chopin, many twentieth-century critics choose to view it in a political light. Larzer Ziff, for example, claims that the novel "rejected the family as the automatic equivalent of feminine self-

Cody 5

Cody quotes opposing views. Note smooth integration of quoted passages. The verbs "claims," "noting," and "states" clearly signal quotations.

fulfillment, and on the very eve of the twentieth century it raised the question of what woman was to do with the freedom she struggled toward" (175). Winfried Fluck, noting Edna's "preference for semi-conscious states of being . . . sleeping, dreaming, dozing, or the moment of awakening" (435), argues that she is enacting "a radical retreat from the imprisonment of all social roles" (435). Marie Fletcher states that "[Edna's] suicide is the last in a series of rebellions which structure her life, give it pathos, and make of the novel . . . an interpretation of the 'new woman'" (172)--"the emerging suffragist/woman professional of the late nineteenth century" (Culley 118). Even in 1899 an anonymous reviewer in the New Orleans Times-Democrat noticed the political implications of the novel, declaring in his own conservative way that

> a woman of twenty-eight, a wife and twice a mother who is pondering upon her relations to the world about her, fails to perceive that the relation of a mother to her children is far more important than the gratification of a passion which experience has taught her is . . . evanescent, can hardly be said to be fully awake. (150)

Cody 6

5   These critics lead us to focus on
the socio-political implications of the
novel, and on the questions it raises
about a woman's role and responsibility:
when if ever does a woman's personal
life become more important than her
children? or, how does Edna embody the
emancipated woman? But I believe that
more than just the social pressure and
politics of the late nineteenth century
were acting on Edna. It was the
inherent instability of her own psyche,
exacerbated by the oppression she
suffered as a woman, that drove her to
swim out to her death at the end of
The Awakening.

6   Despite the feminist undertones
discernible in Chopin's work, a strong
sense prevails that Edna's tragedy is
unique, a result of her own psychology,
not only of societal oppression.
Throughout the novel Chopin describes
Edna's agitated state of mind and drops
hints about her upbringing and family
life before marriage. Upon piecing all
the clues to her personality together
one gets a troubling, stereotypical
picture. Edna's widowed father is a
stern colonel from Kentucky who "was
perhaps unaware that he had coerced his
own wife into her grave" (71). From the
scenes in which he appears one deduces
that he is harsh and authoritative with
his family; the narrator's comment
about his wife implies that perhaps

*Clear
transition
("despite").*

*In this para-
graph and
the next,
Cody devel-
ops her
argument by
analyzing
the text of
the novel.*

Cody 7

he was abusive (no doubt
psychologically, possibly physically)
as well. He gambles compulsively on
horseracing (69), which denotes an
addictive personality. He also
makes his own very strong cocktails--
"toddies"--which he drinks almost
all day long (71). He retains the
appearance of sobriety, however,
which indicates a high tolerance built
up over much time. From this evidence
one may assume that he suffers
from alcoholism.

7   The rest of Edna's family--two
sisters--fit the mold of the
dysfunctional family that a violent,
alcoholic parent tends to create. Her
oldest sister seems to be the hyper-
responsible, over-functioning
"perfect" daughter. She served as a
surrogate mother to Edna and her
younger sister, and is described by
Edna's husband as the only daughter
who "has all the Presbyterianism
undiluted" (66). Edna's younger sister
is, predictably, exactly the opposite:
Leonce Pontellier describes her as a
"vixen" (66). She has rebelled against
all of the rules and expectations that
the eldest daughter obeys and
fulfills. Edna, the middle child, is
hence a curious case. Chopin tells us
that "even as a child she had lived
her own small life all within herself"
(15). In such family situations the

Cody 8

Evidence from experts offered in support of thesis.

middle child is usually rather introverted. Where the two other siblings strive compulsively either to correct or create problems, the sibling in the middle passively escapes from her painful family situation by withdrawing into herself (Seixas and Youcha 48–49).

8   So far this simplistic but relatively reliable delineation of personalities works for Edna's character. Later in life she perpetuates the patterns of her dysfunctional family by marrying a man who almost mirrors her father in personality; he is simply a workaholic rather than an alcoholic. Edna gives birth to two children, "a responsibility which she had blindly assumed" (20) in her typically passive way. The first time she truly examines her role in this marriage and indeed in the world at large occurs on Grand Isle, a resort island where she and her family are vacationing for the summer. There she begins to spend a great deal of time with a young man named Robert Lebrun, and a mutual desire gradually arises between them. This desire, and the general sensuality and openness of the Creole community to which she is exposed, bring about Edna's sexual, artistic, and individual awakening. Although the reader is excited and inspired by this awakening in Edna--a woman learning to shed the fetters

Cody 9

of both her oppressive marriage and
society in general--the way it takes
control of her life is disturbingly
reminiscent of mental illness. She
becomes infatuated with Robert, devotes
an inordinate amount of time to
painting, and seeks out classical
music, which wracks her soul in a
torturous ecstasy.

9   Throughout her awakening, she
experiences myriad moods and feelings
that she had never felt before in her
docile, passive state. Many of these
moods manifest themselves in the form
of mysterious, troubling voices: "the
voices were not soothing that came to
her from the darkness and the sky
above and the stars" (53); "she felt
like one who has entered and lingered
within the portals of some forbidden
temple in which a thousand muffled
voices bade her begone" (84). Behind
the veil of metaphor here one can
detect hints of an almost schizoid
character. Chopin even describes Edna
as two selves, which naturally befits
a woman undergoing an emotional
transformation, but which also
denotes a distinctly schizophrenic
state of mind: "she was becoming
herself and daily casting aside that
fictitious self which we assume like
a garment with which to appear before
the world" (57); "she could only
realize that she herself--her present

Cody 10

self--was in some way different from the other self" (41). Chopin phrases her descriptions of Edna in such a way that they could in fact describe either a woman gaining her emotional autonomy or a woman losing her mind.

10   As compelling as I find the suggestion of Edna's insanity, I must admit that her struggle between self-hood and motherhood is one too common to all women to be passed off as the ravings of a madwoman. As to which interpretation she preferred, Chopin offered few clues. For example, in February 1898 Chopin responded to a question, posed by the society page of the St. Louis Post-Dispatch, about the possible motives for a recent rash of suicides among young high-society women. Rather than the pressure of society as a likely motive, she suggests a "highly nervous" disposition (qtd. in Toth 120). Indeed, she asserts that "leadership in society is a business...there is nothing about it that I can see that would tend to produce an unhealthy condition of mind. On the contrary, it prevents women from becoming morbid, as they might, had they nothing to occupy their attention when at leisure" (qtd. in Toth 120). Perhaps, then, we are to suppose that a combination of psychic instability and extensive leisure, rather than the oppression of her society, caused Edna

Parenthetic reference to an indirect source. (The quotation from Chopin appears on page 120 of Toth's book.)

Cody 11

to take her own life. And yet this same response in the <u>Post-Dispatch</u> includes a counter-question to the editor: "Business men commit suicide every day, yet we do not say that suicide is epidemic in the business world. Why should we say the feeling is rife among society women, because half a dozen unfortunates, widely separated, take their own lives?" (qtd. in Toth 120). Her implicit criticism of the double standard suggests that Chopin was aware of the politics of gender relations in her own society in addition to the existence of an "hysterical tendency" in some women (qtd. in Toth 120). One cannot therefore discount the possibility that Chopin meant Edna's suicide to be in part a reaction to her society's rigid and limiting expectations of women.

11   Chopin received such harsh criticism of Edna Pontellier's sexual freedom and attitude toward family that, when <u>The Awakening</u> was published, if not before, she must have had some idea of how controversial the issue of her protagonist's personal freedom really was: her hometown library banned the book, and Chopin herself was banned from a St. Louis arts club (Reuben). Her critics tend to believe that she sympathized unreservedly with her headstrong heroine; but even the

Citation of online source. (Source is unpaginated, so citation gives only the author's name.)

Cody 12

retraction she published soon after her
novel does not reveal whether she
viewed Edna as oppressed or mentally
ill. Apparently written for the benefit
of her scandalized reviewers, the
retraction ironically relieves Chopin
of all responsibility for Edna's
"making such a mess of things and
working out her own damnation" (159).
Again, as in her ambiguous response to
the Post-Dispatch, Chopin leaves
curious readers unsatisfied, and the
motive of Edna's suicide unclear.

12   It is left to the reader therefore
to decide whether Edna is a martyr to a
feminist cause--the liberation of the
American housewife--or the victim of a
psychological disturbance that drives
her to suicide. I believe that it is
best not to dismiss either possibility.
To begin with, one cannot deny that in
the nineteenth century few options other
than marriage and child-rearing were
open to women. These narrow options were
the result of a societal structure in
which men socially, economically, and
sexually dominated women. In the twenty-
first century we can look back at
Chopin's time and feel confident in
condemning this state of affairs, but
from contemporary criticism of The
Awakening alone, it is clear that this
political view was not so widely
accepted at the turn of the century.
Perhaps Chopin had an unusually clear

Cody 13

and untimely insight into what we now consider the sexism of her society, but she chose to condemn it only implicitly by portraying it as a fact of life against which her unbalanced heroine must struggle and perish. As Larzer Ziff puts it, "Edna Pontellier is trapped between her illusions and the condition which society arbitrarily establishes to maintain itself, and she is made to pay" (175). Chopin fused the political and the personal in Edna Pontellier, who, like most women in the world, suffers not only from the pressures of a society run by and for men, but also from her own individual afflictions.

Sources are listed in alphabetical order by author.

Begin Works Cited list on new page. Continue pagination.

"Works Cited" is centered.

Works Cited

Three hyphens indicate another work by the author named immediately above.

Chopin, Kate. The Awakening. 1899. Ed.
Margaret Culley. New York: Norton,
1976.

---. "Retraction." 1899. Rpt. in The
Awakening. By Kate Chopin. 159.

Short form of citation. Articles by Culley and Fletcher are reprinted in the Norton edition of The Awakening. The full citation for the volume appears under Chopin.

Culley, Margaret. "The Context of The
Awakening." In The Awakening. By
Kate Chopin. 119-22.

Second and subsequent lines of entry are indented 5 spaces.

Fletcher, Marie. "The Southern Woman in
the Fiction of Kate Chopin." Rpt.
in The Awakening. By Kate Chopin.
170-73.

Fluck, Winfried. "'The American Romance'
and the Changing Functions of
the Imaginary." New Literary
History 27.3 (1996): 415-57.
Project Muse. JHU. 1 May 2004.
http://muse:jhu.edu:80/journals/
new literary history /v27/
27.3fluck.html.

On-line source (paginated).

"New Publications." New Orleans Times-
Democrat. Rpt. in The Awakening.
By Kate Chopin. 150.

Signed entry in a reference work with alphabetically arranged entries.

Nissenbaum, Stephen. "Chopin, Kate
O'Flaherty." Notable American
Women, 1607-1950: A Biographical
Dictionary. Cambridge, MA: Harvard
University Press, 1971.

Online source (unpaginated).

Rankin, Daniel S. "Influences Upon the
Novel." Rpt. in The Awakening. By
Kate Chopin. 163-65.

Cody 15

Reuben, Paul P. "Chapter 6: 1890-1910: Kate Chopin (1851-1904)." PAL: Perspectives in American Literature--A Research and Reference Guide. 20 Mar. 1998. http://www.csustan.edu/english/reuben/pal/chap6/chopin.html.

Seixas, Judith S., and Geraldine Youcha. Children of Alcoholism: A Survivor's Manual. New York: Harper, 1985.

Shinn, Thelma J. "Kate O'Flaherty Chopin." American Women Writers: A Critical Reference Guide from Colonial Times to the Present. New York: Unger, 1979 ed.

Journal article. Toth, Emily. "Kate Chopin on Divine Love and Suicide: Two Rediscovered Articles." American Literature 63 (1991): 115-21.

Ziff, Larzer. Excerpt from The American 1890s: Life and Times of a Lost Generation, 279-305. Rpt. in The Awakening. By Kate Chopin. 173-75.

A Brief Analysis of Cody's Use of Sources

In our introductory comments, we noted that Cody uses sources in a range of ways in this essay. Here, we will point to some of the specific ways in which she uses the ideas of others to develop her argument about the novel and to enrich her analysis of it:

- In paragraph 1, Cody alludes to Betty Friedan's concept of the "feminine mystique" to help explain the prevailing interpretation of the novel. Note that the reference to Freidan is general; the idea of the "feminine mystique" is treated as **common knowledge.**

- In paragraph 2, Cody draws on Chopin's biography to help develop the interpretation she'll be arguing against. She's **granting the opposition what's due to it;** she's establishing the merit of the point of view against which she's arguing. (One wouldn't, after all, want to waste time arguing against a foolish position.) She also **quotes the authorities,** the critics Ziff and Rankin, she'll go on to dispute.

- At the end of paragraph 2, Cody **quotes a passage from the novel, evidence** that helps **support** her thesis (stated at the end of paragraph 1) that Edna's suicide in part "resulted from the torments of her individual psyche."

- In paragraphs 3 and 4, Cody **analyzes evidence** from the novel, from contemporary reviews, and from current criticism, that **does not support** her argument, but rather supports the "socio-political" interpretation of *The Awakening*. (Again, she's establishing the merit of the **counterargument.**)

- In paragraph 6, Cody **analyzes** the text of the novel, focusing now on **evidence** that **supports** her position—for example, Chopin's representation of Edna's family members.

- In paragraph 7, Cody refers to what might be called **expert testimony:** a discussion in a psychology textbook that supports her interpretation of Edna's dysfunctional family as a cause of Edna's own disturbed psyche.

- In paragraph 10, Cody quotes from Chopin herself to give a somewhat different perspective on Edna's character; she thereby enriches her analysis of Chopin's protagonist.

- In paragraph 12, Cody uses a quotation from Larzer Ziff, a critic she's been disagreeing with until now, in part to support her larger point. We note that at the end of the essay, she develops a position that strikes a balance between the argument she's been putting forth, and the prevailing view of the novel. Our last impression of Cody, therefore, is that she is a thoughtful and reasonable critic.

A Sample Research Essay (APA Format)

In the following research essay, student Jacob Alexander uses the APA form of in-text citations, which are clarified by a list headed "References." Our annotations in the margins of the essay point to noteworthy features of Alexander's use of sources and of the system of citation; a brief analysis of the essay follows it. For instructions on using the APA citation format, see Chapter 13, "Documenting Sources," pages 330–38.

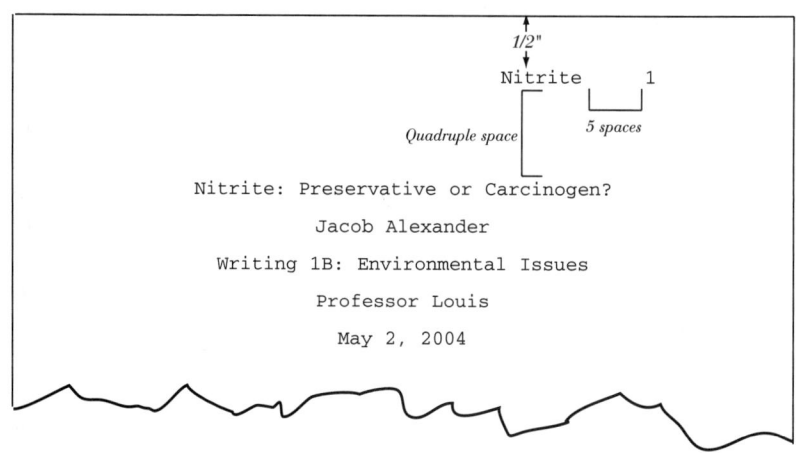

Nitrite   1

Quadruple space   5 spaces

Nitrite: Preservative or Carcinogen?

Jacob Alexander

Writing 1B: Environmental Issues

Professor Louis

May 2, 2004

1/2"

Nitrite   2

Triple space

Abstract appears on separate page after title page. Do not indent first line of paragraph.

Abstract

Quadruple space

← 1" →

Sodium nitrite, added to cured meats and smoked fish as a color fixative, can combine in meat and in the stomach to form a powerful carcinogen. Some argue that restrictions placed in recent years by the FDA on nitrite use have significantly reduced the health threat nitrite poses; however, recent research suggests that it may still be a significant cancer cause. The public must remain cautious about nitrite consumption.

← 1" →

Nitrite   3

Nitrite: Preservative or Carcinogen?

1   According to Julie Miller Jones, a professor of food and nutrition and the author of Food Safety, "average Americans eat their weight in food additives every year" (cited in Murphy, 1996, p. 140). There are approximately fifteen thousand additives currently in use (National Cancer Institute Fact Sheet [NCI], 1996); many of them are known to be dangerous. Of these, nitrites may be among the most hazardous of all. In this country, ham, bacon, corned beef, salami, bologna, lox, and other cold cuts and smoked fish almost invariably contain sodium nitrite. In fact, one-third of the federally inspected meat and fish we consume--more than seven billion pounds of it every year--contains this chemical (Jacobson, 1987, p. 169).

An indirect reference. Alexander consulted Murphy, who quotes Jones.

Citation gives author because Jacobson is not named in the text. Note format: author, date of publication, and page number preceded by a "p."

2   Just how dangerous are nitrites, and why-- if they really <u>are</u> dangerous--does the food industry still use them? Both questions are difficult to answer. Some experts say that nitrites protect consumers from botulism, a deadly disease that can be caused by spoiled food, and that "the benefits of nitrite additives outweigh the risks" (Edlefsen & Brewer, no date). Others argue that the dangers nitrites once posed have been significantly reduced--even eliminated--by restrictions placed on their use by the Food and Drug Administration. Nevertheless, the evidence has long suggested that nitrites are linked to stomach cancer; recent research has

This online source did not provide a date of publication.

Nitrite 4

linked nitrites to leukemia and brain tumors as well (Warrick, 1994; Legator & Daniel, 1995). Perhaps the only certain conclusions one can reach are that the effects of nitrite on the human body are still to some degree uncertain-- and that to protect themselves, consumers must be cautious and informed.

3   That nitrite is a poison has been clear for almost three decades. In 1974, Jacqueline Verrett, who worked for the FDA for fifteen years, and Jean Carper reported on several instances of people poisoned by accidental overdoses of nitrites in cured meats:

> In Buffalo, New York, six persons were hospitalized with "cardiovascular collapse" after they ate blood sausage which contained excessive amounts of nitrites . . . In New Jersey, two persons died and many others were critically poisoned after eating fish illegally loaded with nitrites. In New Orleans, ten youngsters between the ages of one and a half and five became seriously ill . . . after eating wieners or bologna overnitrited by a local meat-processing firm; one wiener that was obtained later from the plant was found to contain a whopping 6,570 parts per million. In Florida, a three-year-old boy died after eating hot dogs with three times greater nitrite concentration than the government allows. (pp. 138-39)

4   The chemical has the unusual and difficult-to-replace quality of keeping meat a fresh-looking pink throughout the cooking, curing, and storage process (Assembly of Life Science, 1982, p. 3). The nitrous acid from the nitrite combines with the hemoglobin in the blood of the meat, fixing its red color so that the meat does not turn the tired brown or gray natural to cured meats.

5   Unfortunately, it does much the same thing in humans. Although most of the nitrite passes through the body unchanged, a small amount is released into the bloodstream. This combines with the hemoglobin in the blood to form a pigment called methemoglobin, which cannot carry oxygen. If enough oxygen is incapacitated, a person dies. The allowable amount of nitrite in a quarter pound of meat has the potential to incapacitate between 1.4 and 5.7 percent of the hemoglobin in an average-sized adult (Verrett & Carper, 1974, pp. 138-39). One of the problems with nitrite poisoning is that infants under a year, because of the quantity and makeup of their blood, are especially susceptible to it.

6   If the consumer of nitrite isn't acutely poisoned (and granted, such poisonings are rare), his or her blood soon returns to normal and this particular danger passes: the chemical, however, has long-term effects, as research conducted in the 1970's clearly established. Nitrite can cause headaches in people who are especially sensitive to it, an upsetting symptom

Nitrite   6

considering that in rats who ate it regularly
for a period of time it has produced lasting
"epileptic like" changes in the brain--
abnormalities which showed up when the rats
were fed only a little more than an American
fond of cured meats might eat (Wellford, 1973,
p. 173). Experiments with chickens, cattle,
sheep, and rats have shown that nitrite, when
administered for several days, inhibits the
ability of the liver to store vitamin A and
carotene (Hunter, 1972, p. 90). And finally,
Nobel laureate Joshua Lederberg points out that,
in microorganisms, nitrite enters the DNA.
"If it does the same thing in humans," he says,
"it will cause mutant genes." Geneticist Bruce
Ames adds, "If out of one million people, one
person's genes are mutant, that's a serious
problem. . . . If we're filling ourselves now with
mutant genes, they're going to be around for
generations" (cited in Zwerdling, 1971,
pp. 34-35).

7   By far the most alarming characteristic of
nitrite, however, is that in test tubes, in
meats themselves, in animal stomachs, and in
human stomachs--wherever a mildly acidic
solution is present--it can combine with amines
to form nitrosamines. And nitrosamines are
carcinogens. Even the food industry and the
agencies responsible for allowing the use of
nitrite in foods admit that nitrosamines cause
cancer. Edlefsen and Brewer, writing recently
for the National Food Safety Database, note that

Nitrite   7

An online source. (The authors and title are named in the sentence; the source has no date or page numbers.)

"over 90 percent of the more than 300 known nitrosamines in foods have been shown to cause cancer in laboratory animals." They continue: "No case of human cancer has been shown to result from exposure to nitrosamines," but they acknowledge that "indirect evidence indicates that humans would be susceptible" (no date).

8   It is important to note that nitrite alone, when fed to rats on an otherwise controlled diet, does not induce cancer. It must first combine with amines to form nitrosamines. Considering, however, that the human stomach has the kind of acidic solution in which amines and nitrites readily combine, and considering as well that amines are present in beer, wine, cereals, tea, fish, cigarette smoke, and a long list of drugs including antihistamines, tranquilizers, and even oral contraceptives, it is hardly surprising to find that nitrosamaines have been found in human stomachs.

9   When animals are fed amines in combination with nitrite, they developed cancer with a statistical consistency that is frightening, even to scientists. Verrett and Carper report that after feeding animals 250 parts per million (ppm) of nitrites and amines, William Lijinsky, a scientist at Oak Ridge National Laboratory,

> found malignant tumors in 100 percent of
> the test animals within six months. . . .
> "Unheard of," he says. . . . "You'd usually
> expect to find 50 percent at the most.
> And the cancers are all over

Nitrite   8

the place--in the brain, lung, pancreas,
stomach liver, adrenals, intestines. We
open up the animals and they are a
bloody mess." [He] believes that
nitrosamines, because of their incredible
versatility in inciting cancer, may be
the key to an explanation for the mass
production of cancer in seemingly dissim-
ilar populations. In other words,
nitrosamines may be a common factor in
cancer that has been haunting us all
these years. (1974, p. 136)

Verrett and Carper (1974, pp. 43-46) list
still more damning evidence. Nitrosamines have
caused cancer in rats, hamsters, mice, guinea
pigs, dogs, and monkeys. It has been proven
that nitrosamines of over a hundred kinds cause
cancer. Nitrosamines have been shown to pass
through the placenta from the mother to cause
cancer in the offspring. Even the lowest levels
of nitrosamines ever tested have produced cancer in animals. When animals are fed nitrite
and amines separately over a period of time,
they develop cancers of the same kind and at
the same frequency as animals fed the corre-
sponding nitrosamines already formed.

10   To address these problems (and in response
to intense public concern), in 1978, the FDA
ruled that a reducing agent, such as ascorbic

This online source did not provide a date of publication.

acid, must be added to products containing
nitrite; the reducing agent inhibits the formation of nitrosamines (Edlefsen & Brewer, no

Nitrite   9

date). And in the last two decades, at least, the furor over nitrite seems as a consequence to have abated. In fact, a 1997 article published by the International Food Information Council Foundation (a group primarily sponsored by the food industry, according to information provided by its Website), celebrates nitrite as a "naturally-derived" substance that, according to the American Academy of Science, has never been found to cause cancer. On the contrary, the anonymous author states, nitrite does many good things for consumers; it may even help to fight cancer: "it safeguards cured meats against the most deadly foodborne bacterium known to man" and helps with "promoting blood clotting, healing wounds and burns and boosting immune function to kill tumor cells."

11   Other experts are less certain that reducing agents have entirely solved the nitrosamine problem. The Consumer's Dictionary of Food Additives notes that one common agent, sodium ascorbate, which is added to the brine in which bacon is cured, "offers only a partial barrier because ascorbate is soluble in fatty tissues" (Winter, 1994, p. 282). But in the wake of several studies it is unclear that "inhibiting" the formation of nitrosamines actually makes nitrites safe to consume.

No citation is given here because all information is included in the sentence itself.

12   The Los Angeles Times reports that one of these studies, conducted by John Peters, an epidemiologist at USC, found that "children who eat more than 12 hot dogs per month have nine

Nitrite   10

times the normal risk of developing childhood

leukemia" (Warrick, 1994). Interestingly, the

study was focused not on nitrites, but rather on

electromagnetic fields. "Dietary exposure to

processed or cured meats was part of a little

side questionnaire to our study on electro

magnetic fields," Peters said. "We were as

surprised as anyone by the hot dogs findings.

An indirect reference. The writer quotes Warrick quoting Peters.

. . . It was the biggest risk for anything we saw

in the study--about four times the risk for

EMF's" (cited in Warrick, 1994).

13   In another of these recent studies, hot

dogs were linked to brain tumors: researchers

found that "children born to mothers who ate at

least one hot dog per week while pregnant have

twice the risk of developing brain tumors, as do

children whose fathers ate too many hot dogs

Authors are named in the sentence and the online source isn't paginated. Only publication date is cited.

before conception" (Warrick, 1994). Dr. M.

Legator and Amanda Daniel comment that "these

studies confirm thirty years worth

of scientific research on the cancer causing

properties of preserved meats and fish" (1995).

14   The question, then, is why nitrite

continues to be used in so much of the meat

Americans consume. Although nitrite adds a small

amount to flavor, it is used primarily for

cosmetic purposes. Food producers are of course

also quick to point out that nitrite keeps

people safe from botulinum in cured meats, an

argument to which the public may be particularly

susceptible because of a number of recent and

serious food scares. Nevertheless, some evidence

suggests that the protection nitrite offers is
both unnecessary and ineffective.

15   Michael Jacobson explains the preservative
action of nitrite:

> Nitrite makes botulinum spores sensitive
> to heat. When foods are treated with
> nitrite and then heated, any botulinum
> spores that may be present are killed. In
> the absence of nitrite, spores can be
> inactivated only at temperatures that ruin
> the meat products. . . . Nitrite's
> preservative action is particularly
> important in foods that are not cooked
> after they leave the factory, such as ham,
> because these offer an oxygen-free
> environment, the kind in which botulinum
> can grow. The toxin does not pose a danger
> in foods that are always well cooked, such
> as bacon, because the toxin would be
> destroyed in cooking.
>
> Laboratory studies demonstrate
> clearly that nitrite can kill botulinum,
> but whether it actually does in
> commercially processed meat has been
> called into question. Frequently, the
> levels used may be too low to do
> anything but contribute to the color.
> (1987, p. 165)

Bratwurst and breakfast sausage are manufactured now without nitrite because they don't
need to be colored pink; bacon is always cooked
thoroughly enough to kill off any botulinum

Nitrite   12

spores present. Certainly there are other ways
of dealing with botulism. High or low temperature prevents botulism. What nitrite undoubt-
edly does lower, however, is the level of care
and sanitation necessary in handling meat.

16   Clearly, the use of nitrite adds immeasur-
ably to the profit-making potential of the meat
industry, but why does the federal government
allow this health hazard in our food? In the
first place, nitrite and nitrate have been used
for so long that it is hard for lawmakers to get
past their instinctive reaction, "But that's the
way we've always done it." Indeed, the Romans
used saltpeter, a nitrate, to keep meat and, as
early as 1899, scientists discovered that the
nitrate breaks down into nitrite and that it is
the nitrite which actually preserves the red

*Note that a
reference to a
single page is
preceded by
"p." and that
a reference to
two or more
pages is
preceded by
"pp."*

color in meats (Jacobson, 1987, pp. 164-65).
Thus, by the time the U.S. Department of Agri-
culture and the Food and Drug Administration got
into the business of regulating food, they
tended to accept nitrite and nitrate as givens.

A second reason for the inadequacy of
regulation is that government mechanisms for
protecting the consumer are full of curious
loopholes. In 1958 Congress passed the Food
Additive Amendment, including the Delaney
Clause, which clearly states that additives
should be banned if they induce cancer in laboratory animals. Unfortunately, however, the
amendment does not apply to additives that were
in use before it was passed, so, since nitrite

Nitrite   13

and nitrate had already been in use for a long time, they were automatically included on the list of chemicals "Generally Recognized as Safe." To complicate matters further, nitrite in meat is regulated by the USDA, while nitrite in fish is under the jurisdiction of the FDA. And these agencies generally leave it to industry--the profit-maker--to establish whether or not an additive is safe. The final irony in this list of governmental errors is that the FDA depends heavily, for "independent" research and advice, on the food committees of the National Academy of Sciences, which Daniel Zwerdling claims are "like a Who's Who of the food and chemical industry" (1971, p. 34). (This, of course, is the organization cited in the anonymous web posting quoted above, the organization that holds that "nitrite levels in cured meat have not been linked to the development of human cancers.")

Because the author is named in the sentence, the citation gives only the date and page number.

17   Clearly, consumers need to be informed; clearly, it is unwise to count on government agencies for protection against the dangers food additives may pose. Some experts continue to argue that nitrite is safe enough; Edelfson and Brewer, for example, cite a 1992 study by J. M. Jones that suggests that drinking beer exposes a consumer to more nitrite than does eating bacon--and that new car interiors are a significant source of nitrite as well.[1] Others recom-

An explanatory footnote.

[1]Presumably the exposure here results from contact, not ingestion.

Nitrite 14

mend caution. One expert advises: "If you must
eat nitrite-laced meats, include a food or
drink high in vitamin C at the same time--for
example, orange juice, grapefruit juice, cran-
berry juice, or lettuce" (Winter, 1994, p.
282). And, in fact, a study by a committee
organized by the National Academy of Science
strongly implies (Assembly, 1982, p. 12) that
the government should develop a safe alternative to nitrites.

18   In the meantime, the chemical additive
industry doesn't seem very worried that alternatives, such as biopreservatives, will pose a
threat to its profits. An industry publication, "Chemical Marketing Reporter," recently
reassured its readers by announcing that
"around 82.5 million pounds of preservatives,
valued at $133 million, were consumed in the
US in 1991." The report also stated that
"though the trend toward phasing out controversial preservatives like sulfites, nitrates
and nitrites continues, natural substitutes
remain expensive and often less than effective, making biopreservatives a distant
threat" (Tollefson, 1995).

References begin on new page

References

Second and subsequent lines of entries are indented five spaces

Assembly of Life Science. (1982). <u>Alternatives to the current use of nitrite in food.</u> Washington, DC: National Academy Press.

Use "n.d." when date is unavailable.

Edlefsen, M., & Brewer, M. S. (n.d.). <u>The national food safety database.</u> Nitrates/Nitrites. Retrieved May 6, 2004, from http://www.foodsafety.org/il/il089.html

Capitalize only the first word in book and article titles.

Hunter, B. T. (1972). <u>Fact/book on food additives and your health.</u> New Canaan, CT: Keats.

International Food Information Council Foundation. (1997). Nitrite: keeping food safe. <u>Food Insight.</u> Retrieved July 15, 2004, from http://ific.org/proactive/newsroom/release.vtml?id=18036

Jacobson, M. F. (1987). <u>Eater's digest.</u> Washington, DC: Center for Science in the Public Interest.

An online version of a newspaper article. Capitalize all important words in newspaper and periodical titles.

Legator, M., & Daniel, A. (1995). Reproductive systems can be harmed by toxic exposure. <u>Galveston County Daily News.</u> Retrieved May 6, 2004, from http://www.utmb.edu/toxics/newsp.htm#canen

An online version of a magazine article. Note that the year precedes the month and date in the parentheses following the author.

Murphy, K. (1996, May 6). Do food additives subtract from health? <u>Business Week,</u> p. 140. Retrieved July 30, 1998, from LexisNexis.

National Cancer Institute (1996, June). <u>NCI fact sheet.</u> Food additives. Retrieved May 4, 2004, from

Nitrite   16

http://nisc8a.upenn.edu/pdghtml/6/eng/

600037.html

Tollefson, C. (1995, May 29). Stability

preserved; preservatives; food

additives '95. Chemical Marketing

Reporter 247(22) SR28. Retrieved

May 6, 2004, from LexisNexis.

Verrett, J., & Carper, J. (1974). Eating may

be hazardous to your health. New York:

Simon and Schuster.

Warrick, P. (1994, June 8). A frank

discussion. Los Angeles Times,

E1. Retrieved May 6, 2004, from

LexisNexis.

Welford, H. (1973). Sowing the wind; a

report from Ralph Nader's Center for

Study of Responsible Law on food

safety and the chemical harvest. New

York: Bantam.

Winter, R. (1994). A consumer's dictionary

of food additives (Updated 4th ed.).

New York. Crown.

Zwerdling, D. (1971, June). Food pollution.

Ramparts, 9(11), 31-37, 53-54.

A book by two authors. Note use of ampersand between authors' names.

Use "p." or "pp." when citing books or newspapers, but not periodicals. Ramparts is a periodical.

A Brief Analysis of Alexander's Use of Sources

Jacob Alexander's **research essay** argues persuasively against eating foods preserved with sodium nitrite even as Alexander acknowledges that the dangers of nitrites haven't been established with absolute certainty. His **balanced, reasonable tone** and his range of **sources** help to establish his credibility. He cites industry and government publications, experts in the field, reference works, news articles, and a variety of other sources. Readers are inclined to trust someone who considers lots of evidence, even evidence that runs counter to his position. We know that at least one reader found his argument convincing: Alexander's writing instructor reports that she hasn't eaten a hot dog since she read his essay.

Here, we will point to some of the specific ways Alexander develops his argument.

- Paragraphs 1–3 capture the reader's attention by **establishing that there is a *problem,*** one that affects almost everyone. Paragraph 1 **introduces the problem** of food additives by quoting an **authority** (a "professor of food and nutrition") and offering a striking piece of information, that people eat their weight in additives each year. Paragraph 2 **develops the problem** by presenting the writer's research questions (how dangerous are additives, and—if they are dangerous—why are they still used?) and offering **evidence** from authorities on both sides. Paragraph 3 **develops the problem further** by presenting frightening **evidence** of deaths due to nitrites.

- Paragraphs 4–10 present the writer's **research** on what nitrites do: how they preserve meat (paragraph 4); how they affect the blood (paragraph 5) and the genes (paragraph 6); and how they may cause cancer in humans (paragraphs 7–10). The writer offers a particularly damning piece of **evidence** in paragraph 7 when he cites the food industry's report that nitrosamines, which form when nitrites and amines combine in the body, cause cancer. The food industry of course profits from preservatives and can be expected to defend nitrites whenever possible, so the admission powerfully supports Alexander's position.

- Paragraphs 11–12 look at the Food and Drug Administration's response, in the 1970s, to public concerns about nitrites and at various experts' current thinking about them. Alexander notes that a bulletin published by a food industry group in the late 1990s celebrates nitrite as a "naturally-derived" substance that may in fact fight cancer—an interesting **counterargument,** but one that seems weak after all the evidence to the contrary. Paragraphs 13–14 present frightening information from current studies that again link nitrites and cancer; the link establishes a **transition** (in paragraph 15) to a discussion of the second part of Alexander's **research question**: why are nitrites still used?

- Paragraphs 16–18 explore and develop this question: botulism-killing nitrites make lower standards of sanitation possible for meat producers and increase industry profits—but given the dangers, why does the *government* permit their use? The answers: long practice, and regulatory loopholes. Paragraph 19 presents Alexander's **conclusion,** that consumers must be wary (we like the touch of **wit** in the explanatory footnote to this paragraph). And paragraph 20—the final paragraph—ends with a chilling **quotation** from a chemical industry publication reassuring its readers that nitrites are here to stay. No summary or further commentary is needed from Alexander; the quotation strikes just the right conclusive note.

PART THREE

A WRITER'S HANDBOOK

CHAPTER ELEVEN

PUNCTUATING SENTENCES

Speakers can raise or lower the volume or pitch of their voices; they can speak a phrase slowly and distinctly and then (making a parenthetical remark, perhaps) quicken the pace. They can wave their arms, pound a table, or pause, meaningfully. But writers, physically isolated from their audience, can do none of these things. Nevertheless, they can embody some of the tones and gestures of speech—in the patterns of their written sentences, and in the dots, hooks, and lines of punctuation that clarify those patterns.

Punctuation clarifies, first of all, by removing or reducing ambiguity. Consider this headline from a story in a newspaper:

SQUAD HELPS DOG BITE VICTIM

Of course, there is no real ambiguity here—only a laugh—because the stated meaning is so clearly absurd, and on second reading we supply the necessary hyphen in *dog-bite.* But other ill-punctuated sentences may be troublesome rather than entertaining. Take the following sentence:

He arrived late for the rehearsal didn't end until midnight.

Almost surely you stumbled in the middle of the sentence, thinking that it was about someone arriving tardily at a rehearsal, and then, since what followed made no sense, you probably went back and mentally added the comma (by pausing) at the necessary place:

He arrived late, for the rehearsal didn't end until midnight.

Punctuation helps to keep your reader on the right path. And the path is your train of thought. If your punctuation is faulty, you unintentionally point the reader off your path and toward dead-end streets and quagmires.

Even when punctuation is not the key to meaning, it usually helps you get your meaning across neatly. Consider the following sentence:

> There are two kinds of feminism—one is the growing struggle of women to understand and change the shape of their lives and the other is a narrow ideology whose adherents are anxious to clear away whatever does not conform to their view.

The sentence is clear enough, but by changing the punctuation it can be sharpened. Because a dash usually indicates an abrupt interruption—it usually precedes a sort of afterthought—a colon would be better. The colon, usually the signal of an amplification of what precedes it, here would suggest that the two classifications are not impromptu thoughts but carefully considered ones. Second, and more important, in the original version the two classifications are run together without any intervening punctuation, but since the point is that the two are utterly different, it is advisable to separate them by inserting a comma or semicolon, indicating a pause. A comma before "and the other" would do, but probably a semicolon (without the "and") is preferable because it is a heavier pause, thereby making the separation clearer. Here is the sentence, revised:

> There are two kinds of feminism: one is the growing struggle of women to understand and change the shape of their lives; the other is a narrow ideology whose adherents are anxious to clear away whatever does not conform to their view.

The right punctuation enables the reader to move easily through the sentence.

Although punctuation helps a reader to move through a sentence, it must be admitted that some of the rules of punctuation do not contribute to meaning or greatly facilitate reading. For example, in American usage a period never comes immediately after quotation marks; it precedes quotation marks, thus:

> "If you put the period inside the closing quotation mark," the writing instructor said, "I will give you an A."

If you put the period after the closing quotation mark, the meaning remains the same, but you are also informing your reader that you don't know the conventions of American usage—conventions all writers in the United States are expected to adhere to. A pattern of such errors will diminish your authority as a writer: Your reader, noticing that you don't know where to put the period in relation to the quotation mark, may well begin to wonder what else you don't know. Conversely, demonstrating that you know the rules will help to gain your reader's confidence and establish your authority as a writer.

A Word on Computer Grammar and Punctuation Checks

Word-processing programs include a tool that can check grammar and punctuation. At your request, the program will flag sentences that look faulty and offer suggestions for correcting mistakes. These programs can be very helpful: They can draw your attention to sentence fragments, to problems with plurals and possessives, even to passive verbs. But they don't catch everything, and they don't always know how to fix the problems they identify.

Our advice: Use the tool if you have it, but don't let it do your editing for you. Check the program's suggestions against your own knowledge and the advice offered in this book.

Three Common Errors: Fragments, Comma Splices, and Run-on Sentences

Fragments and How to Correct Them

A **fragment** is a part of a sentence set off as if it were a complete sentence:

Because I didn't care.

Being an accident.

Later in the week.

For several reasons.

My oldest sister.

Fragments are common in speech, but they are used sparingly in writing, usually for emphasis. A fragment used carelessly in writing often looks like an afterthought—usually because it *was* an afterthought—that is, an explanation or other addition that belongs to the previous sentence.

With appropriate punctuation (and sometimes with no punctuation at all) a fragment can usually be connected to the previous sentence:

Incorrect

Many nineteenth-century horror stories have been made into films. Such as *Dracula* and *Frankenstein*.

Correct

Many nineteenth-century horror stories have been made into films, such as *Dracula* and *Frankenstein.*

Incorrect

Many schools are putting renewed emphasis on writing. Because SAT scores have declined for ten years.

Correct

Many schools are putting renewed emphasis on writing because SAT scores have declined for ten years.

Incorrect

She wore only rope sandals. Being a strict vegetarian.

Correct

Being a strict vegetarian, she wore only rope sandals.

She wore only rope sandals because she was a strict vegetarian.

Incorrect

A fragment often looks like an afterthought. Perhaps because it *was* an afterthought.

Correct

A fragment often looks like an afterthought—perhaps because it *was* an afterthought.

Incorrect

He hoped to get credit for two summer courses. Batik and Hang-Gliding.

Correct

He hoped to get credit for two summer courses: Batik and Hang-Gliding.

Notice in the examples above that, depending upon the relationship between the two parts, the fragment and the preceding statement can be joined by a comma, dash, or colon, or by no punctuation at all.

Notice also that unintentional fragments often follow subordinating conjunctions, such as *because* and *although.* Subordinating conjunctions introduce a subordinate (dependent) clause; such a clause cannot stand as a sentence. Here is a list of the most common subordinating conjunctions:

after	though
although	unless
because	until
before	when
if	where
provided	whereas
since	while

Fragments also commonly occur when the writer, as in the third example, mistakenly uses *being* as a main verb.

How to Correct Comma Splices and Run-on Sentences

An error known as a **comma splice** or **comma fault** results when a comma is mistakenly placed between two independent clauses that are not joined by a coordinating conjunction: *and, or, nor, but, for, yet, so.* If the comma is omitted, the error is called a **run-on sentence.**

Here are some examples of the two errors:

- *Comma splice* (or *comma fault*): In the second picture the man leans on the woman's body, he is obviously in pain.

- *Run-on sentence:* In the second picture the man leans on the woman's body he is obviously in pain.

Run-on sentences and comma splices may be corrected in five principal ways:

1. Use a period to create two sentences:

   In the second picture the man leans on the woman's body. He is obviously in pain.

2. Use a semicolon:

   In the second picture the man leans on the woman's body; he is obviously in pain.

3. Use a comma and a coordinating conjunction (*and, or, nor, but, for, yet, so*):

   In the second picture the man leans on the woman's body, and he is obviously in pain.

4. Make one of the clauses dependent (subordinate). Use a subordinating conjunction such as *after, although, because, before, if, provided, since, though, unless, until, when, where, whereas, while:*

In the second picture the man leans on the woman's body because he is in pain.

5. Reduce one of the independent clauses to a phrase, or even to a single word:

In the second picture the man, obviously in pain, leans on the woman's body.

Run-on sentences and comma splices are especially common in sentences containing transitional words or phrases such as the following:

also	however
besides	indeed
consequently	in fact
for example	nevertheless
furthermore	therefore
hence	whereas

When these words join independent clauses, the clauses cannot be linked by a comma:

Incorrect

She argued from faulty premises, however the conclusions happened to be correct.

Here are five correct revisions, following the five rules we have just given. (In the first two revisions we place "however" after, rather than before, "the conclusions" because we prefer the increase in emphasis, but the grammatical point is the same.)

Correct

1. She argued from faulty premises. The conclusions, however, happened to be correct. [Two sentences]

2. She argued from faulty premises; the conclusions, however, happened to be correct. [Semicolon]

3. She argued from faulty premises, but the conclusions happened to be correct. [Coordinating conjunction]

4. Although she argued from faulty premises, the conclusions happened to be correct. [Subordinating conjunction]

5. She argued from faulty premises to correct conclusions. [Reduction of an independent clause to a phrase]

The following sentence contains a comma splice:

> The husband is not pleased, in fact, he is embarrassed.

How might it be repaired?

The Period

Periods are used to mark the ends of sentences (or intentional sentence fragments) other than questions and exclamations:

> A sentence normally ends with a period.
> She said, "I'll pass."
> Yes.
> Once more, with feeling.

But a sentence within a sentence is punctuated according to the needs of the longer sentence. Notice, in the following example, that a period is *not* used after "pass":

> She said, "I'll pass," but she said it without conviction.

> Periods are used with abbreviations of titles and terms of reference:
> Dr.   Mr.   Mrs.   Ms.
> p., pp. (for "page" and "pages")   i.e.   e.g.   etc.

But when the capitalized initial letters of the words naming an organization are used in place of the full name, the periods are commonly omitted:

> CBS   CORE   IBM   NBA   UCLA   UNICEF   USAF

> Periods are also used to separate chapter from verse in the Bible:
> Genesis 3.2   Mark 6.10

For further details on references to the Bible, see page 268.

The Question Mark

Use a question mark after a direct question:

> Did Bacon write Shakespeare's plays?

Do not use a question mark after an indirect question, or after a polite request:

He asked if Bacon wrote Shakespeare's plays.

Would you please explain what the support for Bacon is really all about.

The Colon

The colon has four uses:

- To introduce a list or series of examples
- To introduce an amplification or explanation of what precedes the colon
- To introduce a quotation (though a quotation can be introduced by other means)
- To indicate time

Now let's look at each of those four uses.

1. The colon may introduce a list or series:

Students are required to take one of the following sciences: biology, chemistry, geology, physics.

2. The colon may introduce an explanation. It is almost equivalent to *namely*, or *that is*. What is on one side of the colon more or less equals what is on the other side. The material on either side of the colon can stand as a separate sentence:

She explained her fondness for wrestling: she did it to shock her parents.

The forces which in China created a central government were absent in Japan: farming had to be on a small scale, there was no need for extensive canal works, and a standing army was not required to protect the country from foreign invaders.

Many of the best of the Civil War photographs must be read as the fossils of earlier events: The caissons with their mud-encrusted wheels, the dead on the field, the empty landscapes, all speak of deeds already past.

—John Szarkowski

Notice in the last example that the writer uses a capital letter after the colon; the usage is acceptable when a complete sentence follows the colon, as long as that style is followed consistently throughout a paper.

3. The colon, like the comma, may be used to introduce a quotation; it is more formal than the comma, setting off the quotation to a greater degree:

> The black sculptor Ed Wilson tells his students: "Malcolm X is my brother, Martin Luther King is my brother, Eldridge Cleaver is my brother! But Michelangelo is my grandfather!"
>
> —*Albert E. Elsen*

4. A colon is used to separate the hour from the minutes when the time is given in figures:

> 9:15   12:00

5. Colons (like semicolons) go outside of closing quotation marks if they are not part of the quotation:

> "There is no such thing as a free lunch": the truth of these words is confirmed every day.

The Semicolon

There are four main uses of the semicolon. Sheridan Baker (in *The Practical Stylist*) summed them up in this admirable formula: "Use a semicolon where you could also use a period, unless desperate." Correctly used, the semicolon can add precision to your writing; it can also help you out of some tight corners.

1. You may use a semicolon instead of a period between closely related independent clauses not joined by a coordinating conjunction:

> All happy families resemble one another; every unhappy family is unhappy in its own fashion.
>
> —*Leo Tolstoy*

> The demands that men and women make on marriage will never be fully met; they cannot be.
>
> —*Jessie Bernard*

> In our fractured culture, we cannot agree on morals; we cannot even agree that moral matters should come before literary ones when there is a conflict between them.
>
> —*Flannery O'Connor*

When a cat washes its face it does not move its paw; it moves its face.

In each of the examples the independent clauses might have been written as sentences separated by periods; the semicolon pulls the statements together, emphasizing their relationship. Alternatively, the statements might have been linked by coordinating conjunctions (*and, or, nor, but, for, yet, so*). For example:

> The demands made upon marriage will never be fully met for they cannot be.
>
> When a cat washes its face it does not move its paw but it moves its face.

The sentences as originally written, using semicolons, have more bite.

2. You *must* use a semicolon (rather than a comma) if you use a *conjunctive adverb* to connect independent clauses. (A conjunctive adverb is a transitional word such as *also, consequently, furthermore, however, moreover, nevertheless, therefore.*)

> His hair was black and wavy; however, it was false.
>
> We don't like to see our depressed relative cry; nevertheless, tears can provide a healthy emotional outlet.
>
> She said "I do"; moreover, she repeated the words.

Take note of the following three points:

- A comma goes after the conjunctive adverb.
- Semicolons (like colons) go outside of closing quotation marks if they are not part of the quotation.
- A conjunctive adverb requires a semicolon to join independent clauses. A comma produces a comma splice:

Incorrect

His hair was black and wavy, however, it was false.

3. You may use a semicolon to separate a series of phrases with internal punctuation:

> He had a car, which he hadn't paid for; a wife, whom he didn't love; and a father, who was unemployed.

4. Use a semicolon between independent clauses linked by coordinating conjunctions if the sentence would otherwise be difficult

to read, because it is long and complex or because it contains internal punctuation:

> In the greatest age of painting, the nude inspired the greatest works; and even when it ceased to be a compulsive subject it held its position as an academic exercise and a demonstration of mastery.

(Often it is preferable to break such sentences up, or to recast them.)

The Comma

The comma (from the Greek word meaning "to cut") indicates a relatively slight pause within a sentence. If after checking the rules you are still uncertain of whether or not to use a comma in a given sentence, read the sentence aloud and see if it sounds better with or without a pause; you can then add or omit the comma. A women's shoe store in New York has a sign on the door:

NO MEN PLEASE.

If the proprietors would read the sign aloud, they might want to change it to

NO MEN, PLEASE

When you are typing, always follow a comma with a space.

For your reference, here is an outline for the following pages, which summarize the correct uses of the comma:

1. with independent clauses, page 261
2. with introductory subordinate clauses or long phrases, page 262
3. with tacked-on subordinate phrases or long clauses, page 262
4. as parentheses, page 263
5. with nonrestrictive modifiers, page 263
6. with a series, page 265
7. with direct discourse, page 266
8. with "yes" and "no," page 266
9. with words of address, page 266
10. with geographical locations, page 266
11. with dates, page 266
12. with other punctuation, page 266

1. Independent clauses (unless short) joined by a coordinating conjunction (*and, or, nor, but, for, yet, so*) take a comma before the conjunction:

> Most students see at least a few football games, and many go to every game of the season.

> Most students seem to have an intuitive sense of when to use a comma, but in fact the "intuition" is the result of long training.

If the introductory independent clause is short, the comma is usually omitted:

> She dieted but she continued to gain weight.

2. An introductory subordinate clause or long phrase is usually followed by a comma:

> Having revised his manuscript for the third time, he went to bed.

> In order to demonstrate her point, the instructor stood on her head.

If the introductory subordinate clause or phrase is short, say four words or fewer, the comma may be omitted, provided no ambiguity results from the omission:

> Having left he soon forgot.

But compare this last example with the following:

> Having left, the instructor soon forgot.

If the comma is omitted, the sentence is misread. Where are commas needed in the following sentences?

> Instead of discussing the book she wrote a summary.

> When Shakespeare wrote comedies were already popular.

> While he ate his poodle would sit by the table.

> As we age small things become killers.

3. A subordinate clause or long modifying phrase tacked on as an afterthought is usually preceded by a comma:

> I have decided not to be nostalgic about the 1950s, despite the hoopla over Elvis.

> Buster Keaton fell down a flight of stairs without busting, thereby gaining his nickname from Harry Houdini.

> By the time he retired, Hank Aaron had 755 home runs, breaking Babe Ruth's record by 41.

With afterthoughts, the comma may be omitted if there is a clear sequence of cause and effect, signaled by such words as *because, for,* and *so.* Compare the following examples:

> In 1601 Shakespeare wrote *Hamlet,* probably his best-known play.

> In 1601 Shakespeare wrote *Hamlet* because revenge tragedy was in demand.

4. A pair of commas can serve as a pair of unobtrusive parentheses. Be sure not to omit the second comma:

> Doctors, I think, have an insufficient knowledge of acupuncture.

> The earliest known paintings of Christ, dating from the third century, are found in the catacombs outside of Rome.

> Medicare and Medicaid, the chief sources of federal support for patients in nursing homes, are frequently confused.

Under this heading we can include a conjunctive adverb (a transitional adverb such as *also, besides, consequently, however, likewise, nevertheless, therefore*) inserted within a sentence. These transitional words are set off between a pair of commas:

> Her hair, however, was stringy.

If one of these words begins a sentence, the comma after it is optional. Notice, however, that the presence of such a word as "however" is not always a safeguard against a run-on sentence or comma splice; if the word occurs between two independent clauses and it goes with the second clause, you need a semicolon before it and a comma after it:

> His hair was black and wavy; however, it was false.

(See the discussion of comma splices on pages 255–57.)

5. Use a comma to set off a nonrestrictive modifier. A nonrestrictive modifier, as the following examples will make clear, is a sort of parenthetical addition; it gives supplementary information about the subject, but it can be omitted without changing the subject. A restrictive modifier, however, is not supplementary but essential; if a restrictive modifier is omitted, the subject becomes more general. In Dorothy Parker's celebrated poem,

> Men seldom make passes
> At girls who wear glasses,

"who wear glasses" is a restrictive modifier, narrowing or restricting the subject down from "girls" to a particular group of girls, those who wear glasses.

Here is a *non*restrictive modifier:

> For the majority of immigrants, who have no knowledge of English, language is the chief problem.

Now here is a restrictive modifier:

> For the majority of immigrants who have no knowledge of English, language is the chief problem.

The first version says—in addition to its obvious message that language is the chief problem—that the majority of immigrants have no knowledge of English. The second version makes no such assertion; it talks not about the majority of immigrants but only about a more restricted group—those immigrants who have no knowledge of English.

Now look at another example:

> Shakespeare's shortest tragedy, *Macbeth*, is one of his greatest plays.

In this sentence, "*Macbeth*" is nonrestrictive because the subject is already as restricted as possible; Shakespeare can have written only one "shortest tragedy." That is, "*Macbeth*" is merely an explanatory equivalent of "Shakespeare's shortest tragedy" and it is therefore enclosed in commas. (A noun or noun phrase serving as an explanatory equivalent to another, and in the same syntactical relation to other elements in the sentence, is said to be in apposition.) But compare

> Shakespeare's tragedy *Macbeth* is one of his greatest plays.

with the misleadingly punctuated sentence,

> Shakespeare's tragedy, *Macbeth*, is one of his greatest plays.

The first of these is restrictive, narrowing or restricting the subject "tragedy" down to one particular tragedy, and so it rightly does not separate the modifier from the subject by a comma. The second, punctuated so that it is nonrestrictive, falsely implies that *Macbeth* is Shakespeare's only tragedy. Here is an example of a nonrestrictive modifier correctly punctuated:

> Women, who constitute 51.3 percent of the population and 53 percent of the electorate, constitute only 2.5 percent of the House of Representatives and 1 percent of the Senate.

In the next two examples, the first illustrates the correct use of commas after a nonrestrictive appositive, and the second illustrates the correct omission of commas after a restrictive appositive:

> Hong Yee Chiu, a Chinese-American physicist, abbreviated the compound adjective *quasi-stellar* to *quasar.*

> The Chinese-American physicist Hong Yee Chiu abbreviated the compound adjective *quasi-stellar* to *quasar.*

6. Words, phrases, and clauses in series take a comma after each item except the last. The comma between the last two items may be omitted if there is no ambiguity:

> Photography is a matter of eyes, intuition, and intellect.
>
> She wrote plays, poems, and stories.
>
> He wrote plays, sang songs, and danced jigs.
>
> She wrote a wise, witty, humane book.

But adjectives in a series may cause difficulty. The next two examples correctly omit the commas:

> a funny silent film
>
> a famous French professor

In each of these last two examples, the adjective immediately before the noun forms with the noun a compound that is modified by the earlier adjective. That is, the adjectives are not a coordinate series (what is funny is not simply a film but a silent film, what is famous is not simply a professor but a French professor) and so commas are not used. Compare:

> a famous French professor
>
> a famous, arrogant French professor

In the second example, only "famous" and "arrogant" form a coordinate series. If in doubt, see if you can replace the commas with "and"; if you can, the commas are correct. In the example given, you could insert "and" between "famous" and "arrogant," but not between "arrogant" and "French."

Commas are not needed if all the members of the series are connected by conjunctions:

> He ate steak for breakfast and lunch and supper.

7. Use a comma to set off direct discourse:

> "It's a total failure," she said.
>
> She said, "It's a total failure."

But do not use a comma for indirect discourse:

> She said that it is a total failure.
>
> She said it is a total failure.

8. Use a comma to set off "yes" and "no":

Yes, he could take Writing 125 at ten o'clock.

9. Use a comma to set off words of address:

Look, Bill, take Writing 125 at ten o'clock.

10. Use a comma to separate a geographical location within another geographical location:

She was born in Brooklyn, New York, in 1895.

Another way of putting it is to say that a comma is used after each unit of an address, except that a comma is *not* used between the name of the state and the zip code.

11. Use a comma to set off the year from the month or day:

He was born on June 10, 1980, at Morristown Memorial Hospital.

No comma is needed if you use the form "10 June 1980."

12. Note the position of the comma when used with other punctuation: If a comma is required with parenthetic material, it follows the second parenthesis:

Because Japan was secure from invasion (even the Mongols were beaten back), its history is unusually self-contained.

The only time a comma may precede a parenthesis is when parentheses surround a digit or letter used to enumerate a series:

Questions usually fall into one of three categories: (1) true-false, (2) multiple choice, (3) essay.

A comma always goes inside closing quotation marks unless the quotation is followed by a parenthesis:

"Sayonara," he said.

"Sayonara" (Japanese for "goodbye"), he said.

The Dash

A dash indicates an abrupt break or pause. It can be typed as two hyphens without hitting the space bar before, between, or after.

1. The words within dashes function as parenthetic material (material that is not essential). However, by setting it within dashes—

an emphatic form of punctuation—the writer gives the material more emphasis than it would get within parentheses:

> The bathroom—that private place—has rarely been the subject of scholarly study.

> The Great Wall of China forms a continuous line over 1400 miles long—the distance from New York to Kansas City—running from Peking to the edge of the mountains of Central Asia.

> The old try to survive by cutting corners—eating less, giving up small pleasures like tobacco and movies, doing without warm clothes—and pay the price of ill-health and a shortened life-span.
>
> *—Sharon R. Curtin*

Note: If the material between two dashes is deleted, the remaindering words still form a grammatical sentence.

2. A dash can serve, somewhat like a colon, as a pause before a series. It is more casual than a colon:

> The earliest Shinto holy places were natural objects—trees, boulders, mountains, islands.

> Each of the brothers had his distinct comic style—Groucho's double-talk, Chico's artfully stupid malapropisms, Harpo's horseplay.
>
> *—Gerald Mast*

A dash is never used next to a comma, and it is used before a period only to indicate that the sentence is interrupted.

Overuse of the dash—even only a little overuse—gives writing an unpleasantly agitated—even explosive—quality.

Parentheses

Let's begin with a caution: Avoid using parentheses to explain pronouns: "In his speech he (Hamlet) says . . ." If "he" needs to be explained by "Hamlet," omit the "he" and just say "Hamlet."

1. Parentheses subordinate material: What is in parentheses functions as a casual aside, less essential than similar material set off in commas, less vigorously spoken than similar material set off in dashes:

> While guest curator for the Whitney (he has since returned to the Denver Art Museum), Feder assembled a magnificent collection of masks, totems, paintings, clothing, and beadwork.

Another caution: Avoid an abundance of these interruptions, and avoid a long parenthesis within a sentence (you are now reading a simple example of this annoying but common habit of writers who have trouble sticking to the point) because the reader will lose track of the main sentence.

2. Use parentheses to enclose digits or letters in a list that is given in running text:

> The exhibition included (1) decorative screens, (2) ceramics, (3) ink paintings, (4) kimonos.

3. Do not confuse parentheses with square brackets. The later are used around material you add to a quotation (see p. 204).

4. For the use of parentheses in documentation, see Chapter 13, "Documenting Sources."

5. Note the position of other punctuation with a parenthesis. The example above under rule 2 is the rare exception to the rule that within a sentence, punctuation other than quotation marks never immediately precedes an opening parenthesis. Note also that in the example under rule 1, the comma *follows* the closing parenthesis:

> While guest curator for the Whitney (he has since returned to the Denver Art Museum), Feder assembled a magnificent collection of masks, totems, paintings, clothing, and beadwork.

If an entire sentence is in parentheses, put the final punctuation (period, question mark, or exclamation mark) inside the closing parenthesis.

Italics

In typewritten material *underlining* is the equivalent of *italic* type:

> *This sentence is printed in italic type.*
>
> This sentence is understood to be printed in italic type.

1. Underline or italicize the name of a plane, ship, train, movie, radio or television program, record album, musical work, statue, painting, play, pamphlet, or book. Do not underline or italicize names of sacred works such as the Bible, the Koran, or Acts of the Apostles, or political documents such as the Magna Carta and the Declaration of Independence. Notice that when you write about a newspaper or periodical whose title begins with the article "the," the convention is to give the article in lower case roman letters. You do not italicize it or underline it; it is not treated as part of the title; for example, the *New Yorker.*

2. Use italics only sparingly for emphasis. Sometimes, however, this method of indicating your tone of voice is exactly right:

> In 1911 Jacques Henri Lartigue was not merely as unprejudiced as a child; he *was* a child.
>
> —*John Szarkowski*

3. Use italics for foreign words that have not become a part of the English language:

> Acupuncture aims to affect the *ch'i*, a sort of vital spirit that circulates through the bodily organs.

But:

> He ate a pizza.
>
> She behaved like a prima donna.
>
> Avoid clichés.

4. You may use italics in place of quotation marks to identify a word:

> Honolulu means *safe harbor.*

5. You may also use italics to identify a word or term to which you wish to call special attention:

> Claude Lévi-Strauss tells us that one of the great purposes of art is that of *miniaturization.* He points out that most works of art are miniatures, being smaller (and therefore more easily understood) than the objects they represent.

Capital Letters

Certain obvious conventions—the use of a capital for the first word in a sentence, for names (of days of the week, holidays, months, people, countries), and for words derived from names (such as pro-French)—need not be discussed here.

1. Titles of works in English are usually given according to the following formula. Use a capital for the first letter of the first word, for the first letter of the last word, and for the first letter of all other words that are not articles, conjunctions, or prepositions:

> *The Merchant of Venice*
>
> *A Midsummer Night's Dream*

Up and Out

"The Short Happy Life of Francis Macomber"

The *Oakland Bee*

2. Use a capital for a quoted sentence within a sentence, but not for a quoted phrase (unless it is at the beginning of your sentence) and not for indirect discourse:

He said, "You can even fool some of the people all of the time."

He said you can fool some people "all of the time."

He said that you can even fool some of the people all of the time.

3. Use a capital for a rank or title preceding a proper name or for a title substituting for a proper name:

She said she was Dr. Perez.

He told President Bush that the Vice President was away.

But:

Why would anyone wish to be president?

Washington was the first president.

4. Use a capital when the noun designating a family relationship is used as a substitute for a proper noun:

If Mother is busy, ask Tim.

But:

Because my mother was busy, I asked Tim.

5. Formal geographical locations (but not mere points on the compass) are capitalized:

North America

Southeast Asia

In the Southwest, rain sometimes evaporates before touching the ground.

Is Texas part of the South?

The North has its share of racism.

But:

The wind came from the south.

Texas is bordered on the north by Arkansas, Oklahoma, and New Mexico.

Do *not* capitalize the names of the seasons:

spring   summer   winter   fall

The Hyphen

The hyphen has five uses, all drawing on the etymology of the word *hyphen*, which comes from the Greek for "in one," "together."

1. Use a hyphen to attach certain prefixes to root words. *All-*, *pro-*, *ex-*, and *self-* are the most common of these (*all-powerful*, *ex-wife*, *pro-labor*, *self-made*), but note that even these prefixes are not always followed by a hyphen. If in doubt, check a dictionary. Prefixes before proper names are always followed by a hyphen:

anti-Semite   pro-NATO   un-American

Prefixes ending in *i* are hyphenated before a word beginning with *i:*

anti-intellectual   semi-intelligible

A hyphen is normally used to break up a triple consonant resulting from the addition of a prefix:

ill-lit

2. Use a hyphen to tie compound adjectives into a single visual unit:

out-of-date theory   twenty-three books   a no-smoking area

eighteenth- and nineteenth-century novels

The sea-tossed raft was a common nineteenth-century symbol of the human tragic condition.

But if a compound modifier follows the modified term, it is usually not hyphenated:

The theory was out of date.

3. Use a hyphen to join some compound nouns:

Scholar-teacher   philosopher-poet

4. Use a hyphen to indicate a span of dates or page numbers: 1957–1959, pp. 162–68.

The Apostrophe

Use an apostrophe to indicate the possessive, to indicate a contraction, and to form certain unusual plurals.

1. The most common way to indicate the possessive of a singular noun is to add an apostrophe and then an *-s:*

a dog's life   a week's work

a mouse's tail   Keats's poems   Marx's doctrines

But some authorities suggest that for a proper noun of more than one syllable that ends in *-s* or another sibilant (*-cks*, *-x*, *-z*), it is better to add only an apostrophe:

Jesus' parables   Sophocles' plays   Chavez' ideas

When in doubt, say the name aloud and notice if you are adding an *-s*. If you are adding an *-s* when you say it, add an apostrophe and an *-s* when you write it. Our own strong preference, however, is to add an apostrophe and an *s* to all proper nouns:

Jones's book   Kansas's highways

Possessive pronouns, such as *his, hers, its, theirs, ours*, do not take an apostrophe:

The cat shed its fur.

The book is hers, not his or ours.

The book is theirs.

(*Exception:* Indefinite pronouns take an apostrophe, as in "one's hopes" and "others' opinions.")

For plurals ending in *-s*, add only an apostrophe to indicate the possessive:

the boys' father   the Smiths' house   the Joneses' car

If the plural does not end in *-s*, add an apostrophe and an *-s:*

women's clothing   mice's eyes

Don't try to form the possessive of the title of a work (for example, of a play, a book, or a film): Write "the imagery in *The Merchant of Venice*" rather than "*The Merchant of Venice*'s imagery." Using an apostrophe gets you into the problem of whether or not to italicize the *s*; similarly, if you use an apostrophe for a work normally enclosed in quotation marks (for instance, a short story), you can't put the apostrophe and the *-s* after the quotation marks, but you can't put it inside either.

2. Use an apostrophe to indicate the omitted letters or numbers in contractions:

She won't.

It's time to go.

the class of '05

3. Until recently an apostrophe was used to make plurals of words that do not usually have a plural, and (this is optional) to make the plurals of digits and letters:

Her speech was full of if's and and's and but's.

Ph.D.'s don't know everything.

Mind your p's and q's. I got two A's and two B's.

He makes his 4's in two ways.

the 1920's

This use of the apostrophe is no longer standard, but it remains acceptable.

Abbreviations

In general, avoid abbreviations except in footnotes and except for certain common ones listed below. And don't use an ampersand (&) unless it appears in material you are quoting, or in a title. Abundant use of abbreviations makes an essay sound like a series of newspaper headlines. Usually, for example, *United States* is better than *U.S.*, except when an adjective: the U.S. army.

1. Abbreviations, with the first letter capitalized, are used before a name:

Dr. Bellini   Ms. Smith   St. Thomas

But:

The doctor took her temperature and eighty dollars.

2. Degrees that follow a name are abbreviated:

B.A.   D.D.S.   M.D.   Ph.D.

3. Other acceptable abbreviations include:

A.D.   B.C.   A.M.   P.M.   e.g.   i.e.

(By the way, *e.g.* means *for example; i.e.* means *that is;* the two ought not to be confused. See pages 284 and 287.)

4. The name of an agency or institution. For instance, the Congress of Racial Equality, International Business Machines, and Southern Methodist University may be abbreviated by using the initial letters, capitalized and usually without periods (CORE, IBM, SMU). It is advisable to give the name in full when first mentioning it (not everyone knows that AARP means American Association of Retired Persons, for instance), and to use the abbreviation in subsequent references.

Numbers

1. Write numbers out if you can do so in fewer than three words: If you cannot, use figures:

> sixteen   seventy-two   ten thousand   one-sixth
> 10,200   10,200,000
> There are 336 dimples on a golf ball.

But write out round millions and billions, to avoid a string of zeros:

> a hundred and ten million

For large round numbers you can also use a combination of figures and words:

> The cockroach is about 250 million years old.

However, if a number begins a sentence, note that it should always be written out:

> Two hundred and fifty million years ago the cockroach first appeared on earth.

2. Use figures in dates, addresses, decimals, percentages, page numbers, and hours followed by A.M. or P.M.:

> February 29, 1900   .06 percent   6 percent   8:16 A.M.

But hours unmodified by minutes are usually written out, followed by *o'clock:*

> Executions in England regularly took place at eight o'clock.

3. Use an apostrophe to indicate omitted figures:

class of '98

the '90s (but: the nineties)

4. Use a hyphen to indicate a span:

1975–79

10–20

In giving inclusive numbers, give the second number in full for the numbers up through ninety-nine (2–5, 8–11, 28–34). For larger numbers, give only the last digit of the second number (101–06; 112–14) unless the full number is necessary (198–202).

5. Dates can be given with the month first, followed by numerals, a comma, and the year:

February 10, 1999

or they can be given with the day first, then the month and then the year (without a comma after the day or month):

10 February 1999

6. B.C. follows the year, but A.D. precedes it:

10 BC

AD 200

The abbreviations B.C. and A.D. are falling out of favor, and are being replaced with B.C.E. ("before the common era") and C.E. ("common era"). Both abbreviations follow the year.

7. Roman numerals are less used than formerly. Capital roman numerals were used to indicate a volume number, but volume numbers are now commonly given in arabic numerals. Capital roman numerals are still used, however, for the names of individuals in a series (Elizabeth II) and for the primary divisions of an outline; lowercase roman numerals are used for the pages in the front matter (table of contents, foreword, preface, etc.) of a book. The old custom of citing acts and scenes of a play in roman numerals and lines in arabic numerals (II.iv.17–25) is still preferred by many instructors, but the use of arabic numerals throughout (2.4.17–25) is gaining acceptance.

CHAPTER TWELVE

USING THE RIGHT WORD

Some things are said or written and some are not. More precisely, anything can be said or written, but only some things are acceptable to the ears and minds of readers. "She don't know nothing about it" has been said and will be said again, but readers who encounter such a sentence will probably judge the speaker as an uneducated person with nothing of interest to say—and immediately tune out.

Although such a double negative is not acceptable today, it used to be: Chaucer's courteous Knight never spoke no baseness, and Shakespeare's courtly Mercutio, in *Romeo and Juliet*, "will not budge for no man." But things have changed; what was acceptable in the Middle Ages and the Renaissance (for example, emptying chamber pots into the gutter) would not be acceptable now. And some of what was once unacceptable has become acceptable. At the beginning of the twentieth century, grammarians suggested that one cannot use *drive* in speaking of a car; one drives (forces into motion) an ox, or even a person ("He drove her to distraction"), but not a machine. A century of usage, however, has erased all objections.

This chapter presents a list of expressions that, although commonly used, set many teeth on edge. Several decades from now some of these expressions may be as acceptable as "drive a car"; but we are writing for today, and we might as well try to hold the attention of today's readers by following today's taste in language.

A Note on Idioms

An idiom (from a Greek word meaning "peculiar") is a fixed group of words, peculiar to a given language. Thus in English we say, "I took a walk," but Germans "make a walk," Spaniards "give a walk," and Japanese "do a walk." (If we think the German, Spanish, and Japanese expressions are odd, we might well ask ourselves where it is that we take a walk to.) If a visitor from Argentina says, in English, that she "gave a walk," she is using *un*idiomatic English, just as anyone who says he knows a poem "at heart" instead of "by heart" is using unidiomatic English.

Probably most unidiomatic expressions use the wrong preposition, as in the following examples:

Unidiomatic	Idiomatic
comply to	comply with
superior with	superior to

Sometimes while we write, or even while we speak, we are unsure of the idiom and we pause to try an alternative—"parallel with?" "parallel to?"—and we don't know which sounds more natural, more idiomatic. At such moments, more often than not, either is acceptable, but if you are in doubt, check a dictionary. (*The American Heritage Dictionary* has notes on usage following the definitions of hundreds of its words.)

In any case, if you are a native speaker of English, when you read your draft you will probably detect unidiomatic expressions such as *superior with*; that is, you will hear something that sounds odd, and so you will change it to something that sounds familiar, idiomatic—here, *superior to*. If any unidiomatic expressions remain in your essay, the trouble may be that an effort to write impressively has led you to use unfamiliar language. A reader who sees such unidiomatic language may sense that you are straining for an effect. Try rewriting the passage in your own voice.

If English is not your first language and you are not yet fluent in it, plan to spend extra time revising and editing your work. Check prepositional phrases with special care. In addition to using a college edition of an English language dictionary, consult reference works designed with

DILBERT reprinted by permission of United Feature Syndicate, inc.

the international or bilingual student in mind. One compact book our students find particularly useful is Michael Swan's *Practical English Usage*, published by Oxford University Press. But don't neglect another invaluable resource: students who are native speakers. They will usually be able to tell you whether or not a phrase "sounds right," though they may not know why.

A Writer's Glossary

a, an   Use *a* before words beginning with a consonant ("a book") or with a vowel sounded as a consonant ("a one-way ticket," "a university"). Use *an* before words beginning with a vowel ("an egg") including those beginning with a silent *h* ("an egg," "an hour"). If an initial *h* is pronounced, *a* is normal ("a history course") but if the accent is not on the first syllable, *an* is acceptable, as in "*an* historian."

above   Try to avoid writing *for the above reasons, in view of the above,* or *as above.* These expressions sound unpleasantly legalistic. Substitute *for these reasons,* or *therefore,* or some such expression or word.

academics   Only two meanings of this noun are widely accepted: (1) "members of an institution of higher learning," and (2) "persons who are academic in background or outlook." Avoid using it to mean "academic subjects," as in "Students should pay attention not only to academics but also to recreation." *Revised:* "Students should pay attention not only to their courses but also to recreation."

accept, except   *Accept* means "to receive with consent." *Except* means "to exclude" or "excluding."

affect, effect   *Affect* is usually a verb, meaning (1) "to influence, to produce an effect, to impress," or (2) "to pretend, to put on," as in "He affected an English accent." Psychologists use it as a noun for "feeling" ("The patient experienced no affect"). *Effect*, as a verb, means "to bring about" ("The workers effected the rescue in less than an hour"). As a noun, *effect* means "result" ("The effect was negligible").

African American, African-American   Both forms are acceptable to denote an American of African ancestry. In recent years these words have been preferred to *black.*

aggravate   "To worsen, to increase for the worse," as in "Smoking aggravated the irritation." Although it is widely used to mean "annoy" ("He aggravated me"), many readers are annoyed by such a use.

all ready, already   *All ready* means "everything is ready." *Already* means "by this time."

all right, alright The first of these is the preferable spelling; for some readers it is the only acceptable spelling.

all together, altogether *All together* means that members of a group act or are gathered together ("They voted all together"); *altogether* is an adverb meaning "entirely," "wholly" ("This is altogether unnecessary").

allusion, reference, illusion An *allusion* is an implied or indirect reference. "As Lincoln says" is a *reference* to Lincoln, but "As a great man has said," along with a phrase quoted from the Gettysburg Address, constitutes an *allusion* to Lincoln. *Allusion* has nothing to do with *illusion* (a deception). Note the spelling (especially the second *i*) in "disillusioned" (left without illusions, disenchanted).

almost See *most*.

a lot Two words (not *alot*).

among, between See *between*.

amount, number *Amount* refers to bulk or quantity: "A small amount of gas was still in the tank." Use *number*, not *amount*, to refer to separate (countable) units: "He did not know the number of gallons that the tank held." Similarly, "A large number of people heard the lecture" (not "a large amount of people"). Note also "an amount of money" but "a number of dollars."

analyzation Unacceptable; use *analysis*.

and etc. Because *etc.* is an abbreviation for *et cetera* ("and others"), the *and* in *and etc.* is redundant. (See also the entry on *et cetera*.)

and/or Acceptable, but a legalism and unpleasant-sounding. Often *or* by itself will do, as in "students who know Latin or Italian." When *or* is not enough ("Scripts for the second season of *The Sopranos* were written by Todd Kessler and/or David Chase") it is better to recast ("Scripts for the second season of *The Sopranos* were written by Todd Kessler or David Chase, or both").

ante, anti *Ante* means "before" (*antebellum*, "before the Civil War"); *anti* means "against" (*antivivisectionist*). Hyphenate *anti* before capitals (*anti-Semitism*) and before *i* (*anti-intellectual*).

anxious Best reserved for uses that suggest anxiety ("He was anxious before the examination"), though some authorities now accept it in the sense of "eager" ("He was anxious to serve the community").

anybody One word ("Do you know anybody here?"). If two words (*any body*), you mean any corpse ("Several people died in the fire, but the police cannot identify any body").

any more, anymore   *Any more* is used as an adjective: "I don't want any more meat" (here *any more* says something about meat). *Anymore* (one word) is used as an adverb: "I don't eat meat anymore" (here *anymore* says something about eating).

anyone   One word ("Why would anyone think that?"), unless you mean "any one thing," as in "Here are three books; you may take any one." *Anyone* is an indefinite singular pronoun meaning *any person:* "If anyone has a clue, he or she should call the police." In an astounding advertisement, the writer moved from *anyone* (singular) to *their* (third person plural) to *your* (second person): "Anyone who thinks a Yonex racquet has improved their game, please raise your hand."

area of   Like *field of* and *topic of* ("the field of literature," "the topic of politics"), *area of* can usually be deleted. "The area of marketing" equals "marketing."

around   Avoid using *around* in place of *about:* "He wrote it in about three hours." See also *centers on.*

as, like   *As* is a conjunction; use it in forming comparisons, to introduce clauses. (A clause has a subject and a verb.)

> You can learn to write, as you can learn to swim.
>
> Huck speaks the truth as he sees it.

Like is a preposition; use it to introduce prepositional phrases:

> He looks like me.
>
> Like Hamlet, Laertes has lost a father.
>
> She thinks like a lawyer.

A short rule: use *like* when it introduces a noun *not* followed by a verb: "Nothing grabs people like *People.*"

Writers who are fearful of incorrectly using *like* resort to cumbersome evasions: "He eats in the same manner that a pig eats." But there's nothing wrong with "He eats like a pig."

Asian, Oriental   *Asian* as a noun and as an adjective is the preferred word. *Oriental* (from *oriens,* "rising sun," "east") is in disfavor because it implies a Eurocentric view—that is, that things "oriental" are east of the European colonial powers who invented the term. Similarly, **Near East, Middle East,** and **Far East** are terms that are based on a Eurocentric view. No brief substitute has been agreed on for *Near East* and *Middle East,* but *East Asia* is now regarded as preferable to *Far East.*

as of now Best deleted, or replaced by *now*. Not "As of now I don't smoke" but "Now I don't smoke" or "I don't smoke now" or "I don't smoke."

aspect Literally, "a view from a particular point," but it has come to mean *topic*, as in "Several aspects should be considered." Try to get a sharper word; for example, "Several problems should be considered," or "Several consequences should be considered."

as such Often meaningless, as in "Tragedy as such evokes pity."

as to Usually *about* is preferable. Not "I know nothing as to the charges," but "I know nothing about the charges."

bad, badly *Bad* used to be only an adjective ("a bad movie"), and *badly* was an adverb ("she sings badly"). In "I felt bad," *bad* describes the subject, not the verb. (Compare "I felt happy," or "I felt good about getting a raise." After verbs of appearing, such as "feel," "look," "seem," "taste," an adjective, not an adverb, is used. If you are in doubt, substitute a word for *bad*, for instance *sad*, and see what you say. Since you would say "I feel sad about his failure," you can say "I feel bad. . . .") But "badly" is acceptable and even preferred by many. Note, however, this distinction: "This meat smells bad" (an adjective describing the meat), and "Because I have a stuffed nose I smell badly" (an adverb describing my ability to smell something).

being Do not use *being* as a main verb, as in "The trouble being that his reflexes were too slow." The result is a sentence fragment. See pages 253–55.

being that, being as A sentence such as "Being that she was a stranger . . ." sounds like an awkward translation from the Latin. Use *because*.

beside, besides *Beside* means "at the side of." Because *besides* can mean either "in addition to" or "other than," it is ambiguous, as in "Something besides TB caused his death." It is best, then, to use *in addition to* or *other than*, depending on what you mean.

between Only English teachers who have had a course in Middle English are likely to know that between comes from *by twain*. And only English teachers and editors are likely to object to its use (and to call for *among*) when more than two are concerned, as in "among the three of us." Note, too, that even conservative usage accepts *between* in reference to more than two when the items are at the moment paired: "Negotiations *between* Israel and Egypt, Syria, and Lebanon seem stalled." *Between*, a preposition, takes an object ("between you and me"): not "between you and I."

biannually, bimonthly, biweekly Every two years, every two months, every two weeks (*not* twice a year, etc.). Twice a year is *semiannually*, i.e., "half yearly." Because *biannually*, *bimonthly*, and *biweekly* are commonly misunderstood, it is best to avoid them and to say "every two. . . ."

Black, black Although one sometimes sees the word capitalized when it refers to race, most publishers use a lowercase letter, making it consistent with *white*, which is never capitalized. See also *African American*.

can, may When schoolchildren asked "Can I leave the room?" their teachers used to correct them thus: "You *can* leave the room if you have legs, but you *may not* leave the room until you receive permission." In short, *can* indicates physical possibility, *may* indicates permission. But because "you may not" and "why mayn't I?" sound not merely polite but stiff, *can* is usually preferred except in formal contexts.

capital, capitol A *capital* is a city that is a center of government. *Capital* can also mean wealth ("It takes capital to start a business"). A *capitol* is a building in which legislators meet. Notice the distinction in the following sentence: "Washington, D.C., is the nation's capital; the capitol ought to have a gold dome."

centers on, centers around Use *centers on*, because *center* refers to a point, not to a movement around.

Chicana, Chicano A Mexican-American (female or male, respectively; the male plural, *Chicanos*, is used for a group consisting of males and females). Although the term sometimes was felt to be derogatory, today it usually implies ethnic pride.

collective nouns A collective noun, singular in form, names a collection of individuals. Examples: *audience, band, committee, crowd, jury, majority, minority, team*. When you are thinking chiefly of the whole as a unit, use a singular verb (and a singular pronoun, if any): "The majority rules"; "The jury is announcing its verdict." But when you are thinking of the individuals, use a plural verb (and pronoun, if any): "The majority are lawyers"; "The jury are divided and they probably cannot agree." If the plural sounds odd, you can usually rewrite: "The jurors are divided and they probably cannot agree."

compare, contrast To *compare* is to note likenesses or differences: "Compare a motorcycle with a bicycle." To *contrast* is to emphasize differences.

complement, compliment *Complement* as a noun means "that which completes"; as a verb, "to fill out, to complete." *Compliment* as a noun is an expression of praise; as a verb it means "to offer praise."

comprise To include, contain, consist of: "The university comprises two colleges and a medical school" (not "is comprised of"). Conservative authorities hold that "to be comprised of" is always incorrect, and they reject the form one often hears: "Two colleges and a medical school comprise the university." Here the word should be *compose*, not *comprise*.

concept Should often be deleted. For "The concept of the sales tax is regressive" write "The sales tax is regressive."

contact Because it is vague, avoid using *contact* as a verb. *Not* "I contacted him" but "I spoke with him" or "I wrote to him," or whatever.

continual, continuous Conservative authorities hold that *continuous* means "uninterrupted," as in "It rained continuously for six hours"; *continually* means "repeated often, recurring at short intervals," as in "For a year he continually wrote letters to her."

contrast, compare See *compare*.

could have, could of See *of*.

criteria Plural of *criterion;* hence it is always incorrect to speak of "a criteria," or to say "The criteria is . . ." Correct: "The criterion is simple"; "the criteria are unfair."

data Plural of *datum*. Although some social scientists speak of "this data," "these data" is preferable: "These data are puzzling." Because the singular, *datum*, is rare and sounds odd, it is best to substitute *fact* or *figure* for *datum*.

different from Prefer it to *different than*, unless you are convinced that in a specific sentence *different from* sounds terribly wrong, as in "These two books are more different than I had expected." (In this example, "more," not "different," governs "than." But this sentence, though correct, is awkward and therefore it should be revised: "These two books differ more than I had expected.")

dilemma A situation requiring a choice between equally undesirable alternatives; not every difficulty or plight or predicament is a *dilemma*. Not "Her dilemma was that she had nowhere to go," but "Her dilemma was whether to go out or to stay home: one was frightening, the other was embarrassing." And note the spelling (two *m*'s, no *n*).

disinterested Though the word is often used to mean "indifferent," "unconcerned," "uninterested," reserve it to mean "impartial": "A judge should be disinterested."

due to Some people, holding that *due to* cannot modify a verb (as in "He failed due to illness"), tolerate it only when it modifies a noun or pronoun ("His failure was due to illness"). They also insist that it cannot begin a sentence ("Due to illness, he failed"). In fact, however, daily usage accepts both. But because it almost always sounds stiff, try to substitute *because of,* or *through.*

due to the fact that   Wordy for *because.*

each   Although many authorities hold that *each,* as a subject, is singular, even when followed by "them" ("Each of them is satisfactory"), some authorities accept and even favor the plural ("Each of them are satisfactory"). But it is usually better to avoid the awkwardness by substituting *all* for *each:* "All of them are satisfactory." When *each* refers to a plural subject, the verb must be plural: "They each have a book"; "We each are trying." *Each* cannot be made into a possessive; you cannot say "Each's opinion is acceptable."

effect   See *affect.*

e.g.   Abbreviation for *exempli gratia,* Latin for "for example." It is thus different from *i.e.* (an abbreviation for *id est,* Latin for "that is"). "E.g." (not italicized) introduces an example: "common pets (e.g., cats, dogs, and birds) have few diseases that can be transmitted to humans." "I.e." (also not italicized) introduces a definition: "Pets (i.e., animals kept for companionship) cost Americans billions of dollars annually." Because these two abbreviations of Latin words are often confused, it may be preferable to avoid them and use their English equivalents.

either . . . or, neither . . . nor   If the subjects are singular, use a singular verb: "Either the boy or the girl is lying." If one of the subjects joined by *or* or *nor* is plural, most grammarians say that the verb agrees with the nearer subject, thus: "A tree or two shrubs are enough," or "Two shrubs or a tree is enough." But because the singular verb in the second of these sentences may sound odd, follow the first construction; that is, put the plural subject nearer to the verb and use a plural verb. Another point about *either . . . or.* In this construction, "either" serves as advance notice that two equal possibilities are in the offing. Beware of putting "either" too soon, as in "Either he is a genius or a lunatic." Better: "He is either a genius or a lunatic."

enthuse   Objectionable to many readers. For "He enthused," say "He was enthusiastic." Use *enthuse* only in the sense of "to be excessively enthusiastic," "to gush."

et cetera, etc.   Latin for "and other things"; if you mean "and other people," you need *et al.,* short for *et alii.* Because *etc.* is vague, its use is usually inadvisable. Not "He studied mathematics, etc." but "He studied mathematics, history, economics, and French." Or, if the list is long, cut it by saying something a little more informative than *etc.*—for example, "He studied mathematics, history, and other liberal arts subjects." Even *and so forth* or *and so on* is preferable to *etc.* Confine *etc.* (and most other abbreviations, including *et al.*) to footnotes, and even in footnotes try to avoid it.

Eurocentric language Language focused on Europe—for instance, the word *Hispanic* when used to refer not to persons from Spain but persons from Mexico and Central and South America, who may in fact have little or no Spanish heritage. (The Latin name for Spain was Hispania.) Similarly, the terms *Near East* and *Far East* represent a European point of view (near to, and far from Europe), objectionable to many persons not of European heritage. See *Asian* and *Hispanic*.

everybody, everyone These take a singular verb ("Everybody is here"), and a pronoun referring to them is usually singular ("Everybody thinks his problems are suitable topics of conversation"), but use a plural pronoun if the singular would seem unnatural ("Everybody was there, weren't they?"). To avoid the sexism of "Everybody thinks his problems . . ." revise to "All people think their problems. . . ."

examples, instances See *instances*.

except See *accept*.

exists Often unnecessary and a sign of wordiness. Not "The problem that *exists* here is" but "The problem here is."

expound Usually pretentious for *explain* or *say*. To *expound* is to give a methodical explanation of theological matters.

facet Literally "little face," especially one of the surfaces of a gem. Don't use it (and don't use *aspect* or *factor* either) to mean "part" or "topic." It is most acceptable when, close to its literal meaning, it suggests a new appearance, as when a gem is turned: "Another *facet* appears when we see this law from the taxpayer's point of view."

the fact that Usually wordy. "Because of the fact that boys played female roles in Elizabethan drama" can be reduced to "Because boys played female roles in Elizabethan drama."

factor Strictly speaking, a *factor* helps to produce a result. Although *factor* is often used in the sense of "point" ("Another factor to be studied is . . ."), such use is often wordy. "The possibility of plagiarism is a factor that must be considered" simply adds up to "The possibility of plagiarism must be considered." *Factor* is almost never the precise word: "the factors behind Gatsby's actions" are, more precisely, "Gatsby's motives."

famous, notorious   See *notorious.*

Far East   See *Asian.*

farther, further   Some purists claim that *farther* always refers to distance and *further* to time ("The gymnasium is farther than the library"; "Let us think further about this").

fatalistic, pessimistic   *Fatalistic* means "characterized by the belief that all events are predetermined and therefore inevitable"; *pessimistic,* "characterized by the belief that the world is evil," or, less gloomily, "expecting the worst."

fewer, less   See *less.*

field of   See *area of.*

firstly, secondly   Acceptable, but it is better to use *first, second.*

former, latter   These words are acceptable, but they are often annoying because they force the reader to reread earlier material in order to locate what *the former* and *the latter* refer to. The expressions are legitimately used in order to avoid repeating lengthy terms, but if you are talking about an easily repeated subject—say, Lincoln and Grant—don't hesitate to replace *the former* and *the latter* with their names. The repetition will clarify rather than bore.

good, well   *Good* is an adjective ("a good book"). *Well* is usually an adverb ("She writes well"). Standard English does not accept "She writes good." But Standard English requires *good* after verbs of appearing, such as *seems, looks, sounds, tastes*: "it looks good," "it sounds good." *Well* can also be an adjective meaning *healthy:* "I am well."

graduate, graduate from   Use *from* if you name the institution or if you use a substitute word as in "She graduated from high school"; if the institution (or substitute) is not named, *from* is omitted: "She graduated in 1983." The use of the passive ("She was graduated from high school") is acceptable but sounds fussy to many.

he or she, his or her   These expressions are awkward, but the implicit male chauvinism in the generic use of the male pronoun ("A citizen should exercise his right to vote") may be more offensive than the awkwardness of *he or she* and *his or her.* Moreover, sometimes the male pronoun, when used for males and females, is ludicrous, as in "The more violence a youngster sees on television, regardless of his age or sex, the more aggressive he is likely to be." Do what you can to avoid the dilemma. Sometimes you can use the plural *their:* "Students are expected to hand in their papers on Monday" (instead of "The student is expected to hand in his or her paper on Monday"). Or eliminate the possessive: "The student must hand in a paper on Monday." See *man;* see also "Avoiding Sexist Language," pages 78–80.

Hispanic, Latina, Latino   A person who traces his or her origin to a Spanish-speaking country is a *Hispanic.* (Hispania was the Latin name for Spain.) But some people object to the term when applied to persons in the Western Hemisphere, arguing that it overemphasizes the European influence on ethnic identity and neglects the indigenous and black heritages. Many who object to *Hispanic* prefer to call a person of Latin-American descent a *Latina* (the feminine form) or a *Latino* (the masculine form), partly because these words are themselves Latin-American words. (The male plural, *Latinos,* commonly is used for a group consisting of males and females.) But many people object that these words too obscure the unique cultural heritages of, say, Mexican-Americans, Cuban-Americans, and Puerto Ricans.

hopefully   Commonly used to mean "I hope" or "It is hoped" ("*Hopefully,* the rain will stop soon"), but it is best to avoid what some consider a dangling modifier. After all, the rain itself is not hopeful. If you mean "I hope the rain will stop soon," say exactly that. Notice, too, that *hopefully* is often evasive. If the president of the college says, "Hopefully tuition will not rise next year," don't think that you have heard a promise to fight against an increase; you only have heard someone evade making a promise. In short, confine *hopefully* to its adverbial use, meaning "in a hopeful manner": "Hopefully he uttered a prayer."

however   Independent clauses (for instance, "He tried" and "He failed") should not be linked with a *however* preceded by a comma. Incorrect: "He tried, however he failed." What is required is a period ("He tried. However, he failed") or a semicolon before *however* ("He tried; however, he failed).

the idea that   Usually dull and wordy. Not "The idea that we grow old is frightening," but "That we grow old is frightening," or (probably better) "Growing old is frightening."

identify   When used in the psychological sense, "to associate oneself closely with a person or an institution," it is preferable to include a reflexive pronoun, thus: "He identified himself with Hamlet," *not* "He identified with Hamlet."

i.e.   Latin for *id est,* "that is." The English words are preferable to the Latin abbreviation. On the distinction between *i.e.* and *e.g.,* see *e.g.*

immanent, imminent   *Immanent,* "remaining within, intrinsic"; *imminent,* "likely to occur soon, impending."

imply, infer The writer or speaker *implies* (suggests); the perceiver *infers* (draws a conclusion): "Karl Marx implied that . . . but his modern disciples infer from his writings that. . . ." Although *infer* is widely used for *imply*, preserve the distinction.

incidence, incident The *incidence* is the extent or frequency of an occurrence: "The incidence of violent crime in Tokyo is very low." The plural, *incidences*, is rarely used: "The incidences of crime and of fire in Tokyo. . . ." An *incident* is one occurrence: "The incident happened yesterday." The plural is *incidents:* "The two incidents happened simultaneously."

individual Avoid using the word to mean only "person": "He was a generous individual." But it is precise when it implicitly makes a contrast with a group: "In a money-mad society, he was a generous individual"; "Although the faculty did not take a stand on this issue, faculty members as individuals spoke out."

instances Instead of *in many instances* use *often*. Strictly speaking an *instance* is not an object or incident in itself but one offered as an example. Thus "another instance of his failure to do his duty" (not "In three instances he failed to do his duty").

irregardless Unacceptable; use *regardless*.

it is Usually this expression needlessly delays the subject: "It is unlikely that many students will attend the lecture" could just as well be "Few students are likely to attend the lecture."

its, it's The first is a possessive pronoun ("The flock lost its leader"); the second is a contraction of *it is* ("It's a wise father that knows his child."). You'll have no trouble if you remember that the possessive pronoun *its*, like other possessive pronouns such as *our, his, their*, does *not* use an apostrophe.

kind of Singular, as in "That kind of movie bothers me." (*Not:* "Those kind of movies bother me.") If, however, you are really talking about more than one kind, use *kinds* and be sure that the demonstrative pronoun and the verb are plural: "Those kinds of movies bother me." Notice also that the phrase is *kind of*, not *kind of a*. Not "What *kind of a* car does she drive?" but "What *kind of* car does she drive?"

Latina, Latino See *Hispanic*.

latter See *former*.

lay, lie *To lay* means "to put, to set, to cause to rest." It takes an object: "May I lay the coats on the table?" The past tense and the participle are *laid:* "I laid the coats on the table"; "I have laid the coats on the table." *To lie* means "to recline," and it does not take an object: "When I am tired I lie down." The past tense is *lay;* the participle is *lain:* "Yesterday I lay down"; "I have lain down hundreds of times without wishing to get up."

lend, loan The usual verb is *lend:* "Lend me a pen." The past tense and the participle are both *lent. Loan* is a noun: "This isn't a gift, it's a loan." But, curiously, *loan* as a verb is acceptable in past forms: "I loaned him my bicycle." In its present form ("I often loan money") it is used chiefly by bankers.

less, fewer *Less* (as an adjective) refers to bulk amounts (also called mass nouns): less milk, less money, less time. *Fewer* refers to separate (countable) items: fewer glasses of milk, fewer dollars, fewer hours.

lifestyle, life-style, life style All three forms are acceptable, but because many readers regard the expression as imprecise, try to find a substitute such as *values.*

like, as See *as.*

literally It means "to the letter," "exactly as stated," and "strictly in accord with the primary meaning; not metaphorically." It is not a mere intensive. "He was literally dead" means that he was a corpse; if he was merely exhausted, *literally* won't do. You cannot be "literally stewed" (except by cannibals), "literally tickled pink," or "literally walking on air."

loose, lose *Loose* is an adjective ("The nail is loose"); *lose* is a verb ("Don't lose the nail").

the majority of Usually a wordy way of saying *most.* Of course if you mean "a bare majority," say so; otherwise *most* will usually do. Certainly "The majority of the basement is used for a cafeteria" should be changed to "Most of the basement is used for a cafeteria." *Majority* can take either a singular verb or a plural verb. When *majority* refers to a collection—for example, a group acting as a body—the verb is singular, as in "The majority has withdrawn its support from the mayor." But when *majority* refers to members of a group acting as individuals, as in "The majority of voters in this district vote Republican," a plural verb (here, "vote") is usually preferred. If either construction sounds odd, use "most," with a plural verb: "Most voters in this district vote Republican."

man, mankind The use of these words in reference to males and females sometimes is ludicrous, as in "Man, being a mammal, breast-feeds his young." But even when not ludicrous the practice is sexist, as in "man's brain" and "the greatness of mankind." Consider using such words as *human being, person, humanity, humankind, people.* Similarly, for "manmade," *artificial* or *synthetic* may do. See also "Avoiding Sexist Language," pages 78–80.

may, can See *can.*

me The right word in such expressions as "between you and me" and "They gave it to John and me." It is the object of verbs and of prepositions. In fact, *me* rather than *I* is the usual form after any verb, including the verb *to be;* "It is me" is nothing to be ashamed of. See the entry on *myself.*

medium, media *Medium* is singular, *media* is plural: "TV is the medium to which most children are most exposed. Other media include film, radio, and publishing." It follows, then, that *mass media* takes a plural verb: "The mass media exert an enormous influence."

Middle East See *Asian.*

might of, might have; must of, must have *Might of* and *must of* are colloquial for *might have* and *must have.* In writing, use the *have* form: "He might have cheated; in fact, he must have cheated."

more Avoid writing a false (incomplete) comparison such as: "His essay includes several anecdotes, making it more enjoyable." Delete "more" unless there really is a comparison with another essay. On false comparisons see also the entry on *other.*

most, almost Although it is acceptable in speech to say "most everyone" and "most anybody," it is preferable in writing to use "almost everyone," "almost anybody." But of course: "Most students passed."

myself *Myself* is often mistakenly used for *I* or *me,* as in "They praised Tony and myself," or "Professor Chen and myself examined the dead rat." In the first example, *me* is the word to use; after all, if Tony hadn't been there the sentence would say, "They praised me." (No one would say, "They praised myself.") Similarly, in the second example if Professor Chen were not involved, the sentence would run, "I examined the dead rat," so what is needed here is simply "Professor Chen and I examined. . . ."

   In general, use *myself* only when (1) it refers to the subject of the sentence ("I look out for myself"; "I washed myself") or (2) when it is an intensive: ("I myself saw the break-in"; "I myself have not experienced racism").

nature You can usually delete *the nature of,* as in "The nature of my contribution is not political but psychological."

Near East See *Asian.*

needless to say The reader may well wonder why you go on to say it. Of course this expression is used to let readers know that they are probably familiar with what comes next, but usually *of course* will better serve as this sign.

Negro Capitalized, whether a noun or an adjective, though *white* is not. In recent years *Negro* has been replaced by *black* or *African-American*.

neither . . . nor See *either . . . or*.

nobody, no one, none *Nobody* and *no one* are singular, requiring a singular verb ("Nobody believes this," "No one knows"); but they can be referred to by a plural pronoun: "Nobody believes this, do they?" "No one knows, do they?" *None*, though it comes from *no one*, almost always requires a plural verb when it refers to people ("Of the ten people present, none are students") and a singular verb when it refers to things ("Of the five assigned books, none is worth reading").

not only . . . but also Keep in mind these two points: (1) many readers object to the omission of "also" in such a sentence as "She not only brought up two children but practiced law"—it's preferable to write "She not only brought up two children but she also practiced law"—and (2) all readers dislike a faulty parallel, as in "She not only is bringing up two children but practices law." ("Is bringing up" needs to be paralleled with "is also practicing.")

notorious Widely and unfavorably known; not merely famous, but famous for some discreditable trait or deed.

not . . . un- Such an expression as "not unfamiliar" is useful only if it conveys something different from the affirmative. Compare the frostiness of "I am not unfamiliar with your methods" with "I am familiar with your methods." If the negative has no evident advantage, use the affirmative.

number, amount See *amount*.

a number of Requires a plural verb: "A number of women are presidents of corporations." But when *number* is preceded by *the* it requires a singular verb: "The number of women who are presidents is small." (The plural noun after *number* of course may require a plural verb, as in "women are," but the subject of the sentence is *the number*, which itself remains singular; hence its verb is singular, as in "is small.")

of Be careful not to use *of* when *have* is required. Not "He might of died in the woods," but "He might have died in the woods." Note that what we often hear as "would've" or "should've" or "must've" or "could've" is "would have" or "should have" or "must have" or "could have," *not* "would of," etc.

off of   Use *off* or *from:* "Take if off the table"; "He jumped from the bridge."

often-times   Use *often* instead.

old-fashioned, old-fashion   Only the first is acceptable.

one   British usage accepts the shift from *one* to *he* in "One begins to die the moment he is born," but American usage prefers "One begins to die the moment one is born." A shift from *one* to *you* ("One begins to die the moment you are born") is unacceptable. As a pronoun, *one* can be useful in impersonal statements such as the sentence about dying, at the beginning of this entry, where it means "a person," but don't use it as a disguise for yourself ("One objects to Smith's argument"). Try to avoid *one;* one *one* usually leads to another, resulting in a sentence that, in James Thurber's words, "sounds like a trombone solo" ("If one takes oneself too seriously, one begins to . . ."). See also *you.*

one of   Takes a plural noun, and if this is followed by a clause, the preferred verb is plural: "one of those students who are," "one of those who feel." Thus, in such a sentence as "One of the coaches who have resigned is now seeking reinstatement," notice that "have" is correct; the antecedent of "who" (the subject of the verb) is "coaches," which is plural. Coaches have resigned, though "one . . . is seeking reinstatement." But in such an expression as "one out of a hundred," the following verb may be singular or plural ("One out of a hundred is," "One out of a hundred are").

only   Be careful where you put it. The classic textbook example points out that in the sentence "I hit him in the eye," *only* can be inserted in seven places (beginning in front of "I" and ending after "eye") with at least six different meanings. Try to put it just before the expression it qualifies. Thus, not "Presidential aides are only responsible to one person," but "Presidential aides are responsible to only one person" (or "to one person only").

oral, verbal   See *verbal.*

Oriental   See *Asian.*

other   Often necessary in comparisons. "No American president served as many terms as Franklin Roosevelt" absurdly implies that Roosevelt was not an American president. The sentence should be revised to "No other American president served as many terms as Franklin Roosevelt."

per Usually it sounds needlessly technical ("twice per hour") or disturbingly impersonal ("as per your request"). Preferable: "twice an hour," "according to your request," or "as you requested."

per cent, percent, percentage The first two of these are interchangeable; both mean "per hundred," "out of a hundred," as in "Ninety per cent (or percent) of the students were white." *Per cent* and *percent* are always accompanied by a number (written out, or in figures). It is usually better to write out *per cent* or *percent* than to use a per cent sign (12%), except in technical or statistical papers. *Percentage* means "a proportion or share in relation to the whole," as in "A very large percentage of the student body is white." Many authorities insist that *percentage* is never preceded by a number. Do not use percentage to mean "a few," as in "Only a percentage of students attended the lecture"; a percentage can be as large as 99.99. It is usually said that with *per cent, percent,* and *percentage,* whether the verb is singular or plural depends on the number of the noun that follows the word, thus: "Ninety percent of their books are paperbacks"; "Fifty percent of their library is worthless"; "A large percentage of their books are worthless." But some readers (including the authors of this book) prefer a singular verb after *percentage* unless the resulting sentence is as grotesque as this one: "A large percentage of the students is unmarried." Still, rather than say a "percentage . . . are," we would recast the sentence: "A large percentage of the student body is unmarried," or "Many (or "Most," or whatever) of the students are unmarried."

per se Latin for "by itself." Usually sounds legalistic or pedantic, as in "Meter per se has an effect."

pessimistic See *fatalistic.*

phenomenon, phenomena The plural is *phenomena;* thus, "these phenomena" but "this phenomenon."

plus Unattractive and imprecise as a noun meaning "asset" or "advantage" ("When he applied for the job, his appearance was a plus"), and equally unattractive as a substitute for *moreover* ("The examination was easy, plus I had studied") or as a substitute for *and* ("I studied the introduction plus the first chapter").

politics Preferably singular ("Ethnic politics has been a strong force for a century") but a plural verb is acceptable.

precede, proceed   To *precede* is to go before or ahead ("*X* precedes *Y*"). To *proceed* is to go forward ("The spelling lesson proceeded smoothly").

prejudice, prejudiced   *Prejudice* is a noun: "It is impossible to live entirely without prejudice." But use the past participle *prejudiced* as an adjective: "They were prejudiced against me from the start."

preventative, preventive   Both are acceptable but the second form is now used by writers on medicine ("preventive medicine"); *preventative* therefore has come to seem amateurish.

principal, principle   *Principal* is (1) an adjective meaning "main," "chief," "most important" ("The principal arguments against IQ testing are three"), and (2) a noun meaning "the chief person" ("Ms. Murphy was the principal of Jefferson High") or "the chief thing" ("She had so much money she could live on the interest and not touch the principal"). *Principle* is always a noun meaning "rule" or "fundamental truth" ("It was against his principles to eat meat").

prior to   Pretentious for *before.*

protagonist   Literally, the first actor, and, by extension, the chief actor. It is odd, therefore, to speak of "the protagonists" in a single literary work or occurrence. Note also that the prefix is *proto*, "first," not *pro*, "for"; it does *not* mean one who strives for something.

quite   Usually a word to delete, along with *definitely, pretty, rather,* and *very. Quite* used to mean "completely" ("I quite understand") but it has come also to mean "to a considerable degree," and so it is ambiguous as well as vague.

quotation, quote   Quotation is a noun, quote is a verb. "I will quote Churchill" is fine, but not "these quotes from Churchill." (In fact, "quote" as a noun is gaining acceptance but avoid this usage because it offends many readers.) And remember, you may *quote* one of Hamlet's speeches, but Hamlet does not *quote* them; he says them.

rather   Avoid use with strong adjectives. "Rather intelligent" makes sense, but "rather tremendous" does not. "Rather brilliant" probably means "bright"; "rather terrifying" probably means "frightening," "rather unique" probably means "unusual." Get the right adjective, not *rather* and the wrong adjective.

the reason . . . is because   Usually *because* is enough (not "The reason they fail is because they don't study," but simply "They fail because they don't study"). Similarly, *the reason why* can usually be reduced to *why.* Notice, too, that because *reason* is a noun, it cannot neatly govern a *because* clause: not "The reason for his absence is because he was sick," but "The reason for his absence was illness."

rebut, refute To rebut is to argue against, but not necessarily successfully. If you mean "to disprove," use *disprove* or *refute.*

in regard to, with regard to Often wordy for *about, concerning,* or *on,* and sometimes even these words are unnecessary. Compare: "She knew a great deal in regard to jazz"; "She knew a great deal about jazz." Compare: "Hemingway's story is often misunderstood with regard to Robert Wilson's treatment of Margot Macomber"; "In Hemingway's story, Robert Wilson's treatment of Margot Macomber is often misunderstood."

relate to Usually a vague expression, best avoided, as in "I can relate to Hedda Gabler." Does it mean "respond favorably to," "identify myself with," "interact with" (and how can a reader "interact with" a character in a play?). Use *relate to* only in the sense of "have connection with" (as in "How does your answer relate to my question?"); even in such a sentence a more exact expression is preferable.

repel, repulse Both verbs mean "to drive back," but only *repel* can mean "to cause distaste," "to disgust," as in "His obscenities repelled the audience."

respectfully, respectively *Respectfully* means "with respect, showing respect" ("Japanese students and teachers bow respectfully to each other"). *Respectively* means "each in turn" ("Professors Arnott, Bahktian, and Cisneros teach, respectively, chemistry, business, and biology").

sarcasm Heavy, malicious sneering ("Oh you're really a great friend, aren't you?" addressed to someone who won't lend the speaker ten dollars). If the apparent praise, which really communicates dispraise, is at all clever, conveying, say, a delicate mockery or wryness, it is irony, not sarcasm.

seem Properly it suggests a suspicion that appearances may be deceptive: "He seems honest (but . . .)." Don't say "The book seems to lack focus" if you believe it does lack focus.

semiannually, semimonthly, semiweekly See *biannually.*

sexist language Language that is not gender-neutral. For example, the use of *he* with reference to females as well as to males ("When a legislator votes, he takes account of his constituency"), like the use of *man* for all human beings ("Man is a rational animal"), is now widely perceived as sexist. See the entries on *he or she; man, mankind;* and *s/he.*

shall, will, should, would The old principle held that in the first person *shall* is the future indicative of *to be* and *should* the conditional ("I shall go," "We should like to be asked"); and that *will* and *would* are the forms for the second and third persons. When the forms are reversed ("I will go," "Government of the people . . . shall not perish from the earth"), determination is expressed. But today almost nobody adheres to these principles. Indeed, *shall* (except in questions) sounds stilted to many ears.

s/he This relatively new gender-free pronoun ("As soon as the student receives the forms, s/he should fill them out") is sometimes used in place of *he or she* or *she or he*, which are used to avoid the sexism implied when the male pronoun "he" is used to stand for women as well as men ("As soon as the student receives the forms, he should fill them out"). Other, less noticeable and therefore better ways of avoiding sexist writing are suggested under *he or she*. See also "Avoiding Sexist Language," pages 78–80.

simplistic Means "falsely simplified by ignoring complications." Do not confuse it with *simplified*, whose meanings include "reduced to essentials" and "clarified."

since, because Traditional objections to *since*, in the sense of "because," have all but vanished. Note, however, that when *since* is ambiguous and may also refer to time ("Since he joined the navy, she found another boyfriend") it is better to say *because* or *after*, depending on which you mean.

situation Overused, vague, and often unnecessary. "His situation was that he was unemployed" adds up to "He was unemployed." And "an emergency situation" is probably an emergency.

split infinitives The infinitive is the verb form that merely names the action, without indicating when or by whom performed ("walk," rather than "walked" or "I walk"). Grammarians, however, developed the idea that the infinitive was "to walk," and they held that one should not separate or split the two words: "to quickly walk." But almost all authorities today accept this usuage. Notice, however, that often the inserted word can be deleted ("to really understand" is "to understand"), and that if many words are inserted between *to* and the verb, the reader may get lost ("to quickly and in the remaining few pages before examining the next question conclude").

stanza See *verse*.

subjunctive For the use of the subjunctive with conditions contrary to fact (for instance, "If I were you"), see the entry on *was, were*. The subjunctive is also used in *that* clauses followed by verbs demanding, requesting, or recommending: "She asked that the students be prepared to take a test." But because this last sort of sentence sounds stiff, it is better to use an alternative construction, such as "She asked the students to prepare for a test."

than, then   *Than* is used chiefly in making comparisons ("German is harder than French"), but also after "rather," "other," and "else" ("I'd rather take French than German"; "He thinks of nothing other than sex"). *Then* commonly indicates time ("She took German then, but now she takes French"; "Until then, I'll save you a seat"), but it may also mean "in that case" ("It's agreed, then, that we'll all go"), or "on the other hand" ("Then again, she may find German easy"). The simplest guide: Use *than* after comparisons and after "rather," "other," "else"; otherwise use *then*.

that, which, who   Many pages have been written on these words; opinions differ, but you will offend no one if you observe the following principles. (1) Use *that* in restrictive (that is, limiting) clauses: "The rocking chair that creaks is on the porch." (2) Use *which* in nonrestrictive (in effect, parenthetic) clauses: "The rocking chair, which creaks, is on the porch." (See pages 263–65.) The difference between these two sentences is this: In the first, one rocking chair is singled out from several—the one that creaks; in the second, the fact that the rocking chair creaks is simply tossed in and is not added for the purpose of identifying the one chair out of several. (3) Use *who* for people, in restrictive and in nonrestrictive clauses: "The women who were playing poker ignored the men"; "The women, who were playing poker, ignored the men." But note that often *that*, *which*, and *who* can be omitted: "The creaky rocking chair is on the porch"; "The women playing poker ignored the men." "The women, playing poker, ignored the men." In general, omit these words if the sentence remains clear.

their, there, they're   The first is a possessive pronoun: "Chaplin and Keaton made their first films before sound tracks were developed." The second, *there*, sometimes refers to a place ("Go there," "Do you live there?"), and sometimes is what is known in grammar as an introductory expletive ("There are no solutions to this problem"). The third, *they're*, is a contraction of "they are" ("They're going to stay for dinner").

this   Often refers vaguely to "what I have been saying." Does it refer to the previous sentence, the previous paragraph, the previous page? Try to modify it by being specific: "This last point"; "This clue gave the police all they needed."

thusly Unacceptable; *thus* is an adverb and needs no adverbial ending.

till, until Both are acceptable, but *until* is preferable because *till*—though common in speech—looks literary in print. The following are *not* acceptable: *til, 'til, 'till.*

to, too, two *To* is toward; *too* is either "also" ("She's a lawyer, too") or "excessively" ("It's too hot"); *two* is one more than one ("It's two feet long").

topic of See *area of.*

toward, towards Both are standard English; *toward* is more common in the United States, *towards* in Great Britain.

type Often colloquial (and unacceptable in most writing) for *type of*, as in "this type teacher." But *type of* is not especially pleasing either. Better to write "this kind of teacher." And avoid using *type* as a suffix: "essay-type examinations" are essay examinations; "natural-type ice cream" is natural ice cream. Sneaky manufacturers make "Italian-type cheese," implying that their domestic cheese is imported and at the same time protecting themselves against charges of misrepresentation.

unique The only one of its kind. Someone or something therefore cannot be "rather unique" or "very unique" or "somewhat unique." Instead of saying "rather unique," say *rare*, or *unusual*, or *extraordinary*, or whatever seems to be the best word.

U.S., United States Generally, *United States* is preferable to *U.S.*, except when used as an adjective (U.S. Air Force).

usage Don't use *usage* where *use* will do, as in "Here Vonnegut completes his usage of dark images." *Usage* properly implies a customary practice that has created a standard: "Usage has eroded the difference between *shall* and *will.*"

use of The use of *use of* is usually unnecessary. "Through the use of setting he conveys a sense of foreboding" may be reduced to "The setting conveys . . ." or "His setting conveys. . . ."

utilize, utilization Often inflated for *use* and *using*, as in "The infirmary has noted that it is sophomores who have most utilized the counseling service." But when one means "find an effective use for," *utilize* may be the best word, as in (here we borrow from *The American Heritage Dictionary*), "The teachers were unable to utilize the new computers," where *use* might wrongly suggest that the teachers could not operate the computers.

verbal Often used where *oral* would be more exact. *Verbal* simply means "expressed in words," and thus a *verbal agreement* may be either written or spoken. If you mean spoken, call it an *oral agreement.*

verse, stanza A *verse* is a single line of a poem; a *stanza* is a group of lines, commonly bound by a rhyme scheme. But in speaking or writing about songs, usage sanctions *verse* for *stanza*, as in "Second verse, same as the first."

viable A term from physiology, meaning "capable of living" (for example, referring to a fetus at a stage of its development). Now pretentiously used and overused, especially by politicians and journalists, to mean "workable," as in "a viable presidency." Avoid it.

was, were Use the subjunctive form—*were* (rather than *was*)—in expressing a wish ("I wish I were younger") and in "if-clauses" that are contrary to fact ("If I were rich," "If I were you . . .").

we If you mean *I*, say *I*. Not "The first fairy tale we heard" but "the first fairy tale I heard." (But of course *we* is appropriate in some statements: "We have all heard fairy tales"; "If we look closely at the evidence, we can probably agree that. . . .") The rule: Don't use *we* as a disguise for *I*. See pages 91–93.

well See *good.*

well known, widely known Athletes, performers, politicians, and such folk are not really *well known* except perhaps by a few of their friends and their relatives; use *widely known* if you mean they are known (however slightly) to many people.

which Often can be deleted. "Students are required to fill out scholarship applications which are lengthy" can be written "Students are required to fill out lengthy scholarship applications." Another example: "*The Tempest*, which is Shakespeare's last play, was written in 1611"; "*The Tempest*, Shakespeare's last play, was written in 1611," or "Shakespeare wrote his last play, *The Tempest*, in 1611." For the distinction between *which* and *that*, see also the entry on *that.*

while Best used in a temporal sense, meaning "during the time": "While I was speaking, I suddenly realized that I didn't know what I was talking about." While it is not wrong to use *while* in a nontemporal sense, meaning "although" (as at the beginning of this sentence), it is better to use *although* in order to avoid any ambiguity. Note the ambiguity in: "While he was fond of movies he chiefly saw westerns." Does it mean "Although he was fond of movies," or does it mean "During the time when he was fond of movies"? Another point: Do not use *while* if you mean *and;* "First-year students take English 1-2, while sophomores take English 10-11" (substitute *and* for *while*).

who, whom Strictly speaking, *who* must be used for subjects, even when they look like objects: "He guessed who would be chosen." (Here *who* is the subject of the clause "who would be chosen.") *Whom* must be used for the objects of a verb, verbal (gerund, participle), or preposition: "Whom did she choose?"; "Whom do you want me to choose?"; "To whom did he show it?" We may feel stuffy in writing "Whom did she choose?" or "Whom are you talking about?" but to use *who* is certain to annoy some reader. Often you can avoid the dilemma by rewriting: "Who was chosen?"; "Who is the topic of conversation?" See also the entry on *that.*

whoever, whomever The second of these is the objective form. It is often incorrectly used as the subject of a clause. Incorrect: "Open the class to whomever wants to take it." The object of "to" is not "whomever" but is the entire clause—"whoever wants to take it"— and of course "whoever" is the subject of "wants."

who's, whose The first is a contraction of *who is* ("I'm everybody who's nobody"). The second is a possessive pronoun: "Whose book is it?" "I know whose it is."

will, would See *shall* and also *would.*

would "I would think that" is a wordy version of "I think that." (On the mistaken use of *would of* for *would have*, see also the entry on *of.*)

you In relatively informal writing, *you* is ordinarily preferable to the somewhat stiff *one:* "If you are addicted to cigarettes, you may find it helpful to join Smokenders." (Compare: "If one is addicted to cigarettes, one may. . . .") But because the direct address of *you* may sometimes descend into nagging, it is usually better to write: "Cigarette addicts may find it helpful. . . ." Certainly a writer (you?) should not assume that the reader is guilty of vices ("You should not molest children") unless the essay is clearly aimed at an audience that admits to these vices, say a pamphlet directed to child molesters who are seeking help. Thus, it is acceptable to say, "If you are a poor speller," but it is not acceptable to say, to the general reader, "You should improve your spelling"; the reader's spelling may not need improvement. And avoid *you* when the word cannot possibly apply to the reader: "A hundred years ago you were faced with many diseases that now have been eradicated." Something like "A hundred years ago people were faced . . ." is preferable.

your, you're The first is a possessive pronoun ("your book"); the second is a contraction of *you are* ("You're mistaken").

CHAPTER THIRTEEN

DOCUMENTING SOURCES

Documentation

One purpose of documentation is to enable your readers to retrace your steps, to find your source and to read what you read—whether you read it in the library, on the Internet, or in your local newspaper. To make this possible, you must give your readers enough information to locate and identify each source you cite. For books, this information generally includes the following:

- Author
- Title
- Publisher
- Date and place of publication
- Page numbers

Electronic sources require this information (at minimum):

- Site address
- Date on which you accessed the information

The way this information is presented varies from discipline to discipline: Sociologists, for example, present the date of publication more prominently than do historians; engineers usually list their sources by number at the end of a research work and in order of their appearance in the text; and literary critics list sources alphabetically by authors' names. In the following pages we discuss in detail two of the most widely used systems of documentation: the Modern Language Association (MLA) and the American Psychological Association (APA). At the end of this chapter we provide information on where you can obtain guidance on other systems of documentation.

MLA Format

Citations Within the Text

Brief parenthetic citations within the body of the essay are made clear by a list of your sources, entitled Works Cited, appended to the essay. Thus, an item in your list of Works Cited will clarify such a sentence in your essay as

> According to Angeline Goreau, Aphra Behn in her novels continually contradicts "the personal politics she had defended from the outset of her career as a writer" (252).

This citation means that the words inside the quotation marks appear on page 252 of a source written by Goreau, which will be listed in Works Cited. More often than not the parenthetic citation appears at the end of a sentence, as in the example just given, but it can appear elsewhere in the sentence. Its position will depend in part on your ear, and in part on the requirement that you point clearly to the place where your source's idea ends and your point begins. (In the following example, the idea that follows the parenthetic citation is not Gardiner's, but the writer's own.)

> Judith Kegan Gardiner, on the other hand, acknowledges that Behn's work "displays its conflicts with patriarchal authority" (215), conflicts that appear most notably in the third volume of Love Letters.

Seven points must be made about these examples:

1. Quotation marks: The closing quotation mark appears after the last word of the quotation, *not* after the parenthetic citation. Since the citation is not part of the quotation, the citation is not included within the quotation marks.

2. Omission of words (ellipsis): If the quoted words are merely a phrase, as in the example above, you do not need to indicate (by an ellipsis—three spaced periods) that you are omitting material before or after the quotation. But if the quotation is longer than a phrase, and is not a complete sentence, you must use an ellipsis to indicate that you are omitting material. If you omit material from the middle of a sentence, indicate the omission with an ellipsis. If you omit material from the end of the sentence, indicate the omission with an ellipsis followed by a period, the sentence period. If you omit a whole sentence, the sentence period comes first, followed by an ellipsis. If you omit material from the middle of one sentence to the end of another, the sentence period *follows* the ellipsis. If the ellipsis is followed by a parenthetical citation, the sentence period follows the parenthesis. (For more on ellipses, see page 204.)

3. Addition of words: On occasion, you'll need to add a word or two to a quotation in order to clarify its meaning. If you must make such an addition—and such additions should be kept to a minimum because they're distracting—enclose the word or words in square brackets, *not* parentheses. If the quotation contains a misspelling or other error, transcribe it as it appears in the source, and insert the word *sic* (Latin for "thus," as in "thus the word appears in the source; it's not *my* error") in italics and in square brackets: [*sic*]. Smith writes, "Jane Austin [*sic*] led an uneventful life."

4. Punctuation with parenthetic citations: Look again at the two examples given a moment ago. Notice that if you follow a quotation with a parenthetic citation, any necessary period, semicolon, or comma *follows* the parenthetic citation. In the first example (citing page 252 in Goreau), a period follows the citation; in the second (citing page 215 in Gardiner), a comma. In the next example, notice that the comma follows the citation.

```
Johnson insists that "these poems can be interpreted

as Tory propaganda" (72), but his brief analysis is

not persuasive.
```

If, however, the quotation itself uses a question mark or an exclamation mark, this mark of punctuation appears *within* the closing quotation mark; even so, a period follows the parenthetic citation.

```
Jenkins-Smith is the only one to suggest doubt:

"How can we accept such a superficial reading of

these works?" (178). He therefore rejects the

entire argument.
```

5. Two or more titles by one author: If your list of Works Cited includes more than one work by an author, you will have to give additional information (either in your comment or within the parenthetic citation) in order to indicate *which* of the titles you are referring to. We will go further into this on page 308.

6. Long (or "block") quotations: We have been talking about short quotations, which are not set off but are embedded within your own sentences. Long quotations, usually defined as more than three lines of poetry or four lines of prose, are indented ten spaces from the left, as in the example below.

```
Janet Todd explains Behn's reverence for the Stuart

monarchy:

          She  was  a  passionate  supporter  of  both

          Charles  II  and  James  II  as  not  simply

          rulers  but  as  sacred  majesties,  god-kings

          on  earth,  whose  private  failings  in  no  way

          detracted  from  their  high  office.  .  .  .

          For  her,  royalty  was  not  patriarchal

          anachronism  as  it  would  be  for  liberated

          women  writers  a  hundred  years  on,  but  a

          mystical  state.  (73)
```

In introducing a long quotation, keep in mind that a reader will have trouble reading a sentence that consists of a lead-in, a long quotation, and then a continuation of your own sentence. It's better to have a short lead-in ("Janet Todd explains Behn's reverence for the Stuart monarchy"), and then set off a long quotation that is a complete sentence or group of sentences and therefore ends with a period. To set off a quotation, begin on a new line, double-space and indent ten spaces (or one inch) from the left margin, and do *not* enclose the quotation within quotation marks. Put a period at the end of the quotation (since the quotation is a complete sentence or group of sentences and is not embedded within a longer sentence of your own), hit the space bar twice, and then, on the same line, give the citation in parentheses. Do *not* put a period after the parenthetic citation that follows a long quotation.

7. Citing a summary or a paraphrase: Even if you don't quote a source directly, but use its point in a paraphrase or a summary, you will give a citation:

```
Goreau notes (89-90) that Behn participated in pub-

lic life and in politics not only as a writer: In the

1660s she went to Antwerp as a spy for Charles II.
```

The basic point, then, is that the system of in-text citation gives the documentation parenthetically. Notice that in all but one of the previous examples the author's name is given in the student's text (rather than within the parenthetic citation). But there are several other ways of giving the citation, and we shall now look at them.

Author and Page Number in Parenthetic Citation

```
Heroines who explore their own individuality (with

varying degrees of success and failure) abound in

Chopin's work (Shinn 358).
```

It doesn't matter whether you summarize (as in this example) or quote directly; the parenthetic citation means that your source is page 358 of a work by Shinn, listed in Works Cited, at the end of your essay.

Title and Page Number in Parentheses   If, as we mentioned earlier, your list of Works Cited includes two or more titles by an author, you cannot in the text simply give a name and a page reference; the reader would not know to which of the titles you are referring. Let's assume that Works Cited includes two items by Larzer Ziff. In a sentence in your essay you might specify one title, saying something like, "For example, Larzer Ziff, in *The American 1890's*, claims. . . ." If, however, you do not mention the title in your lead-in, you will have to give the title (in a shortened form) in the parenthetic citation:

```
Larzer Ziff, for example, claims that the novel

"rejected the family as the automatic equivalent of

feminine self-fulfillment" (American 175).
```

Notice in this example that *American* is a short title for Ziff's book *The American 1890's: Life and Times of a Lost Generation.* The full title is given in Works Cited, as is the title of another work by Ziff, but the short title in the parenthetic citation is enough to direct the reader to page 175 of the correct source named in Works Cited.

Notice also that when a short title and a page reference are given in parentheses, a comma is *not* used after the title.

Author, Title, and Page Number in Parentheses We have just seen that if Works Cited includes two or more works by an author, and if in your lead-in you do not specify which work you are at the moment making use of, you will have to give the title as well as the page number in parentheses. Similarly, if for some reason you do not in your lead-in mention the name of the author, you will have to add this bit of information to the parenthetic citation, thus:

```
At least one critic has claimed that the novel

"rejected the family as the automatic equivalent of

feminine self-fulfillment" (Ziff, American 175).
```

Notice, again, that a comma does *not* separate the title from the page reference; but notice, too, that a comma *does* separate the author's name from the title. (Don't ask us why; ask the Modern Language Association. Or just obey orders.)

A Government Document or a Work of Corporate Authorship Treat the issuing body as the author. Thus, you will probably write something like this:

```
In Food Resources Today, the Commission on Food Con-

trol, concludes that there is no danger (36-37).
```

A Work by Two or Three Authors If a work is by *two or three authors*, give their names, either in the parenthetic citation (the first example below) or in a lead-in (the second example):

```
Where the two other siblings strive compulsively

either to correct or create problems, the sibling in

the middle passively escapes from her painful family
```

> situation by withdrawing into herself (Seixas and Youcha 48-49).

or

> Barnet, Bellanca, and Stubbs suggest that the most efficient way to learn about your library's on-line resources is to consult a reference librarian (365).

If there are more than *three authors*, give the last name of the first author, followed by "et al." (an abbreviation for *et alii*, Latin for "and others"):

> Gardner et al. found that . . .

or

> Sometimes even higher levels are found (Gardner et al. 83).

Parenthetic Citation of an Indirect Source (Citation of Material That Itself Was Quoted or Summarized in Your Source) Suppose you are reading a book by Jones, and she quotes Smith, and you wish to use Smith's material. Your citation will be to Jones—the source you are using—but of course you cannot attribute Smith's words to Jones. You will have to make it clear that you are quoting not Jones but Smith, and so your parenthetic citation will look like this:

> (qtd. in Jones 84-85)

Parenthetic Citation of Two or More Works A semicolon, followed by a space, is used to separate two sources:

> Some scholars have speculated that Poe died of rabies, not alcoholism (Walk 44; Hayward 173).

A Work in More Than One Volume This is a bit tricky.

1. If you have used only one volume, in Works Cited you will specify the volume, and so in your parenthetic in-text citation you will need to give only a page number—as most of our examples illustrate.

2. If you have used more than one volume, your parenthetic citation will have to specify the volume as well as the page:

```
Landsdale  points  out  that  nitrite  combines  with

hemoglobin to form a pigment which cannot carry oxy-

gen (2: 370).
```

The reference is to page 370 of volume 2 of a work by Landsdale.

3. If, however, you are citing not a page but an entire volume—let's say volume 2—your parenthetic citation would be

```
(vol. 2)
```

Or, if you did not name the author in your lead-in, it would be

```
(Landsdale, vol. 2)
```

Notice also some other points:

- When citing a volume and page, the volume number, like the page number, is given in arabic (not roman) numerals.
- The volume number is followed by a colon, then a space, then the page number.
- Abbreviations such as "vol." and "p." and "pp." are *not* used, except when citing a volume number without a page number, as illustrated in the last two examples.

An Anonymous Work   For an anonymous work, give the title in your lead-in, or give it in a shortened form in your parenthetic citation:

```
Official Guide to Food Standards includes a statis-

tical table on nitrates (362).
```

or

```
A  statistical  table  on  nitrites  is  available

(Official Guide 362).
```

But double-check to make sure that the work is truly anonymous. Some encyclopedias, for example, give the authors' names quietly. If initials follow the article, these are the initials of the author's name. Check the alphabetic list of authors given at the front or back of the encyclopedia.

A Literary Work   Because classic works of literature are widely available, and your readers may have at hand editions different from the one that you have read, you can help them locate the material (if they wish to check it) by giving information—for instance, a chapter number—in addition to a page reference. The following forms are customary.

1. A novel. In parentheses give the page number of the edition you specify in Works Cited, followed by a semicolon, a space, and the relevant additional helpful information, such as the chapter number, or the book number (some novels are divided into "books," which themselves are then divided into chapters).

```
Chopin in The Awakening describes the Pontelliers'

house as "charming" (69; ch. XVII).
```

or

```
George Eliot characterizes Glegg effectively when in

The Mill on the Floss she says that his "ordinary

tone" was one of "sharp questioning" (235; bk 3,

ch. 4).
```

2. A play. Most instructors want the act, scene, and (if the lines are numbered) line numbers, rather than a page reference, thus:

```
The  Ghost,  in  his  first  encounter  with  Hamlet,

speaks of "Murder most foul" (1.5.28).
```

This reference is to line 28 in the fifth scene of the first act.

If you are quoting a few words within a sentence of your own, immediately after closing the brief quotation give the citation (enclosed within parentheses), and, if your sentence ends with the quotation, put the period after the closing parenthesis.

```
That Macbeth fully understands that killing Duncan

is not a manly act but a villainous one is clear

from his words to Lady Macbeth: "I dare do all that

may become a man" (1.7.46). Moreover, even though he

goes on to kill Duncan, he does not go on to deceive

himself into thinking that his act was noble.
```

If, however, your sentence continues beyond the citation, after the parenthetic citation put whatever punctuation may be necessary (for instance, a comma may be needed), complete your sentence, and end it with a period.

```
This is clear from his words, "I dare do all that

does become a man" (1.7.46), and he never loses his

awareness of true manliness.
```

3. A poem. Preferences vary, and you can't go wrong in citing the page, but for a poem longer than, say, a sonnet (fourteen lines), most instructors find it useful if students cite the line numbers, in parentheses, after the quotations. In your first use, preface the numerals with "line" or "lines" (not in quotation marks, of course); in subsequent citations simply give the numerals. For very long poems that are divided into books, such as Homer's *Odyssey*, give the page, a semicolon, a space, the book number, and the line number(s). The following example refers to page 327 of a title listed in Works Cited; it goes on to indicate that the passage occurs in the ninth book of the poem, lines 130 to 135.

```
(327; 9.130-35)
```

Long quotations (more than three lines of poetry) are indented ten spaces. As we explained on page 305, if you give a long quotation, try to give one that can correctly be concluded with a period. After the period, hit the space bar three times, and then, on the same line, give the citation in parentheses. As good an example as any of the absurdity and yet the pathos of T. S. Eliot's Prufrock are these line, from near the end of the poem:

> Shall I part my hair behind? Do I dare to eat a peach?
> I shall wear white flannel trousers, and walk upon the beach.
> I have heard the mermaids singing, each to each.
> I do not think that they will sing to me. (122–25)

Notice that the period here is given at the end of the quotation, *not* after the parenthetic citation of lines 122–25.

A Personal Interview   Probably you won't need a parenthetic citation, because you'll say something like

```
Cyril Jackson, in an interview, said . . .
```

or

```
According to Cyril Jackson . . .
```

and when your readers turn to Works Cited, they will see that Jackson is listed, along with the date of the interview. But if you do not mention the source's name in the lead-in, you will have to provide it within parentheses:

```
It has been estimated that chemical additives earn

the drug companies well over five hundred million

dollars annually (Jackson).
```

Lectures   If you use in your research essay a distinctive phrase, idea, or piece of information from a class lecture or discussion, you'll want to give the speaker credit for it. If you give a signal phrase such as "In a lecture at NYU, Jones said," the parenthetic citation should include only the date of the lecture; if you don't give a signal phrase, then include the speaker's name, followed by a comma, followed by the date:

```
The Museum world today, is "now parts of show biz"

(Orlofsky, Sep. 20, 2004).
```

The entry for the lecture on the Works Cited list will contain the title of the lecture—if there is one—and the place it was given.

Electronic Sources   Follow the format for print sources. In some cases, page numbers will be available; in others, paragraphs will be numbered; in still others; no number at all will be given. Use what you have, indicating the author's name or the title of the source where necessary, as determined by context. When giving paragraph numbers, use the abbreviation "par." (Use a comma to separate the abbreviation from the author's name or title.)

```
One lawyer argued that Monica Lewinsky was nowhere

near the White House that day (Hedges, pars. 2-3).
```

A Note on Footnotes in an Essay Using Parenthetic Citations

There are two reasons for using footnotes in an essay that chiefly uses parenthetic citations.

1. In a research paper you will of course draw on many sources, but in other kinds of papers you may be using only one source, and yet within the paper you may often want to specify a reference to a page or (for poetry) a line number, or (for a play) to an act, scene, and line number. In such a case, to append a page headed Work Cited, with a single title, is silly; it is better to use a single footnote when you first allude to the source. Such a note can run something like this

```
¹All references are to Mary Shelley, Frankenstein,

afterword by Harold Bloom (New York: Signet, 1965).
```

2. Footnotes can also be used in another way in an essay that documents sources by giving parenthetic citations. If you want to include some material that might seem intrusive in the body of the essay, you may relegate it to a footnote. For example, in a footnote you might translate a quotation given in a foreign language, or in a footnote you might write a paragraph—a sort of mini-essay—in which you offer an amplification of some point. By putting the amplification in a footnote you are signaling to the reader that it is dispensable; it is, so to speak, thrown in as something extra, something relevant but not essential to your argument.

A raised arabic numeral indicates in the body of your text that you are adding a footnote at this point. (The "insert" function of your word-processing program will insert both the raised numeral and the text of your footnote in the appropriate places in your essay; simply click "insert" at the point in the text where you want the footnote to appear, and follow the program's instructions.)

```
Joachim Jeremias's The Parables of Jesus is probably

the best example of this sort of book.¹
```

Usually the number is put at the end of a sentence, immediately after the period, but put it earlier if clarity requires you to do so.

```
Helen Cam¹ as well as many lesser historians held

this view.
```

The List of Works Cited

Your parenthetic documentation consists of references that become meaningful when the reader consults a list entitled Works Cited, given at the end of your essay. We present sample entries below, but see also the list of Works Cited at the end of the documented essay presented in Chapter 10, "Writing the Research Essay" (pp. 212–47).

The list of Works Cited continues the pagination of the essay; if the last page of text is 10, then the list begins on page 11. Your last name and the page number will appear in the upper-right corner, half an inch from the top of the sheet. Next, type "Works Cited," centered, one inch from the top, then double-space and type the first entry. Here are the governing conventions.

Alphabetic Order

1. Arrange the list alphabetically by author, with the author's last name first.

2. List an anonymous work alphabetically under the first word of the title, or under the second word if the first word is *A, An,* or *The,* or a foreign equivalent.

3. If your list includes two or more works by one author, the work whose title comes earlier in the alphabet precedes the work whose title comes later in the alphabet.

Form on the Page

1. Begin each entry flush with the left margin. If an entry runs to more than one line, indent five spaces for each succeeding line of the entry.
2. Double-space each entry, and double-space between entries.

From here on, things get complicated. We will focus on four categories:

- Books (p. 315)
- Articles in journals and newspapers, and interviews and lectures. (p. 322)
- Films, television and radio programs (p. 324)
- Electronic sources (pp. 326–30).

The forms for books are as follows.

Author's Name   Note that the last name is given first, but otherwise the name is given as on the title page. Do not substitute initials for names written out on the title page. (Books by more than one author are treated later in this discussion, pp. 317–18.)

If your list includes two or more works by an author, the author's name is not repeated for the second title but is represented by three hyphens followed by a period and two spaces. When you give two or more works by the same author, the sequence is determined by the alphabetic order of the titles, as in the example below, listing two books by Blassingame, where *Black* precedes *Slave*.

> Bishop, Robert. <u>American Folk Sculpture</u>. New York:
>
>   Dutton, 1974.
>
> Blassingame, John W. <u>Black New Orleans, 1860-1880</u>.
>
>   Chicago: U of Chicago P, 1973.
>
> ---. <u>The Slave Community: Plantation Life in the</u>
>
>   <u>Antebellum South</u>. Rev. ed. New York: Oxford
>
>   UP, 1979.
>
> Danto, Arthur. <u>Embodied Meanings</u>. New York:
>
>   Farrar, 1994.

We have already discussed the treatment of an anonymous work; in a few moments we will discuss books by more than one author, government documents, and works of corporate authorship.

Title of Book Take the title from the title page, not from the cover or the spine, but disregard any unusual typography—for instance, the use of only capital letters, or the use of & for *and*. Italicize or underline the title and subtitle. (The MLA recommends underlining rather than italicizing in texts submitted in courses or for publication because underlining may be more visible to readers.) If you choose to underline the title, use one continuous underline, but do not underline the period that concludes this part of the entry.) Example:

`Frankenstein: Or, The Modern Prometheus.`

A peculiarity: Italicizing is used to indicate the title of a book, but if a title of a book itself includes the title of a book (for instance, a book about Mary Shelley's *Frankenstein* might include the title of her novel in its own title), the title-within-the-title is neither italicized nor underlined. Thus the title would be given as (if italicized)

`The Endurance of Frankenstein`

If it were underlined, it would be

`The Endurance of Frankenstein`

Place of Publication, Publisher, and Date For the place of publication, give the name of the city (you can usually find it either on the title page or on the copyright page, which is the reverse of the title page). If several cities are listed, give only the first. If the city is not likely to be widely known, or if it may be confused with another city of the same name (for instance, Cambridge, Massachusetts, and Cambridge, England), add the abbreviated name of the state or country (Cambridge, MA, or Cambridge, Eng.).

The name of the publisher is shortened. Usually the first word is enough (Random House becomes Random; Little, Brown and Co. becomes Little), but if the first word is a first name, such as in Alfred A. Knopf, the surname (Knopf) is used instead. University presses are abbreviated thus: Yale UP, U of Chicago P, State U of New York P.

The date of publication of a book is given when known; if no date appears on the book, write "n.d." to indicate "no date," (without the quotation marks).

Here are sample entries, illustrating the points we have covered thus far:

> Douglas, Ann. The Feminization of American Culture.
>
> New York: Knopf, 1977.
>
> Early, Gerald. One Nation Under a Groove: Motown and
>
> American Culture. Hopewell, NJ: Echo, 1995.
>
> Feitlowitz, Marguerite. A Lexicon of Terror:
>
> Argentina and the Legacies of Torture. New
>
> York: Oxford UP, 1998.
>
> Frye, Northrop. Fables of Identity: Studies in
>
> Poetic Mythology. New York: Harcourt, 1963.
>
> ---. Fools of Time: Studies in Shakespearian
>
> Tragedy. Toronto: U of Toronto P, 1967.
>
> Kennedy, Paul. Preparing for the Twenty-First
>
> Century. New York: Random, 1993.

Notice that a period follows the author's name, and another period follows the title. If a subtitle is given, as it is for Feitlowitz's book, it is separated from the title by a colon and a space. A colon follows the place of publication, a comma follows the publisher, and a period follows the date.

A Book by More Than One Author   A book written by *two or three authors* is alphabetized under the last name of the first author named on the title page. The names of other authors are given after the first author's name (with last name first) in the normal order, *first name first*.

> Majors, Richard, and Janet Mancini Billson. Cool
>
> Pose: The Dilemmas of Black Manhood in
>
> America. Lexington, MA: Lexington, 1992.

Notice that a comma is put after the first name of the first author, separating it from the names that follow.

If there are *more than three authors*, give the name of only the first, and then add "et al." (Latin for "and others"), without the quotation marks.

> Belenky, Mary Field, et al. <u>Women's Ways of</u>
>
> <u>Knowing: The Development of the Self, Voice,</u>
>
> <u>and Mind</u>. New York: Basic Books, 1986.

Government Documents If the writer is not known, treat the government and the agency as the author. Most federal national documents are issued by the Government Printing Office in Washington (abbreviated to GPO).

> U. S. Congress. Office of Technology Assessment.
>
> <u>Computerized Manufacturing Automation</u>
>
> <u>Employment, Education and the Workplace</u>.
>
> Washington: GPO, 1984.

Works of Corporate Authorship Begin the citation with the corporate author, even if the same body is also the publisher, as in the first example:

> American Psychiatric Association. <u>Psychiatric</u>
>
> <u>Glossary</u>. Washington: American Psychiatric
>
> Association, 1984.
>
> Carnegie Council on Policy Studies in Higher
>
> Education. <u>Giving Youth a Better Chance:</u>
>
> <u>Options for Education, Work, and Service</u>. San
>
> Francisco: Jossey, 1980.

Republished Work After the title, give the date of original publication (it can usually be found on the copyright page of the reprint you are using), then a period, and then the place, publisher, and date of the edition you are using. The example indicates that Rourke's book was originally published in 1931 and that the student is using the Doubleday reprint of 1953.

Rourke, Constance. <u>American Humor</u>. 1931. Garden

City, NY: Doubleday, 1953.

A Book in Several Volumes

Friedel, Frank. <u>Franklin D. Roosevelt</u>. 4 vols.

Boston: Little, 1973.

If you have used more than one volume, in your essay you will (as we explained on pages 308–09) indicate a reference to, say, page 250 of volume 3 thus: (3: 250).

If, however, you have used only one volume of the set—let's say volume 3—in your entry in Works Cited write, after the period following the date, "Vol. 3," as in the next entry:

Friedel, Frank. <u>Franklin D. Roosevelt</u>. 4 vols.

Boston: Little, 1973. Vol. 3.

In this case, the parenthetic citation in the text will be to the page only, not to the volume and page, since a reader will understand that the page reference must be to this volume. But notice that in Works Cited, even though you say you used only volume 3, you also give the total number of volumes.

One Book with a Separate Title in a Set of Volumes   Sometimes a set of volumes with a title makes use also of a separate title for each book in the set. If you are listing such a book, use the following form:

Churchill, Winston. <u>The Age of Revolution</u>. Vol. 3

of <u>A History of the English-Speaking Peoples</u>.

New York: Dodd, 1957.

A Book with an Author and an Editor

Churchill, Winston, and Franklin D. Roosevelt. <u>The

Complete Correspondence</u>. 3 vols. Ed. Warren F.

Kimball. Princeton, NJ: Princeton UP, 1985.

Shakespeare, William. <u>The Sonnets</u>. Ed. William

Burto. New York: NAL, 1965.

If you are making use of the editor's introduction or other editorial material, rather than of the author's work, list the book under the name of the editor, rather than of the author, following the form given below for an introduction, foreword, or afterword.

A Revised Edition of a Book

> Hall, James. Dictionary of Subjects and Symbols in
>
> Art. 2nd ed. New York: Harper, 1979.

A Translated Book

> Allende, Isabel. The Stories of Eva Luna. Trans.
>
> Margaret Sayens Peden. New York: Atheneum,
>
> 1991.

But if you are discussing the translation itself, as opposed to the book, list the work under the translator's name:

> MacAdam, Alfred, trans. Family Portrait with
>
> Fidel: A Memoir. By Carlos Franqui. New York:
>
> Random, 1984.

An Introduction, Foreword, or Afterword

> Wolff, Cynthia Griffin. Introduction. The House Of
>
> Mirth. By Edith Wharton. New York: Penguin,
>
> 1985. vii–xxvi.

Usually a book with an introduction or some such comparable material is listed under the name of the author of the book (here Wharton), rather than under the name of the writer of the introduction (here Wolff), but if you are referring to the apparatus rather than to the book itself, use the form just given. The words *Introduction, Preface, Foreword,* and *Afterword* are neither enclosed within quotation marks nor underlined.

A Book with an Editor but No Author   Anthologies of literature fit this description, but here we have in mind a book of essays written by various people but collected by an editor (or editors), whose name appears on the collection.

> Baldick, Chris, ed. The Oxford Book of Gothic
>
> Tales. New York: Oxford UP, 1993.

A Work in a Volume of Works by One Author   The following entry indicates that a short work by Susan Sontag—an essay called "The Aesthetics of Science"—appears in a book by Sontag entitled *Styles of Radical Will*. Notice that the inclusive page numbers of the short work are cited—not merely page numbers that you may happen to refer to, but the page numbers of the entire piece.

> Sontag, Susan. "The Aesthetics of Science." In
>
> Styles of Radical Will. New York: Farrar,
>
> 1969. 3-34.

A Work in a Collection of Works by Several Authors   There are several possibilities here. Let's assume, for a start, that you have made use of one work in an anthology. In Works Cited, begin with the author (last name first) and title of the work you are citing, not with the name of the anthologist or the title of the anthology. Here is an entry for Coleridge's poem "Kubla Khan," found on pages 501–3 in the second volume of a two-volume anthology edited by David Damrosch and several others.

> Coleridge, Samuel Taylor. "Kubla Khan." The Longman
>
> Anthology of British Literature. Ed. David
>
> Damrosch et al. 2 vols. New York: Longman,
>
> 1999. 2: 501-3.

Now let's assume that during the course of your essay you refer to several works, rather than to only one work in this anthology. You can, of course, list each work in the form just given. Or you can have an entry in Works Cited for Damrosch's anthology, under Damrosch's name, and then in each entry for a work in the anthology you can eliminate some of the data by simply referring to Damrosch, thus:

> Coleridge, Samuel Taylor. "Kubla Khan." Damrosch
>
> 2: 501-3.

Again, this requires that you also list Damrosch's volume, thus:

> Damrosch, David, et al., eds. The Longman Anthology
>
> of British Literature. 2 vols. New York: Long-
>
> man, 1999.

The advantage of listing the anthology separately is that if you are using a dozen works from the anthology, you can shorten the dozen entries in Works Cited merely by adding one entry, that of the anthology itself. Notice, of course, that in the body of the essay you would still refer to Coleridge and to your other eleven authors, not to the editor of the anthology—but the entries in Works Cited will guide the reader to the book you have used.

A Book Review

> Vendler, Helen. Rev. of Essays on Style. Ed. Roger
>
> Fowler. Essays in Criticism 16 (1966): 457-63.

If the review has a title, give it between the period following the reviewer's name and "Rev."

If a review is anonymous, list it under the first word of the title, or under the second word if the first word is *A, An,* or *The*. If an anonymous review has no title, begin the entry with "Rev. of" and then give the title of the work reviewed; alphabetize the entry under the title of the work reviewed.

An Article or Essay—Not a Reprint—in a Collection   A book may consist of a collection (edited by one or more persons) of new essays by several authors. Here is a reference to one essay in such a book. (The essay, by Smith, occupies pages 178–94 in a collection edited by Lubiano.)

> Smith, David Lionel. "What Is Black Culture?"
>
> The House That Race Built. Ed. Wahneema
>
> Lubiano. New York: Vintage, 1998. 178-94.

An Article or Essay Reprinted in a Collection   The previous example (Smith's essay in Lubiano's collection) was for an essay written for a collection. But some collections reprint earlier material—for example, essays from journals, or chapters from books. The following example cites an essay that was originally printed in a book called *The Cinema of Alfred Hitchcock*. This essay has been reprinted in a later collection of essays on Hitchcock, edited by Arthur J. LaValley, and it was LaValley's collection that the student used.

> Bogdanovich, Peter. "Interviews with Alfred
>
> Hitchcock." The Cinema of Alfred Hitchcock.

New York: Museum of Modern Art, 1963. 15-18.

Rpt. in <u>Focus on Hitchcock</u>. Ed. Albert J.

LaValley. Englewood Cliffs, NJ: Prentice,

1972. 28-31.

The student has read Bogdanovich's essay or chapter, but not in Bogdanovich's book, where it occupied pages 15–18. The student actually read the essay on pages 28–31 in a collection of writings on Hitchcock, edited by LaValley. Details of the original publication—title, date, page numbers, and so forth—were found in LaValley's collection. Almost all editors will include this information, either on the copyright page or at the foot of the reprinted essay, but sometimes they do not give the original page numbers. In such a case, you need not give the original numbers in the entry.

Notice that the entry begins with the author and the title of the work you are citing (here, Bogdanovich's interviews), not with the name of the editor of the collection or the title of the collection. In the following example, the student used an essay by Arthur Sewell; the essay was originally on pages 53–56 in a book by Sewell entitled *Character and Society in Shakespeare*, but the student encountered the piece on pages 36–38 in a collection of essays, edited by Leonard Dean, on Shakespeare's *Julius Caesar*. Here is how the entry should run:

Sewell, Arthur. "The Moral Dilemma in Tragedy:

Brutus." <u>Character and Society in Shakespeare</u>.

Oxford: Clarendon, 1951. 53-56. Rpt. in

<u>Twentieth Century Interpretations of Julius</u>

<u>Caesar</u>. Ed. Leonard F. Dean. Englewood Cliffs,

NJ: Prentice, 1968. 36-38.

An Encyclopedia or Other Alphabetically Arranged Reference Work   The publisher, place of publication, volume number, and page number do *not* have to be given. For such works, list only the edition (if it is given) and the date.

For a *signed* article, begin with the author's last name. (If the article is signed with initials, check the volume for a list of abbreviations—it is

usually near the front, but it may be at the rear—which will say what the
initials stand for, and use the following form.)

> Messer, Thomas. "Picasso." Encyclopedia
>
> > Americana. 1998 ed.

For an *unsigned article*, begin with the title of the article.

> "Automation." The Business Reference Book. 1977 ed.
>
> "Picasso, Pablo (Ruiz y)." Encyclopaedia
>
> > Britannica: Macropaedia. 1985 ed.

A Film   Begin with the director's name (last name first), followed by
"dir." Next give the title of the film, underlined, then a period, two spaces,
the form of the recording (e.g., "videocasette," "DVD") the name of the
distributor, the date, and a period.

> Coppola, Sophia, dir. Lost in Translation. DVD.
>
> > Focus Features, 2003.

A Television or Radio Program

> Sixty Minutes. CBS. 31 Jan. 2001.

An Article in a Scholarly Journal   The title of the article is enclosed
within quotation marks, and the title of the journal is underlined to indicate italics.

Some journals are paginated consecutively—the pagination of the second issue begins where the first issue leaves off; but other journals begin
each issue with page 1. The forms of the citations differ slightly. Let's
look first at an article in a *journal that is paginated consecutively:*

> Julie Nelson Christoph. "Reconceiving Ethos in
>
> > Relation to the Personal: Strategies of
> >
> > Placement in Pioneer Women's Writing."
> >
> > College English 64 (2002): 660-79.

Christoph's article occupies pages 660–79 of volume 64, which was published in 2002. (Note that the volume number is followed by a space, and then by the year, in parentheses, and then by a colon, a space, and the page numbers of the entire article.) Because the journal is paginated consecutively, the issue number does *not* need to be specified.

For a *journal that begins each issue with page 1* (there will be four page 1's each year if such a journal is a quarterly), the issue number must be given. After the volume number, type a period and (without hitting the space bar) the issue number, as in the next example.

> Spillers, Hortense J. "Martin Luther King and the
>
> Style of the Black Sermon." The Black Scholar
>
> 3.1 (1971): 14-27.

Spillers's article appeared in the first issue of volume 3 of *The Black Scholar*.

An Article in a Weekly, Biweekly, or Monthly Publication The date and page numbers are given, but volume numbers and issue numbers are usually omitted for these publications. The following example is for an article in a weekly publication:

> Malcolm, Janet. "Gertrude Stein's War." New Yorker
>
> 2 June 2003: 58-81.

An Article in a Newspaper Because a newspaper usually consists of several sections, a section number or a capital letter may precede the page number. The example indicates that an article begins on page 1 of section 1 and is continued on a later page.

> Bennet, James. "Judge Cites Possible Breaches of
>
> Ethics Guidelines by Starr." New York Times 8
>
> Aug. 1998. sec. 1: 1.

An Interview The citation gives the name of the person you interviewed, the form of the interview ("personal," "telephone," "e-mail"), and the date.

> Curley, Michael. Personal interview. 7 Nov. 2003.

A Lecture   In addition to the date of the lecture and the name of the speaker, the citation should include the title of the presentation (if there is one) and the place it was given. If there is no title, use a descriptive word or phrase such as "class lecture," but do not use quotation marks. If the lecture was sponsored by a particular organization or group, give that information before the date.

> Cahill, Patricia A. Class lecture on Othello. Emory
>
>   Univ. 20 Sept. 2003.
>
> McNamara, Eileen. "Truth and Ethics in Writing."
>
>   The Writers Writing for a Living Lecture.
>
>   Wellesley College Writing Program, Wellesley,
>
>   MA. 10 Feb. 1999.

Portable Database Sources   Material obtained from a portable database, such as a CD-ROM, magnetic tape, or diskette, is treated like print material, but with one important difference: You must specify the physical form of the source. This information comes after the underlined title of the source, and before the city of publication.

> Database of African-American Poetry, 1760–1900.
>
>   CD-ROM. Alexandria, VA: Chadwyck-Healy, 1995.
>
> Gates, Henry Louis, and Kwame Anthony Appiah, eds.
>
>   Encarta Africana. CD-ROM. Redmond, WA:
>
>   Microsoft, 1999.

If the database is periodically published and updated, then some additional information is required. You must include the original date of publication of the material you're using, as well as the date of publication for the database. And if the source of the information is not also the distributor (the MLA publishes the CD-ROM version of the MLA International Bibliography, for example, but SilverPlatter distributes it), you must include the distributor's (or vendor's) name as well.

> Odygaard, Floyd D. P. "California's Collodion
>
>   Artist: The Images of William Dunniway."

> Military Images 1995 16.5: 14-19. America:
> History and Life on Disc. CD-ROM. ABC-Clio.
> Winter 1997-98.

On-line Sources Online sources are treated like books and articles, with four major (and many minor) exceptions:

- The **Internet address,** or URL, of the source is given in angle brackets at the end of the entry.
- The **date accessed**—the date on which *you* found the source—is included in the citation.
- **Page numbers** are included in the citation *only* if the source is paginated. (This is often the case with full-text online versions of books and journal articles, in which case the pagination follows that of the print source.)
- Sometime paragraphs are numbered; the citation gives **paragraph numbers** when the sources provides them.

The basic format for an online source is the same as that of a print source, given in the following order:

- Author
- Title
- Publication information (including date of original publication, if applicable)
- Page or paragraph numbers if available.

Then you give additional information—as much as is applicable and available—in the following order:

- Name of database, project, periodical, or site (underlined)
- Number of volume, issue, or version
- Date on which document was published in electronic source
- Name of site sponsor (if applicable)
- Date *you* consulted the material
- Internet address (or URL) in angle brackets. *Note:* The MLA suggests giving the address of the site's search page *instead of the URL* if the URL is very long and would be difficult to transcribe.

Again, keep in mind that one purpose of documentation is to enable your readers to retrace your steps. It may also be useful to keep in mind that like the Internet itself, guidelines for citing electronic sources are continually evolving. Our guidelines are based on the format given in the sixth edition of the *MLA Handbook for Writers of Research Papers* (2003).

Here are some examples:

1. Novel:

> Jewett, Sarah Orne. <u>The Country of the Pointed</u>
>
> <u>Firs</u>. 1910. <u>Bartleby Archive</u>. Columbia U.
>
> 6 Nov. 2003. <http://www.bartleby.com/
>
> 125/1.html>.

2. Journal article:

> Fluck, Winfried. " 'The American Romance' and the
>
> Changing Functions of the Imaginary."
>
> <u>New Literary History</u> 27.3 (1996): 415-57.
>
> <u>Project Muse</u>. JHU. 1 May 1998.
>
> <http://muse:jhu.edu:80/journals/
>
> new_literary_history/v27/27.3fluck.html>.

3. Journal article retrieved from database:

> Picker, John M. "The Victorian Aura of the Recorded
>
> Voice." <u>New Literary History</u> 32.3
>
> (2001):769-86. <u>JSTOR</u>. 11 Nov. 03 <http://
>
> 80-muse.jhu.edu.ezp2.harvard.edu/journals/
>
> new_literary_history/v032/32.3picker.html>.

4. Magazine article (from a print source):

> Murphy, K. "Do Food Additives Subtract from
>
> Health?" <u>Business Week</u> 6 May 1996: 140.

LexisNexis. 12 Nov. 2003 http://
80-web.lexisnexis.com.ezp2.harvard.edu/
universe/form/academic/s_guidednews.html

5. Article in online periodical (no print source):

Green, Laura. "Sexual Harassment Law: Relax and Try
to Enjoy It." Salon 3 March 1998. 20 Oct.
2003. <http://archive.salon.com/mwt/
feature/1998/03/cov_03featurea.html>.

6. Review retrieved from a database:

Sadovi, Carlos. "Working Class Hero." Rev. of
Shutter Island, by Dennis Lehane. Chicago
Sun-Times. 25 Apr. 03. LexisNexis. 11 Nov. 03
<http://80-web.lexis-nexis.com.ezp2.harvard.edu/
universe/form/academic/s_guidednews.html>

7. Article in reference work:

"Chopin, Kate." Encyclopædia Britannica. 2003.
Encyclopædia Britannica Online. 11 Nov. 2003
<http://www.search.eb.com/eb/
article?eu=84515>.

Reuben, Paul P. "Chapter 6: 1890-1910: Kate Chopin
(1851-1904)." PAL: Perspectives in American
Literature--A Research and Reference Guide. 20
March 2003. <http://www.csustan.edu/english/
reuben/pal/chap6/chopin.html>.

8. Personal Web site:

> Mendelsson, Jonathan. Homepage. 8 Jan. 1999.
> <http://www.mit.edu./~jrmendel/index.html>.

9. E-mail:

> Clineff, Kimberly. "Re: Margaret Mead's pho-
> tographs." E-mail to author. 4 May 2003.

10. Posting to a discussion list:

> Searls, Damion. "Re: Fiction Inspired by Woolf."
> VWOOLF@lists.acs.ohio-state.edu. Online
> posting. 30 Oct. 1998.

Although we have covered the most common sources, it is entirely possible that you will come across a source that does not fit any of the categories that we have discussed. For several hundred pages of explanation of these matters, covering the proper way to cite all sorts of troublesome sources, see Joseph Gibaldi, *MLA Handbook for Writers of Research Papers*, 6th ed. (New York: Modern Language Association of America, 2003).

Note: On pages 215–29 we reprint a student's research essay in MLA format.

APA Format

The MLA style is used chiefly by writers in the humanities. Writers in the social sciences and in business, education, and psychology commonly use a style developed by the American Psychological Association. In the following pages we give the chief principles of the APA style, but for full details the reader should consult the fifth edition of the *Publication Manual of the American Psychological Association* (2001).

A paper using the format prescribed by the American Psychological Association will contain brief parenthetical citations within the text and will end with a page headed "References," which lists all of the author's sources. This list of sources begins on a separate page, continuing the pagination of the last page of the essay itself. Thus, if the text of the essay ends on page 8, the first page of references is page 9.

Here are some general guidelines for formatting both the citations within the text and the list of references at the end of the essay.

Citations Within the Text

The APA style emphasizes the date of publication; the date appears not only in the list of references at the end of the paper but also within the paper itself, when you give a brief parenthetic citation of a source that you have quoted or summarized or in any other way used. Here is an example:

```
Statistics for church attendance are highly unreli-
able (Catherton, 1991, p. 17).
```

Note that unlike the MLA, the APA uses commas to separate elements inside the parenthetic citation, and that a "p." precedes the page number. The parenthetic citation may appear at the end of the sentence, or after the clause that contains the references, or after the author's name—whichever placement makes things clearest for the reader. In the example below, the date of publication appears immediately after the author's name; the page reference is given at the end of the sentence:

```
According to Catherton (1991), statistics for church
attendance are highly unreliable (p. 17).
```

The title of Catherton's book or article will be given in your list entitled References. By turning to the list, the reader will learn in what publication Catherton made this point.

A Summary of an Entire Work

```
Catherton (1991) concluded the opposite.
```

Or

```
Similar  views  are  easily  found  (Catherton,  1991;

Brinnin and Abse, 1992).
```

A Reference to a Page or Pages

```
Catherton  (1991,  p.  107)  argues  that  "church

attendance  is  increasing  but  religious  faith  is

decreasing."
```

A Reference to an Author Represented by More Than One Work Published in a Given Year in the References   As we explain in discussing the form of the material in References, if you list two or more works that an author published in the same year, the works are listed in alphabetic order, by the first letter of the title. The first work is labeled *a*, the second *b*, and so on. Here is a reference to the second work that Catherton published in 1997:

```
Boston is "a typical large Northern city" so far as

church attendance goes (Catherton, 1997b).
```

The List of References
Form on the Page
1. Begin each entry flush with the left margin, but if an entry runs to more than one line, indent five spaces for each succeeding line of the entry.
2. Double-space each entry, and double-space between entries.

Alphabetic Order
1. Arrange the list **alphabetically by author.**

2. Give the **author's last name first,** then the initial *only* of the first and of the middle name (if any).

3. If there is more than one author: Name all of the authors, again inverting the name (last name first) and giving only initials for first and middle names. (But do not invert the editor's name when the entry begins with the name of an author who has written an article in an edited book. See the example below, page 335, illustrating "A Work in a Collection of Essays.") When there are two or more authors, use an ampersand (&) before the name of the last author. When there are more than six authors, the seventh and all additional authors are indicated with "et al." Here is an example of an article in the seventh volume of a journal called *Journal of Experimental Social Psychology:*

> Berscheid, E., Hatfield, E., & Bohrnstett, G.
>
> (1971). Physical attractiveness and dating
>
> choice: A test of the matching hypothesis.
>
> Journal of Experimental Social Psychology 7,
>
> 173-89.

4. If there is more than one work by an author: List the works in the order of publication, the earliest first. If two works by an author were published in the same year, give them in alphabetic order by the first letter of the title, disregarding *A*, *An*, or *The*, and their foreign equivalents. Designate the first work as "a," the second as "b." Repeat the author's name at the start of each entry.

If the author of a work or works is also the coauthor of other works listed, list the single-author entries first, arranged by date. Following these, list the multiple-author entries, in a sequence determined alphabetically by the second author's name. Thus, in the example below, notice that the works Bem wrote unassisted are listed first, arranged by date, and when two works appear in the same year they are arranged alphabetically by title. These single-author works are followed by the multiple-author works, with the work written with Lenney preceding the work written with Martyna and Watson.

> Bem, S. L. (1974). The measurement of psychological
>
> androgyny. Journal of Consulting and Clinical
>
> Psychology, 42, 155-62.
>
> Bem, S. L. (1981a). The BSRI and gender schema
>
> theory: A reply to Spence and Helmreich.
>
> Psychological Review, 88, 369-71.
>
> Bem, S. L. (1981b). Gender schema theory: A
>
> cognitive account of sex typing. Psychological
>
> Review, 88, 354-64.

Bem, S. L., & Lenney, E. (1976). Sex-typing and the avoidance of cross-sex behavior. Journal of Personality and Social Psychology, 33, 48-54.

Bem, S. L., Martyna, W., & Watson, C. (1976). Sex-typing and androgyny: Further exploration of the expressive domain. Journal of Personality and Social Psychology, 34, 1016-23.

Form of Title

1. In references to books, capitalize only the first letter of the first word of the title (and of the subtitle, if any) and capitalize proper nouns. Italicize the complete title and type a period after it.

2. In references to articles in periodicals or in edited books, capitalize only the first letter of the first word of the article's title (and subtitle, if any), and all proper nouns. Do not put the title within quotation marks. Type a period after the title of the article. For the title of the journal, and the volume and page numbers, see the next instruction.

3. In references to periodicals, capitalize all important words, as you would usually do. (Note that the rule for the titles of periodicals differs from the rule for books and articles.) Give the volume number in arabic numerals, and underline it. Do *not* use *vol.* before the number, and do not use *p.* or *pp.* before the page numbers.

Sample References
A Book by One Author

Lancaster, R. M. (2003). The trouble with nature: Sex in science and popular culture. Berkeley: University of California Press.

A Book by More Than One Author

Spence, J. T., & Helmreich, R. L. (1978). Masculinity and femininity. Austin: University of Texas Press.

A Collection of Essays

> Bhabha, H. K. (Ed.). (1990). <u>Nation and narration.</u>
>
> London: Routledge.

A Work in a Collection of Essays

> Rogers, B. (1985). The Atlantic alliance. In W. P.
>
> Bundy (Ed.). <u>The nuclear controversy</u> (pp.
>
> 41-52). New York: New American Library.

Government Documents If the writer is not known, treat the government and the agency as the author. Most federal documents are issued by the Government Printing Office in Washington.

> United States Congress. Office of Technology
>
> Assessment (1984). <u>Computerized manufacturing</u>
>
> <u>automation: Employment, education, and the</u>
>
> <u>workplace.</u> Washington, DC: U.S. Government
>
> Printing Office.

An Article in a Journal That Paginates Each Issue Separately

> Swinton, E. (1993, Winter). New wine in old casks:
>
> Sino-Japanese and Russo-Japanese war prints.
>
> <u>Asian Art,</u> 27-49.

The publication is issued four times a year, each issue containing a page 27. It is necessary, therefore, to tell the reader that this article appears in the winter issue.

An Article in a Journal with Continuous Pagination

> Herdt, G. (1991). Representations of homosexuality.
>
> <u>Journal of the History of Sexuality, 1,</u>
>
> 481-504.

An Article from a Monthly or Weekly Magazine

> Chelminsky, R. (2003, April). The Curse of Count
>
> Dracula. <u>Smithsonian</u>, p. 110.

An Article in a Newspaper

> Perry, T. (1993, 16 February). Election to give
>
> Latinos new political clout in San Diego. <u>Los</u>
>
> <u>Angeles Times</u>, sec. A, p. 3.

Note: If no author is given, simply begin with the article title, followed by the date in parentheses.

A Book Review

> Bayme, S. (1993). Tradition or modernity? [Review of
>
> Neil Gillman, <u>Sacred fragments: Recovering the-</u>
>
> <u>ology for the modern Jew.</u>] Judaism, 42, 106–13.

Bayme is the reviewer, not the author of the book. The book under review is called *Sacred fragments: Recovering theology for the modern Jew*, but the review, published in volume 42 of a journal called *Judaism*, had its own title, "Tradition or Modernity?"

Electronic Sources References to electronic sources generally follow the format for printed sources and include the following information:

- Author
- Year of publication (in parentheses)
- Title (and edition, if applicable)

The retrieval statement is given next. This includes the following:

- Date retrieved
- Name and/or the address of the source

(Note that the period does *not* come at the end of an Internet address.)

The examples below follow guidelines set forth in the fifth edition of the *Publication Manual of the American Psychological Association* (2001).

1. Professional or government site:

> Edlefsen, M., & Brewer, M. S. (no date).
>
> Nitrates/nitrites. Retrieved May 6, 2003, from
>
> The National Food Safety Database:
>
> http://www.foodsafety.org/il/il089.htm
>
> National Cancer Institute (1996, June). NCI fact
>
> sheet. Food additives. Retrieved May 4, 2003,
>
> from http://nisc8a.upenn.edu/pdg_html/6/
>
> eng/600037.html

2. Encyclopedia article:

> Muckraker (journ.). (1994–1998). In Britannica
>
> Online. Retrieved January 2, 2003, from
>
> http://www.eb.com:180cgibin/g?DocF=index/mu/
>
> ckr.html

3. Newspaper article:

> Legator, M., & Daniel, A. (1995). Reproductive
>
> systems can be harmed by toxic exposure.
>
> Galveston County Daily News. Retrieved May 6,
>
> 2003, from http://www.utmb.edu/toxics/
>
> newsp.htm#canen
>
> Warrick, P. (1994, June 8). A frank discussion. Los
>
> Angeles Times, E1. Retrieved May 6, 2003, from
>
> LexisNexis.

4. Journal article:

> Tollefson, C. (1995, May 29). Stability preserved;
> preservatives; food additives '95. <u>Chemical</u>
> <u>Marketing Reporter</u> 247(22) SR28. Retrieved May
> 6, 2003, from LexisNexis.

5. Book:

> Riis, J. (1890). <u>How the other half lives</u>. New
> York: Charles Scribner's Sons [Electronic
> Version]. David Phillips. Retrieved September
> 14, 2003, from http://www.cis.edu/amstud/
> inforev/riis/ch#3/html

A Note on Other Systems of Documentation

The MLA style is commonly used in the humanities, and the APA style is commonly used in the social sciences, but many other disciplines use their own styles. The following handbooks discuss the systems used in some other disciplines.

Biology

Council of Biology Editors, Style Manual Committee. *Scientific Style and Format: CBE Style Manual for Authors, Editors, and Publishers in the Biological Sciences.* 6th ed. New York: Cambridge University Press, 1994.

Chemistry

American Chemical Society. *ACS Style Guide: A Manual for Authors and Editors.* 2nd ed. Washington, DC: American Chemical Society, 1997.

Geology

U.S. Geological Survey. *Suggestions to Authors of the Reports of the United States Geological Survey.* 8th ed. Washington, DC: GPO, Department of the Interior, 1997.

Law

The Bluebook: A Uniform System of Citation. 16th ed. Cambridge, MA: Harvard Law Review Association, 1996.

Mathematics

American Mathematical Society. *A Manual for Authors of Mathematical Papers.* 8th ed. Providence, RI: American Mathematical Society, 1990.

Medicine

American Medical Association. *Manual of Style.* 9th ed. Acton, MA: Publishing Sciences Group, 1997.

Physics

American Institute of Physics. *Style Manual for Guidance in the Preparation of Papers.* 4th ed. New York: American Institute of Physics, 1990.

CHAPTER FOURTEEN

PREPARING THE MANUSCRIPT

I love being a writer. What I can't stand is
the paperwork.

—*Peter De Vries*

Basic Manuscript Form

When you submit a piece of writing to your instructor or to anyone else, make sure it looks good. You want to convey the impression that you care about what you've written, that you've invested yourself and your time in it, that the details matter to you.

Much of what follows is ordinary academic procedure. Unless your instructor specifies something different, you can adopt these principles as a guide.

1. Print your essay on $8\frac{1}{2}$-by-11-inch paper of good weight. Use fresh, plain white paper; don't use the reverse sides of an old draft or lab report; avoid fancy or colored paper.

2. Make sure that the printer has enough ink and that the print is dark and clear. One sure way to irritate your instructor is to turn in an essay with nearly invisible print.

3. Do not use a fancy font. Unless your instructor specifies something else, stick to Times or Courier. And use a reasonable point size: Generally a twelve-point font will do.

4. Print your essay on one side of the paper only. If for some reason you have occasion to submit a handwritten copy, use lined paper and write on every other line in black or dark blue ink.

5. Set the line spacing at "double." The essay (even the heading—see item 6 below) should be double-spaced—not single-spaced, not triple-spaced.

6. In the upper left-hand corner, one inch from the top, put your name, your instructor's name, the course number, and the date. Put your last name before the page number (in the upper right-hand corner) of each subsequent page, so the instructor can easily reassemble your essay if somehow a page gets detached and mixed with other papers.

7. Titles. Use this form for your title: Hit the "enter" (or "return") key *once* after the date and then center the title of your essay. We give instructions for punctuating titles in Chapter 11, but we'll reiterate the most important points here. Capitalize the first letter of the first and last words of your title, the first word after a semicolon or colon if you use either one, and the first letter of all the other words except articles, conjunctions, and prepositions, thus:

`Two Kinds of Symbols in `To Kill a Mockingbird

Notice that your own title is neither underlined nor enclosed in quotation marks. (If, as here, your title includes material that would normally be italicized or in quotation marks, that material continues to be so written.) If the title runs more than one line, double-space between the lines.

8. Begin the essay just below the title. (Again, you'll hit "enter" or "return" only once.) If your instructor prefers a title page, begin the essay on the next page and number it 1. The title page is not numbered.

9. Margins. Except for page numbers, which should appear one-half inch from the top of the page, leave a one-inch margin at top, bottom, and sides of text.

10. Number the pages consecutively, using arabic numerals in the upper right-hand corner, half an inch from the top. Do not put a period or a hyphen after the numeral, and do not precede the numeral with "page" or "p." (Again, if you give the title on a separate sheet, the page that follows it is page 1. Do not number the title page.)

11. Paragraphs. Indent the first word of each paragraph five spaces from the left margin.

12. Proofreading. Check for typographical errors, and check spelling. Use your word processor's spell-check program—but don't rely on it exclusively. This program will flag words that are not in its dictionary and offer suggestions for correcting mistakes. (A misspelled word is of course not in the dictionary and thus flagged.) But a word flagged is not necessarily misspelled; it may simply not be in the program's dictionary. Proper names, for example, regularly get flagged. Keep in mind also that most programs cannot distinguish between homophones (*to, too, two; there, their; alter, altar*), nor can they tell you that you should have written *accept* instead of *except*.

13. Print a copy of your essay for yourself and keep it until the original has been returned. It is a good idea to keep notes and drafts too. They may prove helpful if you are asked to revise a page, substantiate a point, or supply a source you omitted.

14. Fasten the pages of your paper with a paper clip in the upper left-hand corner. Stiff binders are unnecessary; indeed, they are a nuisance to the instructor, adding bulk and making it awkward to write annotations.

Double space

Your Name

Your Instructor's Name — *Font is Courier*

Writing 127

April 1, 2004

— *Capitalize main words in title*

Formatting Your Essays: The Right

Center title

Way to Do It

Print your essay on 8 1/2-by-11-inch paper of good weight, and make sure that the printer has enough ink and that the print is dark and clear. Do not use a fancy font. Unless your instructor specifies something else, stick to Times or Courier. And use a reasonable point size: generally a 12-point font will do. The essay (even the heading) should be double-spaced--not single-spaced, not triple-spaced-- and it should be printed on one side of the paper only.

5 spaces, or tab

In the upper left-hand corner, one inch from the top, put your name, your instructor's name, the course number, and the date, all on separate lines. Put your last name before the page number (in the upper right-hand corner) of

← 1" → each subsequent page, so the instructor can easily reassemble your essay if somehow a page gets detached and mixed with other papers. Hit the "enter" (or "return") key <u>once</u> after the date and then center the title of your essay. Capitalize the first letter of the first and last words of your title, the first word after a semicolon or colon if you use either one, and

↑
1/2"
↓

Your name 2

the first letter of all the other words except
articles, conjunctions, and prepositions.
Notice that your own title is neither underlined nor enclosed in quotation marks. If the
title runs more than one line, double-space
between the lines. Begin the essay just below
the title. (Again, you'll hit "enter" or
"return" only once.) If your instructor prefers
a title page, begin the essay on the next page
and number it 1.

Except for page numbers, which should
appear one-half inch from the top of the page,
leave a one-inch margin at top, bottom, and
sides of text. Number the pages consecutively,
using arabic numerals in the upper right-hand
corner, half an inch from the top. Do not put a
period or a hyphen after the numeral, and do not
precede the numeral with "page" or "p."

Indent the first word of each paragraph
five spaces from the left margin.

Fasten the pages of your paper with a
paper clip in the upper left-hand corner. Stiff
binders are unnecessary; indeed, they are a nuisance because they add bulk and make essays
difficult to annotate. Spell-check your essay
and proofread it carefully; make a copy for
yourself, and then turn the essay in.

Using Quotations (and Punctuating Them Correctly)

If you are writing about a text, or about an interview, quotations from your material or subject are indispensable. They not only let your readers know what you are talking about, they give your readers the material you are responding to, thus letting them share your responses. But quote sparingly and quote briefly. Use quotations as evidence, not as padding. If the exact wording of the original is crucial, or especially effective, quote it directly, but if it is not, don't bore the reader with material that can be effectively reduced either by summarizing or by cutting. And make sure, by a comment before or after a quotation, that your reader understands why you find the quotation relevant. Don't count on a quotation to make your point for you.

Here are some additional matters to keep in mind, especially as you revise.

1. Identify the speaker or writer of the quotation. Usually this identification precedes the quoted material (e.g., "Smith says . . .") in accordance with the principle of letting readers know where they are going. But occasionally it may follow the quotation, especially if the name will provide a meaningful surprise. For example, in a discussion of a proposed tax reform, you might quote a remark hostile to it and then reveal that the author of the proposal was also the author of the remark.

2. When you introduce a quotation, consider using verbs other than "says." Depending on the context—that is, on the substance of the quotation and its place in your essay—it might be more accurate to say Smith "argues," "adds," "contends," "points out," "admits," or "comments." Or, again with just the right verb, you might introduce the quotation with a transitional phrase: "In another context Smith had observed that . . ." or "To clarify this point Smith refers to . . . ?" or "In an apparent contradiction Smith suggests. . . ." But avoid such inflated words as "opines," "avers," and "is of the opinion that." The point is not to add "elegant variation" (see page 102) to your introduction of someone else's words, but accuracy and grace. A verb often used *in*accurately is "feels." Ralph Smith does not "feel" that "the term *primitive art* has come to be used with at least three distinct meanings." He "points out," "writes," "observes," or "says."

3. Distinguish between short and long quotations and treat each appropriately. Enclose *short quotations*, four (or fewer) lines of typing, within quotation marks:

Anne Lindbergh calls the harrowing period of the kidnapping and murder of her first child the "hour of
lead." "Flying," she wrote, "was freedom and beauty
and escape from crowds."

Set off *long quotations* (more than four lines of typing). Do *not*
enclose them within quotation marks. To set off a quotation, begin a
new line, indent ten spaces from the left margin, and type the quotation double-spaced:

The last paragraphs of Five Years of My Life
contain Dreyfus's words when he was finally freed:
> The Government of the Republic gives me back
> my liberty. It is nothing to me without
> honor. Beginning with today, I shall
> unremittingly strive for the reparation of
> the frightful judicial error of which I am
> still the victim. I want all France to know
> by a final judgment that I am innocent.

But he was never to receive that judgment.

Note that long quotations are usually introduced by a sentence ending with a colon (as in the above example) or by an introductory phrase,
such as "Dreyfus wrote."

**4. Don't try to introduce a long quotation into the middle of one
of your own sentences.** It is too difficult for the reader to come out of
the quotation and to pick up your thread. Instead, introduce the quotation, as we did above, set the quotation off, and then begin a new sentence of your own.

**5. An embedded quotation (that is, a quotation embedded into
a sentence of your own) must fit grammatically into the sentence of
which it is a part.** For example, suppose you want to use Othello's line
"I have done the state some service."

Incorrect

Near the end of the play Othello says that he "have
done the state some service."

Correct

Near the end of the play Othello says that he has
"done the state some service."

Correct

```
Near the end of the play, Othello says, "I have done
the state some service."
```

6. Quote exactly. Check your quotation for accuracy at least twice. If you need to edit a quotation—for example, in order to embed it grammatically, or to inform your reader of a relevant point—observe the following rules:

- Enclose any words that you add or substitute in square brackets—not parentheses.

```
"In the summer of 1816 we [Mary Wollstonecraft and
Percy Bysshe Shelley] visited Switzerland and
became the neighbors of Lord Byron."
Trotsky became aware that "Stalin would not hesi-
tate a moment to organize an attempt on [his] life."
```

- Indicate the omission of material with ellipses (three periods, with a space between periods and before and after each period).

```
The New York Times called it "the most intensive
man-hunt . . . in the country's history."
```

- If your sentence ends with the omission of the last part of the original sentence, use four periods: one immediately after the last word quoted, and three (spaced) to indicate the omission.

```
The manual says, "If your sentence ends with
the omission of the last part of the original
sentence, use four spaced periods. . . ."
```

Notice that if you begin the quotation with the beginning of a sentence (in the example we have just given "If your" is the beginning of a quoted sentence), you do *not* indicate that material preceded the words you are quoting. Similarly, if you end your quotation with the end of the quoted sentence, you give only a single period, not an ellipsis, although of course the material from which you are quoting may have gone on for many more sentences. But if you begin quoting from the middle of a sentence, or end quoting before you reach the end of a sentence in your source, it is customary to indicate the omissions. But even such omissions need not be indicated when the quoted material is obviously incomplete—when, for instance, it is a word or phrase.

7. Use punctuation accurately. There are three important rules to observe:

- Commas and periods go inside the quotation marks:

  "The land," Nick Thompson observes, "looks after us."

- Semicolons and colons go outside quotation marks:

  He turned and said, "Learn the names of all these places"; it sounded like an order.

- Question marks, exclamation points, and dashes go inside if they are part of the quotation, outside if they are your own.

  Amanda ironically says to her daughter, "How old are you, Laura?"

  (The question mark is part of the quotation and therefore goes inside the quotation marks.)

  Did you really tell your brother "no"?

8. Use single quotation marks for a quotation within a quotation.

The student told the interviewer, "I ran back to the dorm and I called my boyfriend and I said, 'Listen, this is just incredible,' and I told him all about it."

9. Enclose titles of short works in quotation marks. Short works include chapters in books, short stories, essays, short poems, songs, lectures, speeches, and unpublished works (even if long).

Underline, or use italic type, for titles of long works. (Underlining indicates *italic* type, used in print and available on computers but ordinarily not available on typewriters.) Underline (or italicize) titles of published book-length works: novels, plays, periodicals, collections of essays, anthologies, pamphlets, textbooks, and long poems (such as *Paradise Lost*). Underline (or italicize) also titles of films, compact discs, television programs, ballets, operas, works of art, and the names of planes, ships, and trains.

Exception: Titles of sacred works (for example, the New Testament, the Hebrew Bible, Genesis, Acts, the Gospels, the Koran) are neither underlined nor enclosed within quotation marks. To cite a book of the

Bible with chapter and verse, give the name of the book, then a space, then an arabic numeral for the chapter, a period, and an arabic numeral (*not* preceded by a space) for the verse, thus: Exodus 20.14–15. Standard abbreviations for the books of the Bible (for example, Chron.) are permissible in footnotes and in parenthetic citations within the text.

10. Use quotation marks to identify a word or term to which you wish to call special attention. (But italics, indicated by underlining, may be used instead of quotation marks.)

```
By "comedy" I mean not only a funny play, but any
play that ends happily.
```

11. Do not use quotation marks to enclose slang or a term that you fear is too casual. Use the term or don't use it, but don't apologize by putting it in quotation marks, as in these examples.

Incorrect
```
Because of "red tape" it took three years.
```

Incorrect
```
At last I was able to "put in my two cents."
```

In both sentences the writers are signaling their uneasiness; in neither is there any cause for uneasiness.

12. Do not use quotation marks to convey sarcasm. The following sentence should be rewritten:

```
These "politicians" are nothing but thieves.
```

Sarcasm, usually a poor form of argument, is best avoided. But of course there are borderline cases when you may want to convey your dissatisfaction with a word used by others.

```
African sculpture has a long continuous tradition,
but this tradition has been jeopardized by the intro-
duction of "civilization" to Africa.
```

Perhaps the quotation marks here are acceptable, because the writer's distaste has not yet become a sneer and because she is, in effect, quoting.

But it is probably better to change "civilization" to "western culture," omitting the quotation marks.

13. Do not enclose the title of your own essay in quotation marks, and do not underline or italicize it.

Corrections in the Final Copy

Extensive revisions should have been made in your drafts, but minor last-minute revisions may be made on the finished copy. Proofreading may catch some typographical errors, and you may notice some small weaknesses. You can make corrections with the following proofreader's symbols. If you did not find an error in each triangle, look again.

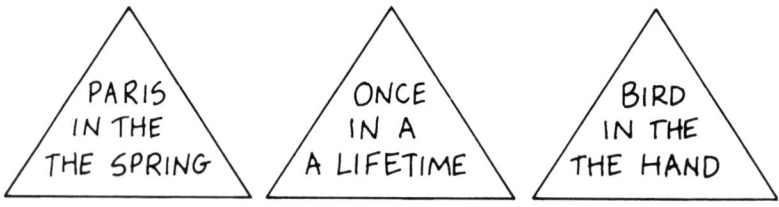

1. *Changes* in wording may be made by crossing through words and rewriting just above them, either on the typewriter or by hand in pen:

```
When I first moved to the United States at the age
                              no
of nine, I had few doubts as to my identity.
```

2. *Additions* should be made above the line, with a caret (^) below the line at the appropriate place:

```
When I  first  moved  to  the  United  States  at  the
      of
age nine, I had no doubts as to my identity.
    ^
```

3. *Transpositions* of letters may be made thus:

```
When I frist moved to the United States at the

age of nine, I had no doubts as to my identity.
```

4. *Deletions* are indicated by a horizontal line through the word or words to be deleted. Delete a single letter by drawing a vertical or diagonal line through it.

When I first moved to the United States at ~~at~~ the

age of nine, I had no doub~~b~~ts as to my identity.

5. *Separation* of words accidentally run together is indicated by a vertical line, *closure* by a curved line connecting the things to be closed up.

When I first/moved to the United States at the age of

nine, I had no dou bts as to my identity.

6. *Paragraphing* may be indicated by the paragraph symbol before the word that is to begin the new paragraph.

When I first moved to the United States at the age

of nine, I had no doubts as to my identity. ¶Within a

year, however, . . .

Last Words

A rich patron once gave money to the painter Chu Ta, asking him to paint a picture of a fish. Three years later, when he still had not received the painting the patron went to Chu Ta's house to ask why the picture was not done. Chu Ta did not answer, but dipped a brush in ink and with a few strokes drew a splendid fish. "If it is so easy," asked the patron, "why didn't you give me the picture three years ago?" Again Chu Ta did not answer. Instead, he opened the door of a large cabinet. Thousands of pictures of fish tumbled out.

Credits

Index

Additional Titles of Interest

Note to Instructors: Any of these Penguin-Putnam, Inc., titles can be packaged with this book at a special discount. Contact your local Allyn & Bacon/Longman sales representative for details on how to create a Penguin-Putnam, Inc., Value Package.

Allison, *Bastard Out of Carolina*

Alvarez, *How the Garcia Girls Lost Their Accents*

Augustine, *The Confessions of St. Augustine*

Austen, *Persuasion*

Austen, *Pride and Prejudice*

Austen, *Sense and Sensibility*

Bloom, *Shakespeare: The Invention of the Human*

C. Brontë, *Jane Eyre*

E. Brontë, *Wuthering Heights*

Burke, *Reflections on the Revolution in France*

Cather, *My Ántonia*

Cather, *O Pioneers!*

Cellini, *The Autobiography of Benvenuto Cellini*

Chapman, *Black Voices*

Chesnutt, *The Marrow of Tradition*

Chopin, *The Awakening and Selected Stories*

Conrad, *Heart of Darkness*

Conrad, *Nostromo*

Coraghessan-Boyle, *The Tortilla Curtain*

Defoe, *Robinson Crusoe*

Descartes, *Discourse on Method and The Meditations*

Descartes, *Meditations and Other Metaphysical Writings*

de Tocqueville, *Democracy in America*

Dickens, *Hard Times*

Douglass, *Narrative of the Life of Frederick Douglass*

Dubois, *The Souls of Black Folk*

Equiano, *The Interesting Narrative and Other Writings*

Gore, *Earth in the Balance*

Grossman, *Electronic Republic*

Hawthorne, *The Scarlet Letter*

Hutner, *Immigrant Voices*

Jacobs, *Incidents in the Life of a Slave Girl*

Jen, *Typical American*

M.L. King, Jr., *Why We Can't Wait*

Lewis, *Babbitt*

Machiavelli, *The Prince*

Marx, *The Communist Manifesto*

Mill, *On Liberty*

More, *Utopia and Other Essential Writings*

Orwell, *1984*

Paine, *Common Sense*

Plato, *The Republic*

Postman, *Amusing Ourselves to Death*

Rose, *Lives on the Boundary*

Rossiter, *The Federalist Papers*

Rousseau, *The Social Contract*

Shelley, *Frankenstein*

Sinclair, *The Jungle*

Steinbeck, *Of Mice and Men*

Stevenson, *The Strange Case of Dr. Jekyll and Mr. Hyde*

Stoker, *Dracula*

Stowe, *Uncle Tom's Cabin*

Swift, *Gulliver's Travels*

Taulbert, *Once Upon a Time When We Were Colored*

Thoreau, *Walden*

Truth, *The Narrative of Sojourner Truth*

Woolf, *Jacob's Room*

Zola, *Germinal*